# Landscape and Identity

MATERIALIZING CULTURE

. . . . . . . . . . . . . . . . . . . . . . . . . . . . . . . . . . . . .

Series Editors: Paul Gilroy, Michael Herzfeld and Danny Miller

# Landscape and Identity

## Geographies of Nation and Class in England

WENDY JOY DARBY

Oxford • New York

First published in 2000 by
**Berg**
Editorial offices:
150 Cowley Road, Oxford, OX4 1JJ, UK
838 Broadway, Third Floor, New York, NY 10003-4812, USA

Berg is the imprint of Oxford International Publishers Ltd.

**Library of Congress Cataloging-in-Publication Data**

A catalogue record for this book is available from the Library of
Congress.

**British Library Cataloguing-in-Publication Data**

A catalogue record for this book is available from the British Library.

ISBN  1 85973 425 1  (Cloth)
       1 85973 430 8  (Paper)

Typeset by JS Typesetting, Wellingborough, Northants.
Printed in the United Kingdom by Biddles Ltd, Guildford and
King's Lynn.

For Penny and Andrew
and
in memory of my sister Veronica

*Ordnance Survey in the Northern Counties*

The Commissioners believe that everything
is named, that land is branded like a beast
to prove its ownership and pedigree:
a word steps softly on the moss's crust,
inks tease rivers out to becks like blue trees;
my letters stitch their banks from mouth to spring
and thread fine serifs through each mountain gill.

Contours whorl like thumbprints, circling my quill;
I dress the map in crocheted black shawls,
string beads of blood between their strands to plot
these common paths a poor man borrows, sweating
in a rich man's fields to raise good walls;

Without a name to bear him witness, I draw
an apronful of stones to mark his spot.

                        Mick North, from
                        *The New Lake Poets*

# Contents

# Part III: Ethnographic

# List of Maps and Figures

## Maps

## Figures

# List of Plates

# List of Abbreviations

*Organizations*
BBC   British Broadcasting Corporation
BMC   British Mountaineering Council
CHA   Co-operative Holidays Association (later name-change to Countrywide Holidays Association)
CC    Countryside Commission (name-change to Countryside Agency, April 1, 1999)
CLA   Country Landowners' Association
CPRE  Council for the Preservation of Rural England (later name-change to Council for the Protection of Rural England)
FLD   Friends of the Lake District
HF    Holiday Fellowship
LDDS  Lake District Defense Society
LDNP  Lake District National Park
MFPS  Manchester Footpath Preservation Society
MTCP  Ministry of Town and Country Planning
NT    National Trust
PDNP  Peak District National Park
RA    Ramblers' Association
SCR   Sheffield Clarion Ramblers
TDA   Thirlmere Defense Association
YMCA  Young Men's Christian Association

*Landscape designations*
AONB  Area of Outstanding Natural Beauty
NNR   National Nature Reserve
SSSI  Site of Special Scientific Interest

*Other*
LDNPP Lake District National Park Plan

# Acknowledgments

This project emerges from a long-standing interest in understanding how landscape functions as a repository of social, economic and political history. Awareness of people's daily engagement with place and the meanings with which they endow it came from my earlier fieldwork as a historic preservationist in the Lake District's Hartsop Valley and through practical experience in landscape conservation and restoration. I am indebted to Christopher Tavener for bringing my landscape-located interests into conjunction with anthropology. The Department of Anthropology at The Graduate Center of the City University of New York provided an environment in which the ideas generated from this intellectual background could flourish, in part through the support and friendship of Ann Berg, Johanna Gorelick and Ian Scoggard. This project profited from detailed discussions and close readings by Joan Vincent, Jane Schneider, Vincent Crapanzano, Gerald Creed, Nathan Gross and two anonymous reviewers for Berg.

Specific funding for this project was provided by the Council for European Studies (1995) and the Wenner-Gren Foundation (1997–8). Virgin Atlantic helped make possible a last field visit. Earlier support by the Royal Oak Society (1986) allowed me to attend the Attingham Summer School, through which I gained an extraordinarily privileged view of (and from) the English country house; a William Kinne Travel Fellowship (1988) awarded by Columbia University made possible numerous visits to England's National Parks. Both sets of experiences bear fruit in this work.

In the field I was assisted by many individuals to whom I am especially grateful. Sonia Ankers, Paula Day, and Marion Canning shared their thoughts, feelings, and time. Sonia invited me to walk with her local group, allowing me to gain very particular insights. Fieldwork was such that I was based everywhere and nowhere. Exacerbating my anxiety within that peripatetic life was the painful knowledge that my sister was dying, the last member of my own English family of origin. For this reason, my gratitude towards the following people, all walkers, for their hospitality to a virtual stranger, carries a deeper emotional tenor. Brian Franks, Peter and Kate Jones, Jane Sweet and Janet Stone, Stella Welford, and Peter and Eileen Willetts welcomed me into their homes. Peter and Eileen Willetts, Stella Welford, and Peter Jones arranged for me to walk with their local groups and to distribute questionnaires to them; Brian Franks rescued me, twice! Stephen Gorton, a friend of long standing, again extended his hospitality whenever I was in the Lake District.

Peter Jones was a consistent source of details I could not track down in New York, while Malcolm Pitt supplied information that I believed unobtainable. Phil Ray kindly volunteered a copy of his uncle's journal, from around 1922, describing a walking tour in the Lake District. John Horne made available a copy of his late mother's 1932 edition of *The Open Road*, which accompanied her on rambles in the 1930s and '40s. My thanks go especially to Colin Doyle, Director of Countrywide Holidays Association, for his kind permission to access the Association's archives held at the Greater Manchester Public Records Office; to Ian Brodie, Secretary of the Friends of the Lake District; and to Catherine Gunningham, Assistant Director of Development at the Ramblers' Association, both of whom were generous with their time and help in furthering the aims of the project. I much appreciated the generous spirit in which walkers agreed to take on a somewhat lengthy questionnaire.

I extend special thanks to Paula Baxter, Rachel Labush, David Ogilvie, Brian Pence, and Penny Sinanoglou for practical assistance in New York, and to David Lindroth for the splendid maps. Given its historical and visual nature, this project could not have proceeded without the holdings of the Columbia University libraries and the unfailing help of their librarians.

Over many years Yani Sinanoglou supported me in all my endeavors. This book could not have been accomplished without him, and it carries my deepest gratitude to him. Finally, Peggy Flinsch has long provided conditions in which my tools of observation have been sharpened. As a young woman some seventy years ago, she 'did' Striding Edge, a precipitous climb up Helvellyn in the Lake District. In the thirty-four years I have journeyed with her here in New York, she has taught by example to face life as the striding edge it really is.

# Foreword: Access Day 1999

Access to the countryside is a hotly debated affair in England. Over the past few years it has moved from localized vocal protests of a few to a national parliamentary debate and imminent legislation. In the process the positions of opposing factions have hardened. These factions represent basic divisions of country and city; they focus on which people and which activities have claim to the landscape. Parts I and II of this work undertake a complex anthropological analysis of the social, symbolic, political, economic and legislative roots that form the tangled historical mass underpinning these contemporary questions of access. They also show how access is bound up in contested myths of national and class-identity formation and the cultural construction of place. Part I shows how the making of the English countryside is intimately connected with the English country house and its unpeopled views, while Part II deals with the struggle to repeople the view. Part III is an ethnographic enquiry into the experience of place and the 'shared symbolic vehicles that give shape to geographical experience and facilitate its communication' (Basso 1996: 109) among groups of people.

Access to the English landscape is at least a dual process of first being able to reach it, and then being able to walk in it. Partial reductions or total removal of rural public transportation systems necessarily limits urban dwellers who do not own cars from achieving that first level of access. This restriction, which in the absence of corrective government policy is policy-by-default, particularly affects the vast majority of ethnic Britons who live in urban centers. Organizations such as Red Rope, the Socialist Walkers and Climbers organization, campaign for the government to open access to more sections of the community by improving public transport. Grass-roots organizations like Earth First! form a broad-based anti-road movement that challenges the expansion of motorways. These privilege the already-privileged car-owning segment of British society at the expense of a countryside diminishing because of the continued encroachment of housing construction. For the car-owning majority, access to the countryside also necessitates access to parking space, further exacerbating problems in popular walking areas such as the Lake District and Peak District National Parks.

The Ramblers' Association (RA) has been in the forefront of efforts to obtain the statutory right of the freedom to roam that has in part been articulated through Access Days meant to highlight local specific issues. In organizing a nationwide access campaign, the RA has drawn upon a tradition of mass protests undertaken by an earlier generation of walkers. But whereas the rallies of the 1930s were working-class, highly confrontational mass *trespasses*, the protest rallies of the 1990s have been relatively non-confrontational, much smaller and predominantly middle-class *events*. The earlier era's militancy has fallen to grass-roots organizations such as Earth First! and the movement to take back the streets.

One of the Access Day 1999 protest walks and rallies particularly represented a spatial and temporal concatenation of access, the English country house and the state. This was the walk and rally that originated in Wendover, Buckinghamshire, an hour's train journey northwest of London. Almost everyone participating in the event arrived in the atomized anonymity of privately owned cars. Following rights of way over farmland, the walk included a rally at Beacon Hill, part of the Chequers estate, the official country residence of the Prime Minister. (Beacon Hill is at one end of the estate, Chequers – the country house – is at the other end.) At the same time that it highlighted a local issue, the rally was intended to bring the national issue of access literally and symbolically to the Prime Minister's country doorstep. Prior to its enclosure in the 1820s, Beacon Hill was common land. The RA would like to have a portion of Beacon Hill made accessible because of the panoramic views over the Vale of Aylesbury from its summit. In addition, Beacon Hill is one of the few remaining areas of chalk downland in the area, much of the rest having undergone agricultural improvement or reverted to scrubland.

Buckinghamshire is one of the 'Home Counties' often presented as the heartland of England. Chequers, the locational and political heart of the heartland, symbolizes party politics, political representation, democratic process and the sheer power of the state: in short, the imagined collectivity of the nation. In 1998, 300 people participated in the same protest walk and rally; the year before, some 1,200. Given the Labour Party's commitment to access legislation – although on

September 19 of 1999 it was not known into which parliamentary session it would be introduced – RA members may have felt that the pressure was off to gather in great numbers. Since numerous other protest walks and rallies were scheduled the same day, people were not bussed in from elsewhere as they had been in previous years. Some 60 people walked the route, the first couple of hours in a downpour. The protest rally took place on the publicly accessible lower slopes of Beacon Hill.

The body of walkers straddled the grassy slopes in a long line looking up at Beacon Hill. Police fanned out from the bottom to the top of the slope some distance away from and facing the walkers. Several police cars were stationed on the nearby road. The BBC, Sky News, and British Satellite News had stationed camera crews at the rally site. The speakers at the rally were Paddy Tipping, Labour MP for Sherwood, and currently Leader of the House of Commons; Dr. Phyllis Starkey, Labour MP for Milton Keynes South West; and Kate Ashbrook, a past Chairman of the RA, present Chairman of the RA Access Committee and the local area's Area Footpath Secretary.

Starkey spoke of a universal entitlement to the countryside as the heritage of everyone, not just of the people who lived and worked there; people from the cities and towns had to be allowed recreational access to the greater countryside as long as they respected the fact that it was a place of work for others; in short, the countryside belonged to no single one faction or group. Tipping, a longtime RA advocate, declared with some warmth that 'we have been fighting for access for over a hundred years and it looks as if the fight is nearly won'. Nodding in the direction of Chequers, and prefacing his remarks by saying that he could not divulge the actual outcome of the meeting, he confided that he had recently been there during the preparation of the Queen's Speech for the opening of Parliament. He repeated that 'we are close to the end of the fight for access' and proposed that given the Millennium, 'access to mountains and heath and downland would be a wonderful gift to the country to take into the new age'. Ashbrook emphasized that the RA position on access to the countryside did not mean granting walkers the right to tramp over crops or through people's gardens, but that people must enjoy the right to reach hill and mountain summits and witness the spectacular panoramic views, as well as simply to enjoy the quiet of the countryside.

A walker softly spoke of Beacon Hill as more than just a place to which Ramblers' wanted access. For, to a number of local druid groups and witch covens, Beacon Hill was a sacred place, one of power. She referred specifically to Cymbeline's Castle, the motte and baily just below the rally point. She complained that 'Christians are allowed their places of worship, but when it comes to non-Establishment religions, they don't get taken seriously. They and [New Age] Travellers are misunderstood.' Given that more than 100,000 people in Britain are estimated to belong to groups that locate the sacred in nature (Lovell 1998: 2), the issue of access has deeper reverberations than might be immediately apparent.

Preceded by police, and observed by police on the upper slopes, after the rally the protesters continued along the public footpath that climbs steeply and then skirts the western flank of Beacon Hill before going into the nearby woods. The police escort was maintained until all the walkers had left the public footpath that works around the Chequers estate.

The interest of private landowners is inimicable to the desires and wishes of the RA; yet this very fact brings them into a common field of relations, especially in the consultation process initiated by the Labour Government through the National Countryside Access Forum established by the Countryside Agency (formerly the Countryside Commission), a process explored in Chapter 6. Out and out conflict has given way to contention that is contained within an established system of relations; legislatively oriented discussions have replaced acts of mass trespass. The politically marginal has been taken into the center. Landscape-located history, events, sentiment, and experience form the lived experience of social geography. It remains to be seen just what kind of social geography the new Countryside Bill will construct, and how it will satisfy all the participants in the debate over access to the countryside.

# Introduction: Envisioning/ Re-Visioning Landscape

In times when subjects of education have multiplied, it may seem at first sight a hardship to lay on the already heavily-pressed student a new science. But it will be found that the real effect of Anthropology is rather to lighten than increase the strain of learning. In the mountains we see the bearers of heavy burdens contentedly shoulder a carrying-frame besides, because they find its weight more than compensated by the convenience of holding together and balancing their load. So it is with the science of Man and Civilization which connects into a more manageable whole the scattered subjects of an ordinary education.

Tylor 1891: v

The construction of identity through recreational participation in valued and symbolic landscapes is a topic little explored in anthropology, even though such activities are assuming an increasingly important role in the lives of many individuals in the affluent countries of Western Europe, Asia, and the United States. Landscape remains largely unproblematized (Hirsch 1995).

Among the questions to be explored here are: How do leisure and exclusion operate as interrelated social and geographical realities based upon class, age, gender or ethnicity? Do England's National Parks represent fifty years of exclusion or inclusion? Whose views of the wider landscape are being preserved for whom? How does one explain the re-emergence of a freedom-to-roam movement now? In considering such questions, this ethnohistorical project takes a transdisciplinary approach to historical class relations and traces various steps in the cultural production of class and national identity as it has operated through landscape and access to it. A politics of access is analyzed

1

through the landscapes of the Lake District and the Peak District, located in the uplands of northwestern England (see Map 1). By bringing fairly wide historical processes into conjunction with local specificities, this work contributes to effecting the magisterially paced, ongoing rapprochement between anthropology and history (Cohn [1980, 1981] 1987; Guha 1987; Mitchell 1997) while it deals with space and viewing in another register than the simply geographical and pictorial (Green 1995).

Running throughout the work as a sub-text are the endnotes. I accord them importance as undergirdings of the whole. From that perspective I concur with the expression that 'God is in the Detail. And in the Footnotes' (Chadwick 1997: 16). One detail (also apparent in the endnotes) that is sufficiently naturalized to require foregrounding here is the extent to which landscape has been a male domain. A male and military gaze lay behind most topographical work; the viewer of landscapes on the European Grand Tour initially was most often male; the art market was dominated by men both as patrons and producers of landscapes; aestheticians who debated categories of landscape and their effects on the mind and feelings were male; early promoters of landscape tourism were male; the discourse of walking and mountaineering reflected a gendered symbolism of landscape; and landscapes – be they representational or actual – were status appendages, much like the wives, mistresses and daughters of the men who held the land and ran the country.

As for walking in the landscape, Anne Wallace has written with great richness about its place in nineteenth-century English literature. Yet there is again an unconscious gendering in her seeing it as

> an extension of Virgilian georgic accomplished by placing the walker in the ideological space vacated by the farmer. The result, which I call 'peripatetic', represents excursive walking as a cultivating labour capable of renovating both the individual and his society by recollecting and expressing past value.
>
> (Wallace 1993: 8, 11)

This work moves beyond the literary framework of an educated elite, to show Wallace's nineteenth-century 'peripatetic' in a more 'pedestrian' light and to bring gender into the picture. It charts how an earlier elite's possession of the landscape by descriptive texts and enclosure is replaced by the dispossessed's regaining access to spaces of excursive walking.

This work contains three parts. The first (Chapters 1–3) delves into an aesthetically informed discourse of nation by tracing out the literary and artistic roots of landscape as an idiom for materializing culture. It brings into focus the eighteenth-century English cultural elite's 'imagined community' of painted, printed and actual unpeopled landscapes. It contextualizes this within the articulation and practices of British nationalism, and within the popularization of the Picturesque. It also uses this imagined community as a point from which to propose a series of related fields of tension within 'polite society,' and between polite society and those immiserated by the enclosure movement.

This first section culminates with the cultural valorization of the Lake District – its movement from empty space to valorized place. It deals with the substitution of mythic memory for real memory and makes the point that the myth-makers are outsiders. Long before its popularity as the Lake District, it was a 'place' for the women, children and men who labored and died there. The experiential intensity of place, wrought through their interaction with the land, can be extrapolated from the clearance of boulder- and stone-strewn valleys to clear fields and construct drystone fieldwalls. It can also be read in the far-flung network of walls over the mountainsides that form one of the most characteristic human-made landscape features of this region.

A verbal counterpart to these physical markers of place exists in the extraordinary number of named crags, outcroppings, ravines, passes and paths, rivulets, falls and tarns, patches of bog, scree slopes, mountain ridges and flanks that predate the nineteenth-century Ordnance Survey. The spatial practices of physical engagement and naming form a double inscription of meaning set down on the landscape, defining it as place long before it became 'The Lake District.'

The second section (Chapters 4–6) continues the process of rendering landscape problematic within a political-economy paradigm. It widens the range of what is brought into view to include the Peak District where the class-based issue of access took on an increasingly strident pitch. The Lake District, around which a version of a homogeneous English national identity was being constructed by an educated elite, paradoxically became the site of cultural differentiation of class participation in this landscape. Both Peak and Lake District landscapes became sounding boards of national sentiment that exposed different claims to history – to the primacy of either pre- or post-Norman Englands.

The politics of access in the Peak District centered on poaching; in the Lake District, on aesthetics. The key to this difference is the vegetative cover. The Peak's moorland heather (*Callunus vulgaris*) is the preferred nesting site for red grouse (*Lagopus lagopus scoticus*) and their major food source. A grouse-shooting elite wanted to protect the grouse being reared on the moors for the kill. This pitted them both against locals who wanted to maintain ancient rights of way across the moors, and walkers from the surrounding industrial towns who wanted to wander at will upon areas of open moorland. Gamekeepers considered walkers inherently dangerous as disturbers of nesting birds and as outright poachers.

Since heather is not an overwhelming part of the Lake District's vegetative ensemble, grouse-rearing was not an issue there. But aesthetics was. Endowed with literary and visual significance since the early 1700s, Lake District landscapes came under threat of massive and permanent damage from rail and mining interests in the nineteenth century. Because opposition to such intrusions was conducted by a highly educated elite, it inaugurated a debate at a national level not only about preservation of these particular landscapes, but also about landscape preservation generally, and especially the preservation of those commons which had survived the depredations of parliamentary enclosures.

From the 1830s through the 1930s, legislative, legal and extra-legal challenges were made to legal, quasi-legal and illegal practices concerning access. The central areas around which these battles were fought were the Lake and Peak Districts. The crosscurrents between actions taken in both areas fueled post-1945 enabling legislation by which ten national parks were established in the uplands of England and Wales between 1951 and 1957. Those parks are: Lake District, Peak District, Dartmoor, Snowdonia (all designated in 1951); Pembrokeshire Coast, North York Moors (1952); Exmoor, Yorkshire Dales (1954); Northumberland (1956); and the Brecon Beacons (1957). These ten parks represent about 9 percent of the land surface of England and Wales (see Map 1). This section also deals with the re-emergence in the 1990s of demands for open access to land both within and outside national parks, and the environmental rhetoric used in contested spatial practices.

The third section (Chapters 7 and 8) moves into the ethnographic present, drawing upon interviews with representatives of national walking organizations and upon participant-observation with walkers in the Lake and Peak Districts and locally-based walking clubs. This peripatetic ethnography examines how social relations are spatialized and how spatial relations are socialized; it investigates the way in which walking is a socially constitutive force shaping personal identity and a sense of community in the face of social fragmentation, global economic restructuring, and European integration.

**Map 1** Location of National Parks

While problematizing the culture of walkers in a highly stratified society (as thickly strewn with class markers as Wordsworth's hills were strewn with daffodils), it becomes apparent that a primary question is whether or not walking groups cross-cut class as they create spaces for new structures of feeling. A gender-centered view of walking is considered, as is ethnic minorities' sense of the English landscape as a landscape of non-identity. The powerful attachment to place, particularly the Lake District, is explored through the voices of three women whose lives have been greatly shaped by engagement with the landscape. Each voice recapitulates a major theme of this work.

The Conclusion considers whether the northern mountainous landscape of the Lake District still functions as another version or vision of England. A London-oriented Home Counties image of the south-east is projected in the literature as the quintessence of the 'Crown Heartland' of 'Deep' England, another example of metonymic misrepresentation, of how 'the South' is especially made to stand for the whole of a country or region (Cosgrove, Roscoe and Nycroft 1996; Fernandez 1988; Wiener 1981; Wright 1985). The Conclusion addresses the issue of whether, under the impact of Britain's social fragmentation and economic restructuring, the idea that certain places are more truly 'England' is an idea put into practice – in this instance – through the practice of walking.

# Part I

# Representational

The representation of landscape is not innocent of a politics. It is deeply embedded in relations of power and knowledge. Part I makes those relations visible by presenting landscape and landscape representations from various interrelated perspectives. This multiple framing helps give voice to silences in landscape images and shows how understanding and experience of landscape and landscape imagery are socially grounded in historically specific notions of exclusion and inclusion. Of central concern is the socio-cultural location of the viewer, the view, and visual and written representations of landscape. Each chapter in this section of the book addresses the political, economic, historic, sentimental or educational underpinnings of the society that produced and consumed landscapes and their representations, and shows how people literally in the same place can inhabit figuratively quite different places. In this respect, Part I produces what might be termed a Foucauldian archaeology of landscape.

Viewed this way, landscape provides a way into the question of culture: its value, its perduration, its categories of worthy and unworthy, and the construction of culture-bound identity-forming myths. It leads to considerations of how culture subsumes the individual at the same time that individual agency helps shape culture, and of how the individual perceives the self as part of a specific culture, especially at periods of doubt caused by social or national trauma, such as agricultural or industrial revolutions, the growth of Empire, war, or the aftermath of war. Operating in a variety of registers, landscape becomes a focus for exploring criteria of inclusion and exclusion: as those criteria are imposed by a specific class, and how they are mediated by gender, aesthetic experience, community or class aspirations.

Part I deals with the conventions and historical context of landscape imagery, examining – within the context of eighteenth-century England – which individuals and classes command what views, and at whose expense. It is concerned with conditions of distance in picturesque scenery and its relationship to social distances. It maps out the social and cultural authority of the culture-bearers, and the prerequisites for understanding a view in terms of other actual, literary or pictorial views. It brings into common focus England's mountainous periphery and the internal sites of tension and debate in the political construction of Britain, showing the deep intertwining of landscape representation and political representation.

# one

# Critical Perspectives:
# The Class/Ification of Views

Operating . . . at the juncture of history and politics, social relations and cultural perceptions, landscape has to be . . . an area of study that blows apart the conventional boundaries between the disciplines.

Bender 1993: 3

## Introduction

What follows constitutes trespass. But I think it is worth the risk. I am searching for what I have come to understand as more or less 'unpeopled landscapes' that have occurred in various cultural arenas. I acknowledge that my trespasses are decidedly more of the hedgerow-hugging variety than deep exploration – indeed I think they would take me precariously too far afield if they were otherwise. And I go pretty far afield as it is. But what I hope to arrive at, for England, is the culturally-valued phenomenon of unpeopled landscapes, and their dissemination in actual and representational form as a medium for the formation of identity. As that overview emerges, so too will its counter-image. Between them, they will help bring into focus a politics of access.

The perspective from which I approach landscape treats it as 'a vast network of cultural codes' (Mitchell 1994). This chapter is informed by the converging influences of two classical texts which legitimated West European landscape-painting as a genre. Those texts are Vitruvius' *de Architectura*, a first-century AD architectural treatise, and the *Idylls* of Theocritus (born 310 BC). Both were given new life in the Renaissance when they were published in Italian and swiftly underwent translation into other European languages.

I come at these two texts through four sets of paired relationships that I view as cultural productions which helped shape reality, rather

11

than merely mimicking it (Barnes and Duncan 1992). Covering a range of media, these four dyadic sets are (1) landscape and early theater, (2) prints and imprints of power, (3) seventeenth-century Italian landscape paintings and the landscapes of eighteenth-century English country seats, and (4) eighteenth-century theater landscape scenery and panoramas. I see these sets as moments in the dialectical processes of class relations from which various cultural productions emerged, productions that themselves served to further mystify class. None of these cultural productions is examined in exhaustive depth – that is not the point of their presence here. Rather, I have striven for simplification without too much distortion. Inevitably, the media that are closer in time to my central argument receive more attention. I am aware that as far as disciplinary 'fields' are concerned there are likely to be irate gamekeepers around. To them I would say that I am not interested in poaching, only in catching sight of the view.

By moving between these four dyadic sets, and drawing upon their interrelated linkages and mutual influences, I show that in eighteenth-century England, the cultural elite shared in an imagined community of painted, printed and actual 'unpeopled landscapes.' In doing so, I subscribe to the view that landscape can be thought of not simply as a noun but also as a verb; that landscape *does*, that it is 'an instrument of cultural power' and is a cultural practice 'by which social and subjective identities are formed' (Mitchell 1994: 1–2) and through which class is expressed. I see the grid of linkages and influences that I trace out below as being part of that 'complex cultural process [whereby] geographical space and the social formation are constructed with . . . hierarchies of high and low,' registers that 'are continually structured, legitimated and dissolved by reference to the vertical symbolic hierarchies which operate in . . . other domains' (Stallybrass and White 1986: 2–3). By following how the elite's cultural imagery diffused down the social scale, naturalizing itself on the way into 'what Marx called a "social hieroglyph," an emblem of the social relations it conceals' (Mitchell 1994: 15), I set the scene for my larger argument concerning the nineteenth- and early-twentieth-century struggle for the democratization of 'the view' through a peopling of the landscape. This then, is where trespass begins.

## Landscape and Early Theater

The traditional art-historical paradigm states that with rare exceptions, classical and medieval landscape representations were 'landscapes of symbols', rather than 'landscapes of fact' capable of conveying impressions of sensation (Clarke 1949). What to our sensibilities are modern landscapes, that is those reflecting a sense of space and the effects of light, first occurred in fifteenth-century Flemish and Italian art. This shift was driven by empirical observation, scientific curiosity and mathematical calculation (Clark 1949; Jackson 1980; Rosand 1988). The advent of scientific perspective in Renaissance Italy made it possible to represent expansive high views and deep vistas in mathematically correct terms, an accuracy that is said not to be found outside of Europe. The complacency and innocence of that paradigm, which posits a European linear progression to a new way of seeing that produces 'real' landscapes, has been criticized as ideological mystification (Barrell 1980; Bermingham 1986; McWilliam and Potts 1983; Mitchell 1994). For that 'new way of seeing' could be manipulated to obscure as much as it revealed.

While geometry and mathematics are the scientific roots of the 'perspectival gaze in which the observer is always outside and above the action' (Bender 1993: 10), the observer actually occupies an aestheticized pictorial point of view. Educated hands and eyes construct, receive and interpret one view, while the engaged ground-level laborer constructs, receives and interprets another. Filtered through social and aesthetic categories of high and low, literal and metaphorical 'perspective' is what determines which view is available to whom. Perspective and theater intersected in scenery as the science of perspective enabled new illusions of space to be brought to the stage.[1] Though painted landscape scenery conveyed the illusion of great depths and distances, it was far from realistic. Landscape as a genre entered into Renaissance art theory through architectural discourse, as Italian Renaissance theater drew upon published reworkings of manuscript copies of Vitruvius' *de Architectura* that had survived, to match the mode of drama to stage setting.[2]

This treatise is an exhaustive ordering of architectural spaces, their styles, proportions, construction, decoration and the meaning carried by combinations of those categories. Among his practical instructions on the building of theaters, Vitruvius outlined three modes of theater: tragic, comic, satiric (Vitruvius 1960: 150). Tragedy was to be played against architectural elements associated with public buildings – reflecting the heroic deeds of public figures; comedy was to be played against domestic architectural elements – reflecting the activities of private citizens; while satiric plays – involving an idealized world of shepherds and peasants, nymphs and satyrs – were to be staged against landscape. Landscape was not an appropriate backdrop for significant human action. That belonged to the realm of city and citizen.

Landscape was also assigned the lowest point on the scale of genres of painting; indeed it did not even warrant discussion in the first Renaissance treatise on painting (Rosand 1988). Nevertheless, it was the critical element in Theocritus' *Idylls*, an extensive pastoral poem which had long been a source of inspiration to other writers. Virgil's *Eclogues* (written *c*. 42–37 BC) expanded upon the *Idylls*, translated them from Greek to Latin, imbued them with a moral direction, and transposed them from Sicily to an imagined Arcadia (Rosand 1988; Short 1991; Tayler 1961). The publication in Italian of Sannazaro's *Arcadia* in 1540 not only brought this pastoral aesthetic to a wider European audience, but acted as an impetus to its pictorial expression. The works of Leonardo da Vinci, Giorgione, Titian and their circles, enabled landscape to begin to evolve (though not in any linear fashion), as an independent subject matter with its own priorities and aesthetic (Cafritz, Gowing and Rosand 1988). As a genre of painting, landscape underwent transformation from an aesthetic based upon vastness of scale capable of inspiring a religious or quasi-religious experience in the observer, to a classicized, Arcadian aesthetic that was literally more down-to-earth.

Evidence that the metaphor of landscape-as-theater had common currency among European reading elites can be found in the frequency with which the word 'theater' appears in the titles of sixteenth and seventeenth-century printed works relating to land. These include cosmographies, geographies, collected illustrations of cities, and manuals of land-use instruction. In the latter category, both Theocritus and Virgil have the status of 'founding citations' (Short 1991). In the meanwhile, and in conjunction with the emergence of merchant capitalism, the landscape-as-theater metaphor entered vernacular usage and theater itself became less a matter of spatial illusion and magical spectacle, and more a matter of drama or psychological confrontation (Jackson 1980). The human passions and interests presented on stage are an example of the 'detailed and candid dissection of human nature' (Hirschman 1977: 15) that preceded capitalism's harnessing or suppression of them.

The perspectival gaze served mercantile capitalism's ordering and codifying drive in various ways. One is the wide range of subject matter encompassed within the metaphor which, apart from land-related topics, ran the gamut from theaters of lace patterns to theaters of mechanical engineering.[3] A second is the practical application of this new landscape perspective to the technical practices of cartography and land surveying that became invested with artistic concerns of light as well as linear and aerial perspective. The cartographic record of the Venetian Republic's shift from a maritime economy to the capitalization of estates (Cosgrove 1988) is a good example of this art of capitalism.

The perspectival gaze operated in two quite different modes. One was representational, allowing three dimensions to be realistically conveyed on a single plane, so that the actual experience of space was made available to the audience. The second was political, where European expansion was achieved through the mastery of all that was figuratively and literally surveyed. Although the 'irregularity of the natural landscape . . . disqualified it as a preferred stage' (Rosand 1988: 23) for significant human action in ancient and Renaissance theater, the natural landscape did submit to such action in the subsequent world of politics and economics, 'triangulation by triangulation, war by war, treaty by treaty' (B. Anderson 1991: 173).

Space is linked to concepts of power. Whether examined as forms of discourse, representation or physical reality, landscape and territory are embedded in relations of power and knowledge (B. Anderson 1991; Barnes and Duncan 1992; Bowen 1981; Darian-Smith, Gunner and Nuttall 1996; Foucault 1980; Harley 1988; Parmenter 1994). The early Renaissance sense of space, articulated through perspective, allowed for a visual appropriation of landscape. At the same time a parallel (as well as unparalleled) political appropriation of territory began (Wolf 1982). The imposition of intellectual order upon unruly though soon enough to be ruled continents, was marked by a flurry of classificatory enumeration, categorization and mapping (Cosgrove 1988; Hodgen 1964; Thomas 1983), the investigative modalities by which knowledge was gathered, ordered and transformed into technologies of control (Cohn 1996), and by which collections of artifacts, antiquities and art were put together.

Such processes transformed neutral geographical territory into culturally defined landscapes, generating and naturalizing the identities ascribed to them and their inhabitants (Darian-Smith *et al.* 1996; Smith 1985). Print capitalism was a major means for the dissemination of those cultural landscapes. For as trade and commerce followed the flag, and new territories were surveyed and described in rational, scientific and economic ways of seeing, engravings of the new territories' landscapes worked themselves back into the theater as stage sets.

# Prints and Imprints of Power

A common language permeating all levels of society is central to the concept of imagined community (B. Anderson 1991). While the vernacular printed word was a shared sign, a sort of new-style communion wafer absorbed not into the body but the mind, there was an important pictorial component to print-capitalism as well. Indeed the printed image is an even more democratic 'language', being more immediately accessible to the less literate and illiterate (P. Anderson 1991; Atherton 1974; Newman 1987). If the discourse of landscape can be posited as the nonarbitrary sign of an imagined community's language (Mitchell 1994), then topographical illustrations must be its purest expression.

Medieval and early Renaissance landscape depictions are most often presented as colorful panoramas revealing or supporting a divine order. Landscape paintings of the High Renaissance operate within the more intimate scale and setting of the pastoral. Under the impact of European exploration and colonization, landscape depictions revealing or supporting a divine order (in some cases, a Protestant one) viewed through the values and interests of mercantile capitalism, were incorporated into 'the black and white of the printed word or the steel engraving' (Jackson 1980: 72).

English topography of the seventeenth and early eighteenth centuries was particularly robust. It reflected the long-established importance assigned to empirical observation, the role of professional draughtsmen who surveyed and described lands both at home and abroad, and their patronage by antiquaries (Smith 1985). An ever-increasing audience was presented with illustrated accounts of voyages of discovery and exploration – that all-encompassing gaze ranging over a panoramic 'world' landscape. The cultural commodification of landscape can be seen in the production of collections of prints, illustrated books, journals, and newspaper articles that both fueled and serviced widespread public interest in such accounts. For example, charts of Captain Cook's voyages in the Pacific appeared in the *Gentleman's Magazine* throughout 1773–75. Interest in exotic landscapes was paralleled by a similar interest in landscapes of home. English illustrated county histories far outnumbered their European counterparts (Harris and Jackson-Stops 1984).

The word 'imprint' has multiple meanings. It can refer to the publisher's name and address that appears on a book's frontispiece (an illustration generally facing the title-page),[4] the physical mark of a house on the land, the culturally indelible mark of a particular class, or an immutable 'impression' – also part of the vocabulary of the world of books and prints. A concatenation of all these meanings is gathered up in a single type of printed image. Known as bird's-eye views, these prints of the imprints of power epitomize the perspectival gaze. Although found across Europe, those under consideration here relate only to the English landscape. Indeed 'bird's-eye view' is one definition of 'landscape' in English usage (*Oxford English Dictionary* 1971).

The folio-sized *Nouveau théâtre de la Grande Bretagne* (Kip and Knyff 1708) published in London, is what might be called the ultimate illustrated and cross-county history. An opening essay describing the various seats is written in French, thereby further confirming the distance that separated the reading elite for whom it was intended from the more democratic language of the printed image. Subscriptions were paid by members of the nobility and aristocracy to ensure that their country seats were drawn and engraved for the *Théâtre*. Its eighty double plates (45 × 30 cm.) have litanies of titles and ranks set below them in English.[5] (Did the publisher realize that it would never do to have one's place in the *Théâtre* without being accorded one's placement in the cultural hierarchy in a language that one could be sure was understood?)

The bird's-eye views of palaces and country seats visually dominate their surrounding countryside, as the elite who inhabited them dominated the country socially, politically and economically (see figures 1 and 2):

> When the Duke of Beaufort dined in state in the saloon behind the central frontispiece at Badminton, he was at the hub of a web of converging avenues stretching far into the surrounding countryside, underlying the fact that all the local avenues of power and influence converged on him – not just as a great landowner and heir of an ancient family, but as Lord Lieutenant and Lord President of Wales.
>
> (Girouard 1980: 145)

Turning plate after plate of the imposing first edition of *Nouveau théâtre*, looking at regimented rows of trees and clipped topiary, symmetrically disposed plinths set with busts, and ranks of statues all centered on one country seat after another, it suddenly becomes apparent that they look for all the world like silent audiences waiting for the empty stages of their vast baroque gardens to be animated. Occasionally groups of men are shown playing bowls, one or two people stroll an immense pathway, the odd carriage with attendant outriders arrives, or the horses and hounds of a hunt stream across distant fields. But for the most part the sets are largely unpeopled (see figures 3–6).

The agricultural setting is depicted as no less empty of people than the immediate surroundings of the country house. If agricultural laborers appear at all, which is rare, and despite the huge amount of labor actually required to bring in the harvest, they do so as a single group of four or five women and men harvesting fields so vast that they couldn't possibly work their way through them by Michaelmas![6] Whether harvesting, raking hay, or loading the harvest wagons, they are literally as well as metaphorically peripheral: set at a distance, on-the-edge indicators of a well-ordered estate, the marginalia of the landed base that was itself the bulwark of the state (see figures 7 and 8). That the base of human labor underpinning this display had to be obscured requires some explanation. And the explanation relates to the eventual peopling of the landscape.

*Nouveau théâtre* can be read as a political and not simply as an aesthetic document. Those who had access to these bird's-eye views, either as subscribers, purchasers, or members of patronage circles receiving individual prints, knew very well that harvesting was a labor-intensive activity. The absence of agricultural laborers in plate after plate when harvest time is the moment presented, has to be more than some kind of artistic oversight, given the topographical specificity underlying the whole project.[7] While some scholars have put such absences down to the landowning elite's nostalgia for preferred landscapes (Prince 1988; Barrel 1980), others have seen it as a telling marker of the fear of collective action (Vardi 1995), or as the ideological functioning of the superstructure (Bermingham 1986).

One way of combining such understandings is to see this theater of prints both as an internally circulating expression of an ideational landscape that carried the social imprint of a dominant class, and as an externally circulating means for the dissemination of that ideational landscape. As for the absence of labor and laborers, a combined understanding brings us to the symbolic dissonance between the high and the low: the numerous statues and plinthed busts radiating in orderly fashion from the country seats, and the paucity of bent or gesturing agricultural workers scattered in the fields. Each is the symbolic inversion of the other. In the following quotation, grotesque 'designates the marginal, the low and the outside from the perspective of [that which is] situated as high, inside and central by virtue of its very exclusions' (Stallybrass and White 1986: 22–3). Of critical importance to this exploration of categories of high and low is Bakhtin's observation of

> the compelling difference between the human body as represented in popular festivity and the body as represented in classical statuary . . . He noticed how the two forms of iconography 'embodied' utterly contrary registers of being. To begin with the classical statue was always mounted on a plinth which meant that it was elevated, static and monumental. In the one simple fact of the plinth or pedestal the classical body signalled a whole different somatic conception from that of the grotesque body which was usually multiple, . . . teeming, always already part of a throng. By contrast, the classical statue is the radiant centre of a transcendent individualism, 'put on a pedestal', raised above the viewer and the commonality and anticipating passive admiration from below. . . . The grotesque body is emphasized as mobile, split, multiple self, a subject of pleasure in processes of exchange; and it is never never closed off from either its social or ecosystemic context. The classical body on the other hand keeps its distance.
>
> (Stallybrass and White 1986: 21–2)

The transcendent individualism encoded in the country house depended in part upon its agricultural base even while it depended upon the repudiation of the 'sweaty vulgar' (Hill 1992: 129) who worked that agricultural base. That repudiation is given further symbolic value in prints delineating authority and social status while simultaneously furthering the identity they helped to establish. Significantly, the true source of wealth supporting this nexus of country, country house, and country-house living was no longer entirely based on agricultural labor, but included trade, commerce and even industry. Such theaters of prints as examined here also served to obscure the social relations of these money-making activities, masking wealth in a rhetoric of land.

Two meanings of 'country' come through clearly in these prints: the territoriality of the nation, and land that was agriculturally productive. The theater of bird's-eye views straddled these linked fields of power in which wealth, territorial, and status elites coalesced. The collection formed a double imprint of power: the country seat as the state in its localized form was 'state/d' over and over again, while the *Théâtre* as an object of material culture was the means of an extended display of status within and between categories of membership in 'the country.' In a process of mutual reinforcement of cultural imagery, the nation,

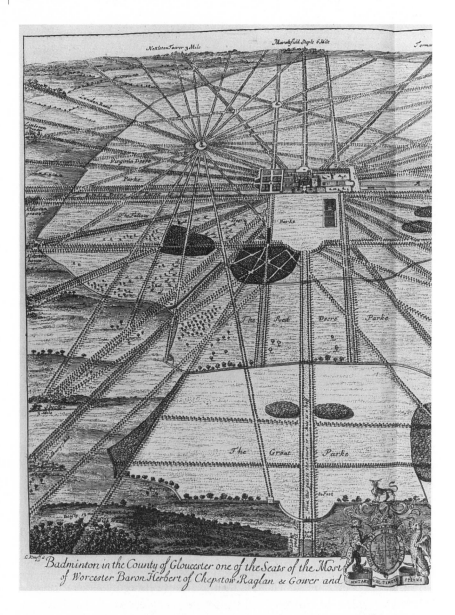

**Figure 1** Plate 12. *Nouveau théâtre de la Grande Bretagne*, "Badminton in the County of Gloucester one of the Seats of the . . . Duke of Beaufort." Avery Architectural and Fine Arts Library, Columbia University in the City of New York

**Figure 2** Plate 12. *Nouveau théâtre de la Grande Bretagne*, "Badminton in the County of Gloucester one of the Seats of the . . . Duke of Beaufort." Avery Architectural and Fine Arts Library, Columbia University in the City of New York

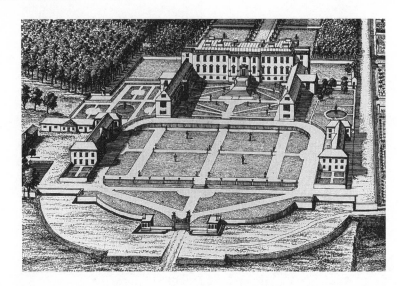

**Figure 3** Plate 41 (detail). *Nouveau théâtre de la Grande Bretagne* "Lowther in the County of Westmorland . . ." Avery Architectural and Fine Arts Library, Columbia University in the City of New York

**Figure 4** Plate 58 (detail). *Nouveau théâtre de la Grande Bretagne*, "Hatley St. George . . . Cambridgeshire." Avery Architectural and Fine Arts Library, Columbia University in the City of New York

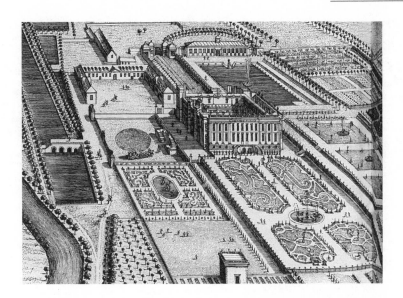

**Figure 5** Plate 17 (detail). *Nouveau théâtre de la Grande Bretagne,* "Chatsworth
. . . Seat of Wm. Duke and Earl of Devonshire . . . " Avery Architectural and Fine
Arts Library, Columbia University in the City of New York

**Figure 6** Plate 17 (detail). *Nouveau théâtre de la Grande Bretagne,* "Chatsworth
. . . Seat of Wm. Duke and Earl of Devonshire . . ." Avery Architectural and Fine Arts
Library, Columbia University in the City of New York

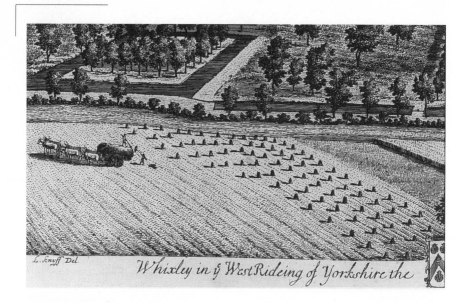

**Figure 7** Plate 78 (detail). *Nouveau théâtre de la Grande Bretagne*, "Whixley in ye West Rideing of Yorkshire." Avery Architectural and Fine Arts Library, Columbia University in the City of New York

**Figure 8** Plate 64 (detail). *Nouveau théâtre de la Grande Bretagne*, "Acklam in Cleveland . . ." Avery Architectural and Fine Arts Library, Columbia University in the City of New York

**Figure 9** Stourhead: view of lake with bridge and Pantheon

**Figure 10** Stourhead: Pantheon 1753–54, Architect, Henry Flitcroft

and those who politically and economically represented the nation, were re-presented through land.

While *Nouveau théâtre* shrank in size (the original 45 × 30 cm. becoming 23 × 36 cm.), a tangle of future editions expanded in scope,[8] going from the original one volume of 1708 to five volumes in 1715, with new editions brought out through the 1720s. The phenomenal popularity of the enterprise speaks to the expanding gentry's entry into land ownership and country-house living in the late seventeenth to mid-eighteenth centuries, and to the importance attaching to gentlemen being well-versed in architectural matters. The widening circle of those whose country seat or seats made it into *Nouveau théâtre* was further enlarged by the practice of distributing individual prints within patronage circles.[9] Cultural capital and landscape were inseparably entwined. Though mercantile wealth did not itself confer cultural capital, it provided the means of acquiring it. With the mercantile elite's literal buying into the aristocracy, property replaced blood in legitimating cultural leadership of the nation, and the landscaping of the English country house reified those power relations (Olwig 1993).

The banker Henry Hoare II (1705–85) helped finance the aristocracy's early eighteenth-century re-landscaping spree (Woodbridge 1989). Axially-planned baroque gardens and forests like those depicted in the *Théâtre* were replaced by open and pseudo-naturalistic parkland. Interest generated on these extensive loans, plus profits from his engagement in the slave trade, helped provide the capital for Hoare's own major landscaping project undertaken at his Wiltshire estate, Stourhead. Now considered the 'jewel in the crown' of Britain's National Trust, Stourhead was rebuilt in classical Roman style and landscaped into a sumptuous vision of Arcadia (see figures 9 and 10). Hoare successfully transformed property in people to status in property, thereby giving physical form to yet another link in the 'mind-forged manacles' (Blake [1794]: Abrams 1986) that obscured social relations based upon slavery abroad or poverty at home.

As the grounds of the English country house lost their rigid axial formality – a style contemporaries associated with France's political system of unbending monarchical absolutism – the aesthetic principles applied to the buildings themselves resulted in structures that were 'the epitome of ordered rectilinear rationality' (Stone and Stone 1986: 239). In the remodeling of both grounds and buildings we meet again the same two major classical texts: Vitruvius' *De Architectura* and Virgil's rendering of Theocritus' *Idylls*. *De Architectura* had been central to Andrea Palladio's (1508–80) fiercely symmetrical reinterpretations of

Roman architecture in and around Vicenza in the Italian Beneto region. Palladianism, the style derived from Palladio's buildings and publications, had been introduced into England by Inigo Jones (1573–1652) in the very early seventeenth century, but a fully-fledged neo-Palladian or neoclassical revival came almost a hundred years later, marked by Colen Campbell's three-volume *Vitruvius Britannicus* (published 1715, 1717, 1725). Engravings of Inigo Jones's classically-inspired buildings were gradually supplemented by illustrations of Campbell's and other neoclassical architects' commissions for members of the English aristocracy, as their great country seats and town houses were remodeled or rebuilt.

## Italian Campagna to English Countryside

Education in the classics shaped cultural perceptions and values that were eventually inscribed in the physical landscape. More widespread formal education of English elite males at the colleges of Oxford and Cambridge exposed them to the aesthetics of classical architecture and to Greek and Roman literature. Such knowledge was considered essential to the acquisition of cultured taste and manners – attributes of a gentleman that mattered more than pedigree (Girouard 1980; Stone and Stone 1986). Study of classical literature and architecture 'functioned as an extra, expensive piece of intellectual equipment to take into the field' (Andrews 1989: 3), and helped to encourage a new appreciation of landscape. It also exposed the well-educated to the oppositional relationship of city and country portrayed in classical literature, which elevated country life to a higher sphere either by transforming the harsh realities of agricultural production into an idealized vision of pastoral serenity (as in Virgil's *Eclogues*) or by locating moral integrity in the work of the rural world (as in Virgil's *Georgics*) (Miles 1980; Williams 1973).

Education and travel combined to reinforce the eighteenth-century Oxbridge elite's way of intellectualizing landscape in pictorial and literary terms. The semi-obligatory Grand Tour to Italy enabled the young English connoisseurs – or *dilettanti* as they were called – not only to purchase antiquities (sometimes fakes) but also to amass their great collections of late seventeenth-century landscape paintings that depicted an idealized and classicized Italian *campagna* often set with figures from classical myths, grottos, temples and architectural ruins (see plates 1 and 2). A Society of Dilettanti was formed in London in 1734 as a dining club for Grand Tour returnees (Cust 1898), young noblemen and men of wealth and position who formed interlocking circles of political and cultural influence, and whose wives and daughters helped cement relations through service at court and elsewhere.[10]

Not simply a question of a few months spent on the Continent, the Grand Tour often involved two, three, or more years during which time young English noblemen and their friends received an education in aesthetics. Even the likes of Dr. Johnson confessed to feelings of inferiority for never having been able to make the Tour (Tashjian, Tashjian and Enright 1990). Especially in Italy, the *dilettanti* collected art works with something approaching abandon,[11] which stimulated a London art market as they and fellow connoisseurs continued to acquire antiquities and paintings.[12]

The baroque setting of the English country house was then reconfigured to accord with the Arcadian aesthetic that informed, and was in turn reinforced by, the acquisition of unrivaled collections of the classicized pastoral paintings of Claude, Poussin, Dughet and their circles.[13] The relandscaping of the English country house thus emerged from an education in a classically rooted pastoral literature (basically Theocritis' *Idylls* by way of Virgil's *Eclogues* and Sannazaro's *Arcadia*), and that literature's pictorial interpretation. The result was neoclassically conceived buildings surrounded by literally picturesque landscaped parks structured along pastoral lines.

As the surroundings of the English aristocracy's and upper gentry's houses began to be relandscaped to conform to the contrived naturalness of this classicized genre of painting, the distinctions between reality and representation were blurred:

> The ultimate 'realism' is achieved ... when the artistic signifier is a landscape garden which is virtually indistinguishable from the surrounding countryside ... When landscape and nature become one with a physical environment, this environment does not cease to bear value-laden, normative meanings concerning the natural. On the contrary, those meanings become even more naturalized because they no longer appear to derive from an artistic scene composed by a subject, an author or artist, but from objective physical reality itself.
>
> (Olwig 1993: 319)

That landscape could function as a theater of power is starkly apparent in Kip and Knyff's evolving engravings. The reconfigured landscape was no less a theater of power than before; it was simply a more natural one that further mystified actual relations of power.

The views through the windows of the great country houses now reflected the paintings hanging in their interiors. So tightly interrelated were Italian pastoral paintings and the English country-house landscapes that they inspired, that those country estates themselves have been considered 'in a manner our oldest and grandest National Gallery' (Blunden 1935: 6). In an inversion of this, and reflecting the popularity of a picturesque landscape aesthetic and panoramas, in 1793 Sir Nigel Gresley commissioned Paul Sandby to decorate the walls of a room in Drakelowe Hall, his Peak District mansion, with a panoramic perspective of the Peak District landscape. Apart from one wall which was given over to a window looking out onto the landscape, the whole room was decorated with a painted panorama of the external view. Fencing, complete with open wicket gates, was set a few inches forward of the walls (see plate 3). Here then is another twist to Olwig's 'ultimate realism'.

But the country-house views, or prospects, could be maintained – whether in reality, literature or art – only by continuing to suppress or gloss over the human labor of the agricultural base from which the landed elite derived a significant proportion of their wealth. What had been artistically left out in the earlier bird's-eye views was now literally taken out. The creation of aesthetically pleasing pastoral landscapes necessitated that agricultural processes, agricultural laborers, and even whole villages be removed from sight to create an unpeopled and picturesque landscape, pristinely available to the privileged viewer.

Aesthetic clearances dovetailed with the economically driven acceleration of parliamentary enclosures, which meant that the impact of enclosure was intense and swiftly deep, leading to a reshaping of the moral order as well as of the visual world.[14] And it was precisely because agriculture was no longer the only source of wealth that aesthetic clearances could be undertaken. It was the implosion of an earlier moral universe that informed the poetry of protest from Goldsmith to John Clare, which articulated 'the sadness and anger of a whole people [for whom the] leaden present and the golden past are not just historical or mythological [but] personal experiences' (Brownlow 1983: 4).

A poetry of protest to so radical an unpeopling of the landscape inevitably followed (Brownlow 1983; Keith 1980; Sales 1983; Williams 1973), epitomized by *The Deserted Village* in which:

> . . . The man of wealth and pride,
> Takes up a space that many poor supplied;
> Space for his lake, his park's extended bounds,

Thus fares the land, by luxury betrayed;
In nature's simplest charms at first arrayed;
But verging to decline, its splendors rise,
Its vistas strike, its palaces surprise;
While scourged by famine from the smiling land,
The mournful peasant leads his humble band;
And while he sinks without one arm to save,
The country blooms – a garden, and a grave . . .

(Goldsmith [1773]; Abrams 1968)

While Malthus was writing about the terrors of overpopulation, depopulation of the land was taking place: raw material of some of Blake's *Songs of Experience.*

As this 'drama of dispossession became a theatre of possession' (Boland 1995), the cultural elite looked beyond their scenic parkland to the enlarged and hedged fields of an improved agricultural landscape.[15] For at the same time that the relandscaping of the English country house was taking place, rights in the commons continued to be extinguished, and village open-fields enclosed by the great sweep of parliamentary enclosures (Beresford 1961; Butlin 1979; Gonner 1912; Mingay 1976). A visible displacement of the lines of power occurred: the layout of the country-house setting became sinuous, while the new and enlarged fields of the enclosure movement took on the rigid lines of the surveyors' rule. The landscape of agricultural improvement also functioned as a site of entertainment for the inhabitants of the country seats as practices of agricultural improvement, considered 'pursuits so truly worthy of a British nobleman' (Young 1771 cited in Stone and Stone 1986: 302), led to the elite's increased involvement with the running of estates and therefore to longer stays in the country.[16]

## Landscape Scenery in Eighteenth-century English Theater and Panoramas, and the Education of an Audience

Another way in which landscape moved into the realm of entertainment was through the theater. Though the meaning of realistic disappears under the shimmering interplay between loam-and-vegetation re-presentations or interpretations of paintings that themselves imaginatively recreated past landscapes of poetry, more realistic landscape representations were called for in the late eighteenth-century

London theater. Realistic in this sense meant accurate representations of great country house landscapes, as well as specific landmark features appearing in illustrated publications such as *The Copper Plate Magazine* and *The Virtuosis Museum* – for whom theater scene-painters doubled as engravers (Parris 1973). And it was theater scene-painters who by the mid-nineteenth century had quit the theater to paint panoramas (Hyde 1988).

Before examining this further, it is necessary to backtrack to Inigo Jones. He had not only introduced classical architecture into England, but as stage-designer for masques at the courts of James I and Charles I he introduced Vitruvius's scenic recommendations to the English stage. Within English theater's prevalent formality of Italianate baroque symmetry (epitomized a hundred years later in the gardens and grounds of Kip and Knyff's *Nouveau théâtre*), Jones designed rustic pastoral 'settings [that] were more natural and . . . more English in tone . . . with their back shutters of tranquil cornfields' (Rosenfeld 1972: 171).[17] As with his introduction of classical architecture, Inigo Jones's sceno-graphic innovations also had to wait until the eighteenth century before being developed in the Drury Lane Theatre and Covent Garden's Theatre Royal, the patent theaters or companies licenced by Charles II after the Restoration.

Meanwhile, landscape scenery found a home in English pantomime which maintained the earlier, *commedia dell'arte* elements of pageant and spectacle. Through its carnivalesque elements, pantomime func-tioned as a site of countenanced transgression of the social order. Here, landscape scenery was the backdrop against which rustics could castigate people of rank (Rosenfeld 1972), in a sort of symbolic reverse conversation between the agricultural workers and classical sculptures depicted in Kip's bird's-eye views. By the mid-eighteenth century, a landscape tradition had been established in the English pantomime. The demand for topographical and historical accuracy (which coincided with the early years of the English Romantic Movement) led to more realistic scenographic representation, including the on-stage burning of (less-than-tranquil?) cornfields, and to criticism if topographical details were not quite right (Backsheider 1993; Funkel 1996; Rosenfeld 1972). Pantomime straddled the outdoors carnivalesque world of the fair, and the indoor world of theaters. Paradoxically, theaters were enclosed sites of assembly within which landscapes took on a special importance.

While the status of Georgian theater was generally low, suspect and unstable, legitimate actors in London moved with ease between licenced patent theaters and the licentious domain of carnivals and fairs (Brewer 1997; Russell 1995; Stallybrass and White 1986). Great actors such as David Garrick made the acting profession respectable, thereby giving theater a role in the development not only of polite public opinion, but a polite public. The notion of cultural semantics hinges upon such displacements between sites of discourse, each having its laws and protocols which serve to code social identity. Moreover,

> ... the most significant kinds of displacement are *across* diverse territories of semantic material and always appear to involve steep gradients, even precipitous leaps, between socially unequal discursive domains ... [that] regulate the body and discursive laws through the formation of manners, habits and attitudes *appropriate* (and it is this 'appropriateness' which is the crucial regulative factor) to each social domain.
>
> (Stalleybrass and White 1986: 198–9)

The social domains of theater audiences and fairground gawkers did not seem to differ much as far as their unruly behavior was concerned. Audiences had to be civilized, they had to refrain from treating the theater as a political arena in which the 'socially encoded hierarchy of box, pit, and gallery' (Russell 1995: 16) was boisterously and sometimes riotously played out. The civilizing process required that the audience be reconfigured from Bakhtin's 'grotesque body' which was 'multiple, teeming, always already part of a throng' (Stalleybrass and White 1986: 21–2), to the stasis of the classical statue. The audience had both to know its place and agree to stay there, silent and still – not milling about, talking and fighting during performances, or conversing with the performers. The Bakhtinian statue also appeared upon the stage, for by the late eighteenth-century, pantomime techniques were used in legitimate theater to convey emotion: 'freezing a moment of particular significance or emotional resonance' by striking poses that were 'readable configurations visually conceived' (Backsheider 1993: 176).

For people of taste, theater became a site for realism in landscape scenery. Major sources for that realism were the highly popular illustrated descriptions of Pacific voyages of discovery (Mitchell 1994; Rosenfeld 1972; Smith 1985), as well as the burgeoning fashion for picturesque touring within Britain (Backsheider 1993). One person in whom these threads met and gained expression was the landscape artist Philippe Jacques de Loutherbourg (1740–1812). A highly respected member of both the Académie des Beaux-Arts and later the Royal

Academy, he was engaged in 1772 by the actor-manager David Garrick as exclusive stage and scenery designer for a pantomime at the Drury Lane Theatre.

The close association between the two men, playwright and stage designer, was 'a process that had not been adopted since the days of Inigo Jones', and through it Loutherbourg went on to become 'one of the most influential stage designers England had ever seen' (Joppien 1973: n.p.). Whether producing scenery in a romantic or picturesque vein (dramatic mountains and raging torrents (see plate 4), topographical sites, and stormy seas and skies) or panoramic views bathed in light, Loutherbourg's scenery was praised by critics in terms of its likeness to seventeenth-century Italian neoclassical paintings (Funkel 1996). Scenery from his numerous and highly popular productions at Drury Lane and Covent Garden's Theatre Royal were copied on the stages of provincial theaters (Rosenfeld 1972), thereby further disseminating the cultural elite's landscape taste to a broader public.[18] It is ironic that some of the scenery Loutherbourg was producing extolled the very virtues so decried by Garrick's friend Oliver Goldsmith, author of *The Deserted Village*.

In his pursuit of realism and the picturesque, Loutherbourg traveled to the Derbyshire Peak District in 1778 to make studies for the following year's Drury Lane pantomime, *The Wonders of Derbyshire*. Apart from Chatsworth, the Duke of Devonshire's seat, with its grand-scale formal garden and expansive park,[19] the wonders were almost entirely geological formations, home-grown versions of curiosities such as those illustrated in Hawkesworth's *Voyages* (1773).[20] As Bernard Smith writes, 'Here, then, in the theatre as in painting, the representation of exotic landscapes and peoples was a harbinger of naturalism' (Smith 1985: 117). *The Wonders of Derbyshire* was the first pantomime

on the British stage which concentrated exclusively on landscape as a form of theatrical representation, and the plot was simply developed as a pretext for a number of changes in scenery . . . The construction of the scenery . . . is particularly interesting in that it no longer follows the tradition of separating wings from borders, but unifies these two elements in a sweeping, oval, coherent curve.

(Joppien 1973: n.p.)

The combination of Loutherbourg's scenographic realism and his stage's 'coherent curve' eventually led to a naturalism that dispensed with actors entirely.

From 1782 to 1793, Loutherbourg sporadically exhibited his *eidophusikon*, a miniature theater devoted to unpeopled landscapes in which scenic effects were the performance (Funkel 1996; Joppien 1973). This presaged the advent of the panorama, with its total grasp of perspective, and later the moving panorama which was incorporated back into pantomime as a moving backdrop. In 1789 Robert Barker's 360° view of Edinburgh and its surroundings, what he called 'nature at a glance,' opened in London. In a manner that recollects the new way of looking attributed to Renaissance perspective painting, the panorama was seen as ushering in 'a new age of verisimilitude . . . in the tradition of illusionistic perspective painting' (Wilcox 1988: 25). In Paris in 1799 the American Robert Fulton exhibited to great and immediate success a 'grandiose, circular panorama of New World scenery, accurate in every detail and without the disturbing presence of a single actor' (Jackson 1980: 77).

From Loutherbourg's 'sweeping, oval, coherent curve' to an all-encompassing inverted panopticon in which the viewer saw no one, the perspectival gaze was now fully realized. Here were theaters without actors, devoted to the display of landscapes without people. Louis Daguerre, scene painter at the Paris Opéra and popular theaters, and inventor of the daguerreotype, went on to produce dioramas which were partial, less-than-360° views. Like Loutherbourg's *eidophusikon*, Daguerre's dioramas placed great emphasis on the effects of light. They were of such startling realism that one contemporary wrote: 'one attempts to leave one's box in order to wander out into the open and climb to the summit of the mountain' (quoted in Newhall 1964: 16). The scattering of figures in some panoramic paintings confirmed to the viewer that indeed it was possible to climb to the summit for the unpeopled view (see figures 11 and 12). Landscape had moved from backdrop to foreground, taking on its own dramatic role in the process.

As a mode of entertainment panoramas and dioramas were initially seen by large numbers of the gentry and middling sorts, either in freestanding rotundas or as scrolling views in the patent theater pantomimes. Their public accessibility broadened during the nineteenth century as theater-scene painters left pantomime production to paint panoramas for the peripatetic world of fair circuits. Scene painters also maintained the panoramas and dioramas shown in provincial cities in rotundas especially built for that purpose, which contained different facilities for various social classes of viewers. As modes of representation they so permeated traditional studio painting that contemporary critics saw panoramists as threatening the academy:

Le panorama est un phénomène populaire qui menace les élites et leur confiscation de la pratique artistique, d'autant plus que très vite les panoramistes vont s'aventurer sur la chasse gardée par excellence des académies, celle des batailles, de la guerre, qu'on peut assimiler de près ou de loin à la peinture d'histoire.

(quoted in Comment 1993: 60)

(The panorama is a popular phenomenon that threatens the elites and their appropriation of artistic practice, the more so since the panoramists will very soon wander into the protected hunting grounds of the academies, those of battles, of war, which one can more or less liken to history painting.)

The architectural and managed vegetative elements in the landscapes depicted by Kip and Knyff look like so many silent audiences waiting for the actors to arrive. The panoramic landscape *was* the actor, silently awaiting its audiences. Bird's-eye views were virtually or entirely unpeopled. They were a cultural production for and about an elite segment of society that relied upon multiple distances of space, language, manners, etc. between itself and the rest of the populace. The earliest panoramas were also virtually or entirely unpeopled. (Later ones often depicted battle scenes and peopled cityscapes.) They were a cultural production aimed at the widest possible audience that, paradoxically, at least in their early stage, gave their audiences the impression of being alone. Indeed, to maintain this effect, the number of viewers admitted at any one time was sometimes limited. Panoramas gained such enormous popularity with the 'humbler classes' that the *Illustrated London News* referred to the phenomenon as a 'panoramania' (Hyde 1988: 11).

Panoramas imbued views and the act of viewing with cultural value and disseminated that value widely. During the nineteenth century several million people in Britain flocked to panoramas by which they toured the Mississippi, criss-crossed Europe, made Polar expeditions, and scaled Mont Blanc (Hyde 1988; Schama 1996; Wilcox 1988). Wilcox states that 'the real success story of the panorama lay not in the creation of great lasting works of art, but in the creation of a new public for art and a new conception of what a work of art could be' (Wilcox 1988: 42). I would take this observation a step further. Paralleling the manner in which the landscape-as-theater metaphor had common currency among an earlier European reading elite, serving to promote mercantile capitalism's perspectival gaze, the widespread and common currency

**Figure 11** John Knox, 1810, "South-western view from Loch Lomond." Oil on canvas, 62.2 × 157.5 cm. Glasgow Museum and Art Gallery

of these 'bird's-eye-views-in-the-round' subtly promoted the shift from pseudo-travel to actual engagement with landscapes.

Here was an engagement rife with commercial possibilities. Travel in Europe had earlier been confined to an aristocratic and Oxbridge elite who toured at a leisurely pace by private carriage over an extended period, relying in part upon political and social letters of introduction to ease their passage. From the late eighteenth-century on, domestic travel became an increasingly popular middle-class leisure activity. Advances in transportation by road and train made touring more comfortable and relatively swift. The eventual cessation of nearly a century of Anglo-French hostilities meant that a burgeoning middle class, already introduced to foreign landscapes and cityscapes by panoramas, could undertake Continental travel via arrangements with Thomas Cook and other similar entrepreneurs. In the case of the 'humbler classes', travel through the unpeopled landscapes of home was done on Shanks's Pony or cheap rail excursions. A more complete exploitation of unpeopled domestic landscapes would have to await the twentieth century – a topic that will be dealt with in the later chapters of this work.

In the meantime, in the process of imbuing landscapes – especially unpeopled ones – with cultural value, panoramas had a function analogous to that which Italian landscape paintings had performed for the gentry. Like those paintings, panoramas became a medium through which specific values circulated at an unremarked-upon level. By introducing large numbers of people to views, and by rendering viewing a culturally valued aesthetic experience, panoramas and

**Figure 12** John Knox, 1810, "South-western view from Ben Lomond." Oil on canvas, 62.2 × 157.5 cm. Glasgow Museums

dioramas represented a transformation of the pattern of exclusion of people from landscape, both at one remove – in the act of viewing landscape representations – and directly – in promoting travel.

## Cultural Mimicry

Whether dealing with seventeenth-century paintings of classicized landscapes, early eighteenth-century black and white bird's-eye views of rigidly organized landscapes, or later eighteenth-century picturesque rolling parkland set with lakes, grottos, Grecian temples and so forth, landscape appears to be the actual as well as abstract repository of an interlocking web of projections rooted in a larger pre-existent ideological system. That system appears to refer constantly back to a time of social stability located temporally as well as geographically in a variety of golden pasts (Barrel 1980; Girouard 1980; Parris 1973; Payne 1994; Stuart 1979; Williams 1973). A semiotic examination of the hidden discourse of power compounded of 'landscape', 'nature', 'culture' and 'nation', combined with an etymological examination of those words so freighted with multiple meanings, reveals the symbolically loaded ideology and fetishized identity between people and landscape (Olwig 1993). The same exercise also shows how a rhetoric of land is capable of carrying political despair and rage (Parmenter 1994).

One aspect of that fetishized identity, unpeopledness, and the extent of its widespread currency in eighteenth-century England, are revealed by examining modes of cultural mimicry for its presence. The late seventeenth through eighteenth centuries saw the rise in English society of what contemporaries called the 'middling sort': merchants, trades-men and, perhaps most importantly, newly proliferating professionals. The middling sort's gentrification through the cultural mimicry of their social superiors is of importance to the argument that an imagined community, constituted around more or less unpeopled landscapes, extended a good way down the social scale. In the context of this chapter, the following quotation speaks to the production in England through cultural mimicry of an aristocratic bourgeoisie – not, as Engels had it, a bourgeois aristocracy:

> What makes the rise of this middling sort so crucial is their attitude towards their social superiors. Instead of resenting them, they eagerly sought to imitate them, aspiring to gentility by copying the education, manners, and behaviour of the gentry. They sent their children to boarding-schools to learn social graces, they withdrew their wives from work to put them in the parlour to drink tea, they patronized the theatres, the music-rooms, the print shops, and the circulating libraries, and they read the newspapers, the magazines, and the novels . . . Their attitude thus provided the glue which bound together the top half or more of the nation by means of an homogenized culture of gentility that left elite hegemony unaffected. . . . However it was achieved, the fact remains that the great strength of the English landed elite was their success in psychologically co-opting those below them into the status hierarchy of gentility.
>
> (Stone and Stone 1986: 291–3)

That the peerage continued to be revered (Wells 1935: 13-15) formed part of the 'glue' of social relations otherwise known as 'snobbery'. I have already shown how more or less unpeopled landscapes formed a specific aesthetic that not only circulated among a cultural elite, but was presented in theater landscape scenery and panoramas where it could be absorbed by the middling sort. Chapters 4 and 5 address how, as the nineteenth century progressed, this aesthetic came to constitute a morally loaded means of class differentiation even as the 'humbler classes' responded to it.

In order to see whether and how the aesthetic of unpeopled land-scapes was presented to a wider reading public, five eighteenth-century English publications have been reviewed. They are the heavily illustrated *Copper Plate Magazine*; Sandby's collection of views published as *The Virtuosis Museum*; the less-illustrated *Britannica Curiosa*;[21] *The London Magazine*, which was reviewed from 1732 until it ceased publication in 1784; and *The Gentleman's Magazine*, also published in London, reviewed from its beginning in 1731 to the mid-1820s.[22]

Through the 1770s, illustrations in *The London Magazine* were noticeable only by their virtual absence. Beginning in the 1770s a series of tipped-in and folded landscape illustrations began to appear, mostly of country seats and their distant prospects. Another series of tipped-in engravings of Scottish counties appeared in 1777–78, reflecting the growing fashion for picturesque landscape tourism. Written descriptions accompanied both series. The same early absence of illustrations, except for an occasional woodcut, holds true for *The Gentleman's Magazine*. Only in the mid-1750s does a series of road maps of Britain appear along with views of fashionable gardens, 'many of which were intended to be taken from the Magazines to be put into "Optical Machines"' (*Gentleman's Magazine* 1821, 5: vii) for further viewing.

Interest in British topography blossoms in *The Gentleman's Magazine* with a series of copperplate illustrations (some of them very large tipped-in fold-outs) that commences in 1787 and runs up to the 1820s. Indeed, the topographical illustrations are considered the most valuable and interesting of the over two thousand illustrations listed in the 1821 cumulative index. Strongly reminiscent of the illustrations of the earlier South Seas voyages are caves, rocks, natural rock arches, standing stones and henges, views of mountains and valleys, cataracts, waterfalls, and 'antient' and gnarled trees (generally oaks). Desolate ruins complete the early Romantic picture. As for the views of foreign countries – hills, bays, cascades, caverns, volcanoes, grottoes, headlands, arched rock formations and mountains are much in evidence.

*The Virtuosis Museum*, a collection of engraved select views of England, Scotland, and Ireland, has no text at all. Its silence speaks of a community of viewers who already share in a discourse of landscape quite possibly shaped through their own experience of landscape. The presence of sketchers in one of the views of mountains supports this idea. Its few examples of townscapes are mostly confined to England. There is just one jarring porticoed Palladian country seat in the whole collection, that of the Earl of Fife. The Romantic taste for ruins, rocky eminences and lonely hills is obvious, as are the stock-in-trade groups of people (seated woman with or without child, man clasping a long walking stick, or man upon horseback) who point the way in, either to the middle ground or to the far distance. These figures are so tiny as to require searching for, yet turning page after page, one begins to guess where they will be positioned and which of the three main types will be raising an arm to the view.

These illustrations reinforce the case for more or less unpeopled landscapes. The reiterated posturing and posing of stock figures resonates with their unnaturalness: their placement merely and consistently conforms to painterly convention. The very definite proscenium arch framing one view carries the image back to the world of stage scenery. Other types of people may appear in the landscape but only to provide local color in an otherwise empty Celtic fringe (the northern Highlands of Scotland, the mountains of Ireland) that is as exotic in its own way as the South Seas. So tartan-kilted men and kirtled women dance to bagpipes in front of a ruined Scottish castle; people living rough in a pole-framed bothie fish in a nearby stream; or Irish women ride in old-style wood-axle donkey carts with solid block-wheels and no superstructure, just a floor. They and the beggars, the knife-grinders, the women with bundles of kindling, are the internally marginalized of Britain, presented to our view as the home-grown primitive, more connected to nature than to civilization. They are Picturesque versions of the earlier peripheral decorative motifs found in Kip's birds-eye view of the great English country estates.

*The Copper Plate Magazine* and *Britannica Curiosa*, by contrast, educated their readership in a unifying national history through the use of illustrations and written descriptions. Framed by reference to the classics, elite culture was presented via the nexus of country seats and actual or representational landscapes. The underpinnings of the world of the *Nouveau théâtre* were being made available to an ever-widening public through such publications. The landscapes depicted or written about are almost always unpeopled. When figures do appear, they are generally of a class engaged in leisure pursuits, or are those in service to that class. The occasional odd rustic may be positioned to lead the eye into the large perspectival view. Very rarely is agricultural work shown, despite its importance in producing some of the very landscapes depicted.

*The Copper Plate's* initial format was tripartite. The first section contained portraits and brief biographies of predominantly English poets, playwrights, philosophers and politicians, followed by a section devoted to engravings of classical myths and historical scenes. This section drew heavily on extended translated selections from Ovid's *Metamorphoses* and Homer's *Odyssey* that were accompanied by illustrations. Other illustrated scenes were of foundational and mythologized moments in British history involving the likes of Kings Canute and Arthur. The third section was comprised of engravings of the country seats of the nobility and gentry, again predominantly English.

Most illustrations are perspective views, though from a less elevated level than Kip and Knyff's aerial ones. In most cases picturesque parkland has replaced the baroque organization of the country seats' immediate surroundings. Little agricultural activity is shown in the larger countryside. Properties such as previously appeared in the *Nouveau théâtre* are jostled by the likes of 'Colonel Onslow's Lodge'. It would seem that unlike now, Onslow was interested in keeping up appearances.

After some years, the amount of text in *The Copper Plate Magazine* was reduced. Its new format included two plates to a monthly number for the price of one shilling (the cost of a gallery seat in a London theater (Russell 1995)). This made it available to a far wider reading public. The industrial revolution and the agricultural underpinnings that made it possible begin to make their appearance in views of northern cities, towns, bridges, working canals and England's first silk mill, as well as agricultural land that had undergone 'improvement'.[23] Illustrations of non-agricultural and non-country-house landscapes are located almost entirely in England's Celtic fringe. There the preferred or valued landscapes are the unpeopled ones which are held up to the tourist gaze as

> bold and terrifick, and delightfully variegated with wood, rocks, and innumerable cascades . . . [that] boast of every species of scenery necessary to mark the sublimest subjects in nature. (*The Copper Plate Magazine* 1794–6 2: 31 text accompanying Plate LXI, n.p.)

There is a widening of subject matter, and an attempt is made to reach a broader public through the change in manner of publication, but mimicry of elite culture is still to the fore, and the publication takes on a guidebook approach to country houses, listing their collections of paintings, drawings, prints, and antiquities. Similarly, *Britannica Curiosa* sets out to redress the lamentable fact that well-to-do young Englishmen know more about the landscapes of Holland and Italy than of England. Published in an octavo pocket-sized format, this fits its function as a guidebook to both the landscapes and the stately homes of England. Descriptions of their art collections are pithy. The following description of paintings at Holkham Hall, Norfolk, gives the tone:

> Titian. Venus. the colouring has gone off, hard and disagreeable. Rubens. Flight into Egypt. A good picture, but the figures disagreeable, especially Mary's who is a female mountain. The drawing appears to be indifferent.

> (*Britannica Curiosa* 1777 4: 248)

# Conclusion

Despite the cultural ambiance of the eighteenth century in which refined taste deplored commerce, high culture received a double impetus from commerce. Commerce produced the capital to be invested in mimicking country living, and turned taste into a commodity. The tensions engendered by commodification of the bourgeoisie's aristocratic yearnings are still apparent some two hundred years later. That one yardstick of taste – indeed of very Englishness itself – is located in landscape, is so naturalized a notion that it is hard to extricate it for viewing. A recent British Rail InterCity poster (see figure 13) unintentionally but brilliantly manages to do so while at the same time capturing how 'the very idea of landscape implies separation and observation' (Williams 1973: 120).

The poster carries a low horizon shot of a ploughed field with one boundary hedge and one tree set against a Constablesque sky. Like the view from a country house, it too is a window-framed view. No farm machinery or workers mar the serenity of the composition. The text that (literally and metaphorically) runs beneath the image emphasizes the privileged view. But the view offered is of course anything but private, being equally on offer to the plebs further along the train in second class.[24] The timeless serenity of the composition is likewise at odds with the high-speed endless succession of momentary pictures that InterCity travel permits – a modernist swift-moving panorama or series of dioramas. But the thrust of the message is that 'the view' conveys a particular class's taste which itself (view and class) embodies England.

Unpeopled landscapes were the product of a strict hierarchical ordering that mystified relations of power. Its mirror image resided in the city-world of carnival and fair – a world with an overwhelming potential for the inversion of hierarchical ordering, a pickpocketing pockmarked close-up world of the exuberantly vulgar, a gawker's paradise. And gawking is so very different from perspectivally gazing. The rest of this study maps out the attempts of the often urban-located 'lower' classes to invade the symbolically charged aestheticized world of actual views and vistas of the 'upper' classes, as the sweaty vulgar challenge the denial of their access to the heights. Along their way to the unpeopled heights are the tensions urban dwellers encountered, and continue to encounter, in crossing the rural middle ground.

An Oxfordshire field as seen from a Bristol to Paddington train.

**English landscape art. A private view. In First Class you can ponder, work, eat, take coffee, or simply enjoy the fact that you have the best private seat for one of the best shows on earth; the English Countryside.**

FIRST CLASS

*INTERCITY*

**Figure 13** British Rail Intercity Poster, "English landscape art. A Private View."
National Railway Museum/Science & Society Picture Library

# Notes

1. 'Scene' and 'scenery' are words borrowed from the theater. In antiquity 'scene' meant the background of a stage (Oxford English Dictionary 1971). The Greek *skene*, Latin *scaena*, French *scène* – all meant or mean 'stage'. 'Landscape' indicated the background or 'scenery' in a portrait, figure-painting or stage set (Oxford English Dictionary 1971). Our own 'scenes of childhood' are a borrowing from the theater made into metaphor (Jackson 1980).

2. *De Architectura* had been copied and recopied through the Middle Ages, with its first printed edition appearing in Rome about 1486 (Summerson 1983).

3. A trawl of Italian, French and English printed books up to 1699 yielded numerous examples. A representative selection includes: theaters of the world: *Theatrum mundi* (1574), *Teatro del cielo e della terra* (1577, 1598, 1620, 1625, 1679, 1697), *Theatri orbis terrarum* (1606) *Théâtre contenant la description . . . de tout le monde* (1587, 1632); theaters of countries: *Nouveau théâtre du monde: L'Afrique* (1681), *Théâtre geographique . . . de France* (1632), *The theatre of the empire of Great Britain, with the prospect of the most famous parts of the world* (1676), *Theatrum sabaudiae* (1682), *Teatro del Belgio* (1696), *Teatro della Turchia* (1683); theaters of cities and architecture: *Teatro delle città d'Italia* 1616), *Il Nuovo teatro delle fabriche et edificii . . . di Roma* (1665, 1699), *Le théâtre des antiquitez de Paris* (1639), *Teatro historico di Velletri* (1644), *Teatro anatomico di Bologna* (1668); theaters of horticulture: *Le Théâtre d'Agriculture et mesnage des champs* (1646), *Théâtre des jardinages* (1663) *Teatro farmaceutico* (1675, 1681, 1686, 1696); theaters of lacemaking, engineering, diet and customs, cookery, etc. *Teatro . . . si rappresentano varij disegni di lavori* (1607, 1616, 1620), *Novo teatro di machine et edificii . . .* (1607, 1656), *Théâtre des instrumens mathematiques & mechaniques* (1578), *Il teatro delle parole . . . commentario & catalogo* (1553), *A theatre of wits, ancient and modern* (1660) *Le théâtre de l'art de charpentier* (1664); and finally, theaters of government, war and church-state relations: *Teatro . . . politico de'governi . . . del regno di Napoli* (1691), *Theatre of God's judgements* (1597) *Il teatro della perfidia . . . dell' Hebreismo* (1689), *Le théâtre de la guerre dans les Sevennes* (1690).

4. 'Frontispiece' is also a word in the architectural vocabulary used to refer to a building's main façade or entryway.

5. A fairly representative example of the now Gilbert-and-Sullivanesque effect is the titling of Plate XII, which is of Badminton, 'one of the seats of the Most Noble & Potent Prince Henry Duke of Beaufort, Marquesse & Earle of Worcester, Baron Herbert of Chepstow Raglan & Gower and Knight of the Most Noble Order of the Garter'. Consuming passion for the niceties of peerage status extended well beyond the peerage itself, as shown by *The Gentleman's Magazine* having devoted eight years (1747–54) to illustrating the complete arms of the peers of England, Scotland and Ireland.

6. Michaelmas, September 29th, was one of the four English Quarter Days when agricultural rents were paid, tenancies began and ended, and magistrates were chosen.

7. In the 1708 *Nouveau théâtre*, groups of four or five agricultural workers appear haymaking in very large fields. In a *c.* 1710–20 oil painting of *Dixton Manor, Haymaking*, twenty-three mowers and some fifty other women and men are depicted at the task. It is 'unique in the genre of prospect painting in focusing on a working field' (Prince 1988: 101).

8. The publication history of *Nouveau théâtre* is difficult to pin down. The publication date of the first edition is either 1707 or 1708; I have used the date of the copy I examined in Columbia's Avery Library. Sometimes the collection is published under the title *Britannica Illustrata*. To further complicate matters, some editions include plates of a date later than the title page with which they are bound; five volumes of plates are bound in three physical volumes and so on; the number of plates varies tremendously; plates are not always drawn or engraved by either Knyff or Kip while some plates are both drawn and engraved by Kip; and some editions include later views of towns, churches, and cathedrals as well as maps.

9. The Duke of Newcastle for instance ordered 400 prints of the engravings of his properties from Kip, while the Duchess of Beaufort ordered multiple prints of hers in order to have them bound in sets and given away (Harris and Jackson-Stops 1984).

10. Among its members were Dukes, Lords and members of the Royal Household, office-holders such as Ambassadors, Lords-Lieutenant of Ireland, Privy Councellors, Lords of the Treasury, and Members of Parliament, a scattering of Bishops, Archbishops and Oxbridge professors who mingled with Directors of the South Sea and the East India companies, wealthy City merchants and fashionable architects and aestheticians.

11. By the 1720s English visitors to Rome were having their portraits painted, often with classical architectural monuments in the backgrounds. In the 1750s Pompeo Batoni (1708–87) became the most sought-after portrait painter. Whether depicted as Ottoman Turks, Rosa's *banditti*, or simply themselves, the English visitors got extraordinary accurate likenesses that cost a great deal less than a similar portrait by Reynolds. Some 160 portraits survive of English tourists, with another 40 of Irish, Scottish and Welsh sitters (Clark 1985). An indication of the sheer quantity of art works being brought back from the Grand Tour is the need for buildings to house those collections. In 1725 the Earl of Burlington designed a villa at Chiswick for his collections; beginning in 1754, the second Lord Egremont formed the South Corridor at Petworth for his collection of Greek and Roman sculpture; and in 1770 Robert Adam added a series of rooms to Newby Hall in Yorkshire to contain William Weddell's collection of Greek and Roman sculpture. A painting by Johan Zoffany (1733–

1810), entitled *Charles Towneley's Library in Park Street* (1781–83), shows a crowded assemblage of part of Towneley's collection of marbles – considered 'the best and most famous English collection of classical sculptures of its day' (Webster 1976: 72) – presided over by Towneley and members of the circle of travelers, antiquaries and public figures. It is in a sense an anglicized version of his earlier painting commissioned for Queen Charlotte, entitled *The Tribuna of the Uffizi* (1772–78). That painting, stupefyingly jam-packed with pictures, statuary and English *dilettanti*, shows the central room of the Florentine Medici gallery which was 'the culminating artistic experience of a Grand Tour' (Webster 1976: 60). The men shown in Zoffany's *Park Street* painting intersect with the patrons of Batoni.

12. The English salesrooms were awash with Italian landscape paintings: 'three hundred landscapes attributed to Dughet' were sold between 1711 and 1759 alone (Andrews 1989: 28).

13. Claude Gelée, called le Lorraine, 1600–82; Nicholas Poussin, 1594–1665; Gaspard Dughet, 1615–75. Dughet was the brother-in-law of Nicholas Poussin in whose studio he worked and whose family name he took. When a Poussin was referred to in the eighteenth century, it was likely to be a Dughet (Andrews 1989).

14. About 85 percent of the eighteenth- and nineteenth-centuries' more than five thousand Enclosures Acts took place between 1750 and 1830. Within that time frame there were two great periods of concentration: the 1760s to 1770s, and 1790s to 1800s. Together they accounted for 80 percent of the total Acts of Enclosure (Turner 1984).

15. For a case study of the range of social and economic consequences of enclosure by one landowning family over a 200-year period that resulted in the eventual consolidation of status in the building of a neoclassical country seat and landscaped grounds in the 1750s, see John Broad (1990) "The Verneys as enclosing landlords".

16. Country entertainment included fox-hunting. Given the larger fields with their hedges that horses could easily jump, it quickly replaced an earlier age's stag-hunting that had relied on the broad axial chases transecting forested land (Girouard 1980; Stone and Stone 1986). Tenant farmers generally had no redress for the damage caused by the passage of the hunt. Walking or driving the circular routes set out in the picturesque grounds was another major source of polite entertainment, as were amateur theatricals.

17. In British English, 'corn' is the term for wheat.

18. Loutherbourg also published topographical works of British scenery: *The Picturesque Scenery of Great Britain* (1801), *The Picturesque and Romantic Scenery of England* (1805).

19. Knyff's 1699 bird's-eye drawing of Chatsworth (Lees-Milne 1968) had appeared in Kip and Knyff's *Nouveau théâtre* (1708), and perspective views of Chatworth appeared in the first edition of *The Copper Plate Magazine* (1778).

20. Loutherbourg was later to be in charge of the scenery and costumes for Covent Garden's pantomime *Omai: or a Trip Round the World*. Produced in 1785, 1786 and again in 1788, the published engravings of Captain Cook's Pacific voyages, and illustrations of Omai's visit to London from Huahine, were reproduced as stage sets and scenery. Covent Garden's 1799 production of 'the play of the voyage' of La Pérouse was also noted for its realistic scenes of geological wonders (Funkel 1996; Smith 1985).

21. The full titles and the dates for which these publications were reviewed are: *"The Copper Plate Magazine, or Monthly Cabinet of Picturesque Prints consisting of Sublime and Interesting Views in Great Britain and Ireland, Beautifully Engraved by the Most Eminent Artists from the Paintings and Drawings of the First Masters"* August 1774 to June 1778, break in publication, then February 1792 to July 1797; *The Virtuosis Museum containing select views, in England, Scotland and Ireland,"* 1778–81; and *"Britannica Curiosa, or a Description of the Most Remarkable Curiosities, Natural and Artificial of the Island of Great Britain . . . Including the Principal seats of the Nobility and Gentry"* 1777, 6 vols.

22. In 1818 Charles St. Barbe, Jr. compiled a descriptive list and index of all the plates and woodcuts in *The Gentleman's Magazine* from 1731 up to and including 1818. It was published in 1821. To see the illustrated world of this magazine in one albeit lengthy glance, complete with its cross-cutting categories, is to catch sight of the early antiquary bringing the arcane and commonplace, the foreign and the homegrown under one perspectival gaze, and to recognize in that the precursive roots of pre-professionalized ethnology and anthropology (Stocking 1987; Urry 1993; Van Keuren 1982) and even sociology, for Herbert Spencer's series *Descriptive Sociology* which began in 1873 was a similar compilation of omnifarious facts (Peel 1971). Indeed, later practitioners of ethnology and anthropology published their work in non-professional periodicals such as *Nineteenth Century*, the *Westminster Review*, and the *Fortnightly Review* (Kuklick 1991) in response to a resurgence of popular interest in folklore and archaeology (Urry 1993).

23. An example is the illustration of the new plantation at Felbrig Hall made 'under the direction of Mr. Kent, author of *Hints to Gentlemen of Landed Property*, who has . . . highly improved the value, as well as the appearance, of the neighbouring waste lands, by judicious inclosure and cultivation' (text accompanying *The Copper Plate Magazine* (1792–94) Vol. I: 1–25 Plate XL n.p.).

24. The 'private view', the 'private seat' and the 'best show on earth' all resonate to theater, and serve to remind us of the landscape-as-theater metaphor and the 'socially encoded hierarchy of box, pit, and gallery' (Russell 1995) quoted earlier.

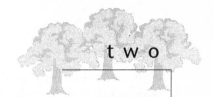

# Landscape of Culture

*The Seasons: Summer, Dawn.*

... Young day pours in apace,
And opens all the lawny prospect wide.
The dripping rock, the mountain's misty top
Swell on the sight and brighten with the dawn.

James Thomson 1727

*The Village, Book I*

... I paint the cot,
As Truth will paint it, and as bards will not ...
Where Plenty smiles – alas! she smiles for few –
And those who taste not, yet behold her store,
Are as the slaves that dig the golden ore;
The wealth around them makes them doubly poor.
Or will you deem them amply paid in health,
Labor's fair child, that languishes with wealth?
Go, then! and see them rising with the sun,
Through a long course of daily toil to run;
See them beneath the dog star's raging heat,
When the knees tremble and the temples beat;
Behold them, leaning on their scythes, look o'er
The labor past, and toils to come explore:
See them alternate suns and showers engage,
And hoard up aches and anguish for their age
... Then own that labor may as fatal be
To these thy slaves, as thine excess to thee.

George Crabbe 1783

# Introduction

The previous chapter showed how members of the English landowning and political aristocracy translated their experience of travel to Italy into physical landscapes at home as they remodeled the surroundings of their country seats to conform to Italian classicized landscape paintings associated with Claude and Poussin. In this sense, those reconfigured pastoral landscapes were literally picturesque. Indeed the word was understood as applicable to any subject suitable for painting.

What this chapter does is first to destabilize any notion that the area we now call the Lake Distict is a monolithic thing. Having established that, it follows the aesthetic debate whereby mountains came to be valorized. This chapter then outlines how a cultural elite's perception of England's mountainous north shifted from empty space to culturally freighted place. It contextualizes this change within the dual social spheres of British nationalism and the Picturesque aesthetic. This chapter delineates through what cultural lenses Lake District landscapes were viewed, and how those views were promulgated in various media to actual and armchair tourists.

# Shifting Contexts

Place is indubitably bound up with personal experience, so much so that landscape may be seen as 'the work of the mind ... built up as much from strata of memory as from layers of rock' (Schama 1996: 7). By contrast, space is unnamed, unhistoried, unnarrativized, at least in the mind and eye of the dominant culture which colonizes space – across both geographical and class distances – by exercising power in the form of naming, mapping, mensurating, and dwelling.

Before turning to the historical specificities of the change from space to place, I want to avoid presenting as either static or monolithic this geographic region that we now know as the Lake District, for paradoxically it has held a 'simultaneous location in both the mid west of Britain and the northwest of England' (Phythian-Adams 1991: 13–18).[1] In a brilliant evocation of movement, Phythian-Adams charts the spatial oscillation of this region over time, as it shifted between northern and western foci that themselves expanded and contracted. As part of the territory of the Brigantes, it first 'looked southeastwards across the Pennines towards the heartland of the Brigantian territory in Yorkshire'. This placed it in the midwest of ancient Britain. As a militarized Roman area, 'the local society was organized to face north,' supplying garrisons along Hadrian's Wall, which served to locate it definitively in what centuries later would be England's northwest. After the Roman departure, through the eleventh century, the region 'was not absorbed into the nascent realm of England,' but 'reverted to its earlier status as a part of the mid west of Britain'.

Invasion and settlement by Norse Vikings, and by peoples from Ireland and the Scottish lowlands, kept the area in a series of client relationships. In the eleventh century it was more formally absorbed into the Scottish royal dynasty, and 'may still have been under Scottish control when the Normans arrived'. Throughout this time it remained firmly situated in mid-western (ancient) Britain, and can be seen more as 'a British and Scandinavian province of the world of the Irish Sea, rather than as an integrated expression of the "English" mainland'.

It was only toward the end of the twelfth century that 'the region cease[d] to represent in practice . . . the southern tip of Scotland . . . [and became] unambiguously . . . established as the northwest corner of England'. However, the area continued to exist for centuries as a veritable battle zone, as the jumping-off point for English attempts to conquer Scotland and the receiving end of devastating Scottish raids. By the seventeenth and eighteenth centuries, under the impact of coal-mining and the development of coastal ports supplying Wales, lowland Scotland and shipping to America, the area 'faced west again, to resume increasingly its long lost role as the mid west of Britain, although now within the context of an Atlantic economy'.

## Knowledge, Aesthetics and Taste

Geologically, England's mountainous periphery can be viewed as part of the Celtic fringe which ran from Cornwall through Wales to northwest Britain. Linguistically, that facet of its Celticness had long since disappeared under the impact of the 'killer' language, English (Phythian-Adams 1991). Throughout the eighteenth century, an Oxbridge-educated cultural elite was involved in an aesthetic debate which transformed the putative space of England's mountainous north into the place of the Lake District. They brought it securely into the English national fold, a position from which it posed 'a serious challenge to the aesthetic supremacy of the European Grand Tour' (Andrews 1989: 153).

In addition to the idealized pastoral landscapes of the Roman *campagna*, the landscapes of the Alps and Apennines had also created deep impressions upon some young Englishmen making the Grand

Tour. Previously viewed as 'crook-shoulder'd' 'excrescences', and 'vast ruins of a broken world', mountains began to elicit a new emotional and imaginative response. Taste changed as appreciation for the irregular in art and in nature challenged classical values of regularity and proportion.[2] This shift did not happen in a vacuum. Fundamental rethinking in theology, philosophy, geology and astronomy taking place over the previous half-century were necessary precursors to this new aesthetic response to wild, rugged nature-in-the-raw (Charlton 1984; Hawes 1982; Nicolson 1959; Schama 1996). Nature was the battle-ground upon which the old verities of religion and religiously under-pinned science were challenged by empirical observation.

From repulsion to valorization is a big leap. Four brief quotations from Englishmen on the Grand Tour may indicate the chasm gradually to be bridged. Typical are such statements as 'Nature has swept up the rubbish of the earth in the Alps', and 'I should like the Alps very much, if it was not for the hills' (Evelyn 1646, Spence 1730, both cited in Charlton 1984: 42). But other Grand Tourers had the impression that they had 'walkd upon the very brink in a literal sense, of Destruction ... The sense of all this produced in me ... a delightful Horrour, a terrible Joy and at the same time that I was infinitely pleasd, I trembled'. These travelers found the Alps endowed with 'magnificent rudeness [full of] glorious desolate prospects' (Dennis 1688, Gray 1739, both cited in Schama 1996: 449).

In 1739 two old Etonian friends set off together on the Grand Tour: Thomas Gray, who later became a major poet, and Horace Walpole, son of the Whig Prime Minister.[3] Though they have been cast in a pioneer role regarding the valorization of mountain landscapes, their rhapsod-izing has usually been placed in the context of earlier excursion poems and aesthetic writings with which they were familiar (Nicolson 1959). Like the Earl of Shaftsbury, they were among those connoisseurs who invested the wild and rugged mountain scenes painted by Salvator Rosa in the previous century with a cultlike status that reminded Grand Tourers of the sublime terror of their own Alpine journeys to Italy. This myopic association of Rosa with 'desolate mountainscapes where brigands set upon unfortunate travellers' was something of an invention, since 'such scenes were actually only a small part of Salvator's output, which was dominated, like [that of] any Baroque artist who sought to be taken seriously, by histories, sacred and classical, and by portraits' (Schama 1996: 454).

Such newly discovered appreciation was not limited to mountains. All aspects of the landscape became valorized during the century's

aesthetic debate. Connoisseurs and moral philosophers grappled with
three problems: the nature of the effects of objects of perception and
consciousness on the mind (i.e. the feelings generated by those objects),
the causes of those effects, and the connection between cause and effect.
The dividing line between moral philosophy and aesthetics is blurred.
Landscape was so politically loaded a realm, that landscape aesthetics
can be considered a mode of political discourse (Bermingham 1994).
Those involved in the debate used landscape aesthetics as a 'paradigm
for the harmonious ordering of society . . . [which allowed] picturesque
landscape paintings to assume a seriously moral political content'
(Rosenthal 1993: 14–15).

The meaning ascribed to the word 'picturesque' changed as aesthetics
became more and more theorized and systematized. It acquired the
definite article, becoming 'the Picturesque' – joining 'the Beautiful' and
'the Sublime' as specific aesthetic concepts to be wrangled over (as in
Addison 1712; Shaftesbury 1723; Hutcheson 1725; Hume 1751; Hogarth
1753; Burke 1757; Gilpin 1791; Price 1794; Knight 1805), and later
explicated (Manwaring 1925; Hussey 1927; Hipple 1957; Nicolson 1959;
Monk 1960; Bermingham 1986; Andrews 1989; Hemingway 1992).

> As the battle subsided, the mountains we see today began to appear to
> men who looked at them with new eyes, seeing them no longer as 'warts,
> and pock-holes in the face of th' earth,' but as the grandest, most majestic
> objects on the terrestrial globe.
>
> (Nicolson 1959: 29)

Aesthetics as applied to landscape held that those which were
cultivated, smooth, calm and harmoniously gradualistic in their variety
were 'Beautiful'. They were bounded, therefore knowable landscapes.
Those that were wild, rugged, and so vast as to lie beyond the imagination's capacity to encompass them, were 'Sublime': their unbounded
prospects led to ideas of eternity and emotions of awe and terror. Most
simply put, regulated nature was Beautiful, wild nature was Sublime.
The Picturesque could be found in either realm and enabled 'the
imagination to form the habit of feeling through the eyes' (Hussey
1927 cited in Monk 1960: 204). The three categories were interrelated,
distinctions between them differing according to various theorists.
Framed in aesthetic categories, landscapes became culturally valued
commodities purveyed in art, poetry, literature, and – as the taste for
foreign mountain landscapes became naturalized – in domestic
tourism.

In large part, geological substructures were literally an underlying and determining factor in whether any particular place could be Beautiful or Sublime. So the scenery of the upland Celtic fringe was Picturesque or Sublime because of its siting on igneous or metamorphic rocks of Paleozoic or Pre-Cambrian age. Conversely, the rolling scenery of the lowlands was Beautiful because of its substrata of Mesozoic or Cainozoic rocks (Appleton 1986; Small 1990; Trueman 1971). The different ages of the two geological categories (necessarily simplified here), and the effects of weathering upon them, inevitably led to two different geomorphologies that in turn supported different types of settlement patterns and ecologies.

Shifts in landscape aesthetics transformed perceptions of England's northern counties of Cumberland and Westmorland from desolate and culturally empty space to desirable culturally loaded place. 'Culturally empty' and 'culturally loaded' here carry the inflection of that

> culture which . . . plume[s] itself on a smattering of Greek and Latin . . . which is begotten by nothing so intellectual as curiosity; it is valued either out of sheer vanity and ignorance, or else as an engine of social and class distinction, separating its holder, like a badge or title, from other people who have not got it.
>
> (Arnold [1869] 1994: 29–30).

## From Space to Place

The transformation of these northern counties was accomplished by the evolving articulation of two phenomena: the rise of British nationalism, and the popularization of the Picturesque aesthetic which valorized the vernacular, the native, and the Celtic. The dynamic interaction of these two spheres created The Lake District as a new site of discourse and metaphorical (though not exclusively metaphorical) assembly. Here the 'emotional, oracular, pastoral, primitive, and subjective elements' (Newman 1987: 120) constituting Romanticism put down their roots. These two spheres should be treated not just as clusters of 'class ideas and ideals sundered from the matrix of places, times and habits which informed them' (Stallybrass and White 1986: 82), but as social spheres delineating the who and the what, the where and the when of how the Lake District was written, mapped, sketched, and painted into existence.

Standing somewhere between the rise of British nationalism and the popularization of the Picturesque and aiding both, was antiquarianism.[4]

Although William Camden's *Britannia* (1586) had to wait until 1695 for translation from Latin to English, Edmund Gibson's enlarged and annotated edition helped precipitate a number of antiquarian publications between 1710 and 1730. While they dealt largely with British or Romano-British artifacts found in the northern and western uplands of England, Scotland and Wales, the surveying in Wiltshire – a south-western county – of Stonehenge, Avebury, and Silbury Hill was being undertaken by William Stukeley in the early 1720s (Piggott 1976). The Camden/Gibson *Britannia* underwent further revision by Richard Gough, and to its edition of 1789 were added more than two hundred illustrations of Roman inscriptions and sculpture from the northwestern counties of England. In this particular articulation of British history, the upland facet of England loomed larger than ever before.

Antiquarian-minded country gentry, clergymen and doctors were still turning to the same desolate and generally uninhabited landscapes as before; but now, through widely disseminated journal articles, guide-books and prints, those landscapes were reframed for them as Pictur-esque. The focus of the class-bound but broadly distributed antiquarian community was thus subtly, or not so subtly, being shifted from myopic consideration of objects in the landscape to the landscape itself. The microcosm of *Britannia's* contributors maps out a triangulation between antiquarianism, the Picturesque, and politics. The connection between antiquarianism and the Picturesque movement can be glimpsed in the fact that Thomas Pennant, author of popular guidebooks for Picturesque tours in Scotland and Wales, worked on both those countries' sections of the 1789 *Britannia*.

A connection between antiquarianism and the political, in the form of the Jacobin threat from Scotland, occurs in the person of General Robert Melville. During the British military campaigns in Scotland, he gathered information on the remains of Roman military fortifications. This formed part of his contribution to the Scottish section of the 1789 *Britannica* (Piggott 1976). A connection between the Picturesque and the political is also offered through Melville, who, after the Battle of Culloden, encouraged and assisted General William Roy in his 1747–55 Highland Survey in which the young Paul Sandby cut his teeth as a draughtsman (Schama 1996).[5] Sandby later contributed to *The Copper Plate Magazine*, and published *The Virtuosis Museum* (1778–81), a collection of his Picturesque views of England, Scotland and Ireland.

It was also General Roy who published in 1793 the period's 'most notable study of Roman military antiquities in North Britain' (Piggott 1976: 121). In a conflation of the military, political, artistic and antiquarian gaze, the dominant culture's exercise of power in nation-building – that is, England's military presence in Scotland to secure 'Britain' – was given further expression in representational technologies of colonizing space. Ironically, those representations in large part recapitulated Roman colonization of the same space.

Given the periodic nature of open hostilities and hostile relations between England and France in the late eighteenth and the early nineteenth centuries, including the French Revolution and the Napoleonic Wars, it was not always easy, possible or advisable for the English to travel abroad for pleasure. Nor was it necessarily easy or possible for them to travel great distances at home. But if they could reach them, England's mountainous northern counties, along with North Wales, were the closest English travelers could get to the *frisson* of the Alps (see figure 14). In 1756 the Society for the Encouragement of Arts 'set up special prizes as a means of encouraging the making of new and accurate maps of the English and Welsh counties' (Colley 1992: 93).

Not only the maps needed remaking. Turnpike acts for improving the English road system nearly quintupled between 1750 and 1790 and 'the appreciation of scenery . . . the perception of the sublime in nature increased in direct ratio to [their] number' (Hussey 1927 cited in Piggott 1976: 122).[6] To convert these new maps into practice required a decent transportation system. Stronger and faster breeds of horses had been produced thanks to the importation of breeding stallions in the early decades of the eighteenth century and an earlier importation of 'Arab' mares.[7] The new technology of steelsprung carriages allowed for regularly scheduled commercially operated journeys that were faster, more frequent and more comfortable.

The Grand Tour had invested foreign landscapes with the ability to rouse sentiment in their viewers, yet travel abroad was hampered. The mountains of 'home', Romano-British antiquities and medieval ruins stood in for foreign landscapes and classical ruins. Just as antiquarianism had been subtly refocused to see the Picturesque landscape, so the Picturesque aesthetic refocused the tourist's look at the landscape to include an antiquarianism gaze – albeit of a romanticized rather than empirical or historically accurate nature. New maps and new perceptions produced a re-visioning of Britain and

a new literature closely connected with improved roads and transport, and summed up in The Tour, so often in search of the Picturesque, in which by now ruins and ancient monuments were essential ingredients. Scotland was soon to be included; Gray had experienced ecstatic emotions among the ... Highlands as early as 1765, and the Road to the Isles, already signposted by Martin Martin in his *Description of the Western Islands*, was opened to a public eager for such novel experiences by Thomas Pennant, who made and published Tours not only of his native Wales, but of Scotland in 1769 and again, with a *Voyage to the Hebrides*, in 1774. This was an immediate success not only at home, but abroad, where for instance German romanticism led to Ebeling's translation published only five years later.

(Piggott 1976: 147–8)

## Scenes and Seeing

The antiquarian William Stukeley, writing in 1725, likened the Lake District's mountains ranged one behind the other to scenic side screens used in the theater, and wrote that a painter did not need to 'go to Italy for variety and grandeur of prospects' (Piggott 1976: 122). How the early connoisseur saw and appreciated the Lake District was deeply influenced by conventions of seventeenth-century Italian landscape painting, an influence that lasted throughout the century.

In a letter to Lord Lyttelton around 1753, John Brown, a Cambridge cleric from Cumberland, found himself unequal to the task of conveying 'the full perfection' of Derwentwater and the Lake District in general. He excused himself, for to do so 'would require the united powers of Claude, Salvator, and Poussin' (cited in Bicknell and Woof 1982: 15). Nearly fifteen years later, his letter was still considered a sufficient statement of what the Lake District was as to warrant its publication as a separate pamphlet. Even at century's end, the Lake District was viewed through an Italian turn of mind. As one visitor to the Lakes wrote in 1792 to a prospective visitor about crossing the Derwent Fells, 'That you may see and have a faint idea of the Alps, and think you have performed as much as Hanibal (*sic*), be sure to start as soon after nine a.m. as possible' (cited in Andrews 1989: 154).

Education in the classics, like familiarity with paintings, endowed landscape with literary associations and transformed local people into artistic embellishments. 'The first sight of a Cumberland shepherd climbing the fells with his flock became more thrilling the more it approximated to a literary prototype: Virgil's *Eclogues* suddenly loomed into the space between the tourist and shepherd' (Andrews 1989: 3). As those returning from the European Grand Tour had sought to construct native versions of Italian landscape paintings on their home estates, so artists like Thomas Smith of Derby (d. 1767) looked for views

**Figure 14** Amos and Harriet Green, 1804, "Views in England, Scotland and Wales: Scene from the Inn at Devil's Bridge with the Fall of the Rhydal." Grey wash over graphite, 32.1 × 41.6 cm. Yale Center for British Art, Paul Mellon Collection

in the Lake District that recalled Italian paintings. If they did not find them, a little judicious rearrangement of various elements did not go amiss. Indeed, after the final pacification of Scotland, kilted Highland raiders (highly reminiscent of Rosa's *banditti*), could give a Picturesque edge to engravings of the Lake District, as in T. Allom's *Honister Crag*. Since the Italian artists' works were known to a wide audience through prints and written commentary, a market for their conventions operated far beyond the range of those with immediate viewing knowledge of the paintings.

There was already a healthy market for engravings of the mountains and moorlands of England and Wales by the late 1740s. But the Lake District had to wait for William Bellers's series of 1752–3 and 1758 and Thomas Smith's three views published in 1761 to enter that market (Thomason and Woof 1986). Taking the issue of supply and demand into a different register, compare one of Thomas Smith's earlier paintings with one of his later engravings. Both are views of Derwentwater. The painting is done from a low viewpoint. Under the watchful eyes of two gentlemen who face out to the viewer, a group of laborers (chopping and sawing newly felled timber) is prominently placed center-foreground. In the later engraving, the laborers have disappeared, the woodlot has been replaced by a suitably picturesque 'antient' and blasted tree, and the two gentlemen-overseers, now much diminished in size due to the quite elevated viewpoint, have their backs to us as they quietly contemplate the view. This rearrangement reflects the popularity of the Picturesque movement and the market for such engravings.

Early elite tourists to the Lake District were 'typically a gentleman or gentlewoman engaged in an experiment in controlled aesthetic response to a range of new and often intimidating visual experiences' (Andrews 1989: 67). If the lower orders were considered to occupy a carnivalesque world of topsy-turvy, then those engaged in the practice of the Picturesque occupied a world occasionally turned back to front. For to see the desired view required turning one's back to it. An oval or round, amber- or silver-tinted convex mirror – called a Claude glass – would be held a little above shoulder height, in which would be captured a framed and miniaturized reversed version of the view.[8] Only the foreground details would be clear. By slowly moving the glass, the 'perfect' Picturesque view could be found. This emulation of an Italian seventeenth-century landscape painting could then be sketched or painted.

Differently tinted transparent glasses allowed the view to be manipulated in other ways. Viewed through a gray- or blue-tinted glass, a bright afternoon scene became a moonlit one; a yellow-tinted glass used in bright sunlight suffused the view with a dawn light (certainly much less tiring than getting up to your viewing station before sunrise!), while a hoarfrost-tinted glass produced approximations of snow scenes (Andrews 1989). This instantaneous manipulation of seasonal or diurnal effects is reminiscent of Loutherbourg's *eidophusikon* in which effects of light, weather and season were not simply theatrical effects, but were the point of the unpeopled landscapes being viewed.

Loutherbourg was one of the three most notable late eighteenth-century painters of Welsh and English mountain scenery, the other two being his friend Thomas Gainsborough and Joseph Wright of Derby. In 1783 Loutherbourg, who had visited Derby a few years earlier to do topographical sketches for the *Wonders of Derbyshire* pantomime at Drury Lane, combined a return visit to Derbyshire with a visit to the Lake District. During the next four years, he exhibited seventeen views at the Royal Academy from material gathered on his Lake District-Derbyshire tour (Hawes 1982; Joppien 1973). These works, mostly of mountain scenery, explored some startlingly different kinds of perspective and were seen by large numbers of people at the Academy exhibitions.

The quintessence of the perspectival gaze is the panorama. One of the earliest extant large-scale panoramas of a Lake District scene was made in the 1770s and may have been intended as the working document for the decoration of a circular room.[9] Others executed either on a smaller scale or as partial panoramas of 180° arcs appeared through the 1830s (Hawes 1982; Thomason and Woof 1986). To gain appropriate vantage points for painting views, artists inexperienced in walking the fells started actually climbing to the tops, sometimes with disastrous results.[10]

Descriptions of the Lake District articulated the antiquarian/Picturesque linkage. William Hutchinson's (1732–1814) *An Excursion to the Lakes . . . in the Years 1773 and 1774* (1776) focuses on the archaeological. Yet, in what is becoming a commonplace, he calls upon Poussin, Rosa and Claude in order to describe the landscape. By bracketing Claude and Thomas Smith, Hutchinson 'naturalizes' foreign artists.

The first actual guidebook to the Lake District to treat it as a place of picturesque mountain scenery was *A Guide to the Lakes* (1778) by Thomas West (c.1720–79), a Jesuit priest. It remained in print for nearly fifty years, variously revised and enlarged, and superseded only by William Wordsworth's *A Description of the Scenery of the Lakes* (1822). William Gilpin (1724–1804) was highly instrumental in popularizing the Picturesque aesthetic through his series of tours through parts of England, Scotland and Wales.[11] Written for an audience beyond the Oxbridge elite, Gilpin provided translations of the many Latin terms he used. Reminiscent of earlier ascriptions of character formation to the influence of mountains, Gilpin wrote in his guide to the Lakes (1786) of 'the great simplicity of this country, and that rigid temperance, and economy, which necessity injoins to all it's inhabitants' (Gilpin cited in Watson 1970: 47).

With all the writing in praise of the Picturesque, it is no wonder that pseudo-druid and classical-style temples began springing up on enthusiasts' estates in the Lake District, particularly on those estates consisting of little islands set in the very lakes (see plate 3 for a vernacular and pre-existing version). These structures reflected both the antiquarian and literary interest in things Druidical and Celtic, and the Italianate taste for landscapes set off by classical ruins. Dorothy Wordsworth for one was 'pained to see the pleasantest of earthly spots [so] deformed by man' (Wordsworth 1802 cited in Bicknell and Woof 1982: 27). Her pain at these un-natural non-national additions to the landscape represents a very different point of view than Hutchinson's, and parallels her brother's concerns about the integrity of the Lake District's vernacular structures.

By the 1780–1790s the Picturesque had been popularized through published guidebooks to the Lakes, collections of engraved views and colored aquatints, maps and surveys, some of which included sets of engraved views. Under the direction of the guidebooks, connoisseurs of the Picturesque followed a circuit of specific viewing stations or vantage points around the mountains and lakes.[12] The views from these stations were considered particularly apt to stir the imagination, to appeal to sentiment, and to lend themselves to picturing and posturing.

Thus began the *embourgeoisement* of the region. Better roads and more comfortable travel meant that in the summers 'coaches of all shapes and sizes rattled along the shores of the Lakes, struggled up steep passes, and now and again, waited at the roadside while passengers jumped out to take a quick sketch of a bewildered shepherd' (Andrews 1989: 153). The Lakes got crowded too as boats took visitors up and down, and, for a price, fired off cannons so one could hear distant waterfalls in the extraordinary silence that followed after the shattering echoes had finished reverberating off the mountains. Carriage rentals, boat rentals, lodging and food, and hires of guides by the day or the week all began to have an impact on the local economy. Prices went up and tourism was blamed for corrupting the locals,

> giving them a taste for pleasures, and gratifications, of which they had no ideas – inspiring them with discontent at home – and tainting their rough, industrious manners with idleness, and a thirst after dishonest means.
>
> (Plumptre 1799 cited in Andrews 1989: 171)

To visit is a transitive verb: that is where the problem sets in. Those visiting in search of the picturesque bumped up against those being visited, who were going about their daily lives rather than existing as picturesque objects in the landscape:

> In early prints of the Lakes it is common to find the people treated as merely part of the scenery. Raiders in Highland dress light bonfires beside Derwentwater, bandits or robbers assemble on Kirkstone; vague, draped figures, melancholy as the mist, pause and ponder on the sands of

> Morecombe Bay. The landscape becomes a landscape with figures, but
> . . . not . . . the solid, shrewd, independent people who could be met at
> every farm and in every inn. Such people did not really suit the scene as
> the tourists saw it.
>
> (Nicholson 1955: 93)

The earliest known published record of a recreational walking tour (of around 250 miles) in the Lake District is *A Fortnight's Ramble in the Lakes* (1792) by Joseph Budworth.[13] Another, far more notable recreational walking trip was made by James Plumptre, a Cambridge cleric, who in 1799 put in 1,174¼ miles walking from Cambridge to the Scottish Highlands and back again via the Lake District. The precise figures came from the pedometer Plumptre carried. He actually carried rather a lot: a set of tinted Claude glasses, sketching pads, watercolor paints and brushes, a telescope, a barometer, maps, and a set of guidebooks (Andrews 1989). Plumptre was a well-seasoned walker, having previously walked to Yorkshire, the Lake District and home to Cambridge via North Wales.

The young William Wilberforce also took a walking tour in the Lake District in 1779 during his long summer break from studies at Cambridge. In one of his diary entries he wrote that 'the Lake District made the rest of the English countryside seem insipid, peaceful and rural in contrast to the majestic, beautiful and sublime lakes' (Wilberforce [1799] 1983: 18) Other entries show that he used a Claude glass and that he found rocky scenes superior, he felt, to those painted by Salvator Rosa. In a letter of October 1, 1818, Wilberforce referred to the Lake District as 'this Earthly Paradise' (Wilberforce [1799] 1983: 20).

## Different Agendas/Genders

An analogy has been drawn between big-game hunting and the way in which Britain's wild mountainous landscapes could be tamed and brought under control by tourists '"capturing" wild scenes, and "fixing" them as pictorial trophies in order to sell them or hang them up in frames on their drawing room walls' (Andrews 1989: 67). An analogy was drawn between the two activities by William Gilpin, one of the leading proponents of picturesque tourism:

> Shall we suppose it is a greater pleasure to the sportsman to pursue a
> trivial animal, than it is to the man of taste to pursue the beauties of

nature: to follow her through all her recesses? to obtain a sudden glance, as she flits past him in some airy shape? to trace her through the mazes of the cover . . .

(William Gilpin 1792, cited in Andrews 1989: 68)

Andrews does not acknowledge the latent sexual imagery of male pursuit, capture, uncovering, and penetration of female nature (consider figure 14 in this regard.) This imagery explodes nearly a century later in Edward Whymper's recounting of a decade of his and other Englishmen's Alpine mountaineering experiences (Whymper 1871). In that work, we learn that mountains 'reveal' their 'shoulders' only to 'coyly' draw a veil of mist over them again; that 'stimulated to make fresh exertions by one repulse after another,' Whymper and friends mount further 'attacks' once they are 'cock-sure' of success; and that faced with peaks 'which yet remained virgin', these men 'assault' and finally 'conquer' them. (Later chapters concerned with the early years of a working-class walking movement and the ethnographic present will pick up this thread of a gendered view of and engagement with landscape.)

## Conclusion

In eighteenth-century England, empirical observations revolutionizing geology and astronomy led to new evaluations of time and nature. Shorn of their earlier theological underpinnings, aesthetic debates led to new evaluations of nature. Resultant changes in taste transformed mountain landscapes, previously feared and avoided, into aesthetically valued spectacles. 'Space' was transformed into 'place' as observed in the Lake District, an early site for landscape tourism thanks to its representation in multiple media, especially prints, and the rise of a cultural nationalism that invested mountainous landscapes of 'home' with new meaning.

In the early eighteenth-century, the 'class view of landscape embodied a set of socially, and finally, economically determined values to which the painted image gave cultural expression' (Bermingham 1986: 3). By the closing decades of the century, landscape as an expression of culture, be it through representation or touring, had become a commonplace among an educated elite and those who aimed to emulate them. The Picturesque movement can be seen as democratic in character because of the value it placed on the local, the vernacular, and the more broadly based engagement with landscape to which it gave rise. Working against this view was the politicization of landscape through parliamentary enclosure, with the concomitant immiseration of the dispossessed.

The practice of cultural mimicry by the middle class was dependent upon the lucrative commercialization of leisure. This is a site of inherent tension. It was the newly dispossessed who were the means whereby leisure was produced, either in terms of producing the profits to fund others' leisure time, or producing the accoutrements of leisure activities. Guidebooks, fiction in which landscape loomed large, books of landscape poetry, individual prints, collections of prints, lending libraries of prints, paper, paints, painting schools, instructional books for painting and drawing, transportation, inns to accommodate tourists – all these things structured a cultural grid of efforts and expectations that connected the least talented Picturesque Tourist sketching away in the rain, to the exhibiting Academician's large-scale paintings. Even those unable to participate directly in this practice of landscape were caught up in it through the efforts and expectations involved in reading the Picturesque and poring over collections of prints.

Thus was a landscape of culture constructed in the Arnoldian sense as a means of class differentiation, a reflection of the absence or presence of cultural capital. Through cultural mimicry, Picturesque touring grew so popular in writing and practice that it finally became the object of satire. The Reverend James Plumptre drew upon his hard-won knowledge of Picturesque tourism and tourists to write his comic opera *The Lakers* (1798). The apogee of Picturesque tourism's satirization came with Thomas Rowlandson's *Dr. Syntax In Search of The Picturesque* (1812), a series of illustrations threaded together by doggerel verse written by William Combe, a hack writer who generally remained anonymous in order to avoid his creditors. In Dr. Syntax's words:

I'll read and *write*, and *sketch* and *print*
And thus create a real *mint;*
I'll *prose* it here, I'll *verse* it there
And *picturesque* it everywhere . . .
With ev'ry other leaf a print
Of some fine view in *aqua-tint* . . .
I will allow it is but trash,
But then it furnishes the cash.

# Notes

1. Since all quotations in this and the following paragraph are from the same article, I give at this one point the page-range from which the quotations are drawn.

2. The reaction against classicism has been seen as emerging in the seventeenth century, with the introduction into England of Indian fabrics and Chinese lacquer work, porcelain and wallpaper, whose decorative elements depended on irregularity and asymmetry. From this perspective it has been suggested that their enormous popularity fostered interest in 'remote times and places' including interest in Celtic and Norse literature, and that in this way 'Orientalism prepared the way for romanticism' (Allen 1937: 256).

3. Horace Walpole had the 'rudeness' of the mountains rather thrust in his face when his lapdog, aptly named Tory, got snatched up by a wolf as it was trotting alongside its master's portered chaise going up Mont Cenis (Schama 1996: 447–8).

4. The Society of Antiquaries of London was founded in 1717, that of Scotland in 1780.

5. Done at 2 inches to the mile, the Highland Survey was intended to facilitate extension of the road system put in under General Wade after the 1715 uprisings (Piggott 1976).

6. *The Gentleman's Magazine* started carrying tipped-in and folded large-size road maps of English and Scottish counties in the mid-1750s. The completion of the first wave of expansion of the turnpike road system coincides with the *Magazine's* carrying numerous engraved views of landscapes, antiquities and ruins.

7. These breeds were the Darley Arabian, Byerley Turk and Godolphin Barb which produced the gentry's hunters and the Cleveland Bay and Yorkshire Coach Horse (Piggott 1976). The influx of new breeds sheds a certain light on the plethora of Stubbs's horse paintings and prints and shows the interweaving of the economic potential to be drawn from new products appearing on the market.

8. The lakes also acted as mirrors on a vastly larger scale. On a calm day, their perfect inversions are still stunning, producing a rather odd and dizzying effect. Take a photograph of this and later you will experience a few second's pause when trying to figure out which way round to hold *your* framed trophy.

9. The surviving six-sheet panorama of Derwentwater, now in the Victoria and Albert Museum, London, is attributed to the amateur Christopher Machell (1747–1827). Accordingly to Southey, one of the Lakeists, he saw a panorama of some twenty or more feet in length of Derwentwater, drawn in 1777 by Thomas Hearne. It was intended as the cartoon for the decoration of a circular

banqueting room for Sir George Beaumont. The room was never built, and the sketch is lost (Thomason and Woof 1986). This would have been a considerably earlier example of the commission Paul Sandby received from Sir Nigel Gresley (see chapter one, footnote 15).

10. The most notable artist of this *oeuvre* was Charles Gough who in April 1805 fell to his death from Helvellyn's Swirrel Edge. When his skeleton was found that July, not only had his dog somehow survived, but she and her newborn litter of pups were at his side. Quite possibly Charles Gough achieved more fame in death than he would have in life, for his sad end and his dog's fidelity provided Wordsworth and Sir Walter Scott with suitably melancholy material for poems. A photograph taken in 1891 by Herbert Bell of Ambleside shows a cairn being set up close to Helvellyn's summit in Gough's memory (Hogg 1974: 27). Here is emplacement in practice: the making of a 'place' out of 'space'.

11. Gilpin's Tours, which were translated into French and German, contained numerous drawings, sketched maps and panoramas, with rather wide latitude being taken with topographical accuracy. His illustrations became almost stock renditions of Claude and Poussin (Bicknell and Woof 1982). His titles showed little originality: *Observations on the River Wye, and Several Parts of South Wales . . . relative chiefly to Picturesque Beauty* (1782); *Observations relative chiefly to Picturesque Beauty . . . particularly the Mountains, and Lakes of Cumberland and Westmoreland* (1786, 2 vols); *Observations, relative chiefly to Picturesque Beauty . . . on several Parts of Great Britain, particularly the High-Lands of Scotland* (1789, 2 vols); *Observations on Forest Scenery, and other Woodland Views (relative chiefly to Picturesque Beauty) . . . of New-forest in Hampshire* (1791, 2 vols), *Three Essays . . . on Picturesque Travel; and, on Sketching Landscape . . .* (1792); *Two Essays . . . on . . . executing rough Sketches* (1804); *Observations . . . on Several Parts of North Wales, relative chiefly to Picturesque Beauty (1809)*. There were in fact so very many guidebooks that they began to be anthologized.

12. The emotional-imaginative response institutionalized in these circuits of viewing stations operated as a secular subconscious parallel to the painted and printed Stations of the Cross. There is the same arousal of emotion through a perambulatory means. Each station required the participant to engage in particular thoughts that – whether Picturesque or religious – involved human contingency and mutability in face of an immutable 'other,' be that Deity or Nature. William Wordsworth's own mystical relationship to his beloved Lake District – that 'blended holiness of earth and sky' – echoed this element of secular pilgrimage.

13. Budworth wrote countryside pieces for the *Gentleman's Magazine* under the pseudonym 'A Rambler' (Bicknell and Woof 1982).

# Landscape of Nation

*London*

I wander thro' each charter'd street,
Near where the charter'd Thames does flow
And mark in every face I meet
Marks of weakness, marks of woe.

In every cry of every Man,
In every Infant's cry of fear,
In every voice, in every ban,
The mind-forg'd manacles I hear:

How the Chimney-sweeper's cry
Every blackning Church appalls,
And the hapless Soldier's sigh
Runs in blood down Palace walls.

But most thro' midnight streets I hear
How the youthful Harlot's curse
Blasts the new-born Infant's tear,
And blights with plagues the Marriage hearse.

William Blake 1794

*The Prelude: Book Seventh, Residence in London – Bartholomew Fair*

For once the Muse's help will we implore,
And she shall lodge us, wafted on her wings,
Above the press and danger of the Crowd,
Upon some shewman's platform. What a shock
For eyes and ears! what anarchy and din
Barbarian and infernal – an phantasma
Monstrous in colour, motion, shape, sight, sound!

... the crowd
Inviting ...
Grimacing, writhing, screaming ...
All out-o'th-way, far-fetched, perverted things
All freaks of Nature, all Promethean thoughts
Of man; his dullness, madness, and their feats
All jumbled up together, to compose
A Parliament of Monsters. Tents and Booths
Meanwhile, as if the whole were one vast mill,
Are vomiting, receiving, on all sides,
Men, Women, three-years' Children, Babes in arms.
Oh blank confusion! true epitome
Of what the mighty City is herself.

William Wordsworth 1805

## Introduction

Earlier I described my approach as being fashioned from 'the linking
threads thrown out to and received back from the socio-political realm
of nation-making', by which I meant the political fiction of Great
Britain. Now I would add: it was a construction against which a very
particular image of 'England' was being woven, one that even today is
oppositional to a rational, political-economy construct.

As this chapter moves into the nineteenth century, so the industrial
revolution and the English Romantic Movement make their appearance.
This chapter attempts to negotiate a series of related fields of tensions.
Insofar as they lent weight to the valorization of Britain's mountainous
areas, it takes on some of the tensions, disjunctions and ambiguities
generated within polite society, between image and counterimage of
London, agricultural/industrial revolutions and the English Romantic
Movement, and between England and Britain. It does so by placing
the discursive site of the Lake District, explored in the previous chapter,
back in the context of the London society that fashioned it. This is
then framed within the then ongoing reconstruction of cultural
nationalisms.

The production and consumption of cultural ideas is dynamic. Supply
and demand are open-ended and open to manipulation. And resistance
creates its own demand in a different register, which then opens up
new avenues of supply.

Literature, like all art, like language, is a collective activity, powerfully conditioned by social forces, what needs to be and what may be said in a particular community at a given time – the field of the anthropologist, perhaps, rather than the psychologist.

(Butler 1982:9)

Similarly, the valorization and consumption of landscape is a dynamic and collective activity, one where 'co-ordinates of geography and class intersect as a network of exclusions' (Stallybrass and White 1986: 108).

Foregrounding landscape allows for another entryway into and between the interactive fields of tension – the social forces – that surrounded the rise of cultural nationalisms and the production of a centralizing nation-state. The Picturesque aesthetic was only one strand in the cultural bundle. The previous chapter extricated that strand for fairly close examination. Now the effort is to reweave it and to make clear how the Picturesque aesthetic carried a time-specific ideology of inequality situated in, and played out through, landscape. This aesthetic operated as a means of class formation

in ways that both arise from, and potentially reshape, the experiences of people and the understandings people form from their experiences. This is the historical dynamic of ideology, which we must try to recover. To do this requires us to situate ideology in the context of culture, and in particular, in the context of contradictions of culture.

(Sider 1986: 154)

Implicit in the chapter title, Landscape of Nation, is consideration of who was deemed worthy of inclusion in the nation through participatory enjoyment in unpeopled landscapes.

## London-based Culture and its Dissemination

As Charles II's (1660–85) exuberantly whoring Court, that sparkled even as it offended, was followed by the boring Courts of domestically-minded William and Mary (1688–1702), Anne (1702–14), and the early Georges (1714–27; 1727–60), the practice of high culture and appreciation of the fine arts was cut loose from court circles. A recent compendious study delineates the mechanics and practices by which high culture ceased to be 'the handmaiden of royal politics' and 'became the partner of commerce' (Brewer 1997: 3).[1] Economic expansion brought a new dynamic to the production of artworks, and to the development of a new, acquisitive audience (Solkin 1992). Social refinement went hand-in-glove with cultivation of the fine arts.[2]

Framed by theories of political economy, an image of England was in the making. English exceptionalism vis-à-vis the Continent was expressed in terms of political freedoms grounded in flourishing commerce, yeoman-farmer freeholders and legislatively favored agriculture (Smith [1776] 1985). Intensified cultivation of the useful arts (commerce, manufactures), aided by scientific and technological improvements and inventions, was producing that 'universal opulence which extends itself to the lowest ranks of the people' (Smith [1776] 1985: 33).[3] But intensification depended upon stability as well as a division of labor, and the flag under whose protection political freedoms and commercial interests grew, flew over the few, not the many:

> . . . if one side of [this] flag is emblazoned with 'Commerce', the other says 'Civilization'. The fabric of the flag is Liberty which if we peer closely at the stitching turns out to be Law. The "market" is *made*, some men must be free to constrain other men and almost all women, thereby to construct progress.
>
> (Corrigan and Sayer 1985: 105)

Wordsworth's *Parliament of Monsters* – the crowd, the passion-ruled mob – threatened stability as, even temporarily, it inverted civil/ized society. Within the Enlightenment's evolutionary model, harnessing the passions defined the rational individual. Passion was an attribute of the unindividuated many, of Bahktin's 'grotesque body'. It was 'cultivated taste [that] extinguishes the passions . . . [and] improves our sensibility' (Hume [1741–2] 1985: 6). Cultivated taste also supported a symbiotic relationship in which the acquisition and performance of social refinement required and generated the commodities provided by the useful arts.[4] Social refinement and commerce were two sides of the same coin, minted by the marketplace's requirements for cooperation and rational interaction.

Freed from the court, and operating with and through the commercial life of the City, London-based culture epitomized the image of England as center of urban modernity and producer of 'universal opulence' (Robbins 1988). But the dark side of eighteenth-century London formed a troubling counterimage. The underbelly of the beast, home to Blake's unforgettable and unforgettably marked faces, showed itself in the suppurating slums and brothels teeming with the impoverished, the diseased, the dispossessed, soldiers and sailors (many of them amputees) discharged from the ongoing series of expensive wars,[5] the orphaned, and the thousands of 'invisible' blacks who lived in London: in short, the preyed-upon and the underclass's own preyers. The proximity in which London's high life and low life existed precluded either's living in ignorance of the other.

This period saw the rise of the literate cosmopolitan man and woman, a person of imagination and feeling whose refinement of social manners could be gauged by his or her informed conversation as much as by dress and other outward signs. Through the pages of the *Spectator*, the *Tatler*, and the *Guardian*, Joseph Addison and Richard Steele led the way in providing the instructive aesthetic that this rapidly expanding segment of 'polite society' needed.[6] The journals and magazines examined for their landscape illustrations in Chapter 1, and the tour guides and collections of prints relating specifically to the Lake District examined in Chapter 2, were part of print capitalism's ever-expanding servicing of a continually recreated and ever-expanding need for leisure pursuits. The Picturesque aesthetic acted not only as a nexus between 'imagination', 'feeling', and 'taste', but also as a locus for their practice.

By the late eighteenth century the blueprint was drawn for profligate consumption and commoditization of culture and leisure. Such self-fashioning of social identity was inevitably a process of exclusion. London-based 'culture' while

> indeed progressive in its best political aspirations, had encoded in its manners, morals and imaginative writings, in its body, bearing and taste, a[n] . . . elitism which was constitutive of its historical being, [and] had engraved in its subjective identity all the marks by which it felt itself to be a different, distinctive and superior class.
>
> (Stallybrass and White 1986: 202)

It was a class that inhabited a city unlike any other. One tenth of the population of England lived in London. One in six eighteenth-century Britons would work there at some point in their lives. London dwarfed all other English cities and British capitals, while its nearly 750,000 inhabitants at mid-century made it the largest city in western Europe (Brewer 1997).

A London-based, broadly accessible cultural life was firmly in place. Art, music, theater, and publishing flourished in the capital's museums, concert halls, enlarged theaters, libraries, coffee houses, print and book shops, literary societies, and drawing rooms. Interlocking circles of people of taste engaged in polite conversation, literary criticism, dancing, painting and musical performance, formed a wide-ranging community deeply involved in the production and consumption of cultural capital. Newspapers, journals and magazines provided the quotidian connective tissue, despite political and religious differences.

By the late eighteenth century, this urban elite's overtly unified and unifying cultural narrative had been replicated in the provinces through the power of the market to fuel differentiation and consolidate identity. Poised between state and civil society, and operating at a national level, a social ensemble of polite society had been in the making. Despite local particularisms, shared practices of culture helped organize social relationships and discipline in provincial cities and towns, and among the country gentry. This was accomplished through a network of pre-existing informal intellectual and religious associational groups, as well as through new sites of assembly which also functioned to displace local particularisms (Stallybrass and White 1986). Though urban in origin, clubs, lodges, assembly rooms, reading and debating societies, all came to exist in the countryside (Morris 1990), and even small towns 'could support an elaborate round of balls, assemblies, concerts, lectures, [and] card parties' (Cunningham 1980: 17). In short, we have the milieu of Jane Austen's novels.

Attributes of culture (books, journals, prints, travel, instruction in dance, painting, music, attendance at the theater, participation in balls and amateur theatricals) and consumption of fashion appropriate to season, place and occasion, furthered the project of replicating this particular cultural narrative while simultaneously creating it. Through its emphasis upon the individual's own imagination and aesthetic experience, the practice of the Picturesque aesthetic cross-cut a number of categories contained within that cultural bundle.[7] In the process, it helped foster a shared identity and sentiment among acquaintances and a larger literate public.

Landscape became a locus of identity formation by virtue of how it was read about, toured through, experienced, viewed physically or in print, spoken about, and painted. Since goods are carriers of cultural meaning, 'who has the goods' becomes part of their meaning. Expressions of taste and leisure practices helped people place themselves and others in their social order (Bourdieu 1984; Mitchell 1994). Eventually, the Picturesque tour became a ritual process by which the cultural valuation of unpeopled landscapes became transferred to the tourist. Touring, whether on foot or by carriage, was a reiterated performative enactment that connected subject and object, while simultaneously transforming Picturesque landscapes into 'goods'.[8]

Used differently by different groups, the Picturesque aesthetic easily rode on the back of the network that it also helped strengthen. It replaced conventions of idealized classicism by stimulating a wider typology of aesthetic considerations of real or representational land-scapes. For some it took the sting out of being provincial, relating provincials to the center by validating the landscapes they lived among. It also helped mythologize the countryside, rendering the gypsy 'an interesting piece of local colour rather than a peripatetic threat to the *status quo*'. Its practice functioned as 'a holding operation' for 'the squirearchy which had lost ground and continued to lose ground in the dynamic of country life' (Andrews 1989: 252 n. 3; Morgan 1983). It helped shape new identity in face of the loss of old ones that were being left behind in the urbanization of England.

Whether in London or the provinces, there was a doubled articulation of tension in the round of opera-, play- and concert-going, of visits to pleasure gardens, and attendance at clubs, balls and assemblies. Internally generated tension was induced by the self-discipline required for membership in polite society. Audiences had to be educated to their role as silent and still spectators, while on stage, momentary frozen poses were taken to convey emotion. Off stage, instruction books demanded the ability 'to hear disagreeable things without any visible tokens of offence or displeasure ... [and] to hear pleasurable things without bursts of joy and frantic distortions of the face'. Entrants into polite society attempted to be neither 'too forward, nor too reserved nor too goodhumoured; but cautious and prudent, cheerful and easy' (Brewer 1997: 111). Drawing, dancing, and music masters taught the new sociable man or woman to harness the passions and thus to achieve success in polite society. To reverse the process of emulation for a moment, Bahktin's classical statue might have stepped down from its country house pedestal to mingle with the middle classes, but it certainly was not going to be allowed to kick up its heels.

Externally generated tension arose from criticism of the practice of worldliness. Avarice, greed, lust, and vanity were bad for the soul, though they were very good for business. The relationship between the slave trade and luxury was loudly proclaimed, in part by the Romantic poets Coleridge, Southey and Wordsworth.[9] The self-promoting creed of mercantilism had led to the oppression of the poor in England and to the unmitigated cruelty of the African slave trade (Baum 1994; Everett 1994; Gerzina 1995).[10] The 'soul' of England, in the form of its old manners and customs, was being sacrificed to self-interest and profit. Polite society, associated with the urban and the urbane cultural narrative, was faulted for being an aesthetic refinement based upon artifice. Its lack of a moral dimension became the focus of opposition. In consequence, another narrative developed, based upon spontaneous sentiment and sentimentalism. But heightened sensibility could tend either towards encouraging benevolence, or to anguished avoidance of human suffering (Everett 1994). Either way, the emphasis on sensibility and sentiment helped foster an aesthetic that responded to the 'cult of rude, wild and authentic nature which . . . put the margins of the nation – the Scottish Highlands and the Welsh hills – at the centre of its taste' (Brewer 1997: 118). This cult was the pursuit of the Picturesque.

## Problems of 'Britain' and 'England'

The period was a vortex of identity construction. The homogenizing process of the production of polite society was taking place along with the not unproblematic development of Britons. But simultaneously, two past versions of England – the Anglo-Saxon and the Norman – were being vociferously argued over by their socio-political heirs. Added to which was nascent cultural nationalism among the constituent parts of Great Britain. All of which was played out against the background of the ongoing Anglo-French rivalry for colonies and colonial wars.

Given that French taste was viewed as underpinning London-based culture, one strand in the argument over what constituted the real England was directed against polite society. As the cultural narrative of polite society was replicated at a national level, it had the effect of producing a 'sense of internal social division along cultural lines' (Newman 1987: 99). Historical reference to the imposition of the Norman yoke by which traditional English liberties had been lost, informed a radical patriotism that agitated against the centralizing state and for political reform (Butler 1988; Evans 1995). Such oppositional patriotism was to give way at the end of the century under the impact of the French Revolution's Reign of Terror. In the meantime, a broad-based anti-French sentiment, and a sense of 'Britain' and 'Britons' was generated in the face of the common enemy, France. Iconographic personification of the nation arose in the form of Britannia. But even this identity was not unproblematic. In relation to the political message she might carry, Britannia could be shown as representing anti-Norman England, or Francophobe Britain (Atherton 1974).[11]

Historical and contemporary issues around Frenchness lined up along class lines that reflected two socio-moral worlds. The ruling class was morally polluted through Gallicism (travel abroad, refined taste, and the trappings of London culture). The recovery of a pre-Norman English identity and assertion of its true principles depended upon the rein-vigoration of rustic virtues, valorization of wild nature, and the shucking-off of all that was foreign (Newman 1987). The recovery of this England-that-once-was stood in stark contrast to the England of political-economy's making, in which local or native community counted for less than profitable foreign trading partnerships and colonial expansion. In the face of curbs upon foreign travel occasioned by the ongoing series of wars with France, London society had turned to and valorized the mountainous areas of the Celtic fringe, and had fashioned the discursive site of the Lake District. Over the course of the eighteenth century, what polite society had fashioned became, for some, the repository of virtues that polite society was perceived as not having.

The overarching political identity of Great Britain as nation-state was in formation in the eighteenth century. The political union of Scotland with England and Wales had begun when James VI of Scotland had ascended the throne of England as James I in 1603. The Act of Union in 1707 formalized a union rife with ambiguities and anger over loss of older identities, as Scottish and Scotland, and English and England gave way to British and Great Britain.[12] Although Britishness was an identity superimposed upon older loyalties, it did not supplant them (Cannadine 1995; Colley 1992; Robbins 1988). Like all identities it was contingent, constructed in relation to a social or territorial other (Sahlins 1989), in this case Catholic France.

The ongoing nature of the deep mutual antipathy bordering on chronic hatred which existed between England and France was only fanned by the Stuart dynasty. Without rehearsing the whole Jacobin/Roman Catholic threat to Protestant England, it should suffice to say that James I's notion that his accession to the throne had led to peace between Scotland and England, was off by nearly a hundred and fifty years. The various late seventeenth- through mid-eighteenth-century Anglo-French wars always carried an undertone of 'French-sponsored Jacobite invasion,' while the 'fact that in 1715 and 1745, hostile Jacobite armies marched into England from Scotland ensured that older memo-ries of cross-border hostilities remained alive' (Colley 1992: 4, 13). As for Ireland, Irish Jacobites had long been fighting the English from within the French armies. The Irish voice that had begun to be raised against Parliament in London in the 1780s eventually erupted in the

Rebellion of 1798 which, aided as it was by the French fleet, certainly did nothing to dispel Anglo-French hostility.[13] At moments when Protestant antagonism towards Catholics coalesced, it cross-cut internal divisions of Welshness, Scotsness, and Englishness and helped cement notions and experience of Britishness (Colley 1992).

However, this view of the construction of British identity focuses on the ties that bound internal divisions together 'rather than the beliefs that rent them asunder' (Brewer 1992:5). Internal dissension was expressed in terms of cultural nationalisms, but Protestantism contained its own schismatic fault lines. What needs to be problematized is the presentation of a monolithic Protestant Britain opposed to Catholic France and its reflected presence in Ireland. What must be acknowledged are the internal divisions of dissenting or nonconforming denominations: Presbyterians, Congregationalists, Baptists, Quakers, Unitarians, and Methodists, Nonconformists and the radical project of Chartism. This theme will be picked up in Chapter 5 when the focus is upon the Midlands.

## Two Versions of England

That there were two versions of England has already been mentioned. It is questionable whether there has ever been a unitary English identity. Initially a construct of the Tudor period, when the 'systematic disinterment of evidence for the Anglo-Saxons – their church, their language and their law-codes' was initiated (Phythian-Adams 1991: 2), 'the English were more likely to identify with their own regions and localities than with the whole country of England *per se*' (Evans 1995: 232). The importance of racial and institutional history was critical. The 'Hengist-and-Horsa racial mystique' (Lowenthal 1991: 208) rooted identity in the Anglo-Saxon race and its democratic institutions.

This mystique underpinned both British, and one version of English, identity.[14] Each was oppositional to the same Other, though that Other was constructed somewhat differently. From the Anglo-Saxon 'English' perspective, the Other was the Norman overlords and their contemporary British heirs. From the British perspective, the Other was the territorially ambitious, overweening, and morally decadent, contemporary French.

Anglo-Saxon primitive democracy (with its Celts, Druids and bards presented as home-grown varieties of the Noble Savage then being met with in the South Pacific), was pitted against the contemporary heirs of Norman overlordship. Contemporary internal social divisions called upon this class divisioning/re-visioning of the past:

On the one hand, a myth of genealogical descent was being elaborated; a myth which traced the 'truly' English community . . . back to the humble Saxons . . . Year by year the vision of a 'truly' English or British racial community with a common past and a common moral, social, cultural and political makeup was pieced together from a maze of scholarly and pseudo-scholarly research, and then fitted with tremendous emotional appeal by associating it with the idealized moral qualities of the Saxon ancestors . . . The political implication . . . was that the innate moral superiority, historic precedence in the British Isles, and Germanic institutional inheritance of 'the people' entitled them to a much larger share of legitimacy and power than they were currently suffered to enjoy by their ('Gallick,' Norman, French) oppressors.

(Newman 1987:117)

At the same time, a quite different version of England was in the making. Elaborated by a discourse of progress and theories of political economy, it was the progressive, 'improving', urbanizing, manufacturing, and industrializing England that was, and remains, interchangeable with Britain. And that pair of conjoined twins has never yet been sundered (Cannadine 1995; Grant and Stringer 1995; Lowenthal 1991). Paradoxically, Enlightenment progressivism served to bring its opposite into sharp intellectual focus: the unimproved, the backward, the quaint – all the things of interest to antiquarians, folklorists, and pursuers of the Picturesque. An Enlightenment evolutionary model of improvement might well be a determining pattern of thought, but a pattern comprises solids and voids, either of which can become the pattern to the other's ground. In terms of landscape and agricultural practice, what the Enlightenment project delineated as needful of improving and modernizing, was for others the bastion of community and repository of lived culture. The center's turn to its own mountainous north, England's Lake District, marks the production of another layer of opposition to that progressive England, as aesthetics and sentiment combined to locate continuity and tradition in the landscape. The spiritual and moral values of paternalistic and benevolent landowner-ship were set against progressive and improving landowners and farmers. Practices of enclosure and eviction broke the time-honored reciprocal bonds of agrarian community. Of course, the reciprocal bonds had been broken many times before, perhaps most notably at a national level in the sixteenth century's enclosure movement.

A fascinating reading of the Enlightenment's project of modernization in relation to landscape/landuse in the Celtic Fringe uses Arthur

Young's *Tour in Ireland ... 1776, 1777, and 1778* (1780) and Samuel Johnson's *A Journey to the Western Island of Scotland* (1775) to reveal political economy's lack of temporality and its threat to indigenous culture:

> For Young, Ireland is a place where a new future can become visible. For the nationalists, it is a place where the outlines of the past can still be glimpsed, where a hidden landscape of historical tradition and emotional attachment can be sensed just beneath the surfaces visible to the modern eye. Such surfaces serve as an accretive national annal, bearing the visible marks of many centuries of continuous human presence. . . . Where both oral and written traditions have been forcibly suppressed, the national landscape becomes crucial as an alternative, less easily destroyed historical record. Agricultural reforms that would erase the surface of the country, to create an economic and political tabula rasa, thus threaten the vestiges of cultural memory.
>
> (Trumpener 1997: 52–3)

The production of a rurally situated traditionalist worldview resulted from the relationship between the Picturesque movement and anti-quarianism.[15] The base of interest in those matters shifted from a cultural elite to a broader-based segment of society. Old or decrepit elements in the landscape (be they people or buildings), ruined field monuments, curiosities such as ancient trees or 'fairy stones', and traditions of speech, dress and manners went into the making of this worldview.[16] The importance of provincial life and local particularities, began to stand out against the gathering importance of urban concentrations. The ruins in the landscape 'stood as the surviving fragments of a native culture whose recovery was a matter of national and regional pride' (Brewer 1997: 582). The English countryside became the locus of timeless stability precisely as it was poised to undergo, or was indeed already undergoing, rapid change with the concomitant transformation of social relations (Bermingham 1986; Newby 1987).

This newly made traditionalist worldview provided raw material for cultural nationalism. It brought new impetus to the collection and valuation of English, Irish, Welsh and Scottish history (mythical or genuine), folk beliefs (such as those concerning the 'little people'), and practices (such as harvest rituals). These histories, beliefs, and practices were rooted in attachment to place, to the magical prior inhabitants of the landscape, indeed to the very magic that had previously been demonized in the Reformation, and denied in Enlightenment thinking

(Schneider 1991).[17] Cultural nationalism was oppositional to the rhetoric of progress and improvement, but Picturesque touring allowed the marketplace to incorporate landscapes of regional resistance. An excursion into those landscapes will bring into focus a non-English context for the statement that to 'persons of pure taste' the Lake District was 'a sort of national property' (Wordsworth [1835] 1984: 133). Doing so helps explicate the notion of cultural nationalism operating through landscape, and indicates the Picturesque aesthetic's range of operation.

## Cultural Nationalism

While the polity of Great Britain was in the making, so too were internal cultural nationalisms, leading to what has recently been termed '"four nations" literary history' (Pittock 1994: 2). Given the 'coercive versions of "Englishness" that were being so assiduously developed at the time' (Lucas 1990: 40), emerging Irish, Welsh and Scottish identities were proactive forms of resistance to the British state. However, they were also subverted by the center's production of a needed peripheral Other (Brydon 1995; Evans 1995). The interconnections between these cultural nationalisms can be sought for and understood in part through the lens of the Picturesque movement.

Britain's unimproved mountainous Celtic fringe supplied appropriately miniaturized Alpine landscapes for the practice of the Picturesque.[18] The Picturesque aesthetic emphasized the individual by its development of sentiment. Images of decay and poverty were central to the aesthetic, but only as peripheral decorative motifs. The development of sentiment was what it was all about, yet engagement with what was seen – the human misery – was not:

> It is, after all, an important feature of the picturesque that the viewer or reader isn't morally, socially or politically implicated in what he/she sees or reads. To go in search of the picturesque is to go in search of merely aesthetic experiences. . . . William Gilpin positively opposed the introduction of what he called 'peasants engaged in their several professions' into picturesque paintings. If beggars and aged men were to appear it should be in a manner that allowed them to be aesthetically absorbed into the scene so that the spectator could indulge thoughts of pleasing melancholy.
>
> (Lucas 1990: 92)

The rise of a political British identity necessitated that advocates of the cultural identity categories (Welsh, Irish, Scottish) not articulate claims to political sovereignty. That was now subsumed in the nation-state.[19] Protestantism, the exigencies of trade, and national defense successfully carried the project forward at all social levels, despite contestation between and within these levels (Colley 1992; Robbins 1988).[20] However, at the same time as the rationale for a more encompassing polity was bringing together 'an expanded social and governing elite which included substantial numbers of Welsh, Scottish and Protestant Anglo-Irish landowners and businessmen' (Evans 1995: 223), ethnic particularities of the older kingdoms were also being explored and documented (Newman 1987; Robbins 1988).[21]

Under the onslaught of centuries of anglicization, Wales had experienced a process of cultural decay and loss of self-confidence. A distinctive Welsh way of life had gradually disappeared, its legal system had been suppressed, the Welsh language had been banned at the administrative level, and the bardic system, almost annihilated in the thirteenth century, had remained in a state of atrophy (Hechter 1975; Robbins 1988). The reinvention of Wales began in the eighteenth century and came to full fruition in the nineteenth. It depended in part upon forgeries and inventions from within that were skillfully intertwined with genuine native Celtic roots (Morgan 1983). But it was the Picturesque aesthetic combined with antiquarianism that helped form the milieu in which such forgeries could be successfully palmed off. Pursuit of the Picturesque, antiquarianism, and the periphery's cultural reinvention of itself were all mutually reinforcing practices.

Fertile confusion reigned. What was Celtic and what was Saxon was unclear. Excavations of the standing stone complexes at Stonehenge, Avebury and Silbury Hill in the 1720s fueled both the Welsh and the tourists' romantic idealization of Druid and Celt. By the mid-1750s, the poet Thomas Gray was crafting a new response to wild nature and remote history. His translations of Norse and Welsh poetry, considered the 'pre-civilised north' (Lucas 1990: 50), were used to promote decentrist cultural nationalism. Gray's turn to the literature of the older north served to break links that traced out for British poetry 'a continuous literary tradition back not (as was and still is customary) through the Normans to Provençal and Latin literature, but to the Welsh and Norse' (Butler 1988: 43). Borrowings from his newly translated Old Norse Edda supplemented eighteenth-century Celtic dramas that contained Druid scenes of the Welsh bards. Gray's immensely popular poem *The Bard* took as its subject the last Welsh bard being hunted down by the English under Edward I. Its importance lay in the fact that historically, political sovereignty as well as culture had resided in the Welsh bards. The poem inspired many paintings and was eventually reimported into Welsh myth-making.[22]

By the late eighteenth century, Picturesque touring to the sparsely inhabited, agriculturally depressed mountains of Wales became increasingly popular. The mountains were suitably formidable without being impossibly so. Outdated agricultural practices and 'primitive' vernacular dwellings supplied acceptably aesthetic images of decay and evidence of the passage of time. Survivals in dress due to poverty were glossed and transformed into national costume. Remnants of bardic poetry were 'Druidical' relicts, the Welsh language was somehow related to Hebrew, and landscape legends were embellished or invented not only for the tourists but also 'to make the Welsh understand that their landscape must be cherished' (Morgan 1983: 86).[23] That the project was successfully carried forward can be judged by the second verse of the nineteenth-century Welsh national anthem. It runs (in translation):

Old mountainous Wales, paradise of bards,
Each cliff and each valley to my sight is fair,
With patriotic sentiment, magic is the sound
Of her rivers and brooks to me . . .

(Morgan 1983: 87)

Bardic 'eulogistic poetry . . . so rooted in the landscape' (Trumpener 1997: 3–4) was an impelling force linking landscape to autonomous cultural nationalism. In their role as keepers of culture, newly known Australian aborigines were likened to Gaelic bards (Smith 1985). The gathering, explication, promulgation, or forging of the bardic tradition was of primary importance to nationalist constructions of Wales, Scotland and Ireland (Piggott 1976; Pittock 1994; Schama 1996; Trumpener 1997). The lynch-pin to the formation of Celtic Scotland, for instance, was James Macpherson's forged indigenous literature, supposedly written by the harp-playing bard Ossian.[24] Yet Scottish identity, initially a Western Highland one, was a 'cultural revolt against Ireland', not England, for it was Irish bardic culture that had historically shaped and dominated the Hebrides. As for Ireland, 'even under the oppressive rule of England in the seventeenth and eighteenth centuries, Celtic Ireland clung to an image of itself as, culturally, an historic nation' ((Trevor-Roper 1983). This had been achieved in part through the active practice of harpistry and a bardic poetry that, in both senses of the word, carried the 'burden' of nation.[25]

If bardic poetry carried 'nation', what did 'nation' carry? A standard dictionary (*Webster's New Collegiate*) shows the following:

> NATION: Middle English *nacioun*, from Middle French *nation*, from Latin *nation-natio* meaning birth, race, nation, from *natus*, the past participle of *nasci* meaning to be born.

*Native* and *nature* are also connected to *nation* by their root in Latin *natus-nasci*:

> NATIVE: Middle English *natif*, from Middle French from Latin *nativus* from *natus* past participle of *nasci* meaning to be born.

> NATURE: Middle English from Middle French from Latin *natura*, from *natus*, the past participle of *nasci* meaning to be born.

When linked with nation, native, and nature, the word landscape has a 'metaphoric, and ideological, potency' that comes from 'the development of a more permanent bond between the nature, or character, of the culture of a particular people and the nature, or character, of the particular areas where they dwell' (Olwig 1993: 310–12). One way in which this more permanent bond is expressed is in the native language, or mother tongue – which connotatively resonates to *natus-nasci*. In relation to the eighteenth-century Celtic fringe, this landscape/language link is central to bardic nationalism. By the end of the century, landscape was a 'version of nature *in* which man most fully experience[d] himself, both in place and in time . . . [and became] . . . a key concept in the shift towards subjective time-consciousness' (Salveson 1965: 14).

The landscape/language link was kept alive through toponymic memory and isolation. Throughout the eighteenth century, the old languages – or in the case of England, dialects – were still being spoken in remote areas (Robbins 1988). Occasionally landscape and language were conflated into iconic expression as, for example, when the Welsh language was depicted on the title page of James Howell's 1659 dictionary 'as a scared wild woodland warrior maiden' (Morgan 1983: 48). But overwhelmingly, languages of nation (Gaelic, Welsh) fell into decay through disuse, outright banning, and inroads made by the killer language, English.[26]

Toponymic memory could be displaced through wholesale clearances, as in the Scottish Highlands. The naming involved in formal mapping could function as a way of silencing the past, as when Gaelic place-names were replaced in the 1824–36 General Ordnance survey of Ireland. Conversely, compilers of the Ordnance Survey took great pains over Welsh orthography (Harley and Walters 1982 cited in Robbins 1988). Local names, including those in the periphery of England, were often ignored or garbled (Wilberforce 1779).[27] On rare occasions, a reverse erasure took place, as when milestones were removed from segments of the British military roads that had penetrated the Scottish Highlands during the Jacobite uprisings (Trumpener 1997). This reverse erasure on military roads also occurred extensively in Ireland, but the social action and power of maps was usually more long-lasting (Harley 1992; Pickles 1992).

Elements in the landscape that indicated the passage of time were of fundamental importance to the Picturesque. Ruins and moss- or ivy-covered structures were melancholy reminders of *tempus fugit*. Mountains spoke of a (newly discovered) geologically deep time scale that by comparison rendered a human lifetime inconsequential. Dawns and sunsets (even if seen through a glass brightly) held the personally measured passage of time. But any ruin, any moss-covered bridge, any old decrepit person, any mountain would do to stimulate imagination and sensation. What emerged was an engagement with memory-over-time that required the particularized, the highly localized ruin, bridge, person, mountain. This shift in focus to close observation of the landscape in the visual arts (Murdoch 1986) forms a parallel to the poetry of particularized place. Such poetry acted as a personal toponymic memory, a recognition of a personal interior isolation or alienation that sought refuge through location in the landscape. That quality of location rendered contingent being poignant. The poignancy of that located memory was memory's triumph over time.

## The English Romantic Movement and the Lakeists

English Romanticism was a term applied retroactively in the mid-nineteenth century to English poets of the late eighteenth and early nineteenth centuries. The formation of a canonical unitary English Romanticism was a product of the 1940s. It has at different times comprised the self-defined Lakeists – Wordsworth, Coleridge and Southey – along with Blake, Byron, Keats and Shelley. All were proponents of an English nationalist aesthetic developed by earlier poets such as Thomson, Shenstone and Cowper. In the last ten to twenty years of the twentieth century, English Romanticism, and particularly its normative figure Wordsworth, underwent critical reexamination (Aers *et al.* 1981; Butler 1982, 1988; Lui 1989; McGann 1983). This has revealed an ideology of poetic displacement and idealization that severs subject matter from its social and economic contexts.

The term English Romanticism has also been used to refer to a broader swath of poetry running from the 1740s to 1790s, when provincialism was exalted; the 1790s to 1815, when provincial landscapes remained the mainstay but post-Revolutionary religious orthodoxy crept in; and 1815 to 1825, when the tone was less provincial and democratic. Within this more extended timeframe, English Romanticism 'tended to oppose the central British state and its institutions' and was preoccupied with 'class, social change, natural religion, regional and national pride, and world revolution' (Butler 1988: 37–41). It was not 'a single intellectual movement but a complex of responses to . . . social pressures' (Butler 1982: 184), arising out of the early stages of the industrial revolution (Aers *et al.* 1981). What resulted was that

> a Romantic structure of feeling – the assertion of nature against industry and of poetry against trade; the isolation of humanity and community into the idea of culture, against the real social pressure of the time – is projected. We can catch its echoes, exactly, in Blake, in Wordsworth, and in Shelley.
>
> (Williams 1973: 79)

Increased levels of literacy, a more extensive publishing industry, and better distribution of printed matter achieved through an extended system of turnpike roads combined to ensure that the provincial middling sort, as well as country gentry, had access to the poetics and politics of English Romanticism. By the end of the eighteenth century, the profound changes wrought in the literate public's appreciation of nature, through the prior half-century's native country or pastoral poetry, allowed for easy absorption of the Lake District as a powerful cultural symbol of stability.

The overt importance attaching to the oppositional voice of poetry, and especially bardic poetry, expressed the deepening sense that poets should speak to and for their community. Yet as a London-based cultural narrative was being replicated in the provinces, the community of *native/nation/nature* was perceived as being shattered under the twin impacts of enclosure and urbanization. By mid-century, England's poets and writers were experiencing a profound crisis about the culture they were giving voice to. Depression, madness and suicides marked the artistic-intellectual community (Butler 1988; Lucas 1990; Newman 1987), while poetry continued to carry the twin motifs of xenophobia and valorization of the English landscape for the rest of the century.

In the face of fragmentation of people and place, landscape answered the felt need for continuity. In extreme instances, this might be expressed as a corpus of allegedly medieval poetry and prose in praise of an English province, but more generally, poets

> beginning with James Thomson (1700–1748), and going on through Thomas Gray (1716–71) to William Blake (1757–1827) and William Wordsworth (1775–1850), replace the 'court' or London or aristocratic discourse of Dryden, Pope, Swift and Gay with a symbolic language exalting provincialism. . . . they express, and further shape, attitudes which are representative of the attitudes of some of the gentry and much of the 'middling orders', especially of the commercial and entrepreneurial classes in eighteenth-century London and the provinces.
>
> (Butler 1988: 41)

Thomson's country poetry exemplifies the first period of English Romanticism in its larger timescale outlined above. His was a generalized countryside, touched by generalized seasons, and evincing generalized emotions. Early tourists to the Lake District had drawn on classical writers to enhance what they saw. From the 1740s on, with the phenomenal popularity of Thomson's *The Seasons*, native literature gained importance in supplying emotive associations.

Unlike bardic poetry, such pastoral poetry falsified the actual relationships of rural communities just as much as and for the same reason that it falsified urban communities (Lucas 1990; Sales 1983; Williams 1973). By the end of the eighteenth century the thrust of the Picturesque was to seek landscapes

> where there are not only no traces of contemporary industrialization, land enclosure and estate improvement, but where the georgic idyll in all its forms is lost and where the terrifying 'levelling' influences from across the channel can never come . . . the Picturesque tourist is now willing to trek hundreds of miles to find a world 'That seems in labours hurry left forgot'.
>
> (Andrews 1989: 66).

Country or pastoral poetry, along with engraved versions of paintings, affirmed the Picturesque, which in turn informed the early works of the Lakeists. In what has been referred to as his poetry of 'domestic anthropology' (Bewell 1989), Wordsworth peopled the Lake District landscape with the marginalized within – the crippled soldier, blind beggar, recluse, mad-woman, gypsy, vagrant – in other words, the abandoned flotsam and jetsam of the early agricultural and industrial revolutions.[28] Not surprisingly perhaps, these marginals formed part of the continuum of human categories then being developed by the centralizing state as the basis for its Poor Law. Wordsworth

> began by wanting to give utterance to those who had been denied their own voices. Such people were no longer to be treated as objects of contemplation, usually from afar, as in the distancing techniques of Thomson's abstractions. Instead, they became subjects: speaking, experiencing. But then Wordsworth began to retreat, figuratively and literally.
>
> (Lucas 1990: 6)

In that retreat, one arrives at Wordsworth's highly particularized 'limited localities' that are lovingly returned to over and over again, as deep familiarity of place and placement is probed and explored (Kroeber 1975). This is why

> Blake's visions of England are liberating and tragically truthful [while] Wordsworth's are increasingly false. From his 'free' place, or 'dwelling', among the Lakes, remote from the city, [Wordsworth] poses as a man speaking *for* men, and particularly for Englishmen and England. This is the ultimate, deeply conservative ambition of pastoral.
>
> (Lucas 1990: 117)

As the previous chapter observed, the valorization of the Lake District preceded by some half-century the Lakeists' exultation of it. However, what had already begun through the Picturesque was to be freighted by the Lakeists with even more national sentiment. The landscape's inhabitants were presented as living examples of what for the rest of the country were merely memories of bygone English virtues: simplicity, temperance, economy and independence (Everett 1994). This was especially so in the case of the statesmen-farmers and their families who were presented as inhabiting a mountain republic (Wordsworth 1835).

The responses to a rural questionnaire on the condition of agricultural laborers in that 'mountain republic' told a different story (Royal Commission 1834). That mountain landscapes were independence-forming places of moral and political refuge was not a new notion. Eighteenth-century writers had themselves revived an earlier self-valorizing literature that had presented Alpine montagnards as figures of 'frugal robustness and artless virtue' and re-promoted them as 'nature's primitive democrats' (Schama 1996: 479–80). Set against this image of a coherent past were the agencies of destruction: the radical alteration to people and place engendered by cataclysmic changes in agriculture, commerce, and industry (Polanyi 1944).

The English Romantic's gaze at and incorporation of the Celtic periphery of Scotland, Wales, and Ireland was accomplished through painterly, poetic, and novelistic renderings. This gaze operated closer to home where it inscribed a particular vision of England upon the Lake District, rendering it a repository of an imagined, or not-so-imagined, past. It was a past that held the core values which the trading/ financial center of London had happily prostituted in the Midlands. The Lake District was made into an icon, a window through which a greater reality or truth could be perceived, be it of God or England – although the two were not necessarily different from one another. This conflation of God, England and the Lake District perhaps reaches its ultimate expression in in two large embroidered panels by Ann Macbeth (1875–1948) who lived in Patterdale, high in the Lake District's central fells. Using local people for her models, Macbeth showed the Hartsop Valley as the site of Christ's nativity and ministry (see plates 5 and 6). Embroidered beneath the portrayal of Christ as The Good Shepherd is the musical notation of Blake's poem *Jerusalem* that accompanies the lines: 'And did those feet in ancient time/ Walk upon England's mountains green?'

Through the poetry of the Lakeists and their circle, and particularly through Wordsworth's *Guide to the Lakes*, the landscape of the Lake District was made known to a wide reading public.[29] It was also made known to a wide viewing public as professional watercolorists began visiting the Lake District in earnest in the first two decades of the nineteenth century and their prolific output reached the market (Beard 1980; Bicknell 1987; Bicknell and Woof 1982, 1983; Rhyne 1986; Tate Gallery 1996). Being bolstered was a version of English national identity, based upon a past (real or mythic) that also rejected the present's perceived destruction of community. The Lake District was a landscape of association, but not the borrowed and idealized Italianate classical landscapes of the south's great country houses, or the exotic 'Oriental' landscapes complete with Chinese pagodas and bridges, or Turkish tents such as at Kew and at Charles Hamilton's Painshill, Cobham, Surrey.[30] And the Lake District certainly stood in the starkest possible contrast to the destroyed landscapes of the manufacturing centers of the Midlands.

In the early nineteenth century, the increasing popularity of the Lake District and its relative proximity to manufacturing centers in the Midlands brought the newly wealthy to the region not just as tourists but as year-round or summer inhabitants. Imposing houses were built in local centers and isolated locations, in both cases with the primary intention of obtaining commanding views of the lakes and mountains.[31] In his *Guide to the Lakes*, Wordsworth railed against industrialists' brash mansions, painted the wrong color and conspicuously sited for the fine views rather than unobtrusively nestled into their landscapes as older vernacular buildings were. He also protested against the proposed intrusion of the railways into the Lake District because they would bring in the day-trippers, the industrial working class.

> The coupling of national landscapes with elite judgement ... was memorably voiced by Wordsworth. He termed the Lake District 'a sort of national property, in which everyman has a right and interest who has an eye to perceive' – but such an eye was formed only gradually, at the court of cultivated taste. Having earlier sought to preserve the Lakes *for* visitors (then a few gentry) Wordsworth ended by protecting them *against* visitors (whose wanton incursions he likened to 'the child's cutting up his drum to learn where the sound comes from').
>
> (Lowenthal 1991: 219)

Under the impact of the agricultural and industrial revolutions' spatial reconstruction of England, the Lake District remained an unutilized or negative space, treated in the following chapters as expressing a previously unexamined manifestation of the capitalist dynamic. A new and unprecedented accumulation of value accrued to this space as it was valorized by an intellectual and artistic elite precisely because it was other than the new urban concentrations of capital. Although a version of an homogenous English national identity centered around the Lake District as a 'sort of national property', it paradoxically led to cultural differentiation of class through contested participation in this landscape.

## Conclusion

The London poems by Blake and Wordsworth that headed this chapter are expressive of the period's urban-centered tensions and anxieties. They stand in contradistinction to the valorization of Britain's mountainous areas, in particular the Lake District. Wordsworth views the 'native culture' of London's St. Bartholomew's Fair from the low but nonetheless distancing height of a 'shewman's platform'. The next Book of the *Preludes* opens on the summit of Helvellyn from which lofty height the poet gazes down at a village fair in the valley far below and ponders with great affection the natural community of people gathered there. Paradoxically, height is no separation here for, remembering the common root of *nat*ion, *nat*ive, *nat*ure, a right relationship exists between people and place.

J.M.W. Turner's exhibition piece of 1798, 'Morning Among the Coniston Fells', is a concatenation of poetry, painting, *nat*ion, *nat*ure and the Lake District landscape. Executed in the vertical format traditionally associated with altarpieces, the painting was accompanied by these lines from Milton:

> . . . ye Mists and Exhalations that now rise
> From Hill or steaming Lake, duskie or grey,
> Til the Sun paint your fleecie skirts with Gold
> In honour to the World's great Author rise.

> (Milton, *Paradise Lost*, Book V, lines 185–8)

Wreathed in their mercantile-authored mists and exhalations, the manufacturing cities and their inhabitants could only exercise a polluting influence upon such scenes. Contemplating 'the stupid herds of modern tourists' that the railways would surely bring into the Lake District, John Ruskin (a nationally-renowned art critic and leading figure in workingmen's education) realized that 'engineers and contractors must live.' But he begged that they might live 'in a more useful and honourable way than by keeping Old Bartholomew Fair under Helvellyn' (Ruskin 1876: 4–6).

The Bakhtinian multiple and grotesque body was present in London, the manufacturing cities of the Midlands and the trading centers of the empire. Polite society responded by seeking refuge in the heights. That the Lake District had become an icon of England can be glimpsed in the way it was 'found' abroad in the early nineteenth century. The following opinion concerned Tasmania, but the Lake District was also seen in the landscapes of Australia and New Zealand:

> The scenery around Newtown is the most beautiful I have seen on this side of the world – very much resembling that of the Cumberland Lakes: the broad and winding estuary of the Derwent flows between lofty and

picturesque hills and mountains ... It seemed like being on the right side of the earth again.

(Meredith 1852 cited in Smith 1985: 291)

Further evidence of the way in which the Lake District functioned as a cultural paradigm is supplied by the inscription of the Picturesque practice of the Lake District upon the landscape of Kandy, a valley city in the central mountainous region of Ceylon (Sri Lanka). Taken by British military forces in 1795, Ceylon was annexed by British treaties in 1802 and 1815. Differences in vegetative cover apart, the two landscapes 'read' the same way, as Lieutenant Colonel Charles Hamilton Smith plainly saw (see plates 7 and 8).

The elevation and topography of Kandy [made] it possible to create a facsimile of the landscape of home ... Kandy was designed to resemble a romanticized image of a pre-industrial England. The landscape model of the English lake district was superimposed upon the mountains and the Kandy lake to recreate a place where English ladies and gentlemen could somehow escape the tropics and the native culture and symbolically return home.

(Duncan 1989: 192)

Promenades, carriage drives, and riding paths were constructed around the newly named Victoria Lake in emulation of Picturesque viewing stations around the Lake District's lakes, while viewsheds were cleared through the jungle to provide suddenly appearing panoramas of the town, the lake, and its surrounding mountains. The result was that

In Kandy, whether one will or not, the mind will go back to the Lake region in England. You will find a calm and quiet beauty, freedom from strain and stress ... and a universal friendliness between all Nature and its lord, which brings up Grasmere, Windermere, Derwentwater, and their spirits – Southey, Wordsworth, Coleridge, and all the rest of the Cumberland immortals.

(Hurst 1890 quoted in Duncan 1989: 194)

Meanwhile, the project of polite society had created a new crowd. This one made its 'pervasive appearance, in the arts and in other records ... not [as] a crowd made up of strangers, as in a London street, still less a threatening mob, but [as] a room full of acquaintances or potential acquaintances at a ball or party' (Butler 1982: 25). This is the crowd well-nigh overwhelmed with its heightened senses and sensibilities, its pride and prejudices, that Jane Austen guides us through. Blake's 'mind-forg'd manacles' were not, indeed are not, the exclusive domain of any one class. None can be automatically exempted from the enslavement of having 'minds already moulded by law, custom and prejudice' (Butler 1988: 57). The site of the Lake District was fashioned by the Picturesque aesthetic and early English Romanticism. For a while it formed one class's retreat from the other. Aesthetic, cognitive and moral standards masked class antagonisms, as landscape representations masked issues of political representation (Helsinger 1994). If the Lake District was indeed 'a sort of national property' as Wordsworth pronounced it to be, then who were the right sort to enjoy it, and who was worthy of inclusion in the nation?

# Notes

1. As the fine arts gained independence from exclusively Court patronage, London became a magnet for Italian, French, Polish, Swedish, German and Dutch composers, musicians, and artists. The production of luxury goods in and around London flourished in large part due to the influx of Huguenots who, despite being prohibited from leaving France, had followed their pastors who *had* been expelled upon the revocation of the Edict of Nantes (1685). Prior to this, Huguenot family networks had dominated the production of the decorative arts for the Court of Louis XIV. The market for the fine arts and luxury goods extended well beyond the aristocracy. People of 'taste', as well as the upper reaches of 'the middling sort', had the disposable income to indulge their taste.

2. The phrase 'hand-in-glove' prompted a train of thought which when pursued, showed that despite all the Societies and Associations for the promotion of home manufactures, English cultivated taste and social refinement did not necessarily support English goods. Originally craft objects subject to sumptuary laws, gloves became one marker of eighteenth-century 'polite' society. Such was the magnitude of the smuggling trade in gloves that The Society for the Encouragement of Arts, Commerce, and Manufactures in Great Britain (founded 1754) offered a Gold Medal for the production of 'superior' gloves that might stem French imports – legal and otherwise. In terms of

cultural mimicry, gloves eventually became ubiquitous in bourgeois society. Yeovil, a center of glove production in the West of England, produced around 300,000 dozen pair a year prior to the 1830s (nearly all from foreign skins, however), despite the more than one and a half million pair legally imported annually from France. As newly invented French machinery replaced craft production in the late 1820s, the English, Scottish and Irish glove industry collapsed, with a corresponding increase in parish poor rates in those countries' glove manufacturing centers. Such political-economy 'progress' was carefully enumerated and roundly condemned (Hull 1834). Not surprisingly, Henry Vincent, a leading Chartist organizer, found the glove-making center of Ledbury, Herefordshire to be a scene of 'poverty and misery in nearly every house' (*Western Vindicator* 1839 cited in Southall 1996: 182) and ripe for organizing.

3. Arts, sciences and commerce were brought into alliance through institutions such as The Society for the Arts mentioned in the previous footnote. Gold medals were awarded in a wide range of endeavors: from drawing and sculpture (to chip away at French dominance of the decorative arts) to experiments in producing dyestuffs (so that British-manufactured cloth would not have to be shipped abroad for dying). Numerous similar societies sprang up around Britain in the mid- to late eighteenth century. Though founded within the trading and commercial community, they generally included members of the patrician class since advantages were to be gained from 'mingling socially with people of rank and influence, with all the prospects this opened up for making useful contacts and good impressions' (Colley 1992: 93). Here were the self-serving 'Courts, Committees, Institutions,/ Associations, Societies, . . . One Benefit-Club for mutual flattery' that Coleridge enumerated in *Fears in Solitude*. Such Manufacturers' Societies and Associations also served to spread some of the risks capitalism posed, such as price fluctuations and shifts in governmental fiscal policy (Morris 1990).

4. The useful arts also supplied the cash necessary to express social refinement on a grand scale, as exampled by Henry Hoare II – see Chapter 1, p. 26.

5. For instance, more than 200,000 men, 'most of them poor, some of them mutilated, all of them trained to violence' (Colley 1992: 101) were demobilized after the Seven Years War (1756–63).

6. Steele's *Tatler* appeared three times a week from 1709 to 1711. It was superseded by Addison and Steele's daily *Spectator* which, priced at one penny, ran from 1711 to 1714. Addison claimed that 3000 copies were distributed daily, with each copy having as many as twenty readers. It was widely distributed around Britain, in private homes as well as debating societies and clubs, and as far afield as New England and the East India Company's offices in Sumatra. Essays from the *Spectator* were also widely reprinted in school texts, manuals of instruction and prose collections (Brewer 1997).

7. Commoditization of the Picturesque aesthetic promoted an intensely private and personal experience of landscape at the same time as it drew large numbers of people into an aesthetic community. New lithographic techniques that allowed illustrations to duplicate more closely watercolor effects (Finlay and Waddell 1996) fed into the explosion of instruction manuals of sketching and watercolor landscape-painting, and a corresponding commercialization of art supplies (Standring 1993). In addition to circulating libraries of prints and drawings, art supply stores provided touring paraphernalia such as the redoubtable James Plumptre carried around with him.

8. Josiah Wedgwood's 952-piece creamware dinner and dessert service made in 1773–4 for Catherine the Great (1729–96), Empress of Russia, represents Picturesque landscapes being literally transformed into goods and commoditized. Every piece was painted with a different view of British landscapes, parks, gardens, and antiquities. The 'Frog Service' as it is known (because of the frog crest on each piece) 'appears to have been the first use of named topographical views on ceramics' (Young 1995: 16). Existing prints were used along with newly commissioned drawings. Decoration of the service had not been completed when it was exhibited at Wedgwood's London warehouse before being shipped to Russia. This allowed 'for influential customers whose estates had not yet appeared on the Service to offer drawings to be copied' (Raeburn 1995: 147). As a consequence of the exhibition's popularity, *The Copper Plate Magazine* was founded in 1774 and *The Virtuosis Museum* in 1778, which 'specifically referred to the Empress's initiative in order to spur the British themselves not to neglect their own country' (Andrews 1989: 35).

9. Although Coleridge ended up a staunch Anglican, he was a radical dissenter when he first met Southey and Wordsworth. It was only an annuity from Thomas and Josiah Wedgwood, sons of the Quaker pottery master Josiah Wedgwood, that persuaded him to not take up a post as a Unitarian minister.

10. As Chapter 4 will show, the metaphors and energy of the anti-slavery movement would be brought into service for the cause of the English laboring poor.

11. Political prints carrying the message of anti-Norman England showed the English aristocracy and government ministers (except Pitt), surrounded by symbols of French culture (tutors, dancing masters, luxury goods, etc.), and as aiding and abetting their French counterparts in the rape, dismemberment, and ruin of Britannia (Atherton 1974; Newman 1987).

12. The northern English counties of Cumberland and Westmorland are an interesting lens through which to see the ambiguities of older identities playing out. Border raids by the Scots had been a semi-permanent feature of existence in these counties for centuries, with counter-raids and attempted conquests of Scotland also being mounted from them. Consequently, a system of border

duty existed for their farming tenantry. As a result of the dynastic yoking of Scotland to England and Wales in 1603, border warfare was presumed to have come to a halt. Based upon that assumption, and arguing that border duty was the underpinning of a system of land tenure that was unusually advantageous to tenantry in this region, James I tried to use the presumed 'peace' as an opportunity to regrant northern crown lands to the great landholding aristocracy on new terms which doubled rent and certain fines. In turn, the great landholders were all too ready to set aside their tenants' low customary rents, and by substituting leases at much higher rents to break their customary manner of inheritance. This issue was addressed in a play performed in 1621 in Kendal (Westmorland), which was considered by the authorities to be seditious. It probably was. It generated a petition to King and Parliament in defense of customary tenant rights, which, it argued, did not depend upon border duty. This in turn precipitated retributive Star Chamber proceedings against the petitioners. In the play, one fool says to another as he comments upon a hell constructed a little below the stage, supposedly containing ravens feeding upon sheep:

> Ravens quotha, no thou art farr by the square, its false landlords makes all that croakinge there, and those sheepe wee poor men, whose right these by their skill, would take awaie, and make us tenants at will, and when our ancient liberties are gone, theile puke and poole, and peele us to the bare bone.

> (Garnett 1621 cited in Campbell 1942)

Though it took some twenty years, the tenantry won their case, and were confirmed in their customary rights of inheritance. Such is the stuff of which not only lingering antagonisms were made, but also myths of this region being the repository of 'old English virtues'.

13. Loutherbourg's sketch of *The British Lion and the French Cock* (reproduced in Colley 1992: 2), dates to *c.* 1797 when he was already a successful and popular figure through his work in the theater. It dramatically captures the spirit of Anglo-French animosity. A hugely muscular lion, teeth bared in a snarl, claws fully extended, pins down with one forepaw a rather scrawny, bulgy-eyed cockerel that appears to have tripped over a set of bagpipes. The lion's other forepaw, raised high, looks set to send the cock to perdition. In the background is the flying debris of a wrecked boat's rigging, while, ranged above the lion's mane, the foaming waves have metamorphosed into Poseidon and his attendants.

14. A glimpse of the interweaving of deep historical continuity can be seen in the founding of the first Anglo-Saxon Professorship at Oxford in 1750. It was funded through a bequest set up by the antiquarian Dr. Richard Rawlingson.

The bequest's income derived from Rawlingson family holdings in the Lake District received from Henry V for services rendered against the French at the Battle of Agincourt (Tashjian, Tashjian and Enright 1990). John Ruskin, in his diatribe against the incursion of the railways into the Lake District, also draws upon this deep history when he likens the strength and virtue of the men working his fields there to those 'who might have fought with Henry the Fifth at Agincourt, without being discerned from among his knights' (Ruskin 1876: 7).

15. As the shift in the aesthetic response to nature did not occur in a vacuum, neither did antiquarianism's glorification of the Celts. It proceeded from a broader intellectual enquiry epitomized by Montesquieu's *Spirit of Laws* (1750) and Rousseau's *Discourse on Inequality Amongst Men* (1753), which were 'enquiries into the origin of man in a context no longer always dominated by the literal text of Genesis; the nature of primitive society, the beginnings of language and literature, the existence of natural law and the earliest development of institutions' (Piggott 1976: 73). In other words, the roots of anthropological enquiry.

16. The material contained in the first few decades of *Man* (Old Series) is strongly reminiscent of this aspect of the eighteenth century. These issues are full of reviews of books such as *Superstitions of the Highlands and Islands of Scotland* (1900, 1: 901), or compendia reviews of Celtic Folklore – including the Ossian literature (1901, 63–4: 79); or illustrated articles such as *Some Scottish String Figures by the Rev. John Gray with nomenclature devised by Drs. Rivers and Haddon* (1903, 3: 117); or articles on oddly-shaped stones in Ireland (1901, 1: 12–13) and perforated stone amulets in England (1093, 8: 17–20). This is professional-journal evidence of the pre-professional antiquarian roots of ethnology and anthropology (Kuklick 1991; Stocking 1987; Urry 1993; Van Keuren 1982).

17. It is no longer possible to ignore the fact that, quite unlooked for, a series of dogs are intruding their way into the endnote narrative. First Horace Walpole's lap dog, Tory, snatched up by wolves as Walpole and Thomas Gray crossed the Alps (Chapter 2, note 3); then the unfortunate painter Charles Gough's virtuous bitch, who stayed by her master's body for months when he fell off Helvellyn (Chapter 2, note 10); and now – as retold in Schneider – the micro-history of a medieval French greyhound-saint, Saint Guinefort, whose tale more or less corresponds to that of the unsainted, and therefore unworshipped, eighteenth-century Welsh hunting dog Gelert. Gelert's wolf-killing abilities (the revenge of Tory?) were invented and his burial cairn built expressly for the benefit of Picturesque tourists. Both resulted in a poem, famous in its time, that

Joseph Haydn set to the tune of Eryi Wen, and within a few years the story returned in Welsh versions to the monoglot Welsh inhabitants of Snowdonia . . . It is a good instance of the kind of complex myth-making which . . . help[ed] very gradually to make the Welsh appreciate the harsh landscape from which they had to scratch a living.

(Morgan 1983: 87)

18. For the range of paintings, drawings, prints and books coming out of this preoccupation with the Picturesque, see the exhibition catalog *Fairest Isle: The Appreciation of British Scenery 1750–1850* (1989) Yale Center for British Art.

19. Similarly, the rise of an imperial British identity necessitated that national identity categories such as Egyptian or Indian not articulate claims to political independence (Said 1979). In either case, the same pattern was imposed: domination followed by hegemony.

20. The political and cultural are forever interwoven. The issue of national defense against French invasion spanned generations; it was not limited to one discrete, relatively brief period of time. It was experienced in political terms in the drawing together of 'Britons' (Colley 1992), and socially as throughout the eighteenth century 'a considerable section of the population experienced military service, if not directly as participants, then indirectly as the relatives and dependents of soldiers and sailors' (Russell 1995). War was felt not only in economic terms (rising food prices and crime resulting from impoverish-ment) but also in cultural terms, as the ongoing series of Anglo-French wars was played out in poetry, novels, plays, prints and broadsides. Much the same situation was to apply in the Great War (Robbins 1988).

21. This is similar to the pattern of the last few years of the twentieth century in which construction of a supranational European Union gave rise to a resurgence of regional and local identity movements (Goddard, Llobera and Shore 1994; Macdonald 1993). As Britain's identity began to give way to a broader European identity, devolution movements became more vocal and, as I explore in later chapters, the English landscape again became the locus for sentiments of national identity.

22. Gray's poem *The Bard* (1757) took as its subject the last surviving Welsh bard, harp in hand, leaping to his death rather than face capture by the English. The 'confrontation of the poet with the power of the state . . . was soon set as a subject for poems and essays in eisteddfodau' (revived bardic gatherings), and was picked up and used in promoting Magyar nationalist literature (Morgan 1983). Both Loutherbourg and Paul Sandby produced paintings based upon Gray's poem. Set to music, *The Bard* was the subject of a maudlin song I had to learn at school in the 1950s! It is only now that I understand just why 'David the Bard' threw himself off the 'White Rock'. It had been a complete mystery to me as a child.

23. In the same way that different occupational groups have different cognitive maps of the same landscape (Frykman and Löfgren 1987), different language groups who occupy the same landscape construct their own cognitive maps. Writing of Welsh speakers in Gwynedd:

> The economic and political history of this corner of Wales have served to perpetuate the divisions between the English, non-Welsh speakers and the local Welsh-speaking Welsh. When Edward I defeated the last of the semi-independent Princes of Gwynedd in the thirteenth century he established a network of castles and English settlements in order to keep the Welsh down. The Edwardian castle towns of Beaumaris, Conwy, Harlech and Criccieth, so popular with tourists, remain to this day centres of anglicisation and are studiously ignored by many Welsh speakers ... It is the castles of the Welsh princes in Deganwy and Dolwyddelan, the graves of legendary heroes and the places associated with eminent Welsh men and women – places seldom on the tourist itineraries – rather than the symbols of English domination, which fill the landscape for the Welsh.
>
> (Bowie 1993: 181)

Given the invention or embellishment of landscape-specific legends for English tourists in the eighteenth century, one can only wonder how much verisimilitude there is to some elements within the Welsh speakers' hidden landscape.

24. The forged Ossianic literature was based upon Irish ballads that were then dismissed as debased reflections of the 'real'. It became the 'source' for revelations about the antiquity of the Highland tartan small kilt. The small kilt was actually designed around 1720 by an English Quaker industrialist, who adapted a larger and looser traditional garment to allow his Scottish foundry workers safe ease of swift working. Without going into the class issues bound up with kilts and trews, suffice it to say that the kilt was banned as it became a symbol of anti-English sentiment because, courtesy of Ossian, it was invested with hoary tradition. An exception was made for the post-1745 anglicized Highland Regiments for whom the kilt was dress uniform (Trevor-Roper 1983).

From an anthropological perspective it is interesting to note that through the posting of Highland regiments to South Africa in the nineteenth century, the Highland short kilt entered the Kalela Dance – where it functioned both as a means of internal differentiation between tribal Selves, and between tribal Self and colonial Other (Mitchell 1956). By the time Mitchell was doing his work on the Kalela Dance, the kilt was no longer being worn in the dance contests. It merely appears as a passing childhood recollection of one of his informants. Given the period's lack of historical research into the invention of traditions at home, there was nothing for Mitchell to notice particularly. Now it is a nicely redoubled image in the construction of identities of resistance.

25. In musical terms, the burden is the chorus or reiterated refrain. At the height of the first period of Irish Celtic revivalism, the Belfast harpists' festival of 1792 similarly reiterated the refrain of cultural and political nationalism. At the festival, cultural revival became linked with demands for Catholic emancipation, while commemorative victory dinners celebrated the anniversary of the Fall of the Bastille (Trumpener 1997: 10).

26. Yet even in the domain of the English language there were formalized points of resistance. Dissenters and, later in the century, radicals produced dictionaries 'of English slang and provincialisms' (Butler 1988: 47).

27. Stephen Gorton, a Lake District resident whom I have known since 1987 (Darby 1988), has lived for many years in a house high in the central fells; it was his parents' summer home. Now 70 years old, he is adamant about maintaining the local voice of place. At the kitchen table poring over 1840s and 1850s Ordnance Survey Maps with me, or out walking, he would often point out mistakes: where the mapped name of a mountain shoulder or scree slope actually belongs to the ridge, or vice versa, or how a local name has been mangled even if left 'in place', or where it has been given no place on the map at all. It is important to him to maintain local knowledge – real memory – against the substitutions imposed by the official world of maps and mapmakers. It is equally important to him that local dialect and distinctively local words be maintained in use. When around local-born people, there is a distinct shift in his pronunciation, and he uses local words that he does not use around me or other people who, like himself, are off-comers (people who were not born in the area).

28. Joan Baum (1994) explores the unstated presence of slavery behind these marginal people who preoccupied both Coleridge and Wordsworth.

29. Wordsworth's *Guide to the Lakes* often uses the language of the Picturesque, but more often operates in the realm of prose poetry, in some instances using, without attribution, Dorothy Wordsworth's writing. The *Guide* first appeared as an anonymous introduction for Joseph Wilkinson's *Select Views in Cumberland, Westmoreland, and Lancashire* (1810). It was later reprinted as *A Topographical description of the Country of the Lakes in the North of England* which appeared as an appendix to Wordsworth's sonnet collection *The River Duddon* (1820). It was then published as a freestanding piece in 1822 as *A Description of the Scenery of the Lakes in the North of England*. The *Description* then went through numerous and enlarged editions up through the 1850s, and has continued to be reissued up through the mid-1980s (Bicknell 1984).

30. The Honorable Charles Hamilton held the lease at Painshill from 1738 to 1773, during which time he managed to bankrupt himself through loans (some from Hoare's Bank) to fund his 200-acre landscaping project (Thacker 1989). It included a tufa-constructed grottoed island, a hermitage, a purpose-

built 'ruined' abbey and a 'ruined' Roman triumphal arch that housed genuine classical antiquities. Staffing the hermitage proved difficult, for although people might be turned into art temporarily, holding the pose proved problematic. An old man on a £700 seven-year contract to play the hermit, lasted only three weeks 'before escaping to a local inn' (Symes 1991: 36).

31. Technical innovations in the production of plate glass allowed for huge panes such as those used for the orangerie built in 1704 at Kensington Palace, London. However, it was the removal of excise duty on glass in 1845 that made picture windows possible for the non-aristocratic wealthy.

# Part II

# Political

Part I posed the question of who merited inclusion in the nation, particularly, but not exclusively, in relation to landscapes freighted with national significance. Part II examines how criteria of exclusion and inclusion are experienced and challenged by people as individuals, as part of a class, as part of a people. It concerns the agency of social actors and the tight fit between political representation and access to landscape. It looks at how open landscapes become sites of protest and contested arenas around which defining myths evolve and, in some instances, how that otherness is also visually represented.

The deeper history of agrarian capitalism is the context for an overview of the past 150 years' legislative history of the protection of open landscapes and linear rights of way, and attempts to secure access to them. The interplay of class and national identities, of religion and leisure, and the antagonism between country and city are analyzed through a materially based view of power relations, and especially through myths of belonging that are rooted in the land. The organization of space is considered as a reflection of class relations. Radicals and Chartists, Non-Conformists, landowners, poachers, reformers and working-class ramblers are some of the social actors who appear in Part II. Their actions undertaken at particular moments and in specific movements to achieve their aims – whether political and social reform or preservation and access – are the histories, events and sentiments that form a multiplicity of contextual framings for an otherwise impersonal legislative history.

# The Politics of Access

The motto of the English nation is 'exclusion'. In this consists our happiness and our pride

William Hazlitt

*The Village Minstrel*

There once were lanes in nature's freedom dropt,
there once were paths that every valley wound –
Inclosure came, and every path was stopt;
Each tyrant fix'd his sign where paths were found,
To hint a trespass now who cross'd the ground . . .

John Clare

*The Earthly Paradise*

Forget six counties overhung with smoke,
Forget the snorting steam and piston stroke,
Forget the spreading of the hideous town . . .

William Morris

*National Trust, Annual Report 1903–4*

To illustrate the way in which people in the great towns value the beauties of nature, it is sufficient to quote the case of a working woman in Sheffield. In sending a postal order for a small sum, she said that after 30 years' work in a Sheffield factory, it was her greatest joy to spend her holidays on the moors, for she found refreshment there. She hopes some day to go as far as Ullswater and Derwentwater [in the Lake District].

quoted in Marsh 1982: 58–9

... the great Romantic criticism of Utilitarianism was running its parallel but altogether separate course. After William Blake, no mind was at home in both cultures, nor had the genius to interpret the two traditions to each other. It was a muddled Mr. Owens who offered to disclose the 'new moral world', while Wordsworth and Coleridge had withdrawn behind their own ramparts of disenchantment. Hence these years appear at times to display, not a revolutionary challenge, but a resistance movement, in which both the Romantics and the Radical craftsmen opposed the annunciation of Acquisitive Man. In the failure of the two traditions to come to a point of junction, something was lost. How much we cannot be sure, for we are among the losers.

E. P. Thompson 1966: 832

## Introduction

Because landscapes, like other material structures, are created and destroyed within an ideological context, understanding them must rest upon the historical recovery of ideologies specific to particular places. The relationship between events and ideas can indeed be exhaustively studied to make landscapes stand clear as material structures. This chapter deals with the political, social and economic embeddedness of access to open landscape in England from the late eighteenth century up to the outbreak of World War II, specifically in relation to the Peak District. Chapter 5 picks up those threads for the Lake District. In each chapter, linking threads thrown out to and received back from the socio-political realm of nation-making will be discussed, along with an examination of tensions in the period of industrialization which resonated with contesting visions of what the nation 'was', 'had been' or 'should be'. This material will introduce the manufacturing towns' re-peopling of the countryside.

The burden of these two chapters is to elucidate a politics of access to open land through examination of local particularities contextualized within the historical interplay of class and national identity. Although differences and similarities in the social uses of nature existed between the Peak and Lake Districts, what happened in one region had direct and indirect effects on developments in the other: events in each region produced a climate of opinion about access that was invested with strong political overtones.

The politics of access is compounded of multi-level interactions between stasis and movement. Conceived of both literally and meta-phorically, they are two poles in a pattern of oscillation that operates in social and geographical terms, as well as within discrete and overarching timeframes. Depending upon any given set of particularities, the state via the law can tacitly and overtly approve and disapprove of both stasis and movement. The actions people do or do not take in their daily lives, depending upon the exigencies of social, geographical, and historical time and place, and the state's interventions or lack thereof, create the shifting field of claims and counter-claims that is the struggle for access.

Access to and movement across the English landscape is but one way of following that struggle. It is a point of view from which can be seen larger issues of domination, incorporation, and contestation. Regardless of when enclosure hedges are torn up, challenges to governmental authority are voiced from the peri-urban commons, lakeside bottles of beer are enjoyed by working-class tourists, or the Derbyshire grouse moors are disturbed by the unemployed – these are actions of the variously dispossessed. All function as markers of class differentiation, indicating who are 'cultivated' and who are not and who possess 'culture' and who do not. It is at the intersections of social place and geographical space that geographies of exclusion are located.

Contested versions of England informed the cultural differentiation of participation in the open landscapes of the commons. In fact, access to the commons was the crucial difference between two versions of England. One was the improving political-economy construct synonymous with Britain. The other was the mythic Anglo-Saxon England of the pre-Norman Yoke. Not only did the deep antiquity of common land signal a pre-manorial system in early Britain, it was both proof and linkage to theories advanced by 'Von Maurer, Sir Henry Maine, Seebohm and others . . . that the common rights now existing are . . . survivals of a system of collective ownership of land . . . the prevalence of which in the early stages of communities has been traced over the greater part of Europe' (Eversley 1910: 5). This proof and linkage was in turn used to buttress legal challenges and parliamentary maneuvers aimed at protecting the few remaining commons.[1]

On the surface what was at stake was an aesthetic nationalism located in landscape, what was to become perhaps a secular religion of the countryside embodied in the aptly named National Trust. At a deeper level, politics, religion and recreation were linked elements in a struggle for access to more than landscape. Undergirding this 'more than landscape' theme are the four great Reform Bills of 1832, 1867, 1884 and 1918 which served to extend gradually the franchise and to bring political emancipation to Catholics and Protestant Nonconformists.

The following six lists, which are selective rather than exhaustive, form a reference point from which to chart a way through the various threads making up this and the next two chapters. They show (1) legislation dealing with rights of way; (2) early footpath preservation societies and rambling organization; (3) organizations concerned with landscape preservation and access; (4) Bills and Acts from 1837 to 1925 having to do with commons, wastes and open landscape and their enclosure and protection from enclosure; (5) Bills, Acts and Parliamentary Committee Reports relating to access to the mountains and open countryside; and (6) Acts, Parliamentary Committees and Parliamentary Committee Reports relating to national parks, and access to and management of the countryside.

## 1.   RIGHTS OF WAY LEGISLATION

1815     Stopping-Up of Unnecessary Roads Act
1833     Select Committee on Public Walks (Documented lack of recreational space.)
1834     Select Committee on Drunkenness (Relationship made between drunkenness and 1833 Committee.)
1835     General Highways Act (Effectively repealed the 1815 Act.)
1933     Rights of Way Act (Simplified 'proving' a footpath by removing criterion of 'indefinite use' and substituting twenty year's continuous use.)
1990     Rights of Way Act, Edward Leigh, MP for Gainsborough and Horncastle (Dealt with farmers' obligations re footpaths and byways.)

## 2.   EARLY FOOTPATH AND RAMBLING ORGANIZATIONS

1824     York Association for the Protection of Ancient Footpaths
1826     Manchester Association for the Preservation of Ancient Footpaths
1856     Keswick and District Footpath Preservation Association (Lake District)
1856     Burnley Footpath Committee
1866     Preston Footpath Association
1866     Carr Hill Road Defense Committee (Nelson, Lancashire)
1866     Bank Top Footpath Association (Blackburn)
1876     Hayfield and Kinder Scout Ancient Footpaths Association (Peak District)
1880     Manchester Young Men's Christian Association Rambling Club
1884     Forest Ramblers Club (London)

1890s    Liverpool Hobnailers
1894    Blackburn and District Ancient Footpaths Association
1894    The Peak District and Northern Counties Footpaths Preservation
        Society
1894    Midland Institute of Ramblers
1897    Co-operative Holidays Association
1900    Sheffield Clarion Ramblers

## 3. PRESERVATION AND ACCESS ORGANIZATIONS

1865    Commons, Open Spaces & Footpath Preservation Society
1883    The Lake District Defense Society
1884    The National Footpaths Preservation Society (Merged in 1899
        with the Commons, Open Spaces & Footpath Preservation
        Society.)
1895    National Trust for Places of Historical Interest or Natural Beauty
        (Made a statutory body in 1907.)
1905    Federation of Rambling Clubs (London)
1922    Manchester and District Federation of Rambling Clubs
1926    Sheffield and District Federation of Rambling Clubs
1926    Council for the Preservation of Rural England (Name changed
        to Council for the Protection of Rural England 1969.)
1930    Youth Hostels Association
1931    National Council of Ramblers' Federation
1934    Friends of the Lake District
1935    The Ramblers' Association

## 4. COMMONS: ENCLOSURE AND PROTECTION

1837    Inclosure Bills – Provision for Public Recreation, Joseph Hume,
        MP for Middlesex
1845    General Inclosure Act (Shifted oversight of enclosure schemes
        from Parliamentary Committees to local enquiries chaired by
        independent Commissioners who were empowered but not
        required to set aside land for recreational use where Commons
        or waste were enclosed.)
1865, 1871, 1876, and each year between 1880 and 1890, Bills or
        Amendments to Bills to repeal the Statute of Merton (defeated)
1887    Thirlmere Act (Set the precedent of giving Select Committee
        status for evidential hearings on landscape preservation issues
        which meant all interested parties could give evidence, not just
        affected landowners.)

1887   Copyhold Act (Introduced in the House of Lords, this Act replaced the Parish Vestry with a Land Commission to consent to new copyholds of waste or Commons; the Land Commission later became the Board of Agriculture.)

1893   Commons Amendment Act (Required Board of Agriculture consent to any enclosure being undertaken under the Statute of Merton, and directed the Board to determine that such enclosure would be of benefit to the public.)

1894   Copyhold Act (Further strengthened tenants' rights of Commons on copyhold land.)

1925   Law of Property Act (Brought Commons located in Urban Districts into the public domain.)

5.   ACCESS TO THE MOUNTAINS AND COUNTRYSIDE

1882   Open Spaces Act, John Lubbock, MP for Maidstone

1884, 1888, 1892 Access to Mountains (Scotland) Bill, James Bryce, MP for South Aberdeen (defeated)

1900, 1906, 1908 Access to Mountains (Scotland) Bill, Annan Bryce, MP for Inverness Burghs (defeated)

1908   Access to Mountains (England, Wales and Ireland) Bill, Charles Trevelyan, MP for Elland, West Riding (defeated)

1920–1930 five Access to Mountains Bills, various MPs (defeated)

1931   Access to Mountains Bill, Ellen Wilkinson, MP for Middlesbrough East (defeated) (Wilkinson was later MP for Jarrow and led the Jarrow Crusade march.)

1937   Access to Mountains Bill, Geoffrey Mander, MP for Wolverhampton East (defeated)

1938   Access to Mountains Bill, Creech Jones, MP for Shipley (defeated)

1939   Access to Mountains Act (Never put into practice.)

1949   The National Parks and Access to the Countryside Act

1983   Greater Access to the Countryside Bill, Tony Baldry, MP for Banbury (Defeated; one of the failed Access Bills introduced each year 1979–85.)

1994   The Criminal Justice and Public Order Act, §70, 71

1996   Access to the Countryside Bill, Paddy Tipping, MP for Sherwood (defeated)

1999   The Queen's Speech at the opening of Parliament introduced a Countryside Bill that would give walkers the right to roam in open countryside, would create two new national parks, and would introduce further measures for wildlife protection.

6. NATIONAL PARKS

1929    National Park Committee set up by Government
1931    Addison Committee Report *Report of the National Park Committee*
1935    CPRE sets up Standing Committee on National Parks
1942    Scott Committee Report *Land Utilization in Rural Areas*
1945    Dower Committee Report *National Parks in England and Wales*
1945    Labour Government sets up Committee on National Parks in England and Wales under chairmanship of Sir Arthur Hobhouse
1947    Hobhouse Committee Report *Report of the National Parks Committee (England and Wales)*
1947    Hobhouse Committee, Access Sub-Committee Report *Footpaths and Access to the Countryside*
1947    Hobhouse Committee, Wildlife Special Conservation Committee Report *The Conservation of Nature in England and Wales*
1947    Town and Country Planning Act
1949    The National Parks and Access to the Countryside Act
1951    Designation of Lake District, Peak District, Dartmoor, Snowdonia National Parks
1952    Designation of Pembrokeshire Coast, North York Moors National Parks
1954    Designation of Exmoor, Yorkshire Dales National Parks
1956    Designation of Northumberland National Park
1957    Designation of Brecon Beacons National Park
1968    Countryside Act
1974    The Sandford Committee Report *National Park Policies Review*
1981    Wildlife and Countryside Act
1991    Countryside Stewardship Scheme

## Im/moral economies

The right to enclose manorial waste land was enshrined in the Statutes of Merton (1235) and Westminster II (1285). They provide that the enclosing lord of the manor leave enough common and waste land, as well as access to it, to enable freehold tenants to exercise their customary rights. Where several manors abutted onto such land, then the access of all the manors' freehold tenants had to be protected. There was no protection of use of commons or waste by villeins (or copyhold tenants as they later became) and non-copyhold tenants. Enclosure of commons and wastes extinguished rights to collect wood (rights of estover), to cut turfs (rights of turbary), to graze animals (rights of herbage), or to fish (rights of pescary). Such rights had provided a slim margin of security to agricultural laborers and their families from the vagaries of seasonal employment.

Proceeding from a broad interpretation of these statutes, the rate of enclosure peaked in the 1450s–1480s. While enclosure of waste accelerated, because of the rising price of wool, great open fields were converted from arable production to more profitable pasture land. Enclosure diminished in the mid-1500s as cereal prices rose and wool prices dropped. An increase in population in the late sixteenth century and rising prices for wool re-accelerated the rate of enclosure. Under the impact of political pressure exerted through riots and armed rebellion, Royal Commissions of Enquiry were set up in 1517, 1548, 1566, 1607, 1630, 1632 and 1635 to determine the extent of conversion of land from arable to pasture. Royal proclamations were issued against enclosure and Parliament legislated against conversion of arable to pasture, even restricting the number of sheep any one man might own (Cantor 1987; Tate and Turner 1978; Wordie 1983); but the enclosure movement remained an inexorable force of dispossession and immiseration for the many and a source of enrichment for the few.

Control of movement across the English landscape has its roots deep within a structure of values that regulates geographical as well as social mobility.[2] Identification with place lies at the heart of this structure of values, central to which is Locke's labor theory of the origin of private property. The landowning class's moral economy was tied to the rise of a highly developed agrarian capitalism that, through its need to force the landless to work for wages, wrought deep changes in relations of community and household. (Roseberry 1991; Williams 1973). Running counter to this deeply im/moral economy was a primitive communism expressed first in the aspirations of the fourteenth-century peasant Great Society and later in the political radicalism of seventeenth-century Diggers and Levellers (Hill 1992, 1996; Williams 1973).[3]

Fixity and proscription of movement was not total. In creating a system of wage labor, early agrarian capitalism established the categories of vagrant and dispossessed. Paradoxically, control of movement enforced mobility, for the most vulnerable had movement thrust upon them as they were expelled from one parish to another to avoid their becoming a charge upon the poor rates. The spring and summer months witnessed a vast but slow ripple of movement the length of England as the towns of the Midlands and the South were provisioned by cattle reared upon the uplands of Scotland, northern England and Wales. For hundreds of years, drovers took their bellowing herds along a network of greenways until, in the nineteenth century, refrigerated railway boxcars transported chilled carcasses to market. Because of their practical knowledge, drovers' evidence was sometimes used in disputes over rights of way. Tinkers, gypsies and fairground people also made their own annual peregrinations round the country, while gangs of fruit pickers walked from North Wales to the southwest and southeast of England to bring in the crops.

Under the impact of scientific agriculture, a new round of agrarian dispossession began slowly in the early eighteenth century. It became a rout as a massive restructuring and re-evaluation of land took place through Parliamentary Acts of Enclosure that affected almost 21 percent of the surface area of England. Three-quarters of these Acts occurred in two periods, the 1760s–70s, and the 1790s–1800s (Turner 1980). Upon enclosure all leases were annulled and agricultural land rents generally doubled, reflecting both a presumption of increased productivity and the shifting of income from the tenant-farmer to the landlord.

Those who were not literally dispossessed might well experience a spatial dislocation as village clearances and field enclosures expunged part of the dense network of traditional pathways that were local signs of place. Enclosure also meant the loss of open spaces where people attended fairs, listened to preachers, took part in political rallies, or played sports. Not that these activities were always separate events. The call for a football match was sometimes the front for getting together enough people to tear down fences around new parliamentary enclosures. Associations such as the Society for the Preservation of Liberty and Property Against Republicans and Levellers were formed in response to such actions (Backscheider 1993), a name redolent with an earlier age's anxiety.

## Threads of Dissenters and Threats of Dissension

Disturbing the surface story of a unified Britain were tensions arising out of the practice of im/moral economies, the formation of cultural nationalisms in Britain's Celtic fringe, Dissenters' voicing of an anti-slavery rhetoric as well as protesting wage-slavery at home, and the extra-parliamentary activity of Radicals and Chartists. Further disturbing the sense of unproblematic Britons was the Dissenters' moral and intellectual culture of otherness, a culture with strong links to radical agendas.

The specific expressions of radicalism that emerged in the 1770s were leveled against 'Old Corruption' – the concatenation of aristocracy, landed interest, Establishment Church, and their combined hold on Parliament. Radical demands for constitutional reform were expressed in The People's Charter. Published in May 1838, it called for universal male adult suffrage, a protected ballot, the dropping of property qualifications for Members of Parliament, payment for MPs, numerically equal electoral districts, and annual parliaments (D. Thompson 1984).

Chartism's social origin lay in political discontent. It not only articulated the anger and distress of disaffected social groups, it also conveyed 'a practicable hope of a general alternative and a believable means of realizing it' (Stedman Jones 1983: 96). It was not a monolithic organization but was responsive to changing circumstances of time and place: it was also manipulable by various interests. The presence of pre-industrial artisanal groups (such as handloom weavers) or factory-located wage workers in the Chartist movement also created internal differentiation along regional lines. Although particularly strong in the Midlands for instance, local particularisms within the region resulted in radical militancy waxing and waning over time (Gadian 1986).

From the late eighteenth century onwards industrial capitalism absorbed the substantial out-migration from the English countryside as the hopeful and hopeless streamed into the new towns to become factory or mill workers, to enter service in the homes of the urban middle class, or to swell the ranks of the unemployed, the unemployable or the criminal underclass while the population of London grew by 20 percent between 1821 and 1841, the population of Birmingham, Leeds, Manchester, and Sheffield grew by more than 40 percent and Bradford's by 65 percent (Williams 1973: 152). Regardless of their socio-economic destination, most people living in industrial towns in the early decades of the nineteenth century remembered country living. In-migration, and not an expanding or even constant birthrate, was the main cause of this explosive urban growth, for given the unsanitary and crowded living conditions, infant mortality rates were high (Burnett 1979; Carter and Lewis 1990).[4]

London culture, so deeply rooted in landed interests, was widespread among the provinces. Yet another socio-cultural life existed, oppositional to it, through which Nonconformists of all stripes achieved success. In the urban manufacturing districts of the Midlands and the north, Unitarians and Quakers in particular formed not only a social, commercial and scientific elite, but were deeply involved in the radical causes that also flourished there. Infused with 'rationalism, enthusiasm, utilitarianism and radicalism bound in a coherent pattern' (Peel 1971: 54) that culture of otherness was composed of Presbyterians, Quakers,

Congregationalists, Methodists, Baptists, Unitarians, Evangelicals and other Dissenting groups. It was given expression through their universities, scientific and literary societies, academies and informal dining circles, Radical Corresponding Societies, Mechanics Institutes and the radical press, as well as through commercial networks such as those of the Quaker bankers, ironmasters and potterymasters. However, as Josiah Wedgwood lamented, commercial success could be painfully dependent upon acceptance within the 'London' culture of taste (Young 1995).

Humanitarian reformism, an anti-slavery stance, and 'sympathy for liberal causes and oppressed races' (Peel 1971: 76) marked the structure of feeling of Dissenting culture. It was not a univocal culture but was nuanced by differences of locality, political agenda and particularities of religious persuasion. Nor was it confined to the provinces but could operate 'within': Thomas Hodgkin, a Quaker physician at Guy's Hospital, was a central figure in the founding of London's Ethnological Society in 1843. Nonconformists – Quakers in particular – formed a substantial part of its antiquarian and philologist members, although the Society's natural scientists tended to have no formal religious beliefs (Van Keuren 1982).

The variety of provincial expression, whether radical or Dissenting, was eventually overwhelmed by the opinions of the metropolis. While rail travel allowed radical speakers to maintain parliamentary contact and to move more swiftly around the country, it also facilitated the provinces' challenge to London being subverted. The British Association for the Advancement of Science, founded in 1831 in York, 'represented the claims of provincial scientific culture over and against those of the metropolis and the ancient universities' (Rudwick 1985: 30). Dissenters could show a strong presence at the Association's annual meetings held in various provincial cities; but those meetings were eventually swamped by speakers from Oxbridge and London who could easily travel to them by train.

One political manifestation of this provincially based Dissenting culture was the Complete Suffrage Union, founded in Birmingham in 1842 by Joseph Sturge, a Quaker corn-factor, railway promoter, philanthropist and abolitionist. It received a great deal of support from Dissenting clergymen and operated most actively in Birmingham, Nottingham, Leicester, and Derby where Herbert Spencer (1820–1903) was its honorary secretary. Spencer's articles on social evolution had appeared in Edward Maill's *The Nonconformist*, a Birmingham newspaper that carried at the same time Union articles directed at reconciling the middle and working classes.

Spencer, the 'father' of sociology, was born into a Wesleyan Methodist family. He epitomized the rejection of the system that rejected Nonconformists. He 'had very little feeling for the antiquity of social creations like the colleges, churches, traditions and local communities which provided emotional bearings for most nineteenth-century English critics of industrialism' (Peel 1971: 212). Rather, Spencer rejoiced in the vigor and innovation of industrialism, which had proved an avenue of scientific and commercial emancipation for many Dissenters. At the same time he railed against the opportunities for 'financial chicanery' and 'speculation and avarice' (Spencer 1855: 9–10) that industrialism provided, especially to the landowning class.

Despite his dislike of elements within that class, Spencer's autobiography provides ample evidence of his love of what they owned and controlled, to wit, the farmland of the Home Counties or the less inhabited mountainous uplands. Long Sunday rambles in the Thames Valley or in Kent, walks around Derby or at the country estates of friends such as Sir John Lubbock and Lord Houghton, provided respite from work. Although he bemoaned damp rooms, dreary sabbaths and 'Celtic indolence' (Spencer 1904 (II): 94), walking holidays in the Highlands of Scotland, the Lake District and Wales fulfilled his craving for mountain scenery. These areas so colored his taste for landscape that even when in the Alps, surrounded by a 'vast panorama of mountains and lakes', he found 'Switzerland . . . far inferior to Scotland' (Spencer 1904 (I): 498–9). The occasion of his getting lost in the Scottish Highlands during a solitary walking holiday in 1862 led Spencer to deplore the quality of maps and to be impressed 'with the heavy responsibility which rests on the makers and publishers of guide-books' (Spencer 1904 (II): 90–1).

Articles concerning the reconciliation of the classes had been the bridge to Spencer's involvement with the Complete Suffrage Union. As a word used to refer to social stratum, 'class' first appeared in the 1740s (Peel 1971). It moved into more general usage in the 1790s and came into universal usage in the 1830s and 1840s. However its meanings were understood, contested, manipulated or constructed, what is apparent is that the shift to universal usage of the word 'class' was paralleled by the growing presence of state responsibility for 'society'.[5] Perhaps the emergent field of sociology, with its laws, regularities and systems approach helped objectify not only society but a class system too. However that may be, the political-moral relationship between social stratification and industrialism is seen by some scholars as having originated in the social experience of middle-class provincials, often Dissenters, contrasting themselves with the landed gentry and aristocracy. *Class* meant mobility, both geographical and social, against the stability of *rank, order* and *estate;* it referred to occupation or role rather than to status; it was achieved by one's actions, not inherited by one's birth.

(Peel 1971: 60)

In this idealized view class replaced 'bonds of deference, loyalty and patronage [with] horizontal political solidarity . . . separated from one another by vertical antagonism' (Peel 1971: 62). Yet those strata were by no means free of contention. Even the Chartist movement was riven by a welter of 'cracks and fractures' (Stedman Jones 1997: 171).

By and large, deference, loyalty and patronage remained the means whereby local societies were governed on a day-to-day basis by Justices of the Peace (with local militia at their disposal). Undermining this was 'the creation of a national politics, linking localities, which could challenge these local polities' (Southall 1996: 178). Of particular interest in this spatialization of politics is the mapping of Feargus O'Connor's journeys in 1838 and 1839 in which he made 147 appearances as he traveled between London and various towns in the Midlands and the North and Scotland. Whit Week 1839 saw him speaking at a mass meeting (with a claimed attendance of half a million) at Peep Green, Yorkshire, at a second meeting organized by the Birmingham Radicals, and at a third mass meeting at Kersal Moor, near Oldham. Advertisements for these meetings urged 'every man, woman, and child within a day's march' or 'within twenty miles' to come to the meeting sites. The 'cry' of the advertisements was 'To the Moor! To the Moor!! To the Moor!!!' (Southall 1996: 181).

The working poor were of inconsequential strength in highly localized societies, but once brought together in their thousands or tens of thousands they formed 'a vast assemblage of moral power . . . capable of being trained to physical purposes' (O'Connor 1839 quoted in Southall 1996: 180–1). In speeches printed in the *Northern Star*, O'Connor likened the meetings to links in a chain. Through speaking at meetings up and down the country, '. . . the links were now perfect. London, Newcastle, Carlisle, Glasgow, and Edinburgh had now become forged as it were together' (*Northern Star* 1838 quoted in Southall 1996: 181). O'Connor's forging of a great chain shaped a social movement that resisted and challenged the establishment's overarching project – the 'forging of Britons'.

## Geographies of exclusion

Just as space was expropriated in the countryside, so too time was appropriated in the new, overcrowded, grim and unsanitary manu-facturing towns. The day's-walk radius of the world shrank to the enclosed and enclosing radius of the factory whistle or bell. Given seventy-hour workweeks, or longer, and the absence of open recrea-tional spaces within the towns (Bailey 1978; Blacksell 1982; Hearn 1978; Reed and Wells 1990; Walvin 1978), whatever commons or ancient rights of way still remained in the nearby countryside became important actual and symbolic resources. In 1833, a Parliamentary Select Com-mittee on Public Walks came to the conclusion that it was the lack of open spaces which was leading the 'humbler classes [to turn to] low and debasing pleasures' (Cunningham 1980: 92). Reformers linked access to recreational landscapes with social reform.[6]

The lack of access to open space was due to footpath closures, enclosure of commons and wastes, and the consolidation and enclosure of open fields. In the towns, previously open public spaces were being taken over as pleasure gardens for the exclusive use of the upper classes. In 1834, Edwin Chadwick, speaking before the Parliamentary Select Committee on Drunkenness said:

> In the rural districts, as well as in the vicinities of some of the towns, I have heard very strong representations of the mischiefs of the stoppage of footpaths and ancient walks, as contributing, with the extensive and indiscriminate inclosure of commons which were play-grounds, to drive the labouring classes to the public-house.
>
> (Chadwick 1834, quoted in Cunningham 1980: 81)

In 1837, Joseph Hume, the radical reformer, proposed that

> In all Inclosure Bills provision be made for leaving an open space sufficient for the purposes of exercise and recreation of the neighbouring population; provided, that in any case where the Committee on the [enclosure] Bill do not make such provision, they be required specially to report to the House their reasons for not complying with the orders of the House.
>
> (Hansard 1837: c.162)

Sir Robert Peel extended the scope of Hume's Bill from 'the neighbour-hood of manufacturing towns' to include all towns and rural popula-tions 'whom it was pleasing to see engaged in athletic and manly exercises, [for although they had] no legal claim . . . [to recreational space] they had a moral right' to it (Hansard 1837: c.162). Peel proposed that central government and local authorities provide equal amounts of funding to secure open spaces in areas undergoing enclosure (Hansard 1837: c.163–4).

There were also more radical approaches to land reform. Feargus O'Connor's Chartist Land Company, founded in 1845, intended to

> return people to enough land to make them eligible to vote. It soon had 70,000 subscribers in 60 branches and a £90,000 share issue. By 1847 there were 600 farmers chosen by ballot, in settlements with names like 'Charterville' and 'O'Connorville' . . . the company was wound up and the estates sold in 1851 after a Parliamentary Enquiry into its activities.
>
> (Reed 1991: 19)

Land Chartism, heir to the Diggers and Levellers, pressed for all working men to have access to small allotments of land upon which to grow foodstuffs (Marsh 1982; Williams 1973), a sort of reconfigured commons. This of course missed the point that by becoming more self-sufficient, the working poor were subsidizing a low-wage system. What the 1842 Select Committee on the Labouring Poor (Allotments of Land) was concerned with, however, was the possibility that a workingman's allotment might be 'an inducement to neglect his usual paid labour' (Reed 1991: 19).

Access to the commons was full of politically charged meaning. The wretched conditions of industrial workers and the equally wretched but differently structured conditions of agricultural laborers formed a potent mix. What emerged were radical petitioning campaigns and intimidatory marches aimed at achieving popular constitutionalism and a Charter of Rights. These were but the most recent manifestations of a form of resistance to an unreceptive state that extended back in English history to the thirteenth-century Peasants' Revolt.[7] Contestation over access to public space, often peri-urban commons, reached its height after 1795. Just as manufactory workers and agricultural laborers were excluded from political power, so a system of local regulations and bylaws excluded them from the public spaces in which they could articulate their political grievances. Judicial regulation was reinforced by the police and militia. Coercive retribution was exercised in employment and housing in the case of agricultural workers living in tied cottages (dwellings that were available only through their jobs).

Steeped in the republicanism of Thomas Paine, and drawing on the lessons of the French Revolution, working-class male and female Radicals and Chartists assembled in formal and informal public spaces. Mass gatherings held on open moorland and commons, in protest against government policy or the introduction of labor-replacing machinery, often had the festive quality of fairs and carnivals. Numerous banners were carried in procession to the mass meetings, as well as the *bonnets rouges* or 'caps of liberty' that were displayed or worn by protestors. These banners and caps were often made by women, who played a significant part in the movement. In an action viewed as transgressing normative gender roles, they made speeches at the rallies, and they were at the forefront of agitation; they also suffered the brunt of deprivation when their husbands were imprisoned or transported to penal colonies. Furthermore, they ensured that their husbands' plight was kept alive in the press, and thus helped keep the Radical cause before the nation (Schwarzkopf 1991).

The mass meetings on moors and commons fed into fears of Midlands-based plots of rebellion,[8] which could only have been exacerbated by the fact that, on the very same moors and commons, citizens – emulating *citoyens-soldats* of the Revolution – drilled at night in preparation for their hoped-for right to bear arms (Epstein 1994; Evans 1995; Gadian 1986). The spectacular quality of military fêtes designed to generate volunteers from beyond the middle class, can be read as a prototype appropriated and inverted by the Chartists. A similar carnival-esque inversion of order and hierarchy accompanied the courtroom defenses of Radical demagogues (Epstein 1994) which, like the mass outdoor gatherings, were theatricalized, performative political utter-ances. Such challenges to governmental authority, loaded as they were with the possibility of armed insurrection, mounted in intensity until they finally spilled over in August 1819 with the Radicals' huge outdoor assembly at St. Peter's Field, Manchester (Epstein 1994; Gadian 1986; Horn 1980; Thompson 1966).[9]

Led by bands and carrying banners, with *bonnets rouges* atop long poles and carrying branches of laurel, between sixty thousand and a hundred thousand well-organized and unarmed people marched into Manchester to the assembly ground. In an era 'where performance, display, and spectatorship were essential components of the social mechanism' (Russell 1995: 17), the pageant-like staging of the Chartist gathering at St. George's Field took on transgressive cultural and political significance. This was not lost on the state in its local manifestation. The mass gathering turned into a riot as, on magistrates' orders, the cavalry sabred through the crowds to arrest the platform speakers. Nine men and two women were killed and hundreds injured in what became known as the Peterloo Massacre.

A month later some thirty thousand people gathered on Hunslet Moor outside Leeds in protest of Peterloo.[10] Among the banners was one that showed a man in chains, 'bending under two immense burdens of *National Debt* and *Taxation*. At the top was written *A Free Born Englishman*, and at the bottom, *Britons never shall be slaves* ' (Wright 1970 cited in Evans 1995: 231).

A Peterloo medallion was designed that presented the working poor's condition of 'wage slavery'. It subverted the iconography of the British Anti-Slavery's official medallion manufactured by Josiah Wedgwood (Baum 1994). A muscular slave is shown in profile, one knee bent to the ground, shackled wrist-to-ankle. Wearing only a loincloth, his clasped hands are lifted in supplication and his head is tilted back as he looks up at an unseen other. The legend, set in a ribbon band beneath him, carries the motto: 'Am I not a man and a brother?'

The Peterloo medallion carries a skull-and-crossbones border centered on three figures. One is a man in rags sitting back on his haunches, arms extended upwards in front of him, palms upraised, head tilted back and mouth wide open in terror. He is looking up at a uniformed soldier in an executioner's mask, whose knees are flexed prior to bringing down the dripping cleaver he holds aloft. Behind these two figures is the body of a worker already slain. To the legend on one side of the medallion's illustration, 'Am I not a man and a brother?', the corresponding legend replies: 'No! – you are a poor weaver!'[11] Weavers could well stand in as an example of the brutal measures taken to advance industrial capitalism:

> On 27 February 1812 George Gordon, Lord Byron, addressed his peers in the House of Lords for the first time. Not yet the famous poet he would become, Byron spoke passionately about the 'unparalleled distress' he had witnessed among textile workers living near his estate in Newgate. His remarks were offered in support of an *unsuccessful* attempt to defeat a bill that sanctioned the use of the death penalty for 'frame-breakers' – those who damaged newly installed textile machinery.
>
> (Nicholson 1991: 22, emphasis added)

In the wake of the Peterloo Massacre and other riots and disturbances, the Government enacted measures to temporarily suspend the Habeas

Corpus Act and curtail free assembly. Fear of revolution through the power of a disciplined mob lay behind such reactions. In this period of national crisis, political dramas were swiftly reflected in stage productions as well as in the general atmosphere in which political dramas played out. When Peterloo was being enacted, Edmund Kean was playing the lead role in *The Carib Chief* at Drury Lane. Though the play was set in the reign of Elizabeth I, the story of a former slave motivated by unabating revenge resonated both to contemporary uprisings in the Caribbean plantations and to the unrest in the industrial north (Baum 1994; Backscheider 1993; Russell 1995).

As reform or revolution was acted out on the stage, there surfaced both fear of the anarchical mob and pride in 'the people'. Tapping into the myth of the pre-Norman Yoke, 'the people . . . [were] cast as those who remembered their ancient rights' and who were the repository of natural sensibility (Backscheider 1993: 223). Paralleling Chartist agitation for an unregulated press, popular and unlicenced theater was generally supported by Chartists as another site in which social tensions could be given expression. Performative aspects of radical culture such as trials were re-staged in fund-raising performances, as were Chartist productions of 'Democratic dramas like *William Tell*' (Thompson 1984: 118). In the theater, in the iconography of Radicals' protests, and in the minds of the literary elite, race and class were becoming linked. Rioting in Jamaica led Southey (one of the Lakeists) to write, 'God grant that the miserable conditions of our own poor may not one day . . . lead to consequences quite as dreadful in this country!' (quoted in Baum 1994: 167).

Against a background of social dislocation, reform or revolution became the overarching issue in England. While print capitalism engendered a national imagining supportive of the state's 'stating' of itself to the landowning class, it also made possible a Radical and radicalizing press. Increased literacy and extended liberty in the mainstream press aided the formation of early labor associations or trade unions for the 'little white slaves in the cotton factory' (Shelley quoted in Baum 1994: 140) and their agricultural counterparts.

Adding to the crisis was the emancipation debate. The Abolition Bill had been passed by Parliament in 1807, but emancipation for the British West Indies had to wait until 1833. As strongly as feelings against 'the trade' ran, public figures such as Byron targeted abolitionists for not addressing the slavery of the immiserated English agricultural laborer and working poor, while Wordsworth wrote that 'though *fettered* slave be none,' England's manufactories and fields 'Groan underneath a weight of slavish toil' (*Humanity* 1829, cited in Baum 1994: 71).

Agricultural discontent expressed in syndicalism, incendiarism and animal-maiming combined with industrial unionism and radical threats of revolution (Archer 1990; Payne 1993; Mingay 1989; Hobsbawm and Rudé 1969). The middle class also saw the need for political and constitutional reform (Helsinger 1994; Horn 1980; Stedman Jones 1983; D. Thompson 1984; E. P. Thompson 1966). The frequency and wide distribution of reform demonstrations speak to the magnitude of the Reform crisis and to the depth and breadth of near-revolutionary discontent. The size of the demonstrations was also impressive: above a hundred thousand in Birmingham and London in the autumn of 1831 and spring of 1832 respectively. Regardless of whether Evangelical Methodism subverted or averted this revolutionary impulse (Olsen 1990), by late 1831

> Britain was within an ace of a revolution which, once commenced, might well (if we consider the simultaneous advance in cooperative and trade union theory) have prefigured, in its rapid radicalisation, the revolutions of 1848 and the Paris Commune.
>
> (E. P. Thompson 1966: 817)

The Reform Bill of 1832 defused the issue by enfranchising members of the middle classes whose homes had an annual rateable value of more than ten pounds. Although the redistribution of Parliamentary seats from depopulated boroughs to the new manufacturing cities helped enfranchise some eight hundred thousand new voters, it was not enough. The fight to extend the franchise and so break the landowning class's political stranglehold on government policy had failed.

The shared radicalism of the middle and working classes shattered upon the First Reform Bill that politicized matters of principle and intensified differentiations of class through defining

> more clearly than at any time before or since in British history, and more clearly than had been done in any other country, [that] a qualification for the inclusion in the political institutions of the country [was] based entirely on the possession of property and the possession of a regular income.
>
> (D. Thompson 1984: 5)

Whereas before 1832 'the people' had been an inclusive term, after 1832 'the people' became synonymous with 'the working classes' (Gadian 1986; Stedman Jones 1983). In the process a working *class* began to coalesce. Of equal importance to that process of differentiation of the working poor was the Poor Law Reform Act of 1834 'which excluded them from relief and distinguished them from the pauper' (Polanyi 1944: 166). Anti-Poor Law riots continued up through the 1840s and mass gatherings of Chartists became even more freighted with revolutionary language in part through 'the open association between the Irish Confederates and the Chartists' (D. Thompson 1984: 323).

Mass demonstrations on the commons, the presence of revolutionary symbols, the delivery of petitions to parliament by vast processions – all these figured in the April 1848 Chartist gathering in London south of the Thames at Kennington Common. Those proponents of 'physical force' within the Chartist movement saw this mass meeting as the rallying point of an armed insurrection. So great was the fear generated by the proposed rally that Queen Victoria was removed to the safety of the Isle of Wight while a strong show of force was mounted in London under the command of the Duke of Wellington.

What had been mooted as a critical juncture in determining whether England would be caught up in the revolutionary fervor sweeping Europe, actually fizzled. Only some twenty thousand Chartists attended the rally which was not allowed to process into London proper. Feargus O'Connor and other Chartist leaders delivered the petition (with its claimed five and a half million signatures) to the House of Commons, but before O'Connor could make his presentation speech a committee rejected it on the grounds of spurious signatures. Neither reform nor revolution was achieved. The would-be intimidatory marchers were themselves intimidated. An exclusionary political process was maintained and Chartists of all stripes were kept in their social and political place.

## Rural myths

From the 1820s on, a middle-class 'vision of peaceful farmland as a synecdoche of national identity' (Hemingway 1992: 298) emerged in reaction to these cumulative undercurrents of division and expressions of massive and deep social unrest. In contrast to the Picturesque or Romantic upland landscape of mountains and ruins, landscape representations looked to the highly cultivated village-centered lowland landscapes of the south-east. Here was the nexus of rurality's golden age of contentment when harmony existed between the various orders of society. A myth of rural England existed in the double sense of the countryside as a place of harmony and of England as still being a rural nation, a green and pleasant land.

This mythic memory was purveyed in paintings and literature to an aristocratic elite and a newly urbanized manufacturing, trading and shopkeeping population of the 'middling sort'. Nostalgia filtered memory of the non-urban past, substituting a myth hugely at variance with the harsh realities of the agricultural laborer. What was forgotten or screened out in the myth-making was the deeply political character of agrarian capitalism's im/moral economy. The myth completely filtered out urbanization. Unintentionally emblematic of this were the 'Transparent Landscape Window Blinds' offered in an 1820s catalogue 'to the Nobility and Gentry' by London's artisanal Co-operative and Economical Society (Thompson 1966: 789).

Paradoxically, the rural myth/myth of the rural was being constructed for an urban middle class, most if not all of whom had either grown up in the countryside or in towns so small that the countryside was a mere short walk away. Myth-making and forgetting were self-reinforcing. One mark of how deep mythic memory ran was the language of 'gracious peer and happy peasant rubbing shoulders', used by the *Pall Mall Gazette* to report upon leisure activities in the 1860s. This has been glossed as

> an attempt by the middle class to appropriate to itself the values of a refined gentry. And this in itself is symptomatic of a profound rejection of urban and industrial civilisation, and of a wish to escape back into a simpler patron-client kind of society.
>
> (Cunningham 1980: 120)

A resurgence of 'Merrie England' sports and pastimes blossomed with archery contests, harvest suppers (transformed by the Establishment Church into religious Harvest Festivals), May Day festivities, and Rush Bearing services.[12] These events were then further mis/represented back to the public through paintings and novels. In them innocence, security and peace were imprinted on particular landscapes and landscape-related activities located in a rural past freighted with 'lost identity, lost relations and lost certainties' (Williams 1973: 139). In the real world, what were actually being lost were ancient rights of way, remnant open spaces in the new manufacturing towns and their nearby countryside, and many of the remaining commons.

While a south-eastern vision of England was being constructed to palliate the anxieties of Victorian society, demands for recreational access to open spaces centered on the uplands of the north-west and the few remaining commons surrounding London. Landscape preservationists' efforts were essentially anti-urban, which seems neither ill-founded nor irrational given the conditions of industrial and manufacturing towns (Lowe 1989). Given the the loss of Empire and status as a world power in the twentieth century, this anti-urban, anti-modern vision of England rapidly gained ground as the country succumbed to a near-fatal case of nostalgia (Hoskins 1955; Howkins 1986; Matless 1993; Miller 1995a; Wiener 1981).

While countryside was being invested with a distinctive ecological importance, it was beginning to be viewed as an urban amenity – a dynamic detectable in many places and at different times (Ching and Creed 1997). In addition, and most importantly, manorial common land around urban areas in late nineteenth-century England was ripe for development. Since the argument could be made that no one any longer grazed a cow or gathered firewood on the commons, it was taken as given that no hardship was incurred. Thus, relying upon the Statute of Merton of some seven hundred and fifty years earlier, Lords of manors encroached upon hereditary rights of access to the commons by issuing new copyholds. These were then either sold for large sums of money to building developers, or through rigged manorial copyhold courts passed directly into the Lord's own hands for agricultural or housing development. Of course from the perspective of urban dwellers, the hardship incurred was the loss of relatively nearby recreational space.

Conflicting uses of land such as these exacerbated already existing tensions between notions of private property and national asset and need. The Copyhold Act of 1887, introduced in the House of Lords, not in the House of Commons, prevented the creation of new copy-holds without the consent of the Land Commission (the forerunner of the Board of Agriculture). A further Bill, again introduced in the House of Lords, became the Commons Amendment Act (1893) which rendered the Statute of Merton redundant by directing the Board of Agriculture that 'it had to be proved to their satisfaction that the inclosure would be of benefit to the public' (Eversley 1910: 211). Public interest had been given precedence over profits from privatization of the commons.

Private property rights and national interests also clashed when it came to ancient monuments. They had moved from being solely objects of antiquarian interest to Picturesque elements in the landscape. Now, through John Lubbock (1834–1913), they were to become formalized as national assets. Lubbock, a Liberal Member of Parliament, had a family pedigree that encompassed intellectual, banking and landed aristocracies (Kuklick 1991; Stocking 1987; Van Keuren 1982). Lubbock was elected to membership in the Royal Institution in 1849, the Geological Society in 1855 and the Royal Society in 1856. He was elected President of the Ethnological Society in 1864 and became the first President of the Anthropological Institute, a position he held from 1871 to 1873.

Lubbock was nationally renowned for his promotion of science education for schoolchildren and workingmen. He also campaigned for a shorter working week and the introduction of bank holidays for 'the newly leisured and newly enfranchised artisan and lower-middle classes' (Kuklick 1991: 108). When elevated to the peerage in 1900, 'he chose his title, Lord Avebury, from a prehistoric site whose megaliths he had studied, and which he subsequently purchased to save from demolition for new buildings' (Stocking 1987: 151).[13] Lubbock sponsored the Act for the Preservation of Ancient Monuments (1882) that set up the first official schedule of protected archaeological sites in Britain, an act that was, not unexpectedly, fiercely challenged as infringing upon rights of ownership.

In 1882 Lubbock brought Ruskin to Avebury. His diary entry records that 'Ruskin had no idea there was such a place and was enchanted by it' (cited in Hutchinson 1914 (I) :188). In fact, the excavations in the 1720s of the standing stone circles of Avebury, Stonehenge and Silbury Hill had fueled the Romantic involvement with antiquarianism. The first Ancient Monuments Act began the process of creating contentious sites of landscape-located archaeology because once these were protected for 'the nation', the public might actually want to visit them![14]

## Locating the Peak District

The Peak District divides into upland gritstone moors in its northern part, and upland limestone hills and dales (pasture land) in its southern part. Folding, faulting and uplifting of Carboniferous Limestone, and grits and shales of the Millstone Grit Series some two hundred to two hundred and fifty million years ago (the late Upper Palaeozoic), have given rise to a landscape of north-south aligned anticlines (folds). Erosion and weathering over the millennia have resulted in a flat plateau called the Peak District Upland Surface. Elevations within that plateau, most notably Kinder Scout, represent remnants of a pre-Cretaceous surface, the Peak District Summit Surface which, once buried, later re-emerged some fifty million years ago. Erosion's cross-cutting of the gritstone folds has led to an upland plateau bounded in places by abrupt escarpments from which there are panoramic views (Small 1990; Trueman 1971). It was access to those panoramic views that was to become an issue.

Situated at the south end of the Pennine uplands some ninety miles south of the Lake District, the roughly 200-square-mile Peak District is surrounded by a roll call of manufacturing towns. Halifax, Huddersfield, Barnsley, Sheffield, Chesterfield, Derby, Stoke-on-Trent, Leek, Maccles-field, Stockport, Manchester, Oldham, and Rochdale tightly ring it round. Forming a second, only slightly more distant ring are Coventry, Birmingham, Wolverhampton, Liverpool, Preston, Bradford, Doncaster, Nottingham and Leicester (see inset, Map 2).

In many of these towns 'the traditional authority of church and state was weak' (Thompson 1984: 6). They were the sites of Chartist mass demonstrations, of agitation for Poor Law and factory reform, of reform of parochial and municipal government; they were also centers of resistance to the crushing of trade unions. The struggle for access to the Peak District may be approached by linking culture and politics, by grounding that struggle in the antagonistic social relations of work.

The rapid and unregulated growth of a market economy had 'crushed multitudes of lives' as it caused 'lethal injury' to social institutions (Polanyi 1944: 82, 157). But the Peak District itself had remained relatively untouched by that market economy's spatial reconstruction of England. Only five to ten percent of its commons and waste and ten to twenty-five percent (in some areas less than ten percent) of its open-field arable land were subject to Parliamentary Enclosure Acts (Turner 1980). So as conditions in the manufacturing towns surrounding it worsened, the Peak District's extensive stretches of heather moorlands stood in even starker contrast.

Not surprisingly then, it was the site of some of the country's bitterest struggles for access to open landscape. A landowning elite looked to the Peak District for the annual slaughter of grouse. The working class from the nearby towns looked to the open moorland for its peace and quietness, as a place to walk, climb, and look at the views. The moors became the site of a symbolic contestation over citizenship by those whose labor was the raw fuel of the manufacturing industries, but who were denied a vote in the political life of the nation.

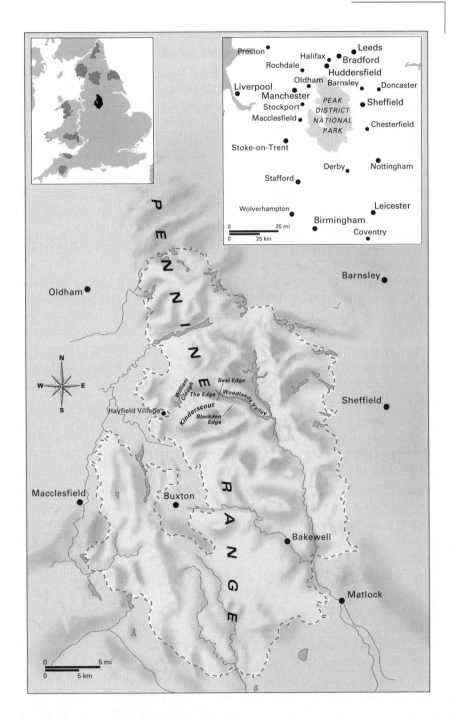

**Map 2** Peak District National Park

# Rural Walks

In addition to the loss of bridleways and footpaths through Parliamentary Acts of Enclosure, the Stopping-Up of Unnecessary Roads Act of 1815 enabled their closure if agreed upon by two Justices of the Peace and confirmed at the next Quarter Sessions. Since rural magistrates generally either were drawn from or received their support from the landowning classes, such closures were not difficult to organize. Mounting legal challenges against them, on the other hand, proved difficult, expensive and time-consuming.

Early footpath preservation societies were extremely numerous and many were highly localized. Some remained in action, often direct; others agitated over years for appropriate legislative protection; still others were ephemeral, coalescing around a particular enclosure or footpath closure and then becoming quiescent or defunct. Founding members and membership in societies that operated beyond the local level tended to be drawn from the professional classes and reformist circles. These included organizations such as the London-based Commons, Open Spaces, and Footpath Preservation Society (Commons Society), founded in 1865, and the National Footpath Preservation Society, founded in 1884. The Commons Society's President was George Shaw-Lefevre, later Lord Eversley, a leading Liberal lawyer and member of every Liberal government between 1868 and 1895.

One of the oldest locally based societies was the Manchester Association for the Preservation of Ancient Footpaths (commonly known as the Manchester Footpaths Preservation Society, or MFPS). It was formed in 1826 in response to the actions of Ralph Wright, a local magistrate and landowner at Flixton, a small village seven miles from Manchester. Wright had two fellow magistrates sign orders extinguishing footpaths running across his fairly modest grounds. Without waiting for Quarter Sessions confirmation, he had the footpaths ploughed up and the land sown. The hedges bordering the footpaths had already been removed in order to give Wright's grounds a more park-like appearance. The locals who used the footpaths were thereby rendered totally visible from his mansion (Taylor 1997; Lee 1976).

A group of neighboring farmers unsuccessfully challenged Wright in Quarter Sessions. They turned for help to Nonconformist radicals in Manchester, out of which association arose the MFPS. Over the next two years, an expensive campaign removed the case from Quarter Sessions into the Court of King's Bench, where it was eventually won.[15] It took another seven years before the General Highways Act (1835) effectively repealed the Stopping-Up of Unnecessary Roads Act. The MFPS represented a new town-based radical liberalism and its challenge to a land-based oligarchy. Among its members were men who had supported the Blanketeers' march on London in 1817 and had also been signatories to a Declaration of Protest against the Peterloo Massacre of 1819 (Taylor 1997).

Agricultural landscapes and commons existed in close proximity to most industrial towns in the early decades of the nineteenth century. But those easily accessible open spaces and footpaths disappeared as the towns expanded.[16] Not that there was a lot of time for recreational walking. Until Saturday afternoons were removed from the regular work schedule in the 1860s, Sundays were the only days when workers could walk out of town and into nearby open farmland. In Manchester for instance, people quickly found themselves in

> . . . meadows, and corn-fields, and parks in the immediate neighbourhood [of the town]. There are so many pleasant footpaths, that a pedestrian might walk completely round the town in a circle, which would seldom exceed a radius of two miles from the Exchange, and in which he would scarcely ever have occasion to encounter the noise, bustle, and dust of a public cart road or paved street.
>
> (Prentice 1851, quoted in Lee 1976: 4)

Depopulation of the countryside had fueled industrial capitalism. Crowded into the urban slums, the original inhabitants of the country-side were again displaced through construction of the railways' vast terminals and surrounding sheds, sidings and marshalling yards. Already appalling slum conditions were further exacerbated by sudden and highly localized increases in population densities as housing was demolished. Until reformers were able to push through Parliamentary regulation, there was no right of rehousing (Carter and Lewis 1990; Dyos and Reeder 1986). Not only urban housing was demolished. Many open areas ringing towns such as Birmingham had been set up as workingmen's allotments. Now they were built over by the stations, goods sheds, and stockpiles of coal needed to fuel the steam engines that drew the trains servicing suburbs and cities. Through the railway system, industrial capitalism reached into the landscape making a connected space of suburbs and slums, and of slums and holiday destinations.

## Religion and Recreation

A social politics that linked religion and recreation emerged in relation to the working poor. The gin palace and the ale house – those other 'spirits of capitalism' – were major sites of working-class recreational activity. In an attempt to wean the lower orders from drink and its attendant ills (not least of which was disruption of factory discipline), religious activity was presented as recreation. Services soon began to be supplemented by Church-based clubs, associations, and outdoor activities such as the Manchester Whit Walks.[17] In 1840, '40,000 school children were transported [by train] from Manchester to avoid the local races' taking place in Whitweek (Walvin 1978: 21). The Whit Walk

> by which the self help movement of the great northern cities extended its members' cultural and spiritual horizons into the Lake District, was held annually in Coniston from the 1830's. Coincidentally, but with some symbolic relevance to events in Thirlmere, the walk was discontinued in 1894.[18]
>
> (Murdoch 1984: 155)

Such a spatialization of authority helped influence perceptions of nature as mill and factory owners, churches and philanthropic organizations attempted to substitute useful pleasures for sinful ones. Temperance excursions introduced extremely large numbers of working-class children to an experience of nature.[19] Many excursions were to the seaside at the literal margins of the nation where the unpeopled view was unowned and indeed unownable, where the perspectival gaze was robbed of its proprietary function.[20] Exposure to the purity of nature was supposed to act as an antidote to the moral degradation of urban squalor. The values encoded in these excursions for the working class were to be more explicitly restated later in the century when walking-holiday organizations overtly linked the moral and the physical.

Courtship practices of 'walking out' had always been sexually loaded. Now walking in the countryside was linked to the development of fellowship and a knowledge of Natural History. This could bolster either a reverential Ruskinian or a rational Darwinian-scientific approach to Nature and God. Recreational walking was popularized among the working class in various Midland towns through weekly newspaper columns that described both nearby and more distant routes (Taylor 1997). Rambling on Sundays, however, faced disapprobation from church and chapel as did other leisure activities.[21]

Depending upon who was doing the organizing, recreational walking could be used to attack the privileges of private property, it could be trumpeted as a medium through which fraternal bonds could be reforged among 'the workers', or it could be used as an occasion for moral education and transmission of middle-class values and aspirations. The upper and middle classes proclaimed that leisure activities such as walking had a 'class-conciliatory function' (Cunningham 1980: 11). Though 'social bonding founded on a mutual interest *can* often transcend economic conflicts and status divisions' (Taylor 1997: 55 emphasis added), it seems somewhat naive to imagine that this was anything more than wishful thinking.

A class-based politics of views and viewing had long surrounded the landowning elite's country house. Picturesque tourism had extended that politics of viewing to the middling sort. Discursive emplacement of the Lake District had been accomplished by the production and distribution of watercolors, prints, paintings, poetry, maps and guide books. (See Chapter 3.) These remained ways of seeing and tools of knowing landscape. A thin veneer of economic development in the Lake District had followed as middle-class tourists had been serviced by new hotels, guides, carriage services, art supply shops, etc. But there it had stopped.

Recreational enjoyment of the landscape in the nineteenth century – especially recreational walking – was different, however, for it precipitated a more active intervention in place. It established that a contentious set of values inhered in the landscape. As the century progressed, it became clear that this contention ultimately derived from the opposition between an ethos of private property and a presumed right that all citizens should have access to the nation's mountains and commons (Hill 1980; Reed 1991; Eversley 1910).

## Grouse, Poachers, and Walkers

Recreational activities are not neutral but may be threatening to the ruling elite. Ultimately, that elite expresses its power and control by initiating, supporting, or suppressing such activities. Hunting and poaching, the legal and illegal sides of the same coin, exemplify the contested claims upon the countryside. Game laws operated against gentry farmers, middle-class landowners, tenant farmers, and agricultural laborers alike. They provided stark illustration of the land-based power structure of the governing class who through patronage and heredity shaped the House of Lords and had a highly visible presence in the House of Commons.

As the Flixton confrontation showed, footpath closures could restrict what comparative freedom of access remained to the laboring classes. What could not be controlled in the same way was game, the protection and pursuit of which pitted the social classes against one another in what has been called 'the most persistent, brutal and bitter conflict the countryside experienced from the mid-18th century onwards' (Archer 1989: 52).[22] For not all recreational walking was innocent. It could also be the opportunity for poaching – which was part sport, part necessity (it was often the only way of putting meat on the table), and always wholly a crime.

The myth of rural peace and plenty was a far cry from reality. A walk in the country could be viewed as a suspicious activity.[23] With the introduction of the *battue*[24] the preservation of game was undertaken in even more earnest in order to ensure the larger 'bags' and the competitive shooting that it facilitated (Cunningham 1980). Though game was viewed by the general community as part of a God-given larger commons available to whoever would and could catch it, to be caught poaching at night could lead to imprisonment, impressment, or transportation. Under the Ellenborough Act of 1803, resisting arrest by a gamekeeper could even lead to the death penalty (Archer 1989; Hay 1975). Legal and extra-legal working-class action to maintain public rights of way not only across commons but also across private land challenged the very roots of a land-based system of power.

Violent confrontations between groups of armed gamekeepers and gangs of poachers in the Peak District lasted well into the late nineteenth century. The Cotton Famine of the 1860s brought many weavers from the mills to the fields for poaching game, while in the 1860s–1880s the conflict over fishing rights 'reached frightening proportions in . . . the Lake District' and elsewhere (Archer 1989: 60–1). The daily movements of agricultural laborers and farmers were carefully watched by gamekeepers because poaching was not only a local problem: there was also an extensive national black market in game.

Whether for walking or poaching, working-class access to the countryside was facilitated by a network of railways that was most densely developed in the Midlands. In a remarkable contraction of space, what had been begun in the 1830s as a means of transporting goods to markets soon came to include passenger travel to resort towns – some of which only became resort towns as the result of railway service being extended to them. The extension of the railway north to the Lake District and Scotland occurred in the 1840s. Cornwall, at the opposite end of the country, was the last county in England to be connected into the railway system in 1859 (Robbins 1988).[25]

As for the Peak District specifically, access to the Peak's moors had been denied in the nineteenth century as a way of protecting grouse from disturbance by working-class walkers and poachers. Chartist rhetoric called for the restoration of pre-Norman rights such as commoners' rights to game. The legally questionable enclosure of commons was viewed as the fundamental infringement upon rights. An ancient right of way across the Peak linked Hayfield Village, in the Hayfield Valley, with Woodlands Valley. It crossed William Clough and the Kinder Scout plateau, waste land that had remained unenclosed until 1836 (see Map 2). This ancient right of way eventually joined up with the Sheffield-to-Manchester highroad. There was nothing remarkable about this except that at a certain point along its length, the right of way crossed the Duke of Devonshire's grouse moors. In 1876 he closed the path, on grounds that it interfered with the grouse shoot. With fifty years' experience behind them, starting with the Flixton footpath case, the Manchester Footpath Preservation Society (MFPS), joined by a newly formed Hayfield and Kinder Scout Ancient Footpaths Association, challenged the Duke's closure of the pathway. Their previous experience notwithstanding, it took twenty years of legal dickering to get the right of way finally reinstated in 1896.

By then the Peak District and Northern Counties Footpaths Preservation Society (the Peak and Northern), had been formed not only to support the issue of access to Kinder Scout, but in response to the wider problem of the public's exclusion from large tracts of common moorland used for the private rearing of grouse (Lee and Houfe 1994). The Peak and Northern's primary objectives were:

(a) The preservation, maintenance and defence of the rights of the public to the use and enjoyment of public highways, footpaths, bridlepaths, bye ways and otherways, vacant spaces, waste lands, and roadside slips, and to right of recreation over commons in the Northern and Midland Counties, particularly in the Peak District;

(b) The prevention of the abuse of such rights, especially trespass and damage to crops and property, and disturbance of game by trespassers.

(Lee and Houfe 1994: 7)

These worthy objectives were fought for – and against – every step of the way. The fight was more than ably carried forward under the auspices of the Clarion Ramblers clubs. The first of them was the Sheffield Clarion Ramblers' (SCR) founded by G.B. Ward in 1900 after he had been dismissed from his position as a Methodist Sunday School teacher for leading Sunday rambles.[26] Ward placed an advertisement for 'fellow-walkers' in the local socialist *Clarion* newspaper. The response enabled him to start a secular Sunday rambling club.[27] Ward's purpose was to re-establish

> the sense of fellowship between men amid the objects of nature [an aim that] quickly brought it into conflict with the powerful vested land interests pursuing their hunting and game shooting privileges which were so widely extended following *the Norman Conquest.*
>
> (Hill 1980: 32, emphasis added)

Where out-and-out organized poaching had been the problem before, an environmental rhetoric was used in the 1920s and 1930s to keep working-class walkers off the moors. Walkers, it was said, damaged the heather and disturbed breeding and nesting grouse, thereby lowering the number of birds making it to maturity to be shot.[28]

A permit system operated across part of Kinder's grouse moors that gave access to the summit. After the deaths of two ramblers in separate winter accidents in 1922, even this limited access was rescinded. Gamekeepers intercepted and chased off those who had come for the panoramic views. By the 1920s, photographs taken of ramblers were being published in regional newspapers with captions offering a £5 reward for anyone who could supply the name, address, and occupation of the persons shown. Writs were served on those identified, restraining them from going onto Kinder Scout (Hill 1980; Taylor 1997). Access to Kinder Scout became a testing ground for the larger open access movement.

Throughout the 1920s joint raids on Kinder Scout were undertaken by Sheffield- and Manchester-based rambling clubs. In 1928 the Socialist-led Sheffield and District Ramblers' Federation organized a mass demonstration on the moors in support of the latest in a series of failed Private Members Bills for Access to Mountains. Attended by some three thousand people, it became an annual event up to 1939 (Taylor 1997). The only way to enjoy Kinder Scout's panoramic views was by trespassing. The situation boiled over in what is still, nearly seventy years later, called 'The Mass Trespass'. In April 1932, amid much publicity, several hundred members of the British Workers Sports Federation, an offshoot of the Young Communist League, trespassed onto Kinder Scout (Taylor 1997; Hill 1980; Rothman 1982). Not wanting to be lumped together with 'the far left', the Manchester Federation of Rambling Clubs had disassociated itself from the trespass.

The trespassers gathered at Hayfield Village, the starting point of the Hayfield/Woodland Valley right of way that the Duke of Devonshire had stopped up in 1876 and which had taken MFPS twenty years to get re-opened. Reminiscent of the reading of the Riot Act to early nineteenth-century Radical gatherings, the Parish Clerk recited the regulations prohibiting the holding of meetings on Hayfield's recreation grounds. The crowd dispersed and reconvened along the Hayfield to Woodlands Valley pathway. Ascending Kinder Scout, the ramblers were met by gamekeepers backed up by a contingent of county police (Taylor 1997; Hill 1980; Rothman 1982).

Six of the trespassers' leaders were arrested and charged with riotous assembly. Their trial quickly became tainted with innuendoes that the trespass was a Jewish-led Communist plot, for three of the six charged were Jews, and British Communist Party newspapers had been found on them. Five of the six received prison sentences. National newspaper coverage of the trial served to place access firmly on the political agenda. Mass demonstrations in the Peak District continued that year, with larger contingents of club-wielding gamekeepers, mounted police and foot police with Alsatian dogs meeting even larger contingents of ramblers (Hill 1980; Rothman 1982).

Apart from sheer class-driven bloodymindedness, private property was at stake, and grouse were the 'red herrings'. A report prepared in 1934 for the Sheffield branch of the Council for the Preservation of Rural England detailed the ownership of the Peak's grouse moors to which access was being refused. Of the seventeen private owners, seven were aristocrats, two were army officers and eight were industrialists (Hill 1980: 35). Trespasses were transgressions of social as well as spatial boundaries. As for rights of way, the 1933 Rights of Way Act could easily be circumvented by a landowner posting notices

> to the effect that he did not intend to dedicate a right of way, thus claiming that public access was only granted as a privilege [and] by erecting notices before a twenty-year period of use was established, it was . . . possible for any owner to prevent a footpath from becoming a right of way.
>
> (Taylor 1997: 255–6)

## Conclusion

Contextualizing access to landscape within multiple frames opens up larger issues of cultural hegemony and the ideologies that go into the making of landscape. It makes clear that unpacking the landscape is a way of studying social, political and economic histories from the bottom up. While a state project was the production and presentation of a unified Britain, looking beneath the surface to the particularities reveals numerous countervailing identities. Set against the 'forging of Britons' were Chartist mass outdoor meetings that 'forged' a chain of the laboring classes from Edinburgh to London. Nonconformists who were also denied full political participation in the life of the nation lent their support to this social movement.

Religion, recreation, and a militant temperance movement functioned separately and together to transmit middle-class values. Temperance excursions and working-class walking or rambling clubs that emerged from the Nonconformist Church, re-introduced vast numbers of people to the land they or their parents had been forced to leave. The contraction of space and time experienced under disciplines of the workplace rendered access to open landscapes and linear pathways even more precious, and led to the founding of localized footpath preservation societies and national organizations for the preservation of the commons. The early Socialist movement was another force in the making of the rambling club movement.

There was no early landscape preservation legislation aimed specifically at the Peak District. Instead, it became the site of working-class direct action to achieve the freedom to roam. By contrast, the Lake District was the object of parliamentary action to preserve its landscape – a landscape without grouse-stocked heather moorland. The Lake District was doubly distanced from the industrial Midlands by miles as well as artistic and literary associations. The 'superior' leisure activities associated with it were solitary fell-walking or touring by people with an informed appreciation of landscape. These were pitted against 'inferior' and 'inappropriate' leisure activities such as day trips to the Lakes by beer-swilling workers who, bereft of aesthetic capital, were brought in on rail excursions from the manufacturing towns of the Midlands.

A predominantly middle-class myth of a rural lowland and cultivated 'Little England' was firmly entrenched by the 1920s and 1930s (Samuel 1989; Miller 1995a), by which time a working-class myth was in evidence of open-air fellowship to be enjoyed in the uncultivated uplands. The open landscape was where the industrial working class went

not to look at nature with the dreaming gaze of poets but to regain good
fellowship amidst the mountains and dales, away from the antagonistic
relationship of the factory.

(Hill 1980: 15)

Factory time-space discipline was the antithesis of the freedom to roam.
And the freedom to roam was viewed by activist ramblers as being in
some way a fundamental right of citizenship, a reassertion of Anglo-
Saxon customary rights to access open land 'without let or hindrance'.
This is not meant to derogate the harsh realities of the manufacturies,
nor the exhilaration of leaving their noisy, dirty time/space confinement for the wind-blown silence of moor or mountain and the
companionship of fellow walkers. It is meant to help catch sight of an
equally backward-looking, nostalgia-laden framing myth, and to show
within what context the deep history of the Norman Conquest is still
sometimes resuscitated.

Recreational or excursive walking evolved into two distinct, class-
bound leisure practices which gave rise to similarly class-bound
preservation movements. Workers' exclusion from the grouse moors
brought a particular impetus to a movement for protection of ancient
linear rights of way and open access to common land. Concern for the
Lake District was drawn from reformist and academic elites who looked
to the Lake District for spiritual refreshment. This gave rise to a
movement for the preservation of landscape which operated at a
national level. This is the material to be explored in the following
chapter.

# Notes

1. Von Maurer (1790–1872) was a German jurist and historian whose work
centered on the Mark as the unit of early German society; Frederic Seebohm
(1833–1912) was a British agricultural and economic historian of the village.
The works of comparative historical jurisprudence written by Sir Henry Maine
(1822–88) – such as *Ancient Law* (1861) – were influential in modern British
social anthropology. His work on custom and law studied the process by which
'the modern modes of European individual ownership had developed through
the aggrandizement of powerful leaders at the expense of the common holdings

of the village community' (Stocking 1987: 126). Although in a different register, it is the issue of custom and law that was to emerge in relation to access.

2. By the fourteenth century, official 'letters of passage' were required before journeying cross-country, and students – placed in the same category as beggars – were liable to be clapped in irons if found wandering in the countryside. Travelers in general and pedestrians in particular were objects of suspicion, potential criminals, while women walking the countryside by themselves bore the additional suspicion of sexual 'wandering'. Even pilgrims needed their letters of authority, while servants or laborers leaving their parish needed certificates to show they were 'at liberty' to seek work elsewhere (Wallace 1993; Williams 1973).

3. The name Diggers was given to the religious sect who wanted to cultivate waste land on a communal basis and thereby 'make restitution of the earth taken and held from the common people' (Hill 1992: 144). The term Levellers comes from the practice of anti-enclosure rioters taking out or 'levelling' enclosing hedges (Thompson 1966).

4. The explosive growth of the manufacturing towns was in part dependent upon the earlier accumulation of capital achieved through the slave trade. 'Between 1701 and 1810, England exported from West Africa over 2 million slaves, about two-thirds of the total number shipped by the three major powers in the slave trade' (Wolf 1982: 198). Depending upon who was doing the trading, the value of slaves in relation to trade goods 'paid' for them, ranged from 4:1 to 6:1. The return on the slave trade between 1620 and 1807 is estimated at being approximately 12 million pounds sterling, 'with perhaps half that sum accruing between 1750 and 1790' (Craton 1974 cited in Wolf 1982: 198). A British mercantilist defending the slave trade wrote that it was 'the first principle and foundation of all the rest, the mainspring of the machine which sets every wheel in motion' (Postlethwayt quoted in Craton 1974: 120, cited in Wolf 1982: 198). Through its generation of capital among merchants and bankers (such as the Hoares – see chapter 1 at p. 26), the slave trade helped set England on its industrializing path. Wealth achieved within a system of mercantile capitalism supplied the initial input required within industrial capitalism.

By the mid-eighteenth century, Liverpool had replaced Bristol as England's primary slave port because of its proximity to the industrial Midlands (Wolf 1982). Indeed Birmingham was 'not only an integral part of the triangle trade, through its cotton industry, but also the center of gun manufacturing for Africa' (Baum 1994: 43). No wonder Coleridge got short shrift when he preached his anti-slavery message there. Whitehaven (a grimly inverted place name if ever there was one) was not only a trading port for Jamaica that sent out some four slave ships a year, it was also – in a reverse flow – one of the Cumbrian ports of entry for a quiet traffic in black children imported into the Lake District (Baum 1994). It was also one of England's most prosperous coal ports. Families such as the Lowthers straddled both businesses.

5. A current debate within British social history concerns the 'linguistic turn' (Joyce 1994; Palmer 1990; Steadman Jones 1997; Vernon 1994). The turn is away from an orthodox intellectual history 'forged though the "experience" of the pre-discursive realm of "prevailing social relations"' (Vernon 1994: 84), to how people make meaning through the cultural narratives available to them, such as 'improvement' or 'liberty'. Within the linguistic turn, the social – including the notion of class – is a discursive construct, not a material outcome of the mode of production.

6. Despite the farsightedness of towns such as Preston which in 1834 enclosed Preston Moor but maintained public access to it (Cunningham 1980), the parks movement that sought to provide public open spaces for working-class families' 'rational' entertainment, could not keep up with the disappearance of open urban space. Octavia Hill, a key figure in the landscape preservation movement, was also a leading figure in urban housing reform – in which she included the need for recreational space. By the 1870s the absence of open space for London's working poor was so extreme that some of the city's graveyards were cleared of their tombstones and the ground laid out with flower beds, grassy areas and walks. In describing the area around Drury Lane in an attempt to pry money loose for more graveyard clearances, Hill presents a prose version of Wordsworth's *Parliament of Monsters* and Blake's anguished faces (Hill 1877: 109). Resting in peace was a luxury denied to some of London's dead working poor.

7. In 1817, more than 500 petitions calling for political reform and signed, their organizers said, by one million people, were to be presented to the Prince Regent in London by the Blanketeers. Starting with the Manchester weavers, the Blanketeers (so-called from the blankets strapped to their backs) were to make their way through the Midlands, picking up disaffected radical workers on the way. The 12,000-strong 'citizens' army' was disbanded by military force soon after leaving Manchester (Epstein 1994; Thompson 1966).

In 1936, 207 unemployed men from Jarrow walked 300 miles to London to present Parliament with a petition signed by 11,572 people. Like the Blanketeers, they all had rolled groundsheets slung round them, for they too were sleeping rough. They were seeking relief from an unemployment rate close to 75 percent that had existed in Jarrow for some fifteen years. Further petitions bearing 90,000 signatures were gathered en route before a final rally in Hyde Park and the presentation of the petitions to Parliament (Pickard 1982). Late twentieth-century marches on London included the Poll Tax march of the late 1980s and the 1998 march of over 100,000 people against the proposed ban on hunting. Both ended with rallies in Hyde Park and presentation of petitions to Parliament.

8. By the end of the century, 'exaggerated middle-class fears of more openly aggressive forms of working-class militancy' led to militaristic voluntary leisure organizations being formed. Here working-class boys and adolescent males received extra-military training under strict middle-class leadership. The Boy's Brigade was even referred to at the time as 'A Juvenile Citizen Army' (Springhall 1977: 14–17).

9. One purpose of the gathering was to petition for the repeal of the Corn Law of 1815 and its various amendments. (It was finally repealed in 1846.) The corn laws forbade the importation of foreign wheat until the price of English wheat was over 80 shillings a quarter. This served to keep prices high. Contemporary perceptions (Cobbett 1830, Committee on Agricultural Distress 1836, Report of Special Assistant Poor Law Commissioners on the Employment of Women and Children in Agriculture 1843, all cited in Burnett 1979) were that the lower classes were being pushed from a bread to a potato diet to enable them to survive on the lowest possible wage. The potato stood as a symbol of degradation, deeply associated with the immiseration of the Irish (Thompson 1966).

10. Hunslett Moor was the site of a similarly sized demonstration in October 1877 protesting a proposed rail line on the Moor. It was led by John De Morgan, an activist dedicated to defense of common lands whose 'brand of radical populism was rooted in a tradition which connected the Chartist era to emerging socialist solutions' (Taylor 1997: 134).

11. In 1788, the captain of the British Fleet in Australia sent some white clay that had been found near Sydney Cove to Sir Joseph Banks, President of the Royal Society (Wetherell and Carr-Gregg 1990). Banks passed it to his friend Josiah Wedgwood, who used the clay to strike a medallion decorated with Grecian figures in relief, with the legend: 'Hope encouraging Art and Labour under the influence of Peace'. This material expression of the arts, sciences, and commerce being brought into institutional alliance to better serve the advancement of British industrial capitalism is the complete antithesis of the hope-less Peterloo medallion. When these two are brought into conjunction with the Anti-Slavery medallion, there becomes clear the role of mercantile and industrial capitalism in its underpinning of slavery abroad and wage slavery at home. Indeed, through both capitalisms' deep disruption of society, one arrives at the Australian penal colonies that received working-class radicals sentenced to transportation, be they Jacobin libertarians, machine-wrecking weavers, unionizing agricultural workers, or poachers (Archer 1989; Epstein 1994; Hay 1975; Thompson 1966). And it was from overseeing the first British settlement in Australia, which was a penal colony, that the white clay of the 'Hope' medallion was discovered.

12. The Rush Bearing ceremony is a tourist attraction at Grasmere's Church, where the Wordsworths are buried. The congregation, led by a marching band and young children carrying rush- and flower-decorated baskets and crosses, processes through the streets. Family, friends and tourists film the event and take photographs. The service of thanksgiving for the beauty and bounty of nature then takes place in the flower-decorated and rush-strewn church.

13. Lubbock actually purchased only a part of the site (Malone 1989). After passing through many changes in ownership, Avebury was finally gathered into one estate and donated to the National Trust in 1943 after a public appeal had raised the money to endow its upkeep by the Trust.

14. For an account of the contested political landscape of Stonehenge see Bender 1993.

15. The Peak and Northern Footpaths Society (which absorbed the Manchester Association for the Preservation of Ancient Footpaths in the 1890s) was still fighting footpath closures in Flixton 150 years later.

16. The common moor outside Oldham 'disappeared under eight cotton mills and two hundred and thirty six houses' (Reed 1991: 17). Within the towns 'even the high palisades that surround ornamental gardens are jealously planked over to prevent the humble operatives from enjoying the verdure of the foliage or the fragrance of the flowers' (Taylor 1841 cited in Cunningham 1980: 82–3).

17. Whit walks took place at Whitsuntide, the week of Pentecost which begins the seventh Sunday after Easter.

18. Thirlmere was the site of a major civil engineering project which reconfigured the lake into a vast reservoir from which water was piped cross-country to Manchester. The controversy surrounding this project is dealt with in the next chapter.

19. In what seems an economy of scale in keeping with the beginning of mass production, the numbers of children and adults taken on excursions are impressive. Multiple-engined trains capable of pulling up to 57 carriages explain how in 'September 1842 2,364 Sunday school scholars and teachers left Preston for an excursion', 'three thousand children travelled from Birmingham to Cheltenham in 1846; a similar number in that year journeyed from Macclesfield to Stockport . . . [and] no fewer than 6,125 parents, children and teachers were taken by train from Norwich to Yarmouth in 1846 . . . [while] a visit to the seaside [was made] by 5,000 working-class children and 3,000 spectators. . .' (Walvin 1978: 19, 50–2).

20. I am indebted to Gerry Boswell for this insight.

21. As late as the 1930s, playing card games on Sundays was not allowed at certain walking holiday centers. Members were beginning to question what the difference was between card games and approved Sunday activities such as tennis (*Comradeship* XXIV, May 1933, "Letters", 4: 15).

22. Game laws were denounced as unconstitutional oppression. Property in game was in part predicated upon an annual £100 income generated from freehold landholdings – a requirement that many wealthy farmers could not meet. Some categories of game belonged to its 'owner' even when it strayed onto other men's land; and some game rights were not tied to ownership of the land at all, so that property rights in the game applied even when that game lived and bred on another man's land. Indeed, the right to take game was at times more exclusive than the right to vote, and the rights of game took supremacy over commoners' rights in the commons (Hay 1975).

23. When Dorothy and William Wordsworth took long walks with Coleridge along the Somerset coast in the summer of 1797, they were thought to be French sympathizers undertaking spying activities in preparation for an invasion (Baum 1994).

24. Introduced in the early nineteenth century, the *battue* is a practice in which beaters flush out the game, driving it towards the lines of guns.

25. The railway network increased in Britain at a remarkable rate: 417 miles of track in 1835, 3,277 miles by 1845, 13,411 miles by 1850, and 30,843 by 1885 (Walvin 1978). Traveling long distances was complicated by the fact that time was a highly localized affair. Divergences from one part of the country to another created havoc for railway companies' timetables. It took an Act of Parliament in 1880 finally to standardize time in Britain (Robbins 1988). Where these long-since abandoned railway lines still exist, their embankments and derelict tracks are now flower-rich life-support systems for butterfly and insect life. As with the U.S. Rails to Trails movement, some abandoned railroad beds have been converted to footpaths and cycling paths. The Peak District's Tissington Trail for instance is the former Ashbourne-to-Buxton railway line. There are splendid views from the Tissington Trail, for rather than being cut into the landscape, it is set upon a high embankment giving a slowed-down version of InterCity travel's 'First Class Views' of the English countryside.

26. Ward's related interests on which he published numerous articles were urban 'infant mortality, the need for pure milk and for infant milk depots' (Prynn 1976: 69). These were to be serviced by the railways that supported the very system responsible for creating the desperate conditions of the cities.

27. Some organizations such as CHA handled the problem of Sunday rambling by incorporating Sunday services in their events. The Young Men's Christian Association-Manchester Rambling Club would undertake 70-mile walks that started on a Saturday afternoon and extended through Sunday evening, while Presbyterian clubs affiliated with the YMCA in Scotland restricted their rambles to Saturday afternoons (Hill 1980).

28. Walkers are still perceived by landowners as a threat to raising grouse. A report prepared for the Ramblers' Association (Watson 1991) directly critiques

a Peak District Joint Planning Board report that relates disturbance of wildlife to recreation. In a review of the scientific literature dealing with walkers' recreational access to the countryside and their impact on birds, the issue of walkers' disturbing the red grouse population is dismissed as a 'red herring' (Phillips 1987 quoted in Sidaway 1990: 16).

# five

# Accessing the Lake District

> ... the *scenic* essence of British identity ... has a profoundly English
> cast. Nowhere else is landscape so freighted as legacy. Nowhere else does
> the very term suggest not just scenery and *genres de vue*, but quintessential
> national virtues.
>
> Lowenthal 1994: 20

## Introduction

Valorized in the eighteenth century through Picturesque tourism, a
new and unprecedented accumulation of value accrued to the Lake
District under the influence of the Lakeists, Wordsworth in particular.
The Lake District was aesthetically valued by an intellectual elite
precisely because it was other than and removed from the new urban
concentrations. On those grounds it was fiercely defended from
proposed industrial encroachment and the incursions of the working
class. Wordsworth's declaration of the Lake District as 'a sort of national
property' was symptomatic of the swirling crosscurrents that existed
between understandings of landscape, nation, and citizen on the one
hand, and private property on the other. Issues of leisure and class
were subsumed in the claim of the landscape's having a national
dimension. That dimension was both expressed and contested in
parliamentary politics, eventually leading immediately prior to the
outbreak of World War II to enactment of legislation that for the first
time gave access to the mountains.

## Location

Situated in the northwestern uplands of England, the Lake District is a
roughly circular domed area only thirty-odd miles in diameter into
which are crowded 180 peaks. The Lake District National Park's 880

square miles is virtually co-terminous with the geographical Lake District. The structural evolution of this central dome has been a process of folding, uplift and erosion. Volcanic activity (during the Ordovician period some five hundred million years ago), glaciation (during the Pleistocene epoch two and a half million years ago), the raising of the earth (during the mid-Tertiary some thirty-five million years ago), and weathering have created a spectacular landscape of barren and exposed crags, cirques (steep-walled, bowl-shaped rock basins scoured by glacial action), arêtes (precipitously steep-sided rocky ridges often forming the crest around one or between two cirques), tarns (bodies of water, often but not always found at the bottom of a cirque, and generally frigidly cold even in summer), and over-deepened U-shaped valleys (Stephens 1990; Trueman 1971). The oldest exposed rocks in the Lake District are the Skiddaw Slates from the Ordovician. Marked by a radial drainage pattern, mountain ridges and valley floors radiate out like spokes in a wheel.

Unlike the Peak District, the Lake District's areas of acid upland moor and heath have not been used extensively for rearing grouse. The Lake District National Park (LDNP) was made up of parts of the old counties of Cumberland, Westmorland and north Lancashire. Local government reorganization in 1974 created the new county of Cumbria within which the LDNP now lies.

## Potatoes and coal

A middle-class tourist trade in the Lake District had given rise to hotels, lodging houses, weekend retreats and country residences. These intrusions were irritants to local literary and artistic circles but not overwhelmingly so. What began to tip the balance was the extension of the railway bringing the Lake District within reach of the Midlands towns. Wordsworth's expressions of moral outrage made little difference, because railways had a central role in economic expansion (Marshall and Walton 1981; Walvin 1978). In a collection of reprints from the *Edinburgh Review* published under the title *Railway Morals and Railway Policy*, Herbert Spencer uses 'the mis-interpretation of the proprietary contract' under which railway corporations operated, to present his views on contract law (Spencer 1855). It is worth quoting in full what Spencer has to say about the linkages between railway stockholders, parliamentarians and landholders because it presents the background against which the defense of the Lake District from railway extensions took place:

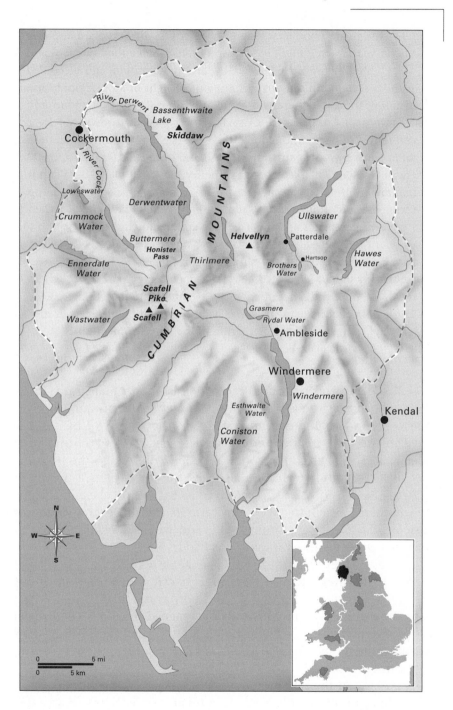

**Map 3** Lake District National Park

Once the greatest obstacles to railway enterprise, owners of estates have of late years been among its chief promoters. Since the Liverpool and Manchester line was first defeated by landed opposition, and succeeded with its second bill only by keeping out of sight of all mansions, and avoiding the game preserves – since the time when the London and Birmingham Company, after seeing their project thrown out by a committee of peers who ignored the evidence, had to 'conciliate' their antagonists by raising the estimate for land from £250,000 to £750,000 ... since then, a marked change of policy has taken place ... When it became known that railway companies commonly paid for 'land and compensation', sums varying from £4000 to £8000 per mile ... when ... preference shares and the like, were granted to buy off opposition – when it came to be an established fact that estates are greatly enhanced in value by the proximity of railways – it is not surprising that country gentlemen should have become active supporters of schemes to which they were once the bitterest enemies. ... [and that] in 1845 there were 157 members of Parliament whose names were on the registers of new [railway] companies for sums varying from £291,000 downwards.

(Spencer 1855: 12–14).

Unlike Wordsworth, the political economist Harriet Martineau (1802–76) was enthusiastic about the railway's potential for bringing workers out to the mountainous countryside. Like the Wordsworths, she too lived in the Lake District and 'preached' that its fresh air and wide open spaces were all to the good for people confined to the noisome dirt of factory and town. She also saw the railways as a means of bringing *ideas* into what she perceived as backward Lakeland society, in which the celebrated yeoman farmers had little knowledge of agricultural science nor much skill, and where pockets of squalor matched whatever the distant towns had to offer.

A popular writer,[1] Martineau wrote her guide book to the Lake District (1855) in a straightforward manner. It offers information about inexpensive inns and lodgings and contains a tipped-in foldout panorama with the mountains and ridges named. The book's endpapers carry advertisements for grand hotels around the Lakes, listing their recent patronage by the titled nobility of Europe, and for hotels catering to the middle classes.[2]

As walking in the fells and around the lakes became more popular with a burgeoning middle class, disputes arose over rights of way and footpaths. This led to the founding of the Keswick and District Footpath

Preservation Association in 1856. Protests generated substantial atten-tion: as many as 500 people attended one protest, while some 2,000 attended another (*Manchester Guardian* 1887 quoted in Hill 1980:41). Even allowing for the vagaries of memory (the letter published in the *Manchester Guardian* was recalling events that had taken place in 1857), there obviously were large numbers of walkers (whether from within the Lake District or from outside) to protest footpath closures there.[3]

When further railway extensions to the Lake District were proposed in the 1870s, apart from the likely proliferation of summer residences for industrialists, it was feared that cheap and swift transit would inundate the area with workers from the Midlands. The French peasantry had earlier been likened to potatoes in a sack (Marx [1852] 1972: 123–4). The English industrial proletariat on day excursions to the Lake District were admonished to save their money for holidays nearer home rather than suffer being 'emptied like coals from a sack' into Keswick and Windermere, only to have the railway 'shovel [them] . . . from one station to the other' (Ruskin 1876: 5–8).

People imagined as inanimate objects were a class apart from the educated solitary fell walker. The anticipated stupid tourists were contrasted with the 'Border peasantry of . . . England . . . whose strength and virtue yet survive to represent the body and soul of England before her days of mechanical decrepitude and commercial dishonour' (Ruskin 1876: 5). In all fairness, this kind of polemic was aimed at a mass tourism that was quite extraordinary. Where twenty-five years earlier cheap excursions had transported a few thousand people at a time, now people in the hundreds of thousands were deposited in a town on any one day on holiday occasions (Walvin 1978).

Capable of provoking apoplectic fits among the defenders of the Lake District was the threat of disturbance to the landscape through mining and quarrying. Protoindustrial mines and quarries either had been overlooked in early guidebooks or had functioned as elements in the Picturesque landscape. The mining and quarrying necessary to offset the engineering costs of the railways' various projects operated at quite another magnitude. Resistance to rail and mining interests was con-ducted on both moral-aesthetic and economic grounds. As opposition to such proposals acquired organizational form, Wordsworth's earlier arguments were applied in environmental battles. At one point the railway's opponents were accused of promoting 'a sort of aesthetic Enclosure Bill of their own, which would fence around the rugged majesty of Skiddaw . . . for the benefit of men of taste' (*Westmorland Gazette* 1876, quoted in Marshall and Walton 1981: 208).

Reservoir construction to alleviate the industrial cities' insatiable demand for water constituted another formidable threat to the Lake District. Thirlmere, which had often figured in the Lakeists' poetry, was the site chosen by Manchester Corporation for construction of a reservoir (see Map 3). The project was introduced into Parliament. The Bill's opponents coalesced in 1877 to form the Thirlmere Defence Association (TDA). Promoted by local notables Robert Somervell, a Lake District publisher; John Harward, a landowner at Grasmere; and the Bishop of Carlisle, the TDA was supported by academics, aristocratic landholders, nationally known public figures such as Ruskin and Carlyle, and the Commons Society.

Speaking in support of the Bill during its second reading, Isaac Fletcher, MP for Cockermouth (Wordsworth's Lake District birthplace), paradoxically presented the project as *protecting* the landscape.[4] He said the Corporation's acquisition of Thirlmere's catchment area of

> 11,000 or 12,000 acres of the most beautiful part of Cumberland [would protect it] from the incursions of those aesthetic gentlemen who come down surveying the district and building Gothic villas upon the shores of this beautiful lake.

(Fletcher 1878 quoted in Marshall and Walton 1981: 211)

Under pressure from the reservoir's opponents, notably the Liberal MP William Edward Forster (whose Elementary Education Act of 1870 was foundational to the system of compulsory education), a public or national dimension was claimed for this landscape. As a result, the parliamentary enquiry into Thirlmere was conducted by special committee rather than the usual select committee. This allowed for all interested parties to submit evidence, rather than only those property-owners who would be directly affected (Marshall and Walton 1981). Opposition to the reservoir failed and Thirlmere was drained, enlarged and reconstructed as a reservoir.

To discourage ramblers around Thirlmere, employees and tenants of the water company were 'not allowed to accommodate overnight visitors, and were even forbidden to provide refreshment' (Hill 1980: 39). Not only were the incursions of aesthetic gentlemen repelled, but until 1989 (yes, 1989, not 1889), public access to the environs of Thirlmere was denied. Only then did modern water-treatment facilities allow for the installation of lakeside paths for public use (Welsh 1989). But the Manchester Water Corporation's conifer afforestation program (surely another threat to the Lake District landscape), had by then created great swathes of uninviting gloomy forest devoid of any undergrowth.

The special committee status under which the Thirlmere Act of 1879 was debated set a precedent for later controversial issues. There also emerged from the battle over Thirlmere the fact that *ad hoc* defense committees were insufficient to stop private interests from winning over Parliament. A national voice was needed to defend a property deemed of national importance. Early in 1883 that voice was summoned into being by a proposed railway line over the Honister Pass south of Derwentwater (see Map 3). Intended to service the slate quarries, the possibility was raised that it might also bring tourists into the heart of the isolated fells.

Opponents presented the scheme in the national and provincial press as 'the unnecessary destruction of a national shrine' and national petitions were organized to help protect a landscape described as 'Nature's own English university in the age of great cities' (Marshall and Walton 1981: 214–15). The promoters withdrew their Bill. Another railway was proposed in the summer of 1883, a line to the head of Ennerdale Water. When that Bill squeaked by its second reading and went into committee, it followed the Thirlmere precedent, proceeding into select committee, at which point the railway promoters withdrew it. While an educated elite was successfully defending the Lake District in a rhetoric of national importance justified by literary and painterly associations, local entrepreneurs were presenting the Lake District in terms of its commercial possibilities.[5]

A core group of local notables had been meeting for some time before they founded the Lake District Defence Society (LDDS) in 1883. In an example of the poetics of politics or perhaps the politics of poetics, membership of the LDDS was mainly drawn from the national membership of the Wordsworth Society. Reflecting the national and cultured nature of this otherwise uncultivated landscape, most of the LDDS's nearly 600 members lived outside the region and were drawn from legal, political and academic circles (Marshall and Walton 1981).[6]

Interlocking circles of social reformers, society figures and landscape preservationists joined in the protection of the Lake District. Some of them were quite radical in their challenges to sacrosanct notions of private property and landownership (Lowe 1989, Samuel 1994). The leading lights among them were Hardwicke Rawnsley, John Ruskin, Octavia Hill, and Robert Hunter. Canon Rawnsley, Vicar of Crosthwaite, was one of the local organizers of the LDDS. Before moving to the Lake District he had served as a curate in the slums of Bristol and

London, where he had been introduced to Octavia Hill by her mentor John Ruskin. Hill was deeply involved in housing reform and in the British army cadet movement; she was also a prominent member of the Commons, Open Spaces, and Footpath Preservation Society (Commons Society) which she had brought into the unsuccessful defense of Thirlmere.

Robert Hunter had worked on commons preservation with John Stuart Mill and in government reform with the political economist Henry Fawcett, who was also a member of the Commons Society. Hunter had devised the means (dealt with in the previous chapter) of preventing the creation of new copyholds by which landowners were taking manorial commons into their own hands for housing development. At the time that the LDDS was fending off incursions of the railways, and Rawnsley was leading a faction within that Society to make access part of its formal agenda, the Commons Society under Hunter's direction was attempting to preserve access to London's Epping Forest. In 1895 Hunter, Rawnsley and Hill were founding members of the National Trust for Places of Historical Interest or Natural Beauty (the National Trust).

An inherent conflict in preservation philosophy soon became apparent. As more tourists came into the now publicly valorized Lake District, rights of way to and around the lakes received heavier usage. Footpaths were closed by the very landowners who had supported the LDDS. Once protected from one source of external threats such as mines, railways, or reservoirs, the resource now had to be protected from being 'loved to death' by visitors, second-home builders, and associated servicing infrastructure. This is a peculiarly modern dilemma certainly current and unresolved, today. What is important is that

> It was in Lakeland that some of the earliest challenges were made to the rights of . . . property-owners to develop their land as they saw fit . . . The Lake District had not only become a tourist centre of importance, it had also become a forcing-house for new ideas about the proper relationship between man, property, morality and the environment.
>
> (Marshall and Walton 1981: 219)

## The National Dimension

It was here and in these circumstances that the concept of a national park was formed. Yet who constituted 'the nation'? The Second Reform Bill of 1867 had nearly doubled suffrage to include many workingmen in the towns and cities, but agricultural laborers and miners remained unenfranchised until the Third Reform Bill added about 2 million rural electors in 1884. Until then, and even then, the idea of landscape having national importance faltered on a contradiction: access to landscape functioned as a means of class differentiation.

We have seen in earlier chapters how the great collections of art displayed in the English country house helped reconfigure the great estates' landscapes, which themselves came to be considered works of art comprising a national gallery of (physical) landcapes. By the 1830s a discussion had begun about works of art in general. Were they best held in the great private collections of the English country house for a national governing elite? Should they not form the basis of a democratically accessible national collection? Or should museums be for 'silent, serious, and essentially solitary' viewers (Helsinger 1994: 128) – echoing the elite walker in the Lake District?

In 1860 Ruskin presented his ideas on the subject to a parliamentary committee on national museums. He proposed a system of separate museums for the working class where a minimal presence of keepers would promote an atmosphere allowing workingmen to feel sufficiently at ease to invite their wives and children to accompany them in 'their' museums.[7] While objects of value would be displayed for the working class, the most precious works of art – the national treasures – would not. In this way, 'class difference was to be institutionalized as the just way to provide for the differing viewing needs of all the nation's subjects' (Helsinger 1994: 129–30). National viewing would not create national viewers. It would differentiate the viewing public by class, gender and religion – for the source from which this aesthetic nationalism was to be derived was the inhabitants of the English country house. Participation in aesthetic life was not to be kept from the working class – far from it – but it was to be undertaken within appropriate spaces.

Ruskin's fulminations against the arrival of the aesthetically challenged masses to the Lake District was all about appropriateness too: knowing one's place and staying in it. In relation to the Lake District, Ruskin rhetorically asked reformers supporting the extension of the railways if:

> After all your shrieking about what the operatives spend in drink, can't you teach them to save enough out of their year's wages to pay for a chaise and pony for a day, to drive Missis and the Baby that pleasant 20 miles, stopping when they like, to unpack the basket on a mossy bank? If they can't enjoy the scenery that way, – they can't any way; and all

that your railroad company can do for them is only to open taverns and skittle grounds round Grasmere, which will soon, then, be nothing but a pool of drainage, with a beach of broken gingerbeer bottles; and their minds will be no more improved by contemplating the scenery of such a lake than of Blackpool.

(Ruskin 1876: 5–6)

Better for the working class to deal with the known landscapes of home than to travel great distances to stand before landscapes they could neither recognize nor engage with (the equivalent of class-specific museums). In this Ruskin was reiterating Wordsworth's earlier arguments against the railway's incursion into the Lake District. Class membership was at issue, not participation in the viewing of national treasures, be they objects or landscapes. To facilitate working-class entry into the inner sanctum of museum or Lakeland would be to condone 'matter out of place' (Douglas 1966).

In what at first seems bald contradiction, the landscape was the 'one space for viewing in which Ruskin imagined these subjects could be united' because it and only it 'offered common aesthetic ground to all English subjects' (Helsinger 1994: 139). However – an enormous however – common ground was predicated on having educated the working class to see by subjugating the touch to the gaze. This process of educating the eye to a right way of seeing was to be achieved through the practice of drawing, allowing the working class to become active practitioners of the perspectival gaze. Overt differentiation along class lines was neither initiated in Britain's provincial museums and National Galleries nor put into practice in relation to physical landscapes. In so notoriously class-structured a society as this it was hardly necessary.

The defense of the Lake District landscape was conducted along Wordsworth's notion that it was 'a sort of national property'. But as land came up for sale in an expanding land market, it was realized that, unlike the National Gallery, to which art could be donated and thereby be made literally priceless, no statutory body existed to guarantee the permanent removal of land from circulation. Although the National Trust was founded in 1895, not until 1907 did an Act of Parliament make it a statutory body with the right to hold land in perpetuity. From today's perspective, the National Trust can well be seen as having furthered Ruskin's aims of shaping the right sort of gaze and of having helped shape a national aesthetic that does indeed locate the 'English landscape as the defining space for national viewing' (Helsinger 1994: 126).

Already existing class antagonisms had been intensified by the displacement of agricultural laborers in the great relandscaping of the English country house. It is ironic that the National Trust, through its preservation of the great estates and the families living on them as lifetime tenants of the Trust, can now be described as a vast system of outdoor relief for distressed gentryfolk. Since its inception, the Trust's presentation of a dominant culture devoid of the circumstances of its creation has been avidly consumed. Meaning and experience have been uncoupled, and 'in the process a common set of assumptions and selections from "our" tradition . . . emerge despite the fact of differentiation' (Roseberry 1989: 45). Only recently has the Young National Trust Theatre presented plays at National Trust properties which show how the other half lived. One such production is *Flowers and Slaves* that depicts Chartist campaigners and their country-house-living factory bosses (Turner 1996).

Ruskin's Inaugural Lecture at Oxford in 1870 presented the English landscape as memorializing the local, the sacred, the slow accretion of better pasts. To the educated elite who would form the future governors of Empire, it was described as a landscape that could

> only be enjoyed by cultivated persons; and it is only by music, literature, and painting, that cultivation can be given. . . . the child of an educated race has an innate instinct for beauty, derived from arts practised hundreds of years before its birth.
>
> (Ruskin 1870 quoted in Helsinger 1994: 139)

It was indeed the practice of the Picturesque aesthetic over the previous century or more that had given Ruskin his beloved Lake District.

At the same time Ruskin also projected the English national landscape into the future and onto foreign shores. He urged the nation to 'found colonies as fast and as far as she is able . . . seizing every piece of fruitful waste ground she can set her foot on' (Ruskin 1870 quoted in Helsinger 1994: 139). The expression 'fruitful waste ground' places us squarely in a rhetoric of improving and scientific farming that required a prior dispossession and annihilation of a way of life. To speak of 'seizing . . . waste ground' is to speak within the political mode of the perspectival gaze.

This discursive linking of English and foreign landscapes expresses English nationalism in terms of the British imperial dimension. It also brings an additional dimension to the notion of the English landscape as the defining space for national viewing. The inscription of the Lake

District on the landscape of Kandy and the seeing of the Lake District and other parts of England in Tasmania, Australia and New Zealand were explored in Chapter 3. Together, these literal and metaphorical views epitomize the integration of the political and representational perspectival gaze, as well as the nesting of England within the British Empire.

## Class and Leisure

Nonconformist religion, early socialism and the workers' education movement provided 'stimulus ... [and] guidelines' for the working-class walking movement (Taylor 1997: 85). Rambling clubs varied by the religious affiliation, political ideology, and class membership of their leaders, as well as by the membership they were founded to serve.[8] Not all clubs held the same opinions about rights of way or access to open land. The Scottish Cairngorms Club, founded in 1889, sought to encourage stavaiging (wandering at will), while the Scottish Mountaineering Club, founded in 1890, specifically disassociated itself from rights of way issues. In contrast, The Liverpool Hobnailers, organized in the 1890s, were a collection of 'tough ramblers who used to go out with the intention of walking in areas where access was restricted' (Hill 1980: 25). In an era dominated by an ideology of self-improvement, recreational walking dovetailed with enthusiasm for Natural History. It provided an educational component to rambling and also served to introduce religion into the enterprise.[9]

The Co-operative Holidays Association (CHA) was started by Thomas Arthur Leonard (1864–1948), a Nonconformist clergyman. It had no Church of England equivalent although Natural History clubs operated out of Anglican churches and necessarily went on afternoon or day-long rambles. Its previously unexamined archives provide a way of seeing how a 'mainly working class movement' (CHA, Minutes October 8, 1898) gave its members a view of the landscape.

T.A. Leonard, the minister at Colne Congregational Church, Lancashire, ran a popular Saturday afternoon rambling club for his congregation.[10] Preaching that holidays were an arena in which 'the devil wields no small influence' (Leonard 1891, quoted in Speake 1993: 3), he found a strong antidote in talks on 'wayside flowers and Wordsworth' and the 'sacred purity' of nature in general (Leonard, n.d. c.1910). In June 1891 he took thirty male parishioners on a four-day fell-walking holiday in the Lake District at a cost of twenty-one shillings per person. In 1893, 268 working-class men and women went on Lake District walking holidays with Leonard. Thereafter the figures climbed rapidly: 673 in 1894 and 1,064 in 1895. In 1894 Leonard left the Church to carry his ministry into the running of CHA which became a legal entity in 1897.

In 1897 its cheap walking holidays cost thirty shillings for a full week, just thirteen shillings for a weekend. The Minutes of February 27, 1897 note that at this time CHA 'manageresses [received] 25 shillings a week salary plus third class railway fare [presumably from their home to the CHA House] and laundry allowance'. The Domestic Committee Minutes of the same date indicate that 'The manageress may give permission to any of her servants to join one of the rambles . . . taking into account the character of the servant'. The servants were women. Two years later the Domestic Committee Minutes referred to them as 'helpers'. It is worth noting that male guests were expected to help with the heavy work in kitchen and scullery.

CHA holidays were complemented by evening lectures and lantern slide shows. The Lecturers' Committee, formed in 1895, determined that these lectures were to be

> of an informal character . . . extemporaneous talks upon natural science, history and literature illustrated by local examples [by] gentlemen lecturers; . . . [that] each lecturer be asked to introduce in an out-of-door talk some notable book, by preference one included in the General Introductory Courses of the National Home Reading Union; [and] that the Executive Committee of the N.H.R.U. be asked to grant in the General Course Magazine two pages to be devoted to 1. Holiday Association announcements; 2. answers to queries on scientific and literary topics suggested by the holiday lecture talks; 3. Lecture notes; 4: Recommendations of literature . . . In return for this [the Association] will guarantee 500 additional members to the R.U. or the Association to pay dues to R.U. to that equivalent.
>
> (CHA Minutes, March 24, 1899: 116–17)

CHA also entered into agreement with London Polytechnic to advertise each others' holidays.[11]

CHA holidays included daily morning prayers supervised by Dr. John Brown Paton (1830–1911), a Nonconformist educator involved in the National Home Reading Union.[12] A Dr. Martineau was engaged to work with him on ensuring their suitability (CHA Minutes, October 23, 1897). In all probability this was the Unitarian minister James Martineau

(1805–1900), brother of Harriet Martineau who had herself been a vocal supporter of working-class holidays in the Lake District.[13] Morning prayers were to be read by the local secretary of the group on holiday, but this was to be 'considered quite optional, he shall be asked to do his utmost to get a substitute if he objects to do this duty himself'. Group secretaries were expected to be males.

It is noted in the CHA Minutes of March 24, 1899 that Cannon Rawnsley of the Lake District Defense Society (who later became a Trustee of CHA) had written a sonnet concerning their house at Whitby. Though the sonnet was not read into the Minutes, its closing lines have been published elsewhere. Whereas the bardic nationalism discussed in Chapter 3 dealt with presumed pre-urban harmony between people and place, this piece of Victorian bardic nationalism is infused with a mythic vision of workers in harmony with their place in life:

> The World of Labour – nobler music still
> Than Caedmon knew, our England shall o'er spread.
> For here by Hilda's Abbey on the slope,
> The harps of God begin again their chime
> The chime of love and sympathy of heart.
> I see the workers come awhile apart,
> And go refreshed with music of sweet hope
> For human brotherhood's melodious time.
>
> (Rawnsley 1897 quoted in Speake 1993: 39)

Through connections with people such as Rawnsley, CHA lent its weight to landscape preservation efforts. The Executive Committee in 1898 for instance decided that the Association would sign a protest against a scheme to construct a light railway to Beddgelert, Wales, and determined that 'a request be sent to all the members of the association asking them to communicate with their respective Members of Parliament' about the matter (CHA, Minutes February 19, 1898). Members were everyone who had gone on a CHA holiday.

The holidays attracted such large numbers that it was decided that 'members should come in detachments, with their own officers to keep order'. The suggestion that each week be limited to fifty people was not acted upon (CHA, Minutes, October 23, 1897). So many women wanted to take CHA holidays that it was decided 'not to allow the proportion of females to exceed two thirds of the entire party, and in order to remove a possible hindrance to masculine bookings, the . . .

late booking fee arrangement' was reduced from two shillings and sixpence, to one shilling (Minutes, January 4 and 5, 1897). There is nothing to indicate why men were thought more likely to book holidays at the last moment. Were women booking holidays in relation to their menstrual cycle and therefore less likely to decide spontaneously to go on a holiday? Or was it more difficult for women to organize time away from work at short notice?

Disbursements of CHA's Fresh Air Fund were made in the amount of £7 each to Glasgow, Bradford, Sheffield, Liverpool, Leeds and Manchester, and £4 each to Nottingham and Oldham (CHA, Minutes December 30, 1895). CHA's own Poor Folk's Holidays (which allowed for 'rest and freedom' rather than excursions), were sometimes offered only for women. Reports on these assisted holidays up through the Second World War show that women formed the vast majority of guests.[14]

CHA's walking holidays were so successful that CHA rambling clubs soon proliferated, especially in the Midlands. To keep the clubs in contact CHA published a small-format monthly magazine called *Comradeship*. It contained short articles, book reviews, reminiscences, announcements of births, deaths and marriages of CHA 'folk', photographs of CHA holiday centers, a calendar of its various centers' free holidays, lead articles by CHA officials, and news from CHA clubs.[15]

Despite the large number of women on CHA holidays and at local CHA clubs, a decidedly male tone colored the manner in which walking was written about. It was also a less self-conscious world in which the following passage about walking could appear as entirely innocent of any sexual connotation:

> ... the true lover of nature is one who never "arrives". With growing intimacy his wonder is transformed into delight, and delight into affection. He ... feels more and more at home yet his pursuit is checked by many a baffling unintelligibility ... Behind the soft breath that plays upon his cheek, hidden far below the ... shoulder over which he climbs, lie problems as unfathomable as any he may find. ... Yet man ... continues to penetrate "the labyrinthine walks of truth," convinced that [to do so] will be to know himself.
>
> (*Comradeship* XVII, March 1914, "Open Sesame," 4: 52 )

Gender was variously represented in the *Comradeship* masthead. Initially the masthead was a narrow horizontal band divided into three compartments by bars of heraldic chevrons. The central and largest area showed a young man, rucksack on his back, walking stick in one hand, facing a young woman carrying a sprig of oak leaves. The man gazes beyond the woman, the woman looks directly out at us. Their right arms are extended towards each other, hands clasped in a gesture of fraternal 'comradeship'. Behind them, more or less filling the frame, stands a tree with distant mountains and cliffs and the sea on either side. Each smaller side compartment contains an oak sapling. One has books propped around its base, the other is surrounded by flowers among which is propped a rucksack bearing the initials CHA above its buckle clasp. The design is unsigned.

By 1924 the masthead had been enlarged and changed. Two young men and one young women are seated on a grassy knoll overlooking the sea. A book is next to the woman. Another woman, wrapped in a cape, stands behind the group, also gazing out to sea. The only visible footwear are walking shoes rather than boots. There is one lone pine tree on their knoll. On one side of the background are mountains, on the other are seacliffs and foreshore. Beneath them, undergirding their resting place as it were, is the title *Comradeship* flanked by rucksack and open book.[16]

By 1932, a full-page cover replaced the horizontal masthead. The foreground is dominated by an enormous oak, its branches extending slightly beyond the sea-girt island-realm on which it is set. In the middle distance and to one side is a ruined castle, on the other a church-spired village. Mountains form the backdrop. Flying up from castle keep and village, and surrounding the tree, are birds. Arching over the tree is the word *Comradeship*, while in the tree is a ribbon band bearing the legend 'The Magazine of the Co-operative Holidays Association'. This frames a heart-shaped device at the center of the oak tree, in which the letters CHA are intertwined. Comradeship and love of country are met in the organizational presence of the CHA.

The oak tree has a long symbolic presence in English history (Thomas 1983). Over time it has been appropriated by both kings and rebels, reflecting different political visions. As for the sea, the increasing space it occupies in the masthead pictures, from its minor presence in the 1911 version to its dominance and defining significance in 1932, constitutes an expression of insularity at variance with CHA's political vision. CHA was a corporate member of the League of Nations Union and gathered signatures at its various houses for presentation to the Disarmament Conference in Geneva in February 1932 (*Comradeship* XXIII, December 1931, "World Disarmament", 2: 5). It had long used its house magazine to preach its creed: 'It is part of the work of CHA to help forward the international movement' and to this end it suggested that people learn French or German to allow communication with their 'fellows' when on trips abroad (*Comradeship* V, September 1911, "CHA", 1: 3). By 1913 CHA had forty-two holiday centers, five of them in Ireland, five on the Continent (Taylor 1997).

During the First World War, *Comradeship* seemed blessedly free of excesses of jingoistic patriotism, even when appeals were made for members to take in Belgian war refugees.[17] The magazine carried correspondence from CHA members serving in the forces including, as one might expect, accounts of their experiences as walkers within the foreign landscapes where they saw duty. A letter written on Boxing Day 1914 by Private H.H. Granger stationed in India with the Somerset Light Infantry confirms Wordsworth's belief that the Lake District was capable of being taken in by the eye in a way that the Alps with their grander size were not. Private Granger's letter read, in part:

> Three of us . . . climbed Dodabetta in the Nilgirio,[Nilgiri] the highest hill in Southern India. The summit is about 9,000 ft. above sea level. . . . Although Dodabetta is so high, and the prospect from it wide and wonderful, I do not consider it half as imposing as our own lesser hills. It rises in terraces of perhaps 2000 ft. at a time, and these masking each other, never allow the great bulk and towering height of the mountain to be properly appreciated.

> (*Comradeship* IX, October 1915, "Letters", 1: 14)

Part of the upper- and middle-class mystique surrounding the Lake District comes from the early fell-walking and rock-climbing fraternity who, regardless of prior generations of shepherds and locals who had walked and climbed, wrote themselves a central role in the activity. Indeed, the history of leisure activities has been written 'on the assumption that what is new starts from high up the social scale and is diffused downwards' (Cunningham 1980: 10). In a physical reconfirmation of the Lake District's earlier picturesque linkage to the Alps, men such as Leslie Stephens used the Lake District in winter or early spring when snow and ice-cover approximate alpine conditions.[18] Tough rock-climbing had been popular since mid-century, but the early 1880s saw

> a systematic attack on the crags and buttresses of the Lake Country by most of the expert climbers of the day. The conquest of almost all the major peaks in the Alps meant that the climbing fraternity turned increasingly to rock climbing, as opposed to pure and simple mountaineering.

> (Lefebure 1977: 249)

In doing so the alpinists developed some of the great Lake District climbs. Photographs taken by climbers were made into postcards and lantern slides and were used to illustrate books of rock climbing, further helping to popularize the Lake District (Craig 1992; Lefebure 1977; Milner 1986).

In this period of Empire and exploration, climbing in the Lake District satisfied 'the desire to exert one-self physically . . . [and conferred] the joy of conquest without any woe to the conquered' (Crook 1900, quoted in Milner 1986:109). As more men wanted to climb, a new Climbers' Club was formed in 1898, but it too was drawn from the same professional and university ranks as the Alpine Club. In 1907 the Fell and Rock Climbing Club of the English Lake District was formed, which extended membership to working-class men who could bicycle in from nearby towns. Unlike the Alpine Club, the new association admitted 'Ladies' who were not only eligible for membership, but at a reduced rate.

The issue of class jumps off the pages of a presentation on fell-walking and rock-climbing in the Lake District that was given as part of a symposium in 1984 at the Victoria and Albert Museum. It took place in conjunction with an exhibition entitled *The Discovery of the Lake District* (Murdoch 1984), which appears to have been part of the run-up to the Lake District National Park's unsuccessful nomination as a World Heritage Site.[19] As the following examples from the presentation show, class, diffusion from above, naming and silencing are all intertwined.

Walter Parry Haskett Smith then began his splendid series of new climbs. He was 21 at the time, and quite by accident had chosen Wasdale Head as the base for two reading parties from Oxford. An Old Etonian, an Oxford man, later a barrister, his background was the same as the others in the Alpine Club . . .

In 1888, Cecil Slingsby, A Yorkshire businessman, and a member of the Alpine Club . . . [enjoined] his fellow members 'Do not let us be beaten on our own fells by Outsiders . . . Let us not neglect the Lake District . . . whilst we are conquerors abroad.

Another pioneer was Professor Norman Colie, a brilliant scientist, who . . . led the first ascent of Moss Ghyll, on Scafell, in 1892.

The first of these bolder and more exposed routes was the ascent by Godfrey Solly, a Birkenhead solicitor, of the Eagle's Nest Ridge, direct, on Great Gable (the Napes), in 1892.

Then, in 1890, a new star appeared, perhaps the greatest, Owen Glynne Jones, a man of Welsh origin, *but* born in London. A young schoolmaster of 23 . . . (emphasis added)

In 1914, the Lake District became pre-eminent among the climbing areas of Britain when the ascent of Central Buttress on Scafell was pioneered by a young Manchester man. It was the hardest climb in the land and remained so for the next 20 years.

(Milner 1986: 106–112)

After a succession of the names, places of education, and professions of the elite Alpinists, the young Mancunian appears unnamed, despite his acknowledged achievement. He was, in fact, Siegfried W. Herford, who was killed in the trenches in December 1915.

Having fought for the country in the First World War, the working class wanted access to the country.[20] Cheap train fares and the proliferation of cycling clubs enabled groups of young working- and middle-class people to get out into the open countryside. More relaxed attitudes towards unchaperoned activities and clothing also helped. However, some women still felt constrained to wear knee breeches under skirts: the skirts were removed and packed into rucksacks once the last village on the route had been left behind. Working men from the industrial north, trained on the Peak District climbs, were able to reach the Lake District cheaply and quickly at weekends on motorbikes purchased on Hire Purchase.[21] There they opened up new climbing routes, and imbued the sport with a militantly working-class aura (Cook 1974; Hill 1980; Taylor 1997), particularly when they climbed in socks or barefoot.

Footgear varied from expensive climbing boots with soft iron edge nails available in places such as Chamonix in the Alps, to their 'home-grown' version, the hob-nailed boot. Cheap plimsolls (canvas shoes with rubber soles) were within the reach of almost everyone:

On Scafell Pike . . . we found rubber soles so good – never a slip the whole time. Often we came across rocks with scratches made with hobnails half a yard long, and that in places where we felt never a slip.

(Smith *c*. 1922 n.p.)[22]

But the experience of the fells also depends upon food and lodging. After a strenuous day on Scafell Pike, we were desperate for food and drink, and after a wash had tea specially served for us in the smoke room. As we were finishing that the gong rang for dinner and we – nothing daunted – went in and fell on it like wolves! So we made a non-stop run of tea and dinner.

(Smith *c.* 1922 n.p.)

This kind of touring in the Lake District could be undertaken for minimal cost.

On Friday we had to leave Grasmere after two or three days of the very best. We had splendid fare and the best attention with Mrs. Borwick of Goody Bridge House and paid six shillings a night each for supper, bed and breakfast. Then they say the Lakes are dear! As a matter of fact, this was the usual price all round.

(Smith *c.* 1922 n.p.)

At those rates, £15 could cover a month in the Lakes. A guide for a month in the Alps would cost ten times that amount.

The Lake District was becoming a recreational landscape in which different classes could meet or at least catch sight of each other. Furness Railway posters of *c.* 1910 and 1914 advertised

tourist and week end tickets all the year round with cheap excursions during the summer months from London and principal provincial stations. Illustrated guides, tour programmes, etc. supplied on application to the Superintendent of the Line.

(Lakeside Railway Society)

The Lake District was presented to excursionists in terms of the picturesque scenery its literary and painterly luminaries had celebrated. Some posters depicted the 'English Lake Land' and the 'English Lakes' bathed in moonlight. Others showed picturesque vignettes of the houses or the settings where Romney, Ruskin, Southey and Wordsworth lived (each man's name appearing in the appropriate vignette).

The struggle for spatial and political access had long been intertwined. The Fourth Reform Bill, passed in early 1918 – several months before the end of the War – went some way towards acceding to demands for Woman's Suffrage, women having proved themselves essential to the war effort.[23] The struggle for political access having now been more or less won, working-class voters' struggle for spatial access could insert itself more firmly into the political arena.

## Converging Paths: Linear Access, Open Access, and Landscape Conservation

In order to be considered a legal right of way, a path had to lead from one settlement to another. This interpretation was challenged by the Commons Society in 1900 in the context of Richmond Hill, Surrey. The Society was already involved there in the preservation of Ham and Petersham Commons, a scheme that

> was intimately connected with a movement for saving from defacement, by building, the exquisite and panoramic view of the River Thames and its valley from Richmond Hill – one of the most beautiful features to be found near London – the frequent subject for artists, and the theme of poets.
>
> (Eversley 1910: 232)

The case established that a path leading to a summit or viewpoint could legally be considered a public right of way.

In further efforts to protect 'the middle vista of the view from Richmond Hill', open space societies, County Councils, and Local Authorities put together the moneys to buy out common land which was being enclosed under common law. The Richmond Hill, Petersham, and Ham Act of 1902 was the first piece of legislation 'incorporating the principle of the purchase of a property by a Local Authority, for the purpose of the preservation of a landscape view' (Eversley 1910: 236). The sweaty vulgar, along with their cooler, aesthetically-minded counterparts, had gained their right to a particular perspective.

The aim of most early footpath preservation societies had been the maintenance or reopening of local linear ancient rights of way. The push for open access was more a development of the late-nineteenth century. In order to campaign more successfully for open access to moors and commons, rambling clubs began to federate in the early years of the twentieth century. Thus the London-based Federation of Rambling Clubs (FRC), an offshoot of the Commons Society, affiliated with clubs in Bristol, Cardiff, Darlington, and Newcastle. In 1926, after the interruption of the First World War, some two dozen working-class rambling clubs in the Sheffield area completed the process of federating. By then, there was also a Manchester Federation of thirty-eight rambling clubs (Holt 1995). In 1931 The National Council of Ramblers' Federation was formed from eleven regional federations.

Demands for open access and political access developed along intertwined trajectories. Walking clubs grew politically sophisticated in their tactics, using parliamentary politics to achieve their aims. Thus the Manchester and District Federation of Rambling Clubs, formed in 1922, canvassed candidates in that year's General Election asking 'in the event of your election will you be willing to co-operate in the introduction of a Bill to give free public access to moors and mountains?' (cited in Hill 1980: 57).

During these years of industrial unrest, English agriculture suffered dramatically from world competition. At a time of sustained economic and social crisis, land-use planners recognized that recreational access would have to be accommodated within the economic and strategic changes occurring in the countryside (Rogers 1989; Taylor 1997). Hunger, homelessness and unemployment were much more deeply felt in the north than in the south where a seemingly indifferent Government was located. Down-and-out tramps, hunger marches, homelessness and massive unemployment co-existed with an upper-class idealization of 'tramping' (Wright 1985). That kind of 'tramping' was associated with the long-distance solitary walker (often a university man), small groups of Oxbridge reading parties, or the likes of Leslie Stephens's Sunday Tramps. In other words, 'tramping' had a pronounced southern-counties slant to it.

Uneven distribution of the social effects of the General Strike of 1926 and the 1930s Great Depression meant that not only was the south-east of England relatively unaffected economically, but even that it prospered. Suburban housing, or 'ribbon development' as it was called, was serviced by the introduction of a national electricity grid, an extended railway network and automobiles. As the middle class moved into suburbia, its wealthier sector moved further out into the countryside.

Concrete and hedgeless arterial roads, massive and densely placed roadside advertising hoardings (billboards), petrol stations, towering electricity pylons, and overhead electricity and telephone lines all went into supporting encroaching acres of 'bungaloid scurf', while roads, cars, and motorized buses allowed picnicking urban lower-class day-trippers to spread their litter further and faster (Bunce 1994; Jeans 1990; Jeffrey 1983; Lowerson 1980; Newby 1987).[24] The 'uglification' of England created a new impetus among the landowning upper classes to preserve the landscape. Suburbanites, for their part, did not necessarily care for some of the agricultural practices that produced the scenery they were so pleased to invade (Miller 1995a).

Access began to be cloaked in aesthetic rhetoric. The impetus for landscape preservation was given organizational form in the Council for the Preservation of Rural England (CPRE), an umbrella organization founded in 1926 from some forty constituent groups, representing a variety of land-related interests.[25] It was supported by 'a body of intellectuals who wrote vigorously in defence of the countryside' (Jeans 1990: 251) and acted as a *de facto* lobbying group. In an ambiguous twist presaging the heritage industry, the tourist industry welcomed preservation since the timeless English landscape was such a draw for newly motorized tourism, especially by foreign visitors.

There is an ironic double bind implicit in the goals of preservation, namely that whatever is considered special and worthy of preservation becomes marked as interesting to more and more people. In the case of the countryside, ordinary people's interest in it was perceived as the problem. George Macauley Trevelyan (1876–1962), a historian of Britain whose eminently readable books were bestsellers in the 1930s and 1940s, was caught in this double bind. His meliorist view of history – that human agency was capable of rendering history a process of inevitable advancement, progress and improvement – overlooked the dark side of the story. One might attribute his general evolutionary frame of mind to the fact that he was related to both Darwin and Huxley. Cutting across his sunny version of history, however, was a cultural pessimism aimed at urban Britain and its invasion of the countryside. By denigrating the urban and valorizing the countryside, he helped foster the very action he decried (Cannadine 1992; Collini 1992).

A recent biography of Trevelyan (Cannadine 1992) affords a view of the interconnections that existed between intellectual, political and institutional circles. Using that, it is possible to glimpse those inter-connections as they relate to landscape aesthetics, land-use planning, landscape preservation and access. Trevelyan's father, George Otto Trevelyan, was a close friend of James Bryce, sponsor of numerous Bills for access to Scotland's mountains (see list 5, p. 110). The older Trevelyan and Bryce both found spiritual solace in long-distance walking, as eventually did the younger Trevelyan.

As a young man at Cambridge, he had gone on an Easter-vacation reading party to Seatoller in the Lake District's Borrowdale Valley. Starting in 1898 and continuing for nearly two decades with few interruptions, Trevelyan and a group of friends would gather in the Lake District to conduct their own version of Whit Walks. A great admirer of Wordsworth, Trevelyan became actively involved with the National Trust in 1912, especially supporting its efforts in the Lake District. An outspoken critic of proposed roads and electricity pylons in the Lake District, Trevelyan argued that 'German' conifer plantations there would be 'a crime against Nature's local bye-laws' (cited in Cannadine 1992: 156). Over the years, Trevelyan himself purchased land in the Lake District for donation to the Trust.

After the First World War 'many of the great aristocratic estates were broken up and one quarter of England was put onto the market' (Cannadine 1992: 151). Inevitably the work of the National Trust took on particular urgency and Trevelyan spearheaded fund-raising campaigns for the purchase of properties, bringing into the effort influential political friends such as Stanley Baldwin and Ramsay MacDonald, as well as members of the aristocracy and the intellectual elite. Partly through his efforts the Trust's holdings in the Lake District increased by nearly 10,000 acres during the course of the 1920s.

Trevelyan was elected to the National Trust's Council in 1926 and served on its Estates Committee (which he chaired from 1928 to 1949) and its Executive Committee (where he served as Vice-Chairman from 1929 to 1946). As Chair of the Estates Committee in 1941, Trevelyan was in the odd position of receiving from his brother Sir Charles Trevelyan the donation of Wallington Hall, the family's seventeenth-century Northumbrian country seat, and its 13,000-acre estate (Williams-Ellis 1947). Charles Trevelyan, who later served as Secretary of Education in the first two Labour Governments after 1945, had long been involved in parliamentary attempts at landscape preservation and access (see list 5, p. 110). In the Great Depression he had turned some of Wallington's outbuildings into dormitories for the use of the Northumbrian Trampers' Guild; he later donated them to the Youth Hostels Association (Taylor 1997) of which his brother George was the first President.

Through the various offices Trevelyan held in the National Trust, he had in-put into the CPRE. Under pressure from CPRE, the government set up a National Parks Committee in 1929 to consider whether and where one or more national parks might be placed. Its deliberations, contained in the Addison Committee Report (see list 6, p. 111), recommended a two-tier system of Regional Reserves for recreational access and National Reserves for science-driven conservation and observation of nature (Ditt 1996; Holt 1995; Taylor 1997).[26]

Within the general discourse of dislocation and change that engulfed Britain at the time, this debate among planners and preservationists has been read as 'a particular landscaped version of English citizenship' (Matless 1995: 93). Wordsworth had spoken of the Lake District as 'a sort of national property . . . in which everyman has a right and interest, who has an eye to perceive and a heart to enjoy'. Ruskin's aim had been to educate the eye and the heart. Expanding upon the Romantics' ideology of the importance of the non-material values of nature (Ditt 1996), the town and country planning that responded to the uglification of England enforced taste and legislated aesthetics. Certainly,

> By the 1930s a recognizable 'environmental lobby' had emerged, committed to defending the countryside from the threat of urban sprawl and urban ways ... The dilemma which existed between promoting the spiritual pleasure of the countryside and preserving it from the 'madding crowds' of insensitive visitors was never far from the surface ... the countryside needed to be preserved for 'the nation', but *from* 'the public'.
>
> (Newby 1987: 176, emphasis in the original)

As a result of the Addison Committee Report in which the Lake District was slated for designation as a National Reserve, the mechanism for a Cumbrian Regional Planning Scheme was developed in 1932. It gave official recognition to the Lake District as a regional entity cross-cutting the administrative boundaries of the counties of Cumberland, Westmorland, and Lancashire, and called for the establishment of a single planning authority for 'Lakeland'. The Friends of the Lake District (FLD) was soon formed in order to have its say in the protection and preservation of this landscape. Oxbridge members of the Wordsworth Society had been a source of support for setting up the LDDS in the 1880s (see p. 153). Now George Trevelyan helped promote a branch of the FLD at Cambridge.

A photograph of the core organizers and supporters of the Friends of the Lake District taken at the inaugural meeting on June 17th, 1934 includes in the front row, T.A. Leonard (founder of CHA and Holiday Fellowship founded in 1913 as an off-shoot from CHA), and Sir Charles Trevelyan; and in the back row, Patrick Abercrombie, professor of civil design and town planning who was later knighted (see figure 15). The group stands on the top step of a porch of Fitz Park, Keswick. Roland Taylor of Whitehaven, a leading local RA activist stands slightly to one side, and one step below the local and national luminaries of the landscape preservation world. Unlike the other men (except those in clerical dress), Taylor wears neither a three-piece suit nor a tie; his shirt is open at the neck and folded back over what appears to be a sports jacket. His distancing from the main body of worthies visually captures class relationships.[27]

In 1935, under the influence of geographer Vaughan Cornish, who was inspired both by Wordsworth and visits he had made to American and South African national parks (Ditt 1996), CPRE set up a Standing Committee on National Parks. It was composed of representatives from rambling federations, camping, cycling and motoring clubs, and various scientific bodies. The Standing Committee favored the Addison Committee's two-tier approach but the Depression thwarted central government from implementing any of its suggestions.

The rambling federations were split over whether to throw their weight behind national parks and protection of footpaths, or to agitate for open access to mountains, moorland, commons, and private but uncultivated land. In 1935 the National Federation of Rambling Clubs became the Ramblers' Association (RA) and lent its support to the push for National Parks. Other organizations backing national parks were CHA, HF), and the Cyclists' Touring Club. The Manchester Federation declined to be part of the new association since it was committed to championing open access. The Commons Society and CPRE favored negotiated access, while the National Trusts's primary commitment was to preservation of the landscape, not public access (Lowe 1989). Yet that public was much in evidence.

**Figure 15** Inaugural public meeting of The Friends of the Lake District, Fitz Park, Keswick, 17 June 1934, photographer unknown. Friends of the Lake District

**Plate 1** Claude Lorrain, 1663, at Devonshire House by 1761, "Landscape with Mercury and Battus." Oil on canvas, 74 × 110.5 cm. Devonshire Collection, Chatsworth. Reproduced by permission of the Duke of Devonshire and the Chatsworth Settlement Trustees

**Plate 2** Gaspard Poussin, c. 1670–75, at Devonshire House by 1761, "Landscape with a view of Tivoli." Oil on canvas, 47.5 cm. Devonshire Collection, Chatsworth. Reproduced by permission of the Duke of Devonshire and the Chatsworth Settlement Trustees

**Plate 3** Paul Sandby, 1793, "Rural Landscape", The Painted Room, Drakelowe Hall, Derbyshire, 241.3 × 63.5 cm. Victoria and Albert Picture Library

**Plate 4** Philippe de Loutherbourg, c. 1785, "Model Piece: Waterfall from an unidentified production." Pencil, watercolor and gouache, 32.7 cm. × 42.4 cm. Victoria and Albert Picture Library

**Plate 5** Ann Macbeth, c. 1940, "The Nativity." Embroidered silk and wool, blue and clear glass beads on linen, 118 × 141.5 cm. Glasgow Museums and Angus Mitchell

**Plate 6** Ann Macbeth, c. 1940, "The Good Shepherd." Embroidered silk and wool on linen, 122 × 158.5 cm. St. Patrick's Church, Patterdale and Angus Mitchell

**Plate 7** Lt. Col. Charles Hamilton Smith, c. 1809–20, "Views – England and Wales – Vol. I: Head of Ullswater, Patterdale, Helvellyn mountain in the distance, Westmoreland." Watercolor over graphite, image 20.3 × 28.9 cm. Yale Center for British Art, Paul Mellon Collection

**Plate 8** Lt. Col. Charles Hamilton Smith, c. 1809–20, "Views of India and Ceylon, Vol. II: Kandy, Ceylon." Watercolor over graphite, image 21 × 18 cm. Yale Center for British Art, Paul Mellon Collection

Working-class hiking and rambling had moved beyond mere popularity to the point of being a craze. By the early 1930s 'estimates put the number of regular country walkers at over 500,000, with about 10,000 in the Derbyshire Peak district alone during a summer weekend' (Lowe 1989: 122). The size of some of the groups out actually walking together is nothing short of staggering: 200, 300, 700, 800, even 1,600! (Taylor 1997). This more modest example (though still remarkably large by today's standards) is drawn from the Lake District:

> We . . . started our climb at Catbells, then straight along the ridge, over Maiden Moor, Narrow Moor and Eel Crags to Dale Head where we had lunch. While resting we saw our first 'party'. They were then ascending Robinson and against the skyline looked like so many matches. There were, I should imagine, 60–70 in the party.
>
> (Smith *c.* 1922 n.p.)

Bicycles, motor cars and negotiated cheap rail fares for rambling clubs were the means of escape from the cities; a shorter working week and drop in church attendance freed weekends for that escape. One rambler's song captures this feeling:

> I'm a rambler, I'm a rambler from Manchester way
> I get all my pleasure the hard moorland way
> I may be a wage slave on Monday
> But I 'm a free man on Sunday . . .[28]

There was also, of course, the influx of the unemployed. For them, as for their nineteenth-century counterparts, the only cost involved in getting out of the towns and cities was the boot leather or the energy expended on cycling out to the moors.[29]

E.V. Lucas's *The Open Road: A Little Book for Wayfarers*, first published in 1899, was in its fortieth edition by 1932.[30] Such pocket-size anthologies of poetry matched literature to landscape from a youth-hostelling as opposed to a drawing-room perspective. They were part of an efflorescence of nostalgia-laden 'country' literature. In 1932, the country writer S.P.B. Mais undertook a 15,000-mile journey through Britain at the British Broadcasting Corporation's request. Walks done on that journey formed a series of BBC talks broadcast in order to stimulate 'in listeners a desire to explore and rediscover their own island' (quoted in Taylor 1997: 231). Mais obviously struck a responsive chord. When in 1932 he organized a midnight train excursion to see sunrise at

Sussex's Chanctonbury Ring, 16,000 people turned up! Unfortunately, the sun was obscured by clouds (Lowerson 1980).

Given the large number of people walking around the landscape, it is perhaps not surprising to find some friction among ramblers, hikers and trippers. From the perspective of ramblers, hikers and high-minded preservationists, trippers were littering, radio-playing, noisy urbanites. Ramblers (according to a RA publication) viewed hikers as 'townies' who were not as well informed about the countryside as they ought to be (Holt 1995).

Working-class walkers were subject to physical and verbal harassment in the countryside (Holt 1995) and to ridicule in literature. Mary Butts' *Warning to Hikers* (1932) lambastes working-class Midlands walkers with their broad accents, 'bugger'-larded language and inappropriate footwear. They were considered unable to appreciate the real England, for theirs was not the 'deeper authenticity of [Butts's] own green world' (Wright 1985: 121–2). Butts considered the hiking craze – she did not use the word 'rambling' – not as a return to nature, but as an expression of a cult of nature engaged in by 'our new barbarians, bred inside that hideously fabricated world, under conditions that man has never known before' and from which they want to escape (Butts 1932: 15).[31]

Butts's *Warning* conjures up a new bardic nationalism located in the land where escapee urbanites have no 'place'. Once hikers

> ... have taken one step across the line of protection, the belt of urban needs and values each of them carry strapped tight about them, they will find themselves in a world as tricky and uncertain, as full of strangeness, as any wood near Athens. No friendly greenwood, fixed by poets; no wise gnome-tapped mountain; no gracious sea. *The dragon-green, the luminous, the dark, the serpent-haunted.* Will they face it? When the Sirens are back at their business, sisters of the Harpies, the Snatchers? When the tripper-steamer – her bows to the sun – turns into the boat called Millions-of-Years?
>
> Quiet in the woods. They can be very quiet when a wind from nowhere lifts in the tree-tops and through the pine-needles clashing the noise of a harp runs down the trunks into the earth. *And no birds sing.*
>
> (Butts 1932: 36 emphasis in original)

The Duke of York, the future King George VI, entertained a less gloomy and doom-laden view of hikers. In May 1933, he included in a speech "a word in defence of the hiker". Compared with the motorist who "rarely enjoys the loveliness of England . . . those who stride away through woods and over hills, who sleep under the stars in meadows, and who hear the nightingale in its own home . . . really know England"

(cited in Holt 1995: 5)[32]

What about the escapee barbarians themselves? A Miss G.M. Bluck of Camberwell, London, wrote a winning essay for CHA in 1931 entitled *Holidays by Instinct*. She was certainly attuned to something when she wrote of the 'compelling instinct' that caused her to turn away from the

> rich, fat fruitfulness of many Southern counties . . . a smell in the wind, a sunset, a chance remark . . . will bring [the compelling instinct] back fresh and disquieting. Then . . . the north, the mountains and the moors, come to me . . . and London becomes . . . a barren desert of bricked ugliness. . . . There comes a great restlessness, a disgust with all cities and neat suburbs, and toleration of one's lot, and with it peace of mind flies away.
>
> (*Comradeship* XXIII, December 1931, "Holidays by Instinct," 2: 11–12)

As the country moved closer to war, a welcome thought for some was the possibility that some of the new towns of bricked ugliness might be bombed out of existence.

> Come, friendly bombs, and fall on Slough
> It isn't fit for humans now,
> There isn't grass to graze a cow
> Swarm over, Death!
> . . . Mess up the mess they call a town . . .
>
> Betjeman 1937

Paradoxically, it was the Second World War itself that transformed thought about town and country planning, access and recreation, and the need for a system of National Parks, into implementation. For in the wartime Coalition Government, angst about the countryside slammed up against demands for access to it.

# Notes

1. Martineau wrote articles dealing with religious and education topics for the *Monthly Repository*, a forum for Dissenters (Hoecker-Drysdale 1992). She also wrote popular fiction on 'issues of the day' such as *The Rioters* (1829), *Poor Laws and Paupers* (1833–34), and *The Forest and Game Tales* (1845). Inspired by Wordsworth's sonnet *To Toussaint L'Ouverture*, Martineau eulogized the leader of the Haitian revolt against French rule in *The Hour and the Man (1841)* .

2. The Royal Hotel at Bowness for instance, listed 'the late Queen Dowager, the King of Saxony, the Prince of Prussia and the Grand Duke Constantine of Russia' among their recent patrons. Other advertisements include those for artists' supply stores, natural-history guides to flowering plants and mosses of the district, travelling maps, collections of Lake District views, and local art exhibitions.

3. While the following story may well be apocryphal, in which case it is interesting for having been invented at all, the same edition of the *Manchester Guardian* recounted how Wordsworth removed an obstruction blocking a footpath across the fields as he was on his way to dine at Lowther Castle. When the landowner, Sir John Wallace, who was at the same dinner, threatened to horsewhip whoever had knocked down the obstruction, Wordsworth is reported to have risen to his feet and said, 'I broke your wall down, Sir John, it was obstructing an ancient right of way, and I will do it again. I am a Tory, but scratch me on the back deep enough and you will find the Whig in me yet' (*Manchester Guardian* 1887, quoted in Hill 1980: 40).

4. This is the same sort of landscape conservation sleight-of-hand out of which Shell Oil successfully made such mileage a hundred years later (Wright 1985).

5. The English Lake District Association (ELDA) approved of the Honister Pass Bill precisely because it would open up an isolated area to tourists. ELDA was founded in 1877 by 'hotel proprietors and shop keepers to advertise and develop the district, during which period it worked with the Lake District Advertising Association to publicize the area' (Thompson 1946: 34; Berry and Beard 1980). ELDA was also involved in footpath preservation and public access.

6. Fewer than 10 percent of its members were Cumbrians, more than 25 percent lived in London and the Home Counties, with another 25 percent coming from Lancashire, mostly from around Manchester. While there were some industrialists, Oxford and Cambridge supplied 35 members, along with a dozen Americans – mainly academics from the East Coast – while 18 masters from Charterhouse, plus others from Eton, Harrow and Winchester, as well as the headmasters of Rugby and Uppingham were members (Marshall and Walton 1981: 214).

7. Museums set up by anthropologists a little later in the century to cater to the working class were imbued with an ethos of 'slowly, slowly':

> Anthropologists believed that these classes reasoned in the concrete terms characteristic of the more primitive members of the human species. . . . Museums were designed to represent spatial correlates of hierarchical social order and to document the process of evolution. . . . They would observe that examples of each type of artifact, arrayed in a developmental sequence, had been modified very slowly over time. Thus the act of viewing museum displays would impart a clear political lesson: responsible citizens did not press for precipitous change, but recognized that social evolution was necessarily gradual.
>
> (Kuklick 1991: 108 drawing upon Van Keuren 1984)

8. Rambling clubs coming directly out of adult education included the Midland Institute of Ramblers, formed in 1894 by student teachers at the Birmingham and Midland Institute of Adult Education. Natural History associations conducted weekly rambles in the course of following their determining interest, while others tagged on rambling to their central remit, such as the Men's Meeting and Literary Associations of Edinburgh's Wesleyan West End Mission which conducted Saturday summertime rambles (Hill 1980; Taylor 1997).

9. Ruskin's writings were a medium through which the nature–religion link could be established, whether through lectures on his ideas to rambling clubs and adult-education schemes or through the inclusion of rambling in progressive education syllabi (Taylor 1997).

10. Colne had been described in the mid-nineteenth century as being utterly destitute, with close to 25 percent of its inhabitants on parish relief. Not surprisingly, it was a stronghold of Chartism (Gadian 1986).

11. The London Polytechnic grew out of the Youths' Christian Institute (YCI) that was founded by Quintin Hogg in the winter of 1864–5 (when he also started a 'ragged school for boys' which was eventually superseded by compulsory Board of Education schools). The YCI offered technical education and an organized athletics program. It outgrew its home and in 1882 opened as the London Polytechnic in the buildings Hogg purchased from the defunct Royal Polytechnic Institute. In 1886 it became a day school offering instruction in professional, commercial and industrial classes, by which time it also organized for its members holiday tours and accommodations both at home and abroad.

12. As Principal of the Congregational Institute in Nottingham, Paton taught T.A. Leonard and was the first President of CHA (Speake 1993: 35).

13. James Martineau was a member of the Metaphysical Society, a debating club that met for about ten years starting in the late 1860s. It included Roman

Catholics such as Cardinal Manning and agnostics such as Thomas Huxley. Sir John Lubbock was also a member and Herbert Spencer declined membership. The exchange of ideas apparently did little to liberalize James's views. In 1872 he published attacks on Huxley's and Spencer's stands on the general question of Evolution. He also wrote scathing reviews of his sister's work because of the agnosticism it revealed (Hoecker-Drysdale 1992; Spencer 1904).

14.  There were 14 Poor Folk's holidays in May 1897 and 23 in September of the same year, each lasting for ten or eleven days. The process of nominating people for free holidays was open to abuse. In a particularly blatant case in the 1940s, a Mr. Piggott turned out to be charging people seven shillings to nominate them, sending five shillings to CHA as a 'donation' and pocketing the difference. It took a couple of years for Mr. Piggott's scheme to be discovered, at which point he was informed that no further nominations would be accepted from him.

15.  Foundational moments in English history occasionally break into Club reports that unconsciously or otherwise endowed walking with an educative value. A report on a reunion of the York CHA group reads in part:

> the party traversed the historic country known as the Forest of Galtres. Tea was provided at Stamford Bridge, the quaint old East Riding spot where more than 800 years ago King Harold vanquished the hardy Norsemen and from whence he departed to meet his own fate at the hands of the Conqueror at Hastings. Rambles are being continued fortnightly until the end of May.

> (*Comradeship* XV, October 1924, "York Group Report", 5: 16)

16.  The illustrator's signature is barely legible; it may be H.M. Rock.

17.  During the First World War CHA houses in Britain were offered to the British Red Cross as convalescent homes or for use as military or naval hospitals. The CHA house at Dinan was given to the French government for use as an auxiliary Military Hospital.

18.  Leslie Stephens, who founded the London-based Sunday Tramps club in 1879, was also Secretary to the Commons Society in its early years. The London *Times* celebrated the Tramps' 50th anniversary with an article in which it was recounted that when the Sunday Tramps were challenged by gamekeepers for trespassing, they would recite together: 'We hereby give you notice that we do not, nor doth any of us, claim any right of way or other easement into or over these lands and we tender you this shilling by way of amends.' As the article went on to say, 'The effect on the gamekeeper must have been devastating' (*The Times*, 18 January 1930, quoted in Hill 1980: 18).

19.  In the same year as the exhibition and symposium (1984), the British Government ratified the UNESCO convention for the protection of the world's

cultural and natural heritage. In 1985/6 the LDNP was submitted for inclusion to the World Heritage List. It was denied.

20. After the 1914–18 War, it was suggested that open spaces be dedicated as war memorials. The National Trust received three Lake District landscapes for this purpose: Borrowdale's Castle Crag, given by Sir William and Lady Hamer; Scafell Pike given by Lord Leconfield; and Great Gable and Great End given by the Fell and Rock Climbing Club. In 1925 the Master of Magdalene College and Wordsworth's last surviving grandson together purchased additional acreage on Scafell, giving all the land above the 3000 foot level as an addition to the Scafell Pike war memorial (Thompson 1946). The silence of these open spaces and their vistas and views form a complete antithesis to the mind-breaking cacophony and tunnel vision of trench warfare in which men such as Siegfried W. Herford lost their lives.

21. The more widespread acceptance of hire purchase, HP as it was referred to, involved making a small down payment on a generally large consumer object, followed by weekly payments spread out over several years. Though 'it had reached well into the middle strata of working-class life' in the 1890s and early 1900s, 'its use multiplied four times in the period 1918 to 1938, accounting for perhaps two-thirds of all mass-produced articles, and absorbing about £50 million at any one time' (Walvin 1978: 109, 139).

22. At the time of this walking tour, Walter Raymond Smith lived in Bideford, Devon, where he worked as a piano tuner. Although the family think Smith probably left school at 14, there is a poetic quality to some of his descriptive narrative, reflecting both his upbringing as the son of a Methodist preacher and his having attended Devizes Grammar School.

23. Limited suffrage was granted to women: they had to be over the age of 30. With the outbreak of war, militant action by the suffragettes had ceased, and both they and the non-militant suffragists had lent themselves to the war effort. Political and spatial access came together in a particular way through Millicent Garrett Fawcett (1847–1929), leader of the suffragists, and Henry Fawcett of the Commons, Open Spaces and Footpaths Preservation Society.

24. In a manner more than a little reminiscent of Ruskin's fulminations, the *Architectural Journal* trumpeted that 'It will take time to teach the vandalistic *nouveaux riches*, who infest our countryside at weekends, not to leave the remains of their picnics behind', while *Country Life* reported that 'townsmen seem to have the mentality of serfs. They act as uneducated slaves might be expected to act when suddenly liberated. They have no sense of responsibility to the countryside' (cited in Jeans 1990: 259).

25. The CPRE was constituted by various clusters of interest groups: The Country Gentleman's Association, the Central Landowners' Association, the Land Agents' Association and the Surveyors' Institution represented the major

landowners and their servicing professions. The Royal Institute of British Architects and the National Town Housing and Town and Country Planning Association were there looking after built aesthetic (and their own) interests, while the National Trust and the Society for the Preservation of Ancient Buildings added their own gracenotes to the aesthetic corner. Users' interest groups included the Commons and Footpaths Preservation Society, the Royal Automobile Club, and the Automobile Association. 'Local' input was seen to be represented through the National Federation of Women's Institutes, while Local Government was represented by the County Councils Association and the Rural District Councils Association.

26.  Land due to be designated accessible to the public was termed 'regional'; that due to be set aside for scientific observation was termed 'national'. It is as if the public in need of access to land (i.e. that segment of society which did not have its own) did not constitute 'the nation'. This is similar to Ruskin's class-based two-tier system of museums which also correlated with his views on landscape. In each case the Lake District fell into the category of an exclusive 'national' property.

27.  The Friends of the Lake District inaugural photograph provides an amazing contrast to one taken in the summer of 1907 of men in the Manchester Rambling Club 'after an all-night walk'. There they stand in suits, with waistcoats, collars and ties (Hill 1980: 29). In a form of cultural mimicry, working-class men in 1907 were still aping their 'sartorial betters'. Did they really walk through the night in three-piece suits? Were ties donned for the photograph? By 1934, an RA representative could sport a relaxed sartorial distancing from his 'betters' that in turn reflected their imposed and photographically posed social distancing of him. Here was cultural mimicry radicalized.

28.  At the end of a week's walking with a group of women, when we were sitting at supper, Jane Sweet (a past member of the Woodcraft Folk movement) said she had something for me, for my project. She then proceeded to sing a song with a voice that matched her name. She later told me the song was Ewan MacColl's "The Manchester Rambler". I would have given anything to have had my tape recorder with me, but to have asked her to wait and so on would have been to have ruined the delicacy of the moment. The next morning before we all went our separate ways she 'told' me the song, part of which I reproduce here.

29.  The unemployed men of Jarrow for instance 'went for really long walks. A walk to Newcastle was nothing to most of them and . . . they put an awful lot of their time in that way' (interview in Pickard 1982: 48). Such walking experience served the men well on their 300-mile walk to London in 1936.

30. The poems in *The Open Road* are sorted into topics that follow seasonal and life cycles as well as the rhythm of the mundane 'journey'. Sections devoted to poems of winter, spring, summer, and autumn are interspersed with sections dealing with setting out, meeting with 'the lover', companionship on the journey, and a final section entitled 'A Handful of Philosophy'.

31. It was the Youth Hostels Association that catered to the escapee urban 'barbarians', for its overnight charge of one shilling made a week's walking holiday within the range of 'even low-paid clerks and manual workers on thirty- or forty-shilling a week salaries' (Lowe 1989: 123). The YHA was founded in 1931; by 1939 it had 30 hostels and 83,000 members.

32. Holt gives no source for the Duke of York's words – where his speech was given, to whom, and upon what occasion. From its larger context, not reproduced here, it seems his words were quoted in a Parliamentary debate in 1936 concerning physical training. This might be connected with the Duke of York's Summer Camp for Boys. Elsewhere it has been written that the Camp's annual photographs show 'the sharpness of social and physical contrasts [between the Duke's] . . . public school helpers [and] . . . boys of the same age . . . [who were] four or five inches shorter, with large gaps in their front teeth, [and] generally looking a good ten years older' than their public school contemporaries (Lowerson 1980: 270). Holt has possibly appropriated to working-class hikers words that the Duke used about upper-class 'trampers' – and then only if the MP was himself accurately quoting the Duke's earlier speech.

six

# Access/Ability: Private Property and National Parks

*The Scott Report, 1942*

The precept that the countryside is the heritage of all involves the corollary that there must be facility for access to all.

quoted in Hill 1980: 86

*Footpaths and Access to the Countryside Report 1947*

Fostered by the instincts of an urbanised population, torn increasingly from its ancient roots in the soil by the industrial revolution, an urban existence that pushes the primeval background out of sight, that makes it remote and unavailable, that deprives people of intimate contact with it . . . is unlikely to produce adequate men and women.

quoted in Marsh 1982: 13

It has been the professional and semi-professional strata who led the National Parks movement, while on access it was the ordinary ramblers drawn from the industrial towns of the North. There are those who have attributed to these social distinctions the greater success of National Parks than of access. But this is to misread the situation. The right to walk anywhere on uncultivated land makes much greater inroads into the exclusiveness of private ownership than does the right to control the use to which private land can be put. The latter is a negative function, whereas the act of walking anywhere on uncultivated land is very positive.

Hill 1980: 114

Since 25 per cent of finance and a good deal of control [of National Parks] is local, they are only partly National; since they contribute in limited

183

ways and with conflicts to the recreation supply, they are only partly
Parks.

Simmons 1975: 111

## Introduction

Philip Corrigan and Derek Sayer assure us that 'neither the profoundly
cultural content of state institutions and activities nor the nature and
extent of state regulation of cultural forms are adequately addressed in
much of the literature' (Corrigan and Sayer 1985: 2). State regulation
of the culture of leisure and the state's reification and expression of
national character and cultural identity are integumental to the
legislative history of access in England and the National Park system.
Incorporated in this history are the interlocking objectives of the state
and preservation organizations which are no less cultural forms than
the landscapes they protect.

Reflecting an antiquarian interest, early preservation legislation such
as the Ancient Monuments Acts of 1882 and 1913 applied to built
objects in the landscape. As aesthetic-ecological interests gained
legitimacy, built objects and the landscape were 'presented as a collective
inheritance expressing the essential national spirit . . . and the definition
of national identity' (Lowe 1989: 119). Opposition to early preservation
measures had been predicated on the fear that the importance attaching
to the public interest would be at the expense of private property rights.
As public interest gained national prominence through the defense of
the Lake District, a solution to this conflict was negotiated within the
framework of private property relations through the institutional form
of the National Trust:

> . . . the inalienability of the Trust's property can be regarded (and also
> staged) as a vindication of property relations: a spectacular enlistment
> of the historically defined categories 'natural beauty' and 'historic interest'
> which demonstrates how private property simply *is* in the national public
> interest.

(Wright 1985: 52)

The creation of enabling legislation for national parks again raised the
specter that private property rights might in some way be curtailed.
They were not.

This chapter presents an overview of the Parliamentary Committee
work leading to the enabling legislation for designating national parks.

It also develops an overview of the actual legislation itself. It highlights the inherent tensions and conflicts existing within national parks as farming, housing, recreation and nature conservation claims, and those of central and local governments, compete (Clout 1984; Ditt 1996; Healey *et al.* 1988; Holt 1995; Lake District National Park Plan (LDNPP) 1986; Lowe 1988; Mormont 1983; Newby 1987; Rüdig 1995; Simmons 1975; Whitby and Ollerenshaw 1988). It ends with the highly contentious re-emergence of demands for open access in the 1990s, and with the debate surrounding the fundamental nature of private property and the comparative weight to be given to private and public rights in the land.

## Cultural Constructions a.k.a. Definitions

*The commons.* In England, 'the commons', or common land, is not common property. Historically, common land was the unenclosed wasteland (mountain, moor, heath or down) that existed beyond a settlement's arable land, meadowland and pastureland. The Statute of Merton (1235) confirmed the rights of a lord of the manor to the commons. The 1925 Law of Property Act brought into the public domain common land that lay within Urban Districts.[1] There is no legal right of access to common land outside metropolitan areas despite their ongoing *de facto* use (i.e. 'by sufferance'). Agreements with landowners for access to private land, or in the case of commons, agreements with manorial lords, is *de jure* access that may sometimes be limited by season. Though the English manorial system of commons and communal working of open fields are used as the Ur-motif in constructing the tragedy of the commons (Hardin 1977), that motif has been sorely bent out of shape. Strictly regulated, the English commons and the communally tended and cooperatively grazed open fields, were anything *but* available to individual efforts at self-serving economic rationalization or maximization.[2]

*Rights of way.* Regulations abound. All public roads are rights of way. Designated footpaths (for people on foot), bridleways (for people on foot, horseback and bicycle), and byways (all traffic), are also rights of way (Highways Act 1980). Definitive rights of way maps are held at local parish council offices, though paths not shown on them may be public rights of way that have been omitted from the maps. Minimum widths are set for paths and bridleways if these have not been legally recorded. In such cases, a footpath running across a field must be 1 metre wide, a bridleway 2 metres wide. A footpath skirting the edge of a field must be one and a half metres wide, a bridleway three metres wide. Dairy bulls but not beef bulls are banned from fields crossed by public paths. Beef bulls must have their herd with them if they are in fields crossed or skirted by footpaths. The Rights of Way Act (1990) set up specific timeframes within which farmers must restore paths that they have ploughed up. Paths with no legal standing beyond the temporary wish of the landowner are termed permissive paths. They are not definitive rights of way and can be revoked at any time.

*Stiles*. Adding emphasis to the significance of the rights of way are stiles that mark the break in boundary walls and hedges through which a right of way passes. They vary enormously but include decorous and decorative small wrought-iron Victorian gates at the end of a village lane; pairs of narrowly-splayed stones through which only the thinnest and most nimble can easily pass; steep wooden stepladders with handpoles; broad throughstones built into drystone walls; insulated breaks in electric fences (sometimes as discouragingly narrow as 8", in which case they are certainly reportable to the local parish council's footpath officer); and other variously configured wooden step systems in a wide range of repair and disrepair.

*National Parks*. National parks in Britain are not wilderness areas set aside as in the United States, but are lived-in working landscapes which support farming, forestry, extractive industries and a multi-tiered tourist industry. Most land in most national parks is privately owned (Poore and Poore 1987). Inevitably, conflicts occur between economic use and recreational activity, let alone between both of these and nature-conservation objectives. There has never been any serious debate over the desirability of the state's acquiring the freehold of land in national parks, though large acreages in the national parks are already held by organizations such as the National Trust.

## From Committee to Act

The florescence of topographical writing in the two decades leading up to the Second World War had sounded a threnody for the English landscape (Bennett 1993; Slater 1987). In 1940 the Coalition Government's Ministry of Labour launched the

> *Recording Britain* project ... – the 'pictorial Domesday' for which Sir Kenneth Clark mobilized a galaxy of talents to preserve, in watercolour and gouache, tokens of the civilization which an enemy invasion might be expected to destroy.
>
> (Samuel 1994)[3]

Although wartime bomb damage and the possibility of invasion were the overt reasons behind the project, its underlying ethos was closely attuned to the enemy within:

> Photography can do much, but it cannot give us the colour and atmosphere of a scene, the intangible *genius loci* [the spirit of a place]. It is this intangible element which is so easily destroyed by the irresistible encroachment of what we call civilisation: schemes of development, the growth of industry, and the building of reservoirs and aerodromes; [and] by motor roads . . . [The project] shows us exactly what we are fighting for – a green and pleasant land, a landscape whose features have been moulded in liberty, whose every winding lane and irregular building is an expression of our national character. We are defending our very possession of these memorials, but when we have secured them from an external enemy, the existence of these drawings may serve to remind us that the real fight – the fight against all commercial vandalism and insensitive neglect – goes on all the time. There will be little point in saving England from the Nazis if we then deliver it over to the jerry-builders and the development corporations.
>
> (Reed cited in Saunders 1990: 7)

This was the cultural backdrop to the wartime appointment of a Coalition Government Minister of Town and Country Planning. That Ministry (MTCP) set up a Committee on Land Utilisation in Rural Areas chaired by Lord Justice Scott, a past Vice-President of the Council for the Preservation of Rural England (CPRE). The Scott Committee grappled with the social, political and economic ramifications of the rural–urban divide and attempted to negotiate several sets of conflicting interests. These included the economic viability of rural communities and agriculture, aesthetically driven preservation and conservation of the landscape, access to the countryside, and urban sprawl (Miller 1995a).

The Scott Report, *Land Utilisation in Rural Areas*, was published in 1942. It declared that 'the establishment of National Parks in Britain is long overdue' and recommended that 'within the first year' of peace, a National Parks Authority be set up and decisions made on which areas might become National Parks and which might become nature reserves. In 1944 a Government White Paper entitled *The Control of Land Use* 'referred to the establishment of National Parks as part of the programme of post-war reconstruction' (Abrams 1959: 21).[4]

While access was a major bone of contention, so were the administration and funding of the proposed national parks. Another Committee was set up. Chaired by John Dower, its remit was to hear evidence on the 'choice of areas [for National Parks], controls to be imposed, the facilities to be provided, the machinery, powers and technique required, and the necessary co-ordination with other purposes of planning and with the policies and activities of other Departments' (Dower 1945: 6).

In 1945, Sir Norman Birkett, Chairman of CPRE's Standing Committee on National Parks and President of the Friends of the Lake District, gave the Rede Lecture at Cambridge University. Calling Wordsworth into service, Birkett used the opportunity as a platform to push for 'a National Parks Commission'. National Parks would be:

> the regions of our finest landscapes made national possessions by the deliberate choice of the nation . . . preserved by the nation in their natural beauty, made accessible to the people, and particularly cross-country walkers, and brought into the fullest public service consistent with these ends.
>
> (Birkett 1945: 19)[5]

The Dower Report, *National Parks in England and Wales*, was published in April 1945, three months before the General Election that, in an astounding reversal, brought in a Labour Government.[6] In the Report, Dower fully developed the philosophy and concept of national parks and supported access to all uncultivated land. A national park was defined as:

> An extensive area of beautiful and relatively wild country in which, for the nation's benefit and by appropriate national decision and action, (a) the characteristic landscape beauty is strictly preserved, (b) access and facilities for public open-air enjoyment are amply provided, (c) wild life and buildings and places of architectural and historic interest are suitably protected, while (d) established farming use is effectively maintained.
>
> (Dower 1945: 6)

In response to the Dower Report, Lewis Silkin, Minister of Town and Country Planning in the newly elected Labour Government, set up a Committee on National Parks in England and Wales, chaired by Arthur Hobhouse.[7] One of its remits was to design the mechanism for implementation of national park legislation. The Hobhouse Committee's Access Sub-Committee (which like the main Committee included John

Dower among its members), 'recommended that access should be given to all uncultivated land, whether mountain, moor, heath, down, cliff, beach or shore' (Hill 1980: 87). The Hobhouse Committee Reports were published in 1947. They and the Dower Report formed the basis for The National Parks and Access to the Countryside Act of 1949.

In tandem with the Wordsworthian theme of certain landscapes being 'a sort of national property', George Trevelyan met with Silkin and Hugh Dalton, then the Chancellor of the Exchequer in the new Labour Government, to talk about preservation policy. The following year, Dalton's Budget included £50 million to create the National Land Fund. The money was designated to reimburse the Inland Revenue (tax authorities) for land and houses that were given to the nation in payment of death duties (inheritance taxes). Such land and houses would then be passed on to the National Trust. Dalton's resignation, due to a piece of political ineptitude, was lamented by Trevelyan in a letter to the *Times*, in which Dalton's governmental department was singled out for having actually been concerned with preserving the nation against the 'rising tide' of urbanism (Cannadine 1992).

Traditional linkages of marriage and patronage lay just below the surface. Dalton, a supporter of the National Trust and President of the Ramblers' Association, had been a political protégé of Sir Charles Trevelyan, George's eldest brother. John Dower, author of the *Dower Report*, was married to Pauline Trevelyan, Sir Charles's eldest daughter. Sir Julian Huxley, who had chaired The Hobhouse Wildlife Sub-Committee, was a distant cousin of the Trevelyans. Within the family, Mary Trevelyan, George's daughter, became a biographer of Wordsworth.

## The National Parks and Access to the Countryside Act of 1949

This enabling legislation made provision for the future designation of national parks in England and Wales and for access agreements and orders on the types of land recommended by the Hobhouse Committee. It also repealed the 1939 Access to Mountains Act. The two Ministries most deeply involved in the 1949 Act were those of Planning and Agriculture. When Lewis Silkin was appointed to the Ministry of Town and Country Planning, he had found that his press officer was Tom Stephenson, an RA activist and 'an Independent Labour Party colleague of some twenty years before' (Holt 1995: 23).[8] However, the landowners' agricultural lobby far outweighed this 'inside track', and the rambling movement also lost lobbying power after John Dower's death in 1947.

Under the 1949 Act the burden of applying for access rested with local authorities. This meant that access operated on a piecemeal basis and depended on local authorities not dragging their heels.[9] Under an RA-orchestrated public pressure campaign, Silkin was adamant that a clause of the 1939 Act criminalizing some types of trespass not be re-enacted: it was not. The 1949 Act continued to emphasize negotiated access in which local circumstances were given a strong role in structuring restrictions, thereby impairing full implementation of its policy of open access for particular types of open country. Open access to open country might seem a radical departure from the pre-existing network of tightly defined linear rights of way, but an evaluation of the rights granted under the 1949 Act shows otherwise.

First it is necessary to undo the bundle of meanings inhering in 'rights.' Four distinct legal advantages are seen to reside in rights: claims (claim-right), liberties (privileges), powers, and immunities (Hohfeld 1923 cited in Barker and Parry 1996; Radcliffe-Brown 1950).[10] Part V of the 1949 Act entitled the public to open access – the right to wander freely – over upland areas. What it actually provided was that 'where an access agreement or order has been made, an individual who enters without breaking or damaging any wall or fence, and who complies with the relevant bylaws and extensive restrictions contained in [other sections] of the Act *is not to be regarded as a trespasser'* (Barker and Parry 1996: 3, emphasis added). In other words, what was granted was an immunity-right not to be treated as a trespasser, rather than a claim-right of access. This negative quality regarding access again confirmed that public rights to open access 'are to be regarded as *interferences with* established private property rights, the scope and effect of which must be limited and controlled' (Barker and Parry 1996: 4 emphasis in the original).

The Act set up a National Parks Commission authorized to appoint semi-autonomous joint management boards for each park. Half the members were to represent local interests, the other half national interests. It was assumed that the local contingent would resist implementing schemes deemed in the national interest because local funds in part would underpin those schemes. The county councils were indeed loath to surrender administrative control of 'their' park areas to joint management boards. The effects of war on the home front had led to a finely honed ability to 'muddle through somehow'. This skill was now brought into play in the setting up of the national parks under Hugh Dalton, who had returned to office in 1950 as Minister of Town and Country Planning.

Between 1951 and 1957, ten national parks – substantial parts of which were common land – were established in the uplands of England and Wales. The designation of the first four in 1951 (Dartmoor, Lake District, Peak District, Snowdonia) coincided with the Festival of Britain – a celebration of Britain past, present and future. The Festival prompted a series of 13 *About Britain* guidebooks which, as the introduction to each stated, were 'handbooks for the explorer'. Each region's guidebook ended with a series of tours illustrated by strip maps that were acknowledged – in a conflation of the historical and modern – as being modeled on seventeenth-century road maps. The guidebooks were pitched not only for those living in Britain but for the 'overseas visitor' – the Canadians, Australians and New Zealanders who had left, exporting their skills, but who were now coming back to see the heart of the Empire they had recently fought for.

Dartmoor, Northumberland and the Pembrokeshire Coast were the only single-county national parks run by county council committees (MacEwen and MacEwen 1987). The Peak District National Park was the first one designated; it straddled land in six counties. It was administered from the beginning by a joint planning board. The Lake District National Park was the second designated and at the time included land in three counties. It was set up with a special authority drawn from the three county councils, each of which maintained control over its expenditures within the park.[11] Each of the remaining parks was administered by a joint advisory committee with no regulatory power vis-à-vis the county councils – each of which maintained administrative control of 'its' bit of whichever park it was in.

The 1949 Act covered both nature conservation and the management of public access to open country. The areas identified as appropriate for national park designation were extensive areas of great natural beauty that, because of their relation to population centers, afforded opportunities for a large number of people to engage in open-air recreation. Their preservation and the enhancement of their natural beauty were somehow to go hand-in-hand with the promotion of their enjoyment by the public. Just a few years after the parks' designation, Birkett wrote of the Lake District National Park in strong anti-Ruskinian tones:

> it is not a nationalised museum piece over which is written "Please do not touch"; it has not been created by faddists and cranks who worship at the shrine of natural beauty to the extent that they would put it beyond the reach of the ordinary man and woman.
>
> (Birkett 1959: 34)

Hearkening back to the two-tier approach recommended in the Addison Committee Report, the 1949 Act made provision for national nature reserves (NNRs) and sites of special scientific interest (SSSIs) 'to safeguard places with a special flora, fauna, or geology' (Lowe 1989: 125–6). These were to be under the control of the Nature Conservancy, a research and advisory body especially created by Royal Charter in 1949. Public access to NNRs was not encouraged; SSSIs were, and remain, not generally on accessible land. Provision was also made for designation of areas of outstanding natural beauty (AONBs) 'chosen on landscape grounds alone' (Lowe 1989: 125–6).

Increased demand for outdoor recreational space created enormous pressure on the national parks. In response, the 1968 Countryside Act set up country parks, picnic areas and water-based recreation facilities. Although woodland and waterways had come within the definition of open countryside in the 1949 Act, they received more emphasis in the 1968 Act, thereby increasing land potentially available for access agreements. The 1968 Act also created the Countryside Commission out of the National Parks Commission. Recognizing the inherent conflict in the 1949 Act's favoring preservation over agriculture, planning authorities were newly charged by the 1968 Act 'to give due regard to the needs of agriculture and forestry and to the economic and social interests of rural areas' (LDNPP 1986: 3).

Further development and tourist pressures on the national parks led the Government to appoint a review committee in 1971 under the chairmanship of Lord Sandford.[12] The Sandford Committee Report (1974) detailed the extent to which short-term utilitarian considerations had taken precedence over conservation. Road and housing development, extractive industry, reservoirs, increased motorized tourism had all been allowed – even encouraged – to take their toll of the national parks. The Report stated :

> The presumption against development which would be out of accord with park purposes must be strong throughout the whole of the parks; in the most beautiful parts which remain unspoiled it should amount to a prohibition to be breached only in the case of a most compelling national necessity.
>
> (LDNP Plan 1986: 4)

The Government endorsed the recommendations of the Sandford Report while acknowledging the need to address the lack of housing and job opportunities for local communities within the national parks.

A measure of the national parks' success was the staggering increase in their use. This was the recreation explosion feared by both central and local government (Blunden and Curry 1988). In tandem with the increased use of the countryside there occurred an increase in environmental awareness. The mid-1960s to mid-1970s saw the greatest expansion in the founding of national environmental groups in Britain (Lowe and Goyder 1983). Membership in voluntary environmental organizations grew from under 700,000 in 1970 to over 3¾ million in 1990 (Robinson 1992). Starting in the 1970s, and emerging from the realm of polemics to state policy, a fundamental reappraisal of agriculture's role in relation to rural economics occurred (Blunden and Curry 1988; Harvey and Whitby 1988; Hodge 1986; Robinson 1992).

The 1981 Wildlife and Countryside Act addressed the conflict between agricultural intensification and conservation of wildlife and landscape, and introduced the concept of 'management agreements' into the agri-environmental world.[13] The Act incorporated recommendations of the Sandford Report regarding clarification of national parks' statutory powers in relation to agricultural practices, modifications of public rights of way, and the national parks' obligation to prepare maps showing moor, heath, and woodland areas of particular conservation interest.

A remarkably fatuous access Bill was introduced into the House of Commons in 1983 by the Conservative MP for Banbury, Tony Baldry. His Greater Access to the Countryside Bill, which was not given a second reading, proposed giving county councils extended powers to divert footpaths for farmers' convenience, thereby facilitating access to the countryside! In return 'farmers should have a statutory duty to take all reasonable steps to mark the route of any footpath crossing their land' (Hansard 1983 (61) c. 924), which they are obliged to do anyway.

## Constructions of Citizenship

Wordsworth's terming the Lake District a 'sort of national property' prompted the question of who was worthy of inclusion in 'the nation' (Chapter 3). A succession of Reform Bills widened political access to 'the nation' as spatial access to 'the country' was pursued in Parliament (Chapter 4) and, with appropriate *caveats*, won in the post-war era (our current topic).

It is argued that in post-industrial Britain, strong identification with political party, religious affiliation or class membership has been replaced by individualism and 'self-invention' through lifestyle:

What people do with their time is increasingly a reflection of who they feel they are. What we call leisure time, is actually one of the key disposable resources in their lives, and frequently significant therefore in the meanings they give or find in their lives.

(Grove-White 1996: 2)

Recreation has been turned into a commodity and the state has redefined active leisure as no longer an element of citizen rights, but a question of means. This has led to a situation in which

... access to active living is no longer a societal goal for all, but a discretionary consumer good, the consumption of which signifies 'active' citizenship. It furthermore signifies differentiation from the growing mass of 'deviants' who are unwilling or unable to embrace this new construction of citizenship and are, therefore, increasingly denied access to active living and, hence, active citizenship.

(Ravenscroft 1994: i)

Within the arena of 'active living,' rural recreation is given a low place on the state's budgetary totem pole.[14] The sheer numbers of people pouring into the national parks, however, requires that the issue of access be addressed, for were there more generally available access to the countryside, then the parks would bear less of the brunt of visitors. As it is, the daunting numbers of visitors to the national parks lead to almost unimaginable traffic jams, a sort of Los Angeles-freeway scenario transposed to the English countryside. One humorous postcard on sale all over the Lake District shows a single-track road solid with cars backed up over the mountains. The driver of the first car, which is pulling a trailer, is saying to his passenger 'And not another car in sight too!' The Lake District National Park with its 880 square miles receives 20 million visitor days a year (Stanners and Bourdeau 1995). The nearly 600 square miles of the Peak District National Park receive 22 million visitor days a year, and it is within easy reach of some sixty percent of the present population of England. In 1996 the Lake District National Park Planning Board initiated preliminary discussions with what are called 'interested parties' about banning all vehicular traffic in the Park at the height of the summer. The very thought created strong negative responses from the shopkeepers I spoke with in various towns in the Park.

While many tourists never go much beyond the honey pots (tourist attraction areas), hundreds of thousands of people climb and fell-walk.

Not surprisingly, damage to footpaths and other rights of way in the parks is reaching epic proportions. In the Lake District, eroded footpaths appear as great gashes on the fells. In the Peak District, runnels in the peat disfigure sites such as Kinder Scout. Repairing the damage is costly. In some parts of the Lake District, stone slabs have to be helicoptered up the mountains to the repair sites. But then, even as a severely eroded footpath is stabilized, perhaps with a series of huge stone steps, even *more* people are empowered to go further up the mountain, thereby shifting the problem to even more inaccessible sites. In the Peak District, various approaches have been tried in heavily trafficked areas to prevent peat from turning to bog.[15]

One way of relieving pressure on the ten national parks is to open access to other areas. The Inheritance Tax Act of 1984 is supposed to help accomplish this by providing relief from inheritance tax to landscapes designated by the Treasury Department as 'Heritage Land-scapes', that is, those with outstanding scenic, historic or scientific interest. In return, the Heritage Landscape's new owner is expected to provide 'reasonable' public access to the land. The Act does not define what constitutes 'reasonable' public access. Figures for taxes lost to the public purse under this Act vary: one source cites £65 million between 1984/5 and 1995/6 (Whitby 1997), whereas another cites £90 million foregone between 1983/4 and 1991/2 (Pearlman 1992).

The Heritage Landscape inheritance tax relief project is a particularly clear example of the class-based, class-biased relation between landed property-owners and the state. Landowners are not obliged to institute rights of way on Heritage Landscapes, nor are Heritage Landscapes publicly listed. This makes even local knowledge – indispensable to their access/ability – even less likely. Quite clearly, there is no *quid pro quo* to the nation for taxes foregone.

Rural recreation has been promoted as an alternative, though as yet uncosted, economic activity. Access is presented as an 'income elastic' good, that is, one upon which more money is spent as incomes increase (Whitby 1997). However, costing of rural recreation is being brought into play (Watkins 1996). A quasi-market approach was introduced into agri-environmental policy in 1991 in England through the centrally funded Countryside Stewardship Scheme. Under this scheme, what a farmer seeks to sell for scheme payments is an environmental output deemed by the Countryside Commission (CC) to enhance the amenity value of the landscape (Lloyd 1992, Fraser 1996). Access is one of those amenities or public goods that are 'frequently produced as joint products (often unintended) with other (possibly private) goods' (Whitby 1997: 3). In other words, farmers' economic returns on growing crops or raising livestock are not matched by any economic return 'for providing access on traditional rights of way' crossing their property (Whitby 1997: 3).[16] By late 1997 there were over 1,200 Stewardship scheme agreements containing permissive access routes (Cooke and Gough 1997) that could be revoked at any time.

Site visits have revealed that less access has been purchased than the figures would indicate. In addition, some new access routes are poorly signed, making them difficult or impossible to find and use; some are even blocked. The Ramblers' Association (RA) has thus challenged the touted success of access purchases within this new property market. There is no public listing of farmers who have entered into Stewardship access contracts, so knowledge of access is something of a hit-or-miss affair. In short, a public policy geared towards commodification of access only served to re-privilege and re-legitimize rights of private property.

Some view the central government's funding of Stewardship farmland access as tacit presumption against open access, despite statements to the contrary. And, given the market-economy approach, there 'is a strong case for the assertion that the access question will become more, not less, important as we become wealthier' (Whitby 1997: 5). Here access and citizenship meet, and Corrigan and Sayer's concern with the 'profoundly cultural content of state institutions and activities [and] the nature and extent of state regulation of cultural forms' (with which this chapter opened) can be seen at the level of practice.

Starting in 1985 with a single protest walk at Edale, the RA subsequently organized local protest walks across the country each September to highlight areas where access is forbidden. They have been billed as Forbidden Britain Days, Woodland Walks Days, Open Britain Days and, most recently, Access Days. By whatever name, they occasioned much press and television coverage for the RA, not all of which was friendly. The RA's new-found overt combativeness was directly linked in some articles to its 'communist' roots in the 1932 Mass Trespass (Farndale 1995), and has provided material for writers, cartoonists and photographers.[17] The day after the Government proposed the greatest extension of the public right to roam in open country, cartoonists responded (see figures 16 and 17). In an indication of how naturalized the Ramblers'-driven access issue had become, landscape imagery was used to carry other political messages (see figure 18). At issue in this case was whether shareholders in the privatised utilities would receive dividends under a Labour Government. Whatever mileage the RA's confrontational stance gave cartoonists, it also managed to alienate some of its more conservative members.

In December 1995 the RA published a consultation document entitled *A Draft Access to the Countryside Bill*. It sought freedom to roam on foot in open country (as defined in the 1947 and 1968 Acts), except where particular conditions required temporary prohibition orders such as shooting (limited to twelve days in any calendar year), exceptional weather conditions likely to result in fire, lambing, and the protection of floral or faunal restoration efforts (RA 1995).

As defined in the draft Bill, open country included woodlands, cliffs, riversides and foreshores, and brought Forestry Commission woods back into the open country category on a statutory footing. Included in this last category were many of the woods sold off by the Commission over the years to which access had been subsequently rescinded. The freedom to roam that the draft Bill sought categorically did not include the freedom to tramp across agricultural land sown to crops or people's gardens. However, opponents to the draft Bill sought to present it otherwise, and again, cartoonists had a field day.

**Figure 16** Charles Griffin, 27 February 1998, "Excellent, Simkin . . ." *The Express* (London) University of Kent at Canterbury, Centre for the Study of Cartoons and Caricature, and Charles Griffin

**Figure 17** Steve Bell, 27 February 1998, "No rights, no roams . . ." *The Guardian* (London) University of Kent at Canterbury, Centre for the Study of Cartoons and Caricature, and Steve Bell

**Figure 18** Nicholas Garland, 19 September 1989, "Privatisation – Keep Out." *The Independent* (London), University of Kent at Canterbury, Centre for the Study of Cartoons and Caricature, and Nicholas Garland

In a barely concealed attempt to forestall possible access legislation, a counter-proposal, called *Access 2000*, was issued in November 1996 by The Country Landowners' Association (CLA) (MacNicol 1996). This called for a process of lengthy assessment leading to voluntary agreements. Giving tacit support to the notion that access is an interference with private property rights, *Access 2000* turned aside any notion of a claim-right to access, and placed itself behind the quasi-market approach. CLA openly acknowledged later that it 'does not support the creation of a statutory Right to Roam' (Etchell 1997 n. p.)

The British Mountaineering Council (BMC) entered the debate by publishing its own *Access Charter* in February 1997, a much less sophisticated document than the RA's draft *Access Bill*. What is interesting from the perspective of this ethnohistorical work is something in the BMC's *Charter* notes which reads as if it were from the 1833 Committee on Public Walks mentioned in the previous chapter:

(1) Climbing, mountaineering and hillwalking, in common with other forms of countryside recreation are of great benefit

(1.3) to society in general: by enhancing the mental, physical and spiritual health of individual participants these activities help promote a healthier nation; by *engendering a spirit of adventure* and self-reliance, the wider community benefits in many ways, from crime reduction to the stimulation of enterprise.

(BMC 1997 n.p., emphasis added)

Manifestations of that 'spirit of adventure' have led to intergenerational use-issues in the national parks, where there is a statutory presumption of 'quiet enjoyment'. Controversy has been caused by the growing popularity of mountain biking, much of it motorized,[18] the use of off-road vehicles and the presence of motorboats on the lakes. Military low-flight training exercises over the LDNP have been an unresolved use issue for years.

After a year's consultation with RA members and numerous organizations, an Access to the Countryside Bill was introduced into Parliament in 1997 by Paddy Tipping, MP for Sherwood and a longtime RA member. It did not get past its first reading, which was much as RA had expected, given a Conservative Government. Prior to the general election of 1997, the leaders of all three political parties committed themselves to access legislation in the following session, although without detailing exactly what form that legislation would take. Tipping introduced the RA Access Bill again in 1998, this time under the new

Labour Government; but once again there was no real debate and it did not get beyond its first reading.

In February 1998 The Government issued a consultation paper, *Access to the open countryside in England and Wales*. It gave landowners three months to come up with a voluntary code for access to private uncultivated land – mountain, moorland, heath and registered common land, but not including the woodlands, cliffs, riversides and foreshores as the RA had hoped. The Countryside Commission (CC) – the Government's countryside and landscape advisor – responded that 'access on this scale will represent a significant cultural change' and that

> Open access legislation should provide three freedoms ... freedom for the public to explore open countryside on foot without any unnecessary constraints on their free movement; freedom for individual owners and occupiers to close this land temporarily on accepted grounds where this is necessary for land management reasons – without seeking prior approval; and freedom for the statutory agencies to limit access if this is essential to protect particularly sensitive wildlife or historic sites.
>
> (CC: 1 June, 1998: 1)

The CC saw the need for 'education and persuasion [in order] to ensure that visitors and landowners respond positively and constructively to the new arrangements', and suggested that such education be introduced into 'the National Curriculum' (CC, 1 June, 1998: 1). What could speak more clearly of the 'profoundly cultural content of state institutions and activities' (Corrigan and Sayer 1985: 2).

At the same time, CC pushed for a 'more flexible approach' to linear rights of way, one that would be less expensive, less time-consuming, less confrontational. Its proposed *Paths 21* would be a cost-effective 'network of paths that meets the needs of the next century, and not one that is the result of historic demand' (CC 12 June, 1998: 1). Could this be a return to Tony Baldry's 1983 failed Greater Access to the Countryside Bill, which would have putatively rationalized legal rights of way out of existence, replacing historic paths with ones more convenient to the farmers?

*Paths 21* is part of a new look at countryside planning that calls into question certain received ideas. It allows that under this new kind of planning there will not be as much countryside left.[19] This, when more and more people are seeking access? When one can hardly open a British newspaper without reading of a new motorway tearing up some piece of common land fought for and protected in the past? When the Council for British Archaeology has felt compelled to call for farm subsidies to be linked with environmental protection in order to prevent farmers receiving 'Class Consents' permitting them to deep-plough Mesolithic, Roman and Civil War sites with impunity?

Greenbelts are being brought under the same economic scrutiny to determine whether they 'help or hinder sustainable development, [what] their impact [is] on the *efficient* use of resources (land, minerals, water, etc.), [and whether] they help us think and plan sensibly for the long term' (CC, 19 September 1998: 1, emphasis added). 'Efficiency' from whose perspective? In the same web document there is a proposal to 'create the right setting for towns'. All towns should:

> sit in well managed countryside. Development plans need restraint policies on urban growth and positive objectives for the countryside around towns. Every town and city should develop a Greenspace programme, so that everyone, *including socially excluded groups*, has access to, and is able to enjoy, open space near their homes.

> (CC, 19 September 1998: 1, emphasis added)

Is this perhaps not also a way of keeping the socially excluded groups in place and out of the wider English countryside? This is after all the group most affected by the lack of public transportation into the open landscape. Perhaps they will settle for Millennium Greens for which the CC obtained a £10 million grant from the National Lottery? By the year 2000, a Charitable Trust will be administering and maintaining in England some 250 community-based and -organized Millennium Greens.

Vociferous demands for open and linear access within and beyond national park boundaries have been met by equally vociferous protests over urban infringement on a country way of life. (By all those 'uneducated visitors' from the cities and towns, perhaps?) An economic argument has been advanced against proposed bans on foxhunting, conjuring up the specter of unemployed saddlers, hunt tailors, grooms and dog handlers, and the putting down of hunting packs.[20] In July 1997 a crowd estimated at 100,000 demonstrated against a Private Member's Bill that would have banned the hunting of wild mammals with dogs. In March 1998, over 250,000 'country' people, led by red-coated huntsmen, descended upon Hyde Park in a march organized by The Countryside Alliance. The presence of landowning interest groups served to undercut the presentation of 'The Countryside March', as it was called, as representing rural workers. Nothing could quite disguise the fact that it was a protest against the introduction of legislation that would ban foxhunting.[21]

Sections of The Criminal Justice and Public Order Act (1994) were a response to hunt saboteurs. Section 68 of the Act made a new criminal offence of aggravated trespass, by which was meant trespass with the intent to intimidate persons engaging in lawful activity on land or to obstruct or disrupt that activity. But a wider net was cast through Sections 70 and 71 of the Act that dealt with 'trespassory assemblies.' These are defined as groups of twenty or more persons intending to assemble 'on land in the open air to which the public has no right of access or only a limited right of access.' Those exercising their rights under the 1949 Act could thus be caught in the sweep of Sections 70 and 71 of the 1994 Act.[22]

The antagonism between country and town can be seen in the November 1995 launching of the Countryside Movement, an organization whose posters indicated that they were dedicated to 'Putting the Country's Side' on issues of recreational access, the national importance of farmers, and farmers' role as the real people who take care of the countryside.[23]

Another indicator of the conflict between agriculture and leisure is the

> growing tendency to confine a large proportion of countryside leisure pursuits to officially defined and administered recreation areas, in a controlled extension of the notion of national parks. [Although it has produced] substantial benefits to outdoor recreational amenity . . . it has also, ironically, helped to perpetuate the practice of exclusion from vast tracts of open countryside, as well as the 'stopping-up' of public rights of way, particularly in arable districts and around the urban fringes.
>
> (Taylor 1997: 275)

Conversely, the CC acknowledges the tremendous economic value of recreational activities in the countryside, particularly leisure walking which generates 'up to £2 billion of visitors spending for the local economy" (Ashcroft 1998: 2). The central dilemma is that rural communities cannot get the economic benefits of tourism and recreational activities such as walking, without bearing the burden of increased access.

Cutting across the the push and pull of proposals for access legislation and counter proposals meant to forestall such action, the Government issued its *Access to the Countryside in England and Wales: Framework for Action* in March 1999 and a consultation paper *Improving Rights of Way in England and Wales* in July 1999. They outlined the Government's intention to legislate access to open countryside and extend the present network of rights of way. Local and national level 'access forums' were to be set up, bringing together all interested parties for consultative input to a proposed Countryside Bill that, among other things, would establish a statutory right of access and the freedom to roam over certain types of open uncultivated land. The Government hedged as to when that Bill would be introduced into Parliament. However, the Queen's speech of November 17th, 1999 introduced that Countryside Bill thus advancing the long struggle for access and freedom to roam. The relative weight of contesting interests will determine the shape of the final piece of legislation and its (probably phased) implementation at national and local level.

## Conclusion

Private property relations are rooted in control of and access to land. Tensions inevitably preceded proposals for superimposing national parks on private land. Even the great stretches of common land that fall within national park boundaries are not necessarily open to all comers. Indeed, they never have been. Paradoxically, a cultural nationalism rooted in landscape fostered a rural–urban divide, while aesthetics, agriculture and recreation make for an uneasy partnership of interests. Attempts to order these multiple sets of conflicting needs and demands seem only to have codified the conflicts, not settled them. Perhaps no settlement is possible, or perhaps the cost of the settlement is too high. Questions of public good tend to get short shrift in the market place.

The long history of denial of access to and control of movement across the English landscape is a process still very much in the making. In as densely populated and highly urbanized a country as England, open land is an extremely scarce resource. Contestation, state regulation and ultimately commoditization of that resource is hardly surprising. English NGO's and policy-makers remain locked in historically determined, narrowly conceived ideas of leisure, and 'have difficulty in according leisure its true social significance' (Grove-White 1996: 2). The following ethnographic chapters explore the social significance of fell-walking – one aspect of leisure which is dependent upon access.

As regards recreational walking,

> ... acclamation of the substantial practical achievements and social and political significance of a British outdoor movement, founded on a locally nuanced progressive core ideology, does not represent a Whiggish or triumphalist affirmation of the irreversible consummation of an idea. Many of the objectives continue to be frustrated, while gains are often counteracted by losses. Regressive conservative forces within the movement itself, sustained by a strong compromising tendency, have militated persistently against the unified effort needed to pursue the interests of walkers, mountaineers, and touring cyclists. Footpath and access campaigners are fighting much the same battles at the end of the twentieth century as they were in the 1820s.
>
> (Taylor 1997: 273–4)

If the same battles are being fought, the introduction of a Countryside Bill in late 1999 carried them into a new arena.

# Notes

1. Urban Districts were defined as a county's smaller towns. The larger towns and the cities were county boroughs – administrative 'islands' within a county. (Pepler 1950).

2. The commons tend to be either demonized (the source of economic hardship, the remedy for which is privatization) or romanticized (everyone working on the commons in social harmony and ecological equilibrium). Common property does not necessarily equate to open access; the commons are often highly managed and regulated. The central question, as is shown in various edited collections of commons studies, is 'who gets access to what, and when' (Acheson and McCay 1987; Bromley 1992; Lees and Ortiz 1992; Taylor 1995).

3. Like the pseudo-travel afforded by panoramas, selections from *Recording Britain* were exhibited around the country in an attempt to cut down on what its organizers termed 'unnecessary' holiday train travel and petrol use. The term 'Britain' was a misnomer, for only England and Wales were covered and even then Wales was far from adequately addressed. A separate scheme dealt with Scotland. The project was undertaken with money from the American-funded Pilgrim Trust (Mellor, Saunders and Wright 1990). George Trevelyan

persuaded the Pilgrim Trust also to make donations to the National Trust for the purchase of properties and land (Cannadine 1992). He returned the favor as it were when, at the suggestion of Helen Lowenthal of the Victoria and Albert Museum, he helped organize the Attingham Summer School. Under the aegis of the National Trust, and with Trevelyan supervising the tutorials, in 1952 the first group of American collectors and scholars toured National Trust and privately owned great eighteenth-century English country houses, viewing their collections, architecture and settings in highly privileged conditions.

4. Abrams' edited collection of articles on the National Parks is interesting for the affinal and organizational connections it reveals. At the time of its publication Abrams was Secretary of the National Parks Commission; the book was dedicated 'To the Memory of John Dower and H.H. Symonds'.

John Dower (1899–1947), an architect involved in planning, had been the Honorary Drafting Secretary to CPRE's Standing Committee on National Parks. When invalided out of the armed forces, he served as a wartime civil servant in the Ministry of Works and Planning and the Ministry of Town and Country Planning where he undertook work central to the planning of national parks. He also designed hostels in the Lake District for the YHA, and was architect to the National Camps Board.

Reverend Symonds (1885–1958) had been Drafting Secretary to CPRE's Standing Committee on National Parks, Vice President of the Friends of the Lake District, a Member of the Lake District Planning Board, Vice President of the Ramblers' Association, and Vice President of the Merseyside Youth Hostels Association.

5. A mark of the audience Birkett was addressing is that an extensive quotation from Wordsworth's *Preludes* with which the lecture ends is not referenced as being Wordsworth at all. That presumption of knowledge carried through into publication.

6. The revenge of the 'bungaloid scurf' was heard in India in the sudden sound of cheering that carried to a British Army officer's bungalow set uphill from the rank and file's barracks. It turned out to be occasioned by the news of Winston Churchill's ousting from power, and the election of a Labour Government (personal communication, Joan Vincent).

7. After a brief stint as MP for Wells in 1923–4, Hobhouse (1886–1965) had been a member of Somerset County Council from 1925, and its Chairman since 1940. He became Chairman of the County Councils Association in 1946. The county councils did not want to give up park-planning authority to joint planning boards because they would also be giving up the central government funds slated for the parks. Coming from the County Councils Association, it was assumed that Hobhouse would be able to negotiate this problem.

8. In a sort of celebration of the Act that promised to bring access within reach, 1949 also saw the publication of *Lovely Britain: A description in words*

*and pictures of the beauties and interests of the British countryside* co-edited by Stephenson and S.P.B. Mais.

9. The authority vested in local government to negotiate access agreements has been used infrequently: 'The House of Commons Environment Committee (1995) reports about 48 such agreements in the national Parks' (Whitby 1997). An Access Agreement to the Peak District's Kinder Scout was only signed in 1958, seven years after the designation of the Peak District National Park. This brought its panoramic views into public access 58 years after the securing of the panoramic views from London's Richmond Hill (see Chapter 4). Differently timed protection of views for different classes of viewers.

10. The interwar period saw the 'search for order' through engagement in studies of law and disorder. Hohfeld was one of the numerous scholars engaged in such comparative or historical jurisprudence, some of whose work entered anthropology (Vincent 1990).

11. Only with the reorganization of local government in 1974 was the multi-county council planning board replaced by the Lake District Special Planning Board–National Park Authority. Set now entirely within the new county of Cumbria, the park includes parts of four District Councils. Most of the common land in the LDNP came within the former Lakes Urban District, which through the 1925 Law of Property Act ensured public access to many of the fells and mountains. Unlike the rest of the national parks, 41.3 percent of the land within the LDNP is publicly owned (Poore and Poore 1987). This does not mean, however, that there is unrestricted access to all of that land.

12. At the time of his appointment, Lord Sandford, the Reverend John Cyril Edmondson (b.1920), had served as Parliamentary Secretary in the Ministry of Housing and Local Government, and was the Parliamentary Under-Secretary of State in the Department of the Environment. He remained involved in regional planning and environmental education up through the 1980s, including serving in an advisory capacity to Countrywide Holidays Association (the renamed Cooperative Holidays Association – CHA – founded by the Reverend T.E. Leonard). Sandford was also Vice President of the Youth Hostels Association from 1979 to 1990.

13. Management agreements as they operated for quite a while in England paid farmers to *not* do environmentally damaging things which in many cases they would not have thought of doing were it not for specific Ministry of Agriculture subsidies *to* do those things.

14. Curiously enough, the Ordnance Survey's recently-released CD-ROM, *Interactive Atlas of Great Britain*, covering the country at the scale of 1 inch to 10 miles, and 1 inch to 4 miles (plus zoom capacity), does not show footpaths.

15. These have included wooden walkways set on styrofoam support pads. Unfortunately, the styrofoam soon started to break apart at the edges. Another approach was introduced on the coast-to-coast walk in the Yorkshire Dales

National Park in 1996. Infra-red 'rambler-counters' were installed on stiles to monitor usage. When usage went beyond what was considered the path's environmentally sustainable capacity, walkers were directed on to other less fragile routes (Wainwright 1996).

16. While the purchase of new permissive access routes is one thing, paying farmers to produce the public goods of access to traditional rights of way begs the question of traditional rights of way being just that – legal rights of way. Some farmers maintain that they suffer an economic loss through access (traditional and definitive, or new and permissive) for which they want preemptive grant aid. Economic losses come about through gates being left open which allows livestock to wander and damage crops, and costs the farmer time in gathering livestock together again; footpaths not being kept to, causing growing crops to be trampled; and unleashed dogs harrying livestock.

17. Cartoons have portrayed access in relation to class, privacy, political party and religion. One by Jak, published in the *Evening Standard* on 30 September 1991, showed three shotgun-carrying landowners outside one of their stately homes. By the side of a 'no trespassing' notice board are the bodies of ramblers, Ordnance Survey maps in hand, neatly stretched out like so many brace of grouse or pheasant. The caption reads, 'Not a bad bag old boy, after all it was only our first ramblers shoot!' Rights of way have on occasion been illegally built over. This has given rise to cartoons showing ramblers demanding to pass through dining rooms or bathrooms (usually with buxom women in the tubs) because they have discovered that a right of way passes through the house. Other cartoons play on that part of the Lord's Prayer which goes, 'forgive us our trespasses as we forgive those who trespass against us'. Other cartoons work on the theme of trespassing ramblers about to be shot at, executed, or taken hostage by farmers. A 1930s illustration has recently been reissued as a postcard. Showing ramblers kicking, punching and throttling gamekeepers, its caption reads 'Even the Little Steepingford Ramblers' Association was not without its hooligan element'. It inverts a photograph taken during the 1932 Mass Trespass at Kinder Scout and published in the *Sheffield Daily Telegraph* (reproduced in Hill 1980), which shows ramblers bent around and helping an injured gamekeeper who had twisted his ankle.

18. The English landscape has been rendered strangely personal in being portrayed as '*disadvantaged* in its ability to provide for this sport' (emphasis added) unlike the 'the desolate wilderness areas of the United States' in which the sport arose (McGowan 1996: 2). The same author dismisses the controversy about mountain-bike use in national parks as a 'perceptual problem' on the interpersonal level because it is based solely on anecdotal evidence. But he acknowledges that a real problem exists in relation to erosion and disturbance of wildlife. A group I was walking with in the Lake District was forced off a steep mountain track by several motorized mountain bikers. One bike broke

down as it was being gunned over a boulder. Its owner could not get it to work again. The group broke into cheers as it was realized that he would have to carry the thing for the rest of the day.

19. Somehow there will be a 'net environmental gain from all development. . . . Though [the countryside] may not be quite as extensive, it should grow in quality to compensate for what is lost in quantity' (CC, 19 September 1998: 1).

20. The anti-hunt movement, which grew stronger in the late twentieth century, received a major boost at one point when the National Trust reluctantly banned stag hunting on all NT property. Whereas in the past fox-hunting was a countryside ritual enactment of power and possession, in the contemporary landscape it smacks of nostalgia and dispossession. Perhaps the still-maintained tradition in the Lake District of only following the hounds on foot maintains an element of a more democratic localized culture. Given the terrain, there are no scarlet-clad hunters thundering around on horseback. If you want to hunt with Lake District hounds, then you have to be prepared to make it up the fellsides. On the occasion I bumped into a Lake District hunt, the fox was not caught.

21. A week later, the Bill failed to make it to the statute books as opponents introduced hundreds of amendments and made lengthy speeches that used up the allotted debate time. Given that sightings of foxes are now quite common in urban settings in England, perhaps the fox is playing the Country-side Alliance at its own game and is moving into town.

22. Also at stake are intergenerational use-issues. Mass outdoor festivals of Travellers exist outside the official discourses of countryside leisure activities. Such festivals do speak to leisure preferences of a generation that is discounted and whose activities are now criminalized. The hedging-around of access privileges the already privileged, and promulgates their point of view. The Travellers' festivals are another instance of mass gatherings of the disaffected.

23. A national advertising campaign introducing the Countryside Movement featured posters that juxtaposed large artwork images with contrary messages. An image of the Yorkshire Dales was captioned 'While You're Trying to Save the Brazilian Rainforest The British Countryside is Disappearing'; an outsize image of a hand cupped around a small dead mammal carried the caption 'the Killer is a Male, White Collar Worker, Probably in His Late Forties Who Lives and Works in an Industrial Town'; a portrait of a man in a rubber apron was captioned 'George Roberts, Head Slaughterman and Animal Lover.' The message they carried was that the five million or so people who live and work in rural Britain have been unable to make their voices heard in countryside matters even though they are the 'best qualified to look after it'. CM wanted to 'start the process of rebuilding the understanding that used to exist between town and country'.

# Part III

# Ethnographic

Your life depends to some extent on your shoes; care for them properly. But a quarter of an hour each day is enough, for your life depends on several other things as well.

René Daumal 1974: 118

"To ___ on Her First Ascent to the Summit of Helvellyn":

Inmate of a mountain-dwelling,
Thou has clomb aloft, and gazed
From the watch-tower of Helvellyn;
Awed, delighted, and amazed . . .
Maiden! now take flight; – inherit
Alps or Andes, they are thine . . .
For the power of hills is on thee,
As was witnessed by thine eye
Then, when old Helvellyn won thee
To confess their majesty!

William Wordsworth 1816

I have been examining the shifts and turns in the cultural production of identity as it takes place in and through landscape, especially in relation to the Lake District and the Peak District. The point of this prologue is to locate fell-walking in the Lake District as I have experienced it doing fieldwork in the spring, summer and autumn months of 1995, 1996 and 1997. In addition to pleasantly warm dry weather that is perfect for walking, I also experienced walking and scrambling in driving rain, sleet, light snow flurries, and intense summer heat. I know nothing of fell-walking in snow and ice.

In a way there are really two Lake Districts. One I call Wordsworth-shire, compounded of drifts of daffodils, lakeside strolls, the ever-hovering presence of the National Trust's long-ago comforting world of Peter Rabbit and Mrs. Tiggy Winkle, and high teas taken in gleaming dark wood interiors set with chintz and lustreware. Despite the fact that I do know that Dorothy Wordsworth and her brother took famously long walks across the fells, Wordsworthshire exists now as a parallel universe of the bottomlands, and is not much my concern. Rather I am concerned with the Lake District of the horizon-bounding mountain ranges that seem to catch the clouds down to themselves. And unless you have slogged around them all day long in pelting rain, or even in the unusual extreme heat of recent summers, it is hard to get quite the right pitch of their ruggedness – especially if you are an American more likely to think of mountains in terms of 13,000 rather than 3,000 feet.

As has been explained in Chapter 5 in some detail, the Lake District is a roughly circular domed area only thirty-odd miles in diameter into which are crowded 180 peaks. The compactness of the Lake District means that the cumulative ascent in a day's walking can easily go over the 3,000 foot mark although there are only four peaks topping the 3,000 foot mark. Neither they nor the others are to be dismissed lightly.

The fells present themselves a little differently each time you go out on them, depending upon the season, weather conditions, your own level of physical fitness, and, not least importantly, your companions. Bringing the range of my own experience briefly into focus is intended as payment somehow for all the others' 'performances' that I watched. I want to make it clear that I was not simply watching others confronting their limits; I was in that confrontation myself. Consideration and fear sat firmly on my own shoulders as I willed myself up what were sometimes heart-poundingly steep slopes or, even worse, scrambled down frost-fissured crags in fierce blustery wind – whatever the obstacle course of the day held. Under the impact of organic impression, the boundary between the observing would-be ethnographer and the walker-as-informant thinned out. I left the privileged safety of 'audience' and became an at-risk 'fellow-actor' in the performance. My view was not only that of an onlooker but, if you will, also that of inlooker.

Britain gets its weather from the West. Set in the northwestern uplands of England, south of the border with Scotland, the Lake District gets the weather full in the face, with all the force generated by its proximity to the Irish Sea. I quickly learned this during my first fieldwork experience in the late 1980s in the Hartsop Valley, high in the central fells, with its average ninety inches rainfall a year. One year's welcome fires on June evenings and the shock of ground frosts in July, can contrast with the next year's risks of sunburn and dehydration.

The immediacy of weather conditions when walking makes for great awareness of the sky. Generally it is very active with some combination of mist, rain or cloud-cover coming in. Storms can blow up quickly, and temperatures drop rapidly, even at the height of summer. The speed at which the weather comes in can be glimpsed in the towering cloud-plumes carried by air currents breaking around a dod (a foothill). Even on seemingly stable days, weather conditions can vary enormously – both between valleys (one valley can have a hail storm, while another just a few over can be sunny), and within a two-or-three-thousand-foot change in altitude. Given the wrong combination of circumstances, death from hypothermia is a year-round risk, and the Lake District's mountain rescue teams spend almost 20,000 hours a year on their task (Lake District Mountain Rescue Team Association 1995).

But even without such circumstances, severe chilling can be experienced within minutes of stopping as, powered by the breeze, sweat-soaked clothing turns into individually tailored refrigeration units. 'Extras' come out of the backpack: wool sweaters, windproof jackets, wool hats, scarves and gloves. The 'technophiles' scoff at all this, preferring gear woven from synthetic fibers whose micro-filaments wick sweat from the body to the outer surface of the fabric where it can evaporate without any chilling effect. Having listened to the pros and cons of this rather heatedly discussed at just about every rest stop, I eventually invested fifty dollars in a wickable top and can no longer understand the technophobes' technophobia. Given the cost, however, I can understand why at least one manufacturer advertises that the fabric has received an anti-bacterial treatment 'enabling the garment to be used on multi-day activities . . . whilst still retaining some friends' (Karrimor 1994).

If there is one overarching reason why people would choose to push themselves very hard physically, often under unpleasant or even downright nasty conditions, it seems to be the glorious spectrum of views. These vary from phenomenal cloudscapes that complement the onrunning mountain ranges, to sun-shot glimpses through parting rain clouds of the lakes far below, to the non-view experience of walking through a Kurosawa-like, mist-enveloped world. At the other extreme are panoramic days such as one I shared in, rare enough that people in the group who had been walking in the Lake District for over thirty years had never seen the likes of it before. The snow-capped mountains south of Glasgow were clearly visible some seventy miles away to the north, while a quarter turn to the west revealed even further distant mountains in Ireland.

My first week of 'serious walking for purposes of research' was undertaken from Borrowdale, one of the least accessible valleys in the far west of the Lake District. It was my introduction to walking hour after hour in ongoing driving rain. Going up a path through a disused slate quarry in a light drizzle, a wall of stacked debris to the left, an open drop to the right, was nerve-racking. Coming down the same path in pelting rain led me to question my choice of topic. People did this by choice? For their holidays? Later that week, our little group went over Green Gable and came to Windy Gap. The leader, who had taken the activities manager's place just for a couple of days, indicated that I was to go down 'over there' while he attended to someone further back in the line.

I looked at the spot he had pointed to: a steep scree slope (loose surface rock). I genuinely believed he was joking. He was not. It was 'Aaron's Slack,' a 700–800-foot descent to Styhead Tarn. His response to my exclamation, 'How?', was, 'Just lean back, dig your heels in, and go!' So in the heels went and I found myself sliding three to four feet at each footstep as my bodyweight scudded me forward through the scree. I cannot say 'I' established a rhythm, not at all. It was more that the rhythm miraculously established itself. After the first few hesitant steps I ran down, grinning. Beyond the scree was a steep stone pathway down which I sped on a tiptoe run, my boots' rigidity letting me just skip from stone to stone. This was a total in-body experience, a state of grace with no fear, but rather with a heightened awareness of the body moving in perfect alignment with the visually vivid terrain, and an awareness of an observing mind that could see when the ordinary self began grabbing at the experience, threatening to shift me out of the exquisitely balanced moment of now. But 'now' was maintained over and over again as I finally ran down the grassy incline at the bottom and threw myself down to wait for the others far behind me, before swimming in the ice-cold tarn.

I have come to think of that first week's experience as being 'In the Beginning,' and I have to admit it gave me a false sense of my boots, let alone of myself. I somehow *believed* in my boots – *they* knew what they were doing, *they* had their own kind of eyes, *they* took care of me. So on another fieldtrip I asked a walking friend who is not only an extremely accomplished walker but also a climber, to take me to 'do' Striding Edge, an approach to Helvellyn that I had heard so much about but actually knew nothing of. As it turned out, after a long hot slog,

Striding Edge is a sharp, jagged knife-edged arête, one arm of the rim
of a cirque on the north-eastern slope of Helvellyn (one of the four
mountains over 3,000 feet). The other arm of the basin's rim is Swirrel
Edge. Red Tarn sits some 1,800 precipitous and rocky feet below in the
center of the basin. West of Striding Edge is a less steep but deeper
2,300-odd-foot incline to the valley floor.

At the point where I saw my friend wobble on that knife-edge in the
thrust of the wind and have to drop down to his hands and knees, I
had to make my way off the top and down to a parallel footpath.
Regaining my nerve I went back to the top, but it was beyond me to
look at the views. What I saw with my peripheral vision warned me
not to bother. The arête negotiated, there is still a bit of a scramble up
Helvellyn's shoulder to get to the top. Working our way around some
largish patches of snow got us into scree. At one point my leading foot
stepped on a rock that promptly went out from under me and I started
falling down the tarn-side slope. I heard, as if at a great distance,
someone screaming. It was my self spread-eagled as the scree slid
fractionally past my face while I dug in with my boots and fingers for
a hold, which my boots found. In the intense silence, I experienced
sheer incredulity at what had happened and where I now found myself.

My companion climbed down to me, while another man some thirty
or so feet below positioned himself to break my fall if I slipped again. I
was helped off the scree and, tremendously shaken, made to continue
to the top immediately. After a few steps on the sloping top of Helvellyn
I sat down and refused to budge. I would not walk the last couple of
hundred yards to the top of Helvellyn for the much-touted view – all I
could think was 'the mountain can keep its sodding views!' Black and
blue from the top of my boots to the top of my hips and totally drained
of energy, I managed the five-hour walk out over Dollywagon Pike,
down more steep scree to Grisedale Tarn and out through the long
valley in silence, even when I tripped over the rock equivalent of a
toffee paper and went crashing full-length to the ground, just missing
hitting my head on a boulder. I had gone almost full circle – for had
the first fall been longer or on my back, or the second fall worse, it
would have been the Patterdale Mountain Rescue team that would have
been called out, the team founded in 1964 by the Hartsop Valley's Dr.
James Ogilvie, whose ashes had been scattered from the top of Helvellyn
just days before my 'doing' Striding Edge.

Fieldwork 'After the Fall' was literally plagued by nightmares. Even
walking along the simplest of contour tracks provoked anxiety, and
steep scrambles held a kind of terror. It took a while to regain even

some of my previous sense of ease and balance. It is between these two poles of experience, of physical exhilaration and physical terror, that my fieldwork has been undertaken. From within their parameters I have been able to relate to what other fell-walkers expressed about their senses of accomplishment, about pushing up to their limits, and about why they bother doing this. It is due to their camaraderie and encouragement that there is anything to report – for my work in the Hartsop Valley had not prepared me for this kind of fell-walking. It had been carried out under my own steam with no one to see or comment on my lack of experience.

My time in the Hartsop Valley had itself dredged up a then nearly twenty-five-year-old memory of when in the early 1960s, aged seventeen, I had joined a rock-climbing club. Though I was not the only girl there I certainly was an oddity in not being someone's 'bird' (girlfriend). Women climbed by default.[1] Not particularly welcomed, I had continued into the winter until after one disastrously ice-slipping day (I could not afford the proper boots), the man who ran the club devastated me by announcing in earshot of everyone and in unequivocal relation to me, that now he knew what Hannibal had felt like getting the elephants over the Alps.

Only now in reading Simon Schama's *Landscape and Memory*, in which he unpacks Hannibal's act of monumental hubris and its impact on the Romantic taste for 'delightful horror' and 'moralizing mountaineering' (Schama 1996: 422), have I remembered that I had again forgotten. Perhaps it was no coincidence that any mountain-walking in the subsequent twenty-five years had been done in Greece, an environment far away from ice and upper-class Englishmen. Perhaps my choice of topic is somehow trying to get over the Alps again in a more dignified manner. At least I have had better boots on my feet this time in gathering this bird's-eye set of views.

# Notes

1. In a session of the 1974 National Mountaineering Conference entitled 'The Mountaineer and Society,' it is commented upon with a certain degree of self-satisfaction, and couched in terms of the 'healthy heterosexual debauchery that characterises the climbing community today' that 'there are many more

girls' climbing than there used to be. Then, in a shift of terminology, the speaker continued: 'women are not yet on the scene on their own terms . . . but there are now women who are defined as climbers and not just as "so-and-so's-bird"' (Cook 1974). That it required comment shows what rare birds they indeed were.

# Re-Siting/Sighting/ Citing the View

The modern anthropologist Victor Turner operates with a set of opposi-
tions similar to Virgil's in his discussion of the relationship between
the structured, hierarchical world of the city and state, and that of
*"communitas"*, which builds upon a feeling of egalitarian brotherhood.
The two forms of social organisation are, conceptually and experientially,
mutually incompatible, with the result that they must be mediated by
myth and ritual. The passage from one to the other takes place via a rite
which allows one to cross the limen or invisible boundary between them.
A pilgrimage is a very literal form of such passage in which people often
move from urbanised core areas of the state, to rural areas which are
often perceived to be the core of the ancient national homeland of a
given people within a state. Through the process of travelling together
by primitive means and in common dress, people form ties which cross
social boundaries.

Olwig 1993: 326–7

Rambling is . . . a culture and a craft . . . an intense love for one's own
country, the innermost and the most remote parts of it . . . It is a love
. . . which cannot be exhausted, a love which . . . compels a devotion
and adoration which is equal to some men's religion.

Ward 1934–5 quoted in Hill 1980: 32

The National Parks have been called the last jewel in the nation's crown.
Their heartland, "the remote and fortifying Commons", stand aloof and
untouched. Up here, what came to be called "Thatcher's Britain" seems
very small indeed; and a clearer view emerges – it is not "Their" Britain
but Ours.

Reed 1991: 7

We crave the comforts and conveniences of civilisation, but if this means wholly abandoning contact with the visual symbols of the habitat to which we still properly belong, we may become like the lion in its cage ... reduced to the neurotic behavior of pacing backwards and forwards because something is deeply wrong. .... *Exploration*, in short, is one of the most fundamental kinds of survival behaviour, and we are powerfully motivated to put it into practice because it is in our nature to want to do so. .... Placed in this context the great cultural stream of art and literature which fixed attention on the Lake District can be seen, not as some parallel stream of experience, alternative to that of the climber or fell-walker, but as part and parcel of the same thing.

Appleton 1986: 119–22

Man was meant to, designed to roam twenty-odd miles from his cave; all this technology and being by-passed by more up-to-date stuff all the time, all the stress – no! – walking was how it was meant to be, gets you to the elementals – do I hurt, am I hungry, do I want to pee. That's why I love walking – it's just you and your body and the elements.

Martin F. 1996

## Introduction

The preceeding six chapters dealt with historical processes spanning some 250 years in the cultural construction of the Lake District. Those processes turned on the issue of access to and ways of looking at the landscape. Running parallel, and deepening the issue of access to the commons, was the social movement for political access. I now turn to a small-scale study of the popularity of fell-walking in the Lake District among a group of mostly urban people. This is the most recent manifestation of that earlier imagining of, engagement with and accessing to this landscape, this cultural terrain, this version of England.

My multi-sited and locationally mobile ethnography of fell-walkers does not fit the mold of a conventional study of a British community (Arensberg and Kimball 1940; Bell 1994; Cohen 1985; Fox 1967; Frankenberg 1957, 1966; Mewett 1986; Strathern 1981; Williams 1956). It is neither locationally static, nor does it cover an annual cycle, and kinship plays no central role. Far from being an ethnography of the 'involuntarily localized "other"' (Appadurai 1988: 16), it is a study of a dis/located community of feeling made up of people who, returning to the Lake District over years – even decades – demonstrate not only affective affiliation to a non-quotidian locale, but also to the fluid form of this social field. It is also about access, the inclusions and exclusions of community, specifically, temporally bounded communities of walkers. Although conceptualized in quite different registers, access to the landscape, political access, and access to community, individually and jointly articulate a politics of access.

In this re-siting of the field of fieldwork, the feeling of 'local distinctiveness [obtainable through] indigenous perception of the locality' (Cohen 1982: 1) that is of such importance to British social anthropology is turned on its head. For at issue here is the distinctiveness of this upland locality as perceived and experienced by temporary and mostly urban incomers. That this sort of community and locality lacks the 'purity' of a typical fieldsite or object of study speaks to assumptions about the discipline and its practice, the conventions of which are under ever more interrogation (Gupta and Ferguson 1997). This study is not only part of an emergent trend towards multi-sited ethnography, but given its broadly based ethno-historical framing, belongs to a movement to locate such work within an interdisciplinary sphere (Marcus 1995).

## Research Populations and Research Methods

The *General Household Survey* of 1990 revealed that a little more than twenty million people in Britain consider walking as their main outdoor activity. Granted the great variation in meaning – from walking the dog in the local park on a Sunday afternoon, to day-long walks or a week of walking – the figure does indicate to what extent Ramblers' Association local and national activities (such as maintaining footpaths and pushing for access) affect a far greater percentage of the population than the RA membership itself (which stands at around 185,000).

Commercially organized recreational walking outfits advertise in membership-organization magazines, commercial magazines catering to walkers, on maps such as 'Britain for Walkers' (published by the British Tourist Authority), in monthly newspapers put out by separate national parks, through local Tourist Authority bureaus, and on web sites. These sources serve the people who purchase over three million walking holidays in Britain each year. A combination of longevity and early retirement is fueling an ever-expanding market for such leisure activity.

I gathered addresses of walking holiday organizations from a variety of printed and electronic sources and made bookings from among the brochures I was sent, choosing of necessity from among the lowest-priced holidays. The cost per week ranged between £225 and £308 ($360 and $493). I received brochures in which Lake District weeks cost between £600 and £800 ($960 and $1280). Meals, accommodation and size of groups were quite different in those cases; the itinerary was the same. They reflect one aspect of the commoditization of walking. What follows therefore is drawn from a limited segment of the walking holiday market.

Historical research conducted for this and my previous work in the Lake District (Darby 1988) made me want to understand the role of walking holidays and clubs in creating social networks and a sense of community. Given the historical intensity of class antagonism in relation to dispossession from and access to the landscape, I also wanted to see whether walking groups cut across class. Interest in attitudes, beliefs and perceptions about environmentally responsible politics and decline of the environment stemmed from research I had undertaken on regional and local implementation of agri-environmental European Union policy. I thought it might be possible to catch sight of these issues from the ground up. In the course of fieldwork, issues of group dynamics, gender and race became foregrounded.

The core study population consisted of about 120 people with whom I walked some 400 miles in one-, two- and three-week stretches in the Lake District over the course of 1995, 1996 and 1997. None of these people lived in the Lake District. With the exception of six holiday-makers from Western Europe, all the people I walked with were British, and virtually all of them were English. We were on walking holidays (at the lower end of the price range) run by national organizations such as Countrywide Holidays Association (CHA) and the Ramblers' Association (RA), and by privately-run walking outfits. Fellow-walkers are referred to by a first name pseudonym except where permission was given to identify them.

Each group walked together for a week, returning in the evenings to a fixed locale for common evening activities in most cases. The houses varied in style: large Victorian piles situated on their own grounds outside villages; a Swiss-style lodge built in a relatively inaccessible valley by a walking organization in the 1930s at the height of the hiking craze; an early twentieth-century house overlooking Buttermere with wonderful views of the Lake through its enormous plate-glass windows; a converted barn. The weeks started on Saturday afternoons; on one mid-week day off, walkers shopped, visited tourist sites, took their own walks, or rested. At the CHA houses, two or three groups operated simultaneously. Each group of around twelve to twenty-five people, walked at a different level of difficulty (4 to 6 miles a day with 500 to 800 feet of ascent, 7 to 9 miles a day with 2,000 to 2,500 feet of ascent, or 10 to 14 miles a day with 2,500 to 3,000 or more feet of ascent). People were free to move between groups; few did.

To minimize observational and quantitative biases and to obtain means for comparison, I walked with Holiday Fellowship (HF) from their Dovedale, Peak District house, and with locally based walking clubs at Coventry, Oxford, Colwyn Bay (North Wales), and Kendal (in the Lake District). Like CHA, HF offers three walks of different levels each day, and shared evening activities. The comparison population also numbered around 120 people. I complemented participant-observation with a questionnaire survey of both populations (see the Appendix, p. 287). I gave the questionnaire to 110 people. Fifty were completed by people in the core population, and fifty-two in the comparison population. Given the length of the questionnaire – some fifty-six questions – the 97 percent response rate speaks to the interest walkers had in being an object of study.

There were no young families and few people under thirty-five years of age in either population (12 percent of the core and 3.8 percent of the comparison). The average age of the core population was forty-three and there were slightly more males than females (52 percent to 48 percent). Retirees accounted for 20 percent of the group, of whom 2 percent were widowed. The average age of the comparison population was fifty-two, and there were considerably more males than females (59.6 percent to 40.4 percent A comment made to me on several occasions by men in the comparison population was that their wives could no longer do the kind of walking they had done when younger and so only joined some of the shorter walks or the weekend away trips. Retirees accounted for 61.5 percent of this population and 13.5 percent of this population were widowed. Putting single, separated, divorced and widowed into category 'A' and partnered and married into category 'B' showed that both populations had a large minority of people in category 'A' – 44 percent of the core and 35 percent of the comparison population.

A crosstabs comparison of professional, managerial, academic, white-collar, blue-collar and manual worker distribution between the two populations showed no statistically significant difference between them. An interesting disparity between the populations emerged in household income, not in what it actually was – that could not really be determined – but in the missing response rate for this question which jumped from 8 percent for the core to 23.1 percent for the comparison population. Regardless of how the distribution and return of question-naires was organized within the groups forming the comparison population, this single question was avoided – in some groups almost completely.

There were seven income categories. While 45 percent of the core population income responses came into the £20,000–35,000 ($32,000–56,000) category, the average for that population was £17,100 ($27,360). The average of the income data received for the comparison population was £12,627 ($20,203). The lower four categories were quite similar between the two populations, with the exception of a three-fold increase for the comparison population in the £5,000–9,000 ($8,000–14,400) category. The comparison population suddenly 'blanked out' in the upper three categories. When the variable of gender was applied to income data, there appeared an average of £17,500 ($28,000) for male and £16,700 ($26,720) for female members of the core population; and £14,500 ($23,200) for male and £10,750 ($17,200) for female members of the comparison population.

Analysis of responses showed that variations in income had no impact on what was spent on walking gear 'this year' or 'on average': 60 percent spent under £250 ($400), 20 percent spent £251–500 ($400 to $800) and 5 percent spent more than $500 ($800), but that older people spent less. The core population spent more on purchasing walking gear and walking holidays than the comparison population. White-collar workers and older walkers participated more frequently in walks taken in England under the direction of a leader or guide. The frequency went down as income went up, until retirement was factored in. There is an acknowledged courtesy bias in opinion polls. Perhaps indicating an unacknowledged macho bias, there was a correlation between the easier level of walking (such as strolling along a bridle path) and white-collar workers and women; and a correlation between difficult level walks (such as scrambling up steep mountain slopes) and professional men.

The questionnaire ended with a series of twenty-seven statements that operated on a five-point response system with one equaling 'strongly agree' to five equaling 'strongly disagree'. A multivariate regression was run on the data using age, income, gender, marital status and occupation as explanatory variables. I was most interested in responses to three clusters of questions distributed among them. The first cluster focused on attitudes, beliefs and perceptions about environ-mentally responsible politics. Women were in greater agreement with the statements that the environment should receive priority over other issues; white-collar workers were in disagreement with those statements. Since 60 percent of white-collar workers were women, their socio-economic location can be posited as an overriding determinant of their responses. There was no difference in response between the core and comparison populations.

In the cluster of statements that focused on a perceived decline in the environment, white-collar workers disagreed with that basic perception. There was no significant difference by any other variable. Once again, there was no statistically significant difference in response between the core and comparison populations. In the cluster of statements that focused on walking and personal fulfillment, a significant correlation occurred between age and scores, indicating that older people found more fulfillment in their engagement with walking. The core population, with its 74 percent employment/self-employment rate, found less personal fulfillment in walking, as did people in managerial and academic occupational categories.

## Pasts and Presents

As a reiterated performative act, fell-walking creates personal pasts that are located in both time and place. These multiple pasts relate individuals through experiences and memories which are recited to new sets of people, intertwining people with place and forging links that cut across urban/rural, north/south and economic markers of social emplacement. For some of its practitioners, fell-walking's linking process also connects them to historical pasts such as those examined in chapters one through three. Poetry, literature or art associated with particular places in the Lake District form another layer of re-citation and re-sighting of the view.

For some, the fact of organized and organizing groups of walkers resonates quite directly with the history of the struggle for access examined in chapters four and five. For others, that struggle for access is freighted with contemporary social issues of race and gender (topics to be explored later in this and the next chapter). For them, insistence upon and experience of access to the landscape and the mountains is simultaneously a kind of cognitive mapping and a strategy of resistance.

Few of the core population were on their first walking trip in the Lake District. Although I had some familiarity with the Lake District from previous work in the Hartsop Valley, I was a novice at this organized approach to fell-walking. Most people in the core population were not. Some had been reconvening in the Lake District year after year to walk together. They did not see one another outside of the Lake District since they lived in different parts of the country. Over the years some people took walking holidays together not only in the Lake District, but elsewhere too, although again not meeting up outside the walking setting. Others, introduced to fell-walking in the Lake District as children or teenagers, had kept returning, eventually choosing to retire there in a very literal re-siting of themselves in the views they had come to know and love. These few people appeared in my comparison population which included a locally based walking club in the Lake District. Some of the Lake District core population had been taking walking holidays alone with CHA so often over the years that they had come to know other people doing likewise, and so unexpectedly met up on these week-long walks. Within these varying parameters, most people were 'returnees'.

My own different 'returnee' status cannot be exempt from examination (Hastrup 1987). Being born and brought up in England, yet having lived in America for many years, meant that my undertaking fieldwork in the north of England blurred the hierarchical separation of fieldsite and home. I occupied an uncomfortable inside-outsider position: I realized that at some inchoate level, the English landscape has remained the 'home-land' while England as a social entity is now for me a 'foreign' country. The paradox was not lost on me: I was supposedly undertaking a detached viewing of those whose involvement with the landscape I was trying to understand, but I was certainly no fly on the wall. My own reactions to people and place entered into the group dynamics to a lesser or greater extent, depending upon particular circumstances.

While it might be structurally satisfying to separate out individual topics for examination, the experience is that they were all tangled together. I have tried to bring some order to my material both by presenting a discrete week's tangle in and of itself, and also by gathering up the same strand from different weeks and presenting it under its own rubric. But before doing either, I want to frame the walking group as a rite of secular pilgrimage.

## Secular Pilgrimage

Without turning the notion of secular pilgrimage into a Procrustean bed into which any and everything will be made to fit, I do want to suggest that the patterns and processes, and the symbolics of walking create a secular parallel to pilgrimage. The density of the walking routes and walkers in the Lake District, its peripherality, multitudinous viewing points and density of popular routes, construct a secular version of the shrines and way stations in networks of intersecting pilgrimage routes that lead to topographically focused, peripherally sited pilgrimage centers (Turner 1974). Walking groups can be seen as a spatialized actualization of the three-fold classification of rituals of separation, transition and incorporation that bring the individual into the group and govern the movements of people and groups on the land (Van Gennep 1960). Locally based walking groups bring the added dimension of dealing with movement across lifetimes.

The kinds of ritual that Van Gennep addressed have been considered 'incompatible with the structure of modern urban life' (Gluckman 1962: 36–7) due to fragmentation of roles and activities, segregation of conflicts between roles, and the absence of belief that 'specialized ceremonies . . . will mystically affect the well-being of the initiands' (Gluckman 1962: 37). A walking group allows for a breaching of what is for some an urban-generated isolation, at the same time that it functions as a means of withdrawal from the world. Within the rural setting of a group of individuals walking together for a week or more, and their escape from the urban, 'solitude and society cease to be antithetical' (Turner 1974: 203).

Walk leaders spoke of the help and support that the group gives to the lonely and emotionally needy, and the help that is generated through reestablishing a physical grounding in self. Various walk leaders who also had experience in locally based walking clubs expressed the opinion that loneliness was the driving force behind many people's involvement in walking holidays and clubs. As Mark, the chairman of a large locally based walking club, who also leads for a national walking holiday outfit, put it, 'the physical exertion of walking and being in relation to nature helps people come out of their personal problems – the experience of a week's walking can function as a spiritual renewal'. This was summed up by a young man in his thirties who quite evidently to all of us was one of life's wounded.[1] In response to a survey question that asked whether 'you read novels and poetry by authors associated with the areas you walk in', he wrote in the additional comments section:

> I have . . . a particular interest in Wordsworth; I often slip into his poetry while doing other tasks. I think his poems have a quality of healing: he understands anxiety and finds ways of soothing the mind. I like him for presenting Nature as a mysterious creative power to which we can attune our psyches.

In this sense the walking group can be the site of the magico-religious element of existing 'in a special situation for a certain length of time ... between two worlds' (Van Gennep 1960: 18) – although in this case the special situation is not between 'two worlds', but is the movement into a space beyond the ordinary daily structure. This is experienced as restorative of the person, of what is damaged under the technological imperative of the ever-quickening pace of urban living.

Like pilgrimage, walking can be an experience of the process of healing and renewal. (Here I am not considering formalized systems of walking mediation which are clearly more recognizable as ritual.) Any phase in Van Gennep's classification can be more or less empha-sized in any given ritual. Taking the walk-week as a ritual, the transi-tional phase is the extended liminal period in which *communitas* can be experienced. This is the threshold state in which, if the ritual is collective in character, participants 'experience ... a spontaneously generated relationship between leveled and equal ... human beings, stripped of structural attributes' (Turner 1974: 202).

Turner's construct of *communitas*, derived from his pilgrimage data, is defined as anti-structure although 'social structure is *not* eliminated, rather it is radically simplified: generic rather than particularistic relationships are stressed' (Turner 1974: 196). *Communitas* is cosmo-politan in character as opposed to being based on local particularisms, and is experienced as 'a timeless condition, an eternal now' (Turner 1974: 238) in which one day replicates another and repetition transmits social bonds. *Communitas* is not constructed as a collectivity in opposition to another group, nor is Turner concerned with 'spon-taneous behavioral expressions of *communitas* ... such as an English pub [or] ... a group of passengers at play on an ocean voyage' (Turner 1974: 242).

If religious pilgrimage sits at one end of the spectrum of *communitas* and English pub life at the other, perhaps walking groups can be seen to occupy a midpoint that carries reflections of both. It would seem that in societies

> where this is little or no structural provision for liminality, the social
> need for escape from or abandonment of structural commitments seeks
> cultural expression in ways that are not explicitly religious, though they
> may become heavily ritualized.
>
> (Turner 1974: 260)

It has been shown in earlier chapters that access to the landscape and walkers' clubs were cultural expressions and mobile symbolic practices of resistance to work-discipline. The notion of *communitas* reinforces viewing the walking group as a form of secularized pilgrimage. As on entering upon a religious pilgrimage, there is a required loss of status based upon occupation or knowledge. It is the walk leader's occupation and knowledge that renders him (or occasionally, her) exceptional and authoritative. Participants are leveled through the drastic change in activity and the organization of time and space that center on a different set of daily rituals.

As with pilgrimage, it is the activity itself – the dropping away of familiar expectations – that creates the structure of the group, and the potential for a new structure of feeling. The meeting of physical challenges with others leads to a sense of comradeship. Making up for loss of status and power is the symbolic empowerment of the group's arrival 'at the top'. It is the journeying that consolidates community, both synchronically and diachronically.

Particular routes lead to key objects to be seen from specific vantage points. Sighting of those key objects or views is obtained by voluntarily submitting to the discipline of physical exertion. This can be posited as the counterpart to the sacred objects or symbols which

> operate culturally as mnemonics . . . about values, and cultural axioms, whereby a society's deep knowledge is transmitted from one generation to another [and which are often presented] . . . in the setting of "a place that is not a place, and a time that is not a time" (as the Welsh folklorist and sociologist Alwyn Rees once described for me the context of Celtic bardic utterance).
>
> (Turner 1974: 239)

Those once poetically scripted sacred elements in the landscape are now re-cited and re-sited in a secular milieu. Yet it is one that still resonates to the sacred: as Jane put it, 'Walking also has a spiritual side for me. I feel uplifted by standing on top of a mountain – similar to listening to Bach. Everyday niggles seem so much less important'. Another woman said she experienced the space and relative solitude of the mountains as 'a time of emotional and spiritual renewal'.

In a literal reflection of the sacred, one evening as a small group of us were taking the lakeside footpath to the pub, we were stopped in our tracks by the setting sun. The mountains and their perfect reflections in the still water of Buttermere were tinged a fiery golden-orange. We sat down on the grassy banks of the lake and, in silence, 'in a place that was no place, and a time that was no time' watched a progression of colors so intense that I occasionally blinked to make sure I was registering them properly. These ephemeral minutes remained lodged in the brain to be vividly recalled by Walter Smith's journal description of rowing on Buttermere:

> . . . we noticed that the sun was going down and setting the mountains on fire, so we hurriedly set off and pulled into the centre of the lake. There we rested and watched the most wonderful sunset I have ever seen. Starting at gold, the light gradually changed to orange, red, purple and then died away into a luminous sort of grey. It was the sort of evening to give you an 'overcome' sort of feeling.
>
> (Smith *c*. 1922 n.p.)[2]

It was that '"overcome" sort of feeling' that lay behind Eric's saying, 'I'm not religious, but . . .' and then expressing how humbled he felt on the mountaintops. Others voiced such impressions, speaking of their sense of belonging to something much larger than their own individualities, while yet others wrote of it in additional comments on their questionnaires.

Generally when a group arrived at the top and even after people had caught their breath, there would be almost no conversation as people took in the extraordinary views. What conversation there might be was often a verbal mapping of the mountains, ridges or lakes spread out below us. This recitation of place names served to orient people, not just literally to the points of the compass but, it seemed, also to bring the immensity of the landscape back under some kind of control. Then photographs would be taken. Sometimes one or another person would go sit alone by her- or himself, but generally the group stayed together in companionable silence.

Walking groups provide opportunities for the experience of *communitas* in a 'temporal-spatial frame [that] marks off the special kind of reality' (Milner 1955 cited in Douglas 1966: 78–9). However, experienced from below, *communitas* is structured from above – for institutionalization subverts *communitas* back into the structure of the marketplace. It is because of this that outward marks of rank are not entirely eroded. Differences in clothing, the experience of past walks taken in more or less expensive and exotic locations, and expressions of cultural capital prevent the ideal state of *communitas* from being achieved in this secular pilgrimage. Yet something approximating to its levelling mechanisms and the spontaneous arrival of comradeship can be experienced in the walking group because there too, as in pilgrimage, 'an important component of the liminal situation is . . . an enhanced stress on nature at the expense of culture' (Turner 1974: 252). Walking the same territory over many years creates episodic memory, a re-experiencing in the mind of that which is literally a memory embodied through movement. This leads to a sense of recognition and attachment to place, a sense of located identity if not local identity.

## Clothing the Image

Clothing was a medium through which a lack of harmony was expressed. Ritual displays of hi-tech clothing signalled the literal and metaphoric investment some walkers made in image-led market economics. Ritual displays of no-tech clothing signalled resistance to capitalism's commoditization of this leisure activity. Clothing also becomes the locus of memory, associated with past walking trips and weather conditions withstood. Clothing is a serious issue. It can capture the 'moral divide' between fell-walkers and locals (Chapman 1993), and it can make the difference in saving lives.

Given the sudden and fairly extreme variability of weather conditions in the Lake District (as in all mountainous areas), death through hypothermia is a year-round risk. It is not entirely unusual to go, in an hour or two, from being completely sweaty to putting on a 200-Polartec jacket or woolen sweater with a waterproof over it to cut the wind, as well as donning hat, scarf, and gloves, and clambering into waterproof trousers for their warmth and wind-protection. Conversely, it is not entirely unusual to start out on a very crisp May morning through a light dusting of snow, and be walking in a short-sleeved top within a couple of hours. Some walkers attribute the drop in hypothermia-related deaths to the phenomenal increase in the use of hi-tech, lightweight, waterproof outerwear and the heat-retaining properties of fibers such as Polartec even when wet.

The symbolic significance of these material objects, their status distinctions and the posturing they engender offends some walkers. As Paula said to me, 'walking clothes have become casual fashion – walking boots that look like walking boots that wouldn't do the job. Its a sign of wealth to have clothes that are for leisure'. Others, while appreciating their particular attributes, deplore the color pollution created by their sometimes brilliant hues. A cartoon which catches some of these attitudes shows two frowning, angry members of the Keswick Mountain Rescue Team, kitted-up in hi-tech jackets in a blinding snowstorm. Pointing back up the mountain to two people virtually obscured by driving snow, one rescue team member says to the other, 'They refuse to be rescued because our Gore-Tex jackets clash with theirs.'

Responses on the questionnaire survey about hi-tech clothing showed that women disapproved of such clothing more than men. Some walkers resist co-option into this segment of the walking market with a sometimes overt and vocalized defiance, and continue to wear old and patched trousers and jackets or torn woollies. Marion put it this way: 'I went to an exhibition of outdoor wear and I heard two chaps say "And we haven't even tapped the walking market yet." And I thought, "Well you are not tapping me matey!" And I immediately put up a block.' Boots seem to be the exception: almost everyone wears 'proper' walking boots of one type or another. It is rare to see serious adult hill walkers in Wellington boots – rubber boots – although in one or two instances that was the case, due to the cost of 'proper' walking boots.

Boots are the object of much ritualized attention: cleaning off mud and digging out the treads takes place soon after returning from a day's walk; then the boots are placed in a heated boot room to dry out. Leather boots, once dry, are rubbed with mink oil, boot polish or some other waterproofing or polish. Last-minute oiling or buffing takes place in the morning. Some people take a definite pride in polishing their boots until they look like new chestnuts. A lot of this mystique is confined to men, some of whom spoke of learning their boot-polishing skills in the army. This was the source of much joking.

Walkers' magazines are full of articles evaluating boots that the articles' authors put through several hundred miles of testing. The peculiarities of British feet are the topic of a two-page advertisement by Karrimor. A full-page color photograph of a blistered heel catches the eye. Headed in inch-high print, 'Most boots come in continental sizes. The rub is, British feet don't', the copy on the opposite page reads in part:

> At Karrimor we have identified a problem with the walking boots worn by most British people. They don't fit. That's because the accurate fittings we enjoy as children allow our feet to spread naturally. So we British tend to have wider feet than our European counterparts. Unfortunately, the vast majority of walking boot manufacturers are out of step, and make their boots in narrow, continental sizes. We've shunned this narrow-mindedness and made our new Gold Standard K-SBs . . . wider. Specifically for British feet.

> (Country Walking 1996: 38–9)[3]

Its tongue-in-cheek anti-European humor reinforces British 'natural' superiority. Olive, a retired nurse who does volunteer work in Rumanian orphanages, talking about walking solo in Europe said how recreational walking was viewed there as being a 'peculiarly English tradition'.

## A Window on the Past

One thing that has changed in the course of engaging in this tradition is the level of comfort sought in accommodation. In the affluent 1980s, the rather spartan accommodation available at Co-operative Holidays Association centers in the Lake District and around Britain became less desirable, and bookings began to drop. In a move that managed to maintain the impression of continuity while eliminating confusion with the Co-operative movement and its chain of shops, the organization changed its name to Countrywide Holidays Association. The shift from the old-fashioned working-class self-help image of 'the Co-op' to the more expansive ring of 'Countrywide' was a commercially-loaded linguistic turn that reflected the middle-classing of England.

By the mid-1990s, CHA was an organization in the throes of major transition. According to one center's activities manager, it was a transition that would have to be accomplished if the organization were to stay in business at all. CHA had been forced to consolidate its assets by selling a number of its centers. It continued to close others during my period of fieldwork. At the same time, it was engaged in upgrading those centers it retained since fewer people than in the past were prepared to share bathrooms and toilets located down hallways, or find that they were competing with fifty or sixty others in the use of one coin-operated public telephone.

As I began fieldwork in 1995, CHA also instituted a new titled functionary at its centers, that of activities manager. Such managers lead walks and live at the centers either year-round or for the summer season. They have oversight of the volunteer walk leaders and hosts and hostesses who organize evening activities and also lead walks. This professionalization of walk leaders has been accompanied by the addition of substantially more strenuous grades of walks in order to appeal to a more demanding and generally younger segment of the market. As a result CHA now runs some weeks of 16-mile days with up to 5,000 feet of ascent each day.

CHA was also beginning to reorganize its marketing strategy. In 1998, its rather dowdy two-tone flyers and pamphlets were replaced by folio-sized full-color glossy brochures, that also advertised a CHA web page. At the same time, CHA entered into partnerships with for-profit holiday organizations and broadened its scope of specialty holidays that combine walking with tutoring in a range of hobbies such as landscape painting. Also, holidays for the 21–35 age group, family week holidays, and special deals for single-parent families were highlighted. These departures from past practice reflected the changing tastes and social realities of the late twentieth century. All in all a far cry from CHA's nineteenth-century roots in 'cold water Christianity'.

My first week of organized walking was undertaken from CHA's 33-bedroomed Swiss-style guest lodge situated deep in the Borrowdale Valley, which commanded spectacular views. This first week revealed the tensions generated within the organization by the conflict between continuity and change. What was taking place in the microcosm of the Countrywide Holidays Association was a reflection of issues playing out countrywide.

The guests fell into two distinct categories: those who were booked on a week of led walks and evening activities, and those who were using the center either for a week or less from which to conduct their own walks. The first category was composed of mainly over-60-year-olds who generally appeared to be not very fit. They took the gentle level walks. There was just one couple within this group who were younger and fitter and took that week's concurrent intermediate level walks. From the questionnaires it was apparent that people in this group fell into the lower and lowest income brackets (£10,000–15,000 – $16,000–24,000 and even under £5,000–$8,000). They were rather quiet and did not seem to talk a great deal among themselves. When everyone met on the opening Saturday afternoon to introduce themselves, my project generated comments (mystifying to me at the time) from people in this group such as, 'are you from the taxman's office?' (the Internal Revenue Service).

There were only two people under twenty-five: Mary, the activities manager, and a friend of hers who had come for the week's walks in order to visit her. Neither of them participated in the evening activities which were under the direction of Douglas and Rosemary, the 'host' and 'hostess' for the week. They had been hosting for CHA for the past thirty-five years and had been CHA members prior to that. The evening activities involved quizzes, guessing games and spelling bees. There was no ceilidh (an evening of dancing) because, Douglas said, there were not enough people. The Celtic word 'ceilidh' was the word used to describe such evenings at various walking centers in England.

The host and hostess provided a window through which CHA's past history of fellowship and religion could be glimpsed. At our first evening meal Douglas announced in very jolly tones that we were not to sit next to the same person for more than one meal because 'everyone here is good company'. He then proceeded to give a rather lengthy grace. As I looked around during grace I saw that some people seemed, like myself, to be taken aback by this. They were among those who were not booked into the led walks and evening activities.

Conversations with Douglas revealed his perceptions that the fostering of fellowship and community which had been the hallmarks of CHA in 'the old days' had been put aside by the inroads individualism had made in recent years. He told me that up until 1991 he had conducted Sunday evening services on his weeks, and he deeply regretted the passing of that custom. He indicated that there had been a change in Head Office management and hence of policy.[4]

Despite Douglas's attempts to maintain continuity with CHA's past, change had obviously taken place. He regretted that a lunch hamper was no longer carried on walks by the men in the party and that at afternoon teabreaks on the walks the hostess no longer cut up a cake and handed it round, something that he felt had helped define the hostess's role in attending to the well-being of her guests. These were customs which he felt had helped foster a sense of belonging to a group, as had the communal washing-up of dishes after the evening meal. (Perhaps it was in relation to this lost but still remembered past that a notice was prominently posted at the entrance to the kitchen announcing that guests were not allowed to enter the area.) Douglas contrasted this past to current practice whereby everyone picked up her or his own individually bagged lunch and snacks in the morning and carried them her- or himself, eating what was wanted more or less at will.

One arena in which Douglas had not allowed change to encroach was his insistence that no one was to walk in front of him.[5] So walking a step or two behind him, I listened to him voice his regret that the phenomenal growth of Evangelical churches in recent years had taken away the young people who otherwise would have been the new intake for CHA. Douglas's equating the evangelical movement's intake with CHA's lack of a replacement generation was an indicator of his perceptions of what CHA stood for, or more accurately, what it had stood for in his youth. This lack of a younger replacement generation was spoken about by various people over different weeks. It was explained as coming from changes in family structure: that adolescents no longer want to be with their parents and so they are no longer introduced to walking as a family activity. Such thinking presumably lies behind CHA's current efforts to emphasize young people's weeks, young families' weeks, and the introduction of extremely strenuous weeks that would appeal to those who otherwise would dismiss CHA as being for the 'oldsters'.

Those who were using the center as a base for their own walks did not mix with the larger group in the evenings. They were couples and solo walkers who knew the Lake District well. They were in the younger age brackets (36 to 45 and 46 to 55) and in the higher, even highest income bracket (over £50,000–$80,000). One couple were not fell-walkers but were touring in England. They were an Australian opal merchant and his wife. Bob, in his late 50s, had been born in India to English parents but educated in an English public school. Jackie, who was in her early 50s, had moved to Australia as a young girl. They had included the Lake District in their trip to England specifically to see what they called 'Wordsworth's landscape'. They had both been introduced to his poetry at school and felt that they could not possibly be in England without seeing the actual mountains and valleys named by him in his poems. They toured the area by car, only occasionally joining the gentle walks.

Like Jackie and Bob, Ian and Pauline felt they had wandered into some kind of a time warp. A recently retired business couple from the Midlands, they were equipped with the relatively expensive walking gear of which they strongly approved 'provided it was used for actual walking and not High Street posturing'. Ian and Pauline readily voiced exasperation with the anachronistic air that the host cast over the week. Douglas became a metaphor through which Ian could express what he felt was wrong with Britain as a whole. The same arguments were brought to bear on the dowdy nature of the CHA house, the host from a virtually vanished past, and the shambles that had been made of British industry. They included a generalized fear of change and a backward-looking approach to industry, commerce, and social policies, the absence of foresight and vision among the leadership, and lack of willingness to put money into upgrading infrastructure in a timely fashion.

A strong component of CHA's ethos has been to assist those who are unable otherwise to afford holidays. Subsidized and free holidays are funded through donations that are solicited during each CHA week. Discrepancies between the 'haves' and 'have nots' were clearly evident in this week, publicly in clothing, language, and demeanor, and privately through information on the questionnaire. No other CHA week I experienced had anything approaching this concentration of low-income guests. This led me to think that I had booked into a week that had more or less been set aside for assisted and/or invited guests.

This would explain the silence of not openly voicing preferences or dislikes to the on-site management but welcoming changes resulting from others' voicing the same preferences. It might also be an explanation for the initial suspicion with which my project was met – that I might find out something that would jeopardize someone's entitlement to a free or assisted holiday.

Out on a day's walk, this silence was broken by Barbara, a single woman in her early 50s who was a clerical worker. She confided how 'patronizing' she found the host and how the way he 'pushed religion' greatly offended her. Framing it very precisely in her knowledge of CHA's early history, Barbara put it that 'they see us as working-class people who need educating'. Though she was happy to be able to let off steam about this and manifestations of the host's authority over the group, she took extreme care that no one could possibly overhear what she was saying. Barbara's highly conspiratorial air and obvious fear of being overheard seemed to indicate that she thought that were she to be overheard, she might be precluded from returning.  Had she been a paying guest like myself, or like those not on the group being hosted in the evenings by Douglas and Rosemary, she could have voiced her complaints with impunity. As it was, she used class as a social description of hierarchy in which she ranked her own identity and self-class/ification vis-à-vis Douglas and the organization. It was also through the category of class that she made sense of the collective memory of CHA.

Most of the guests on the led-walking party were in their late 60s to early 70s. They had been coming to CHA for decades. For them, the customs whose passing Douglas lamented had been part of the CHA they had known as young people. They much appreciated the hosted evenings organized by Douglas and Rosemary around the games that they had collected over the years. The gentle walks and familiar games provided traces of their individually remembered pasts and gave the impression of belonging again. Unlike Barbara, at least at the level of voicing, most of the guests knew their place in the social order as it operated in this particular field – this tail end of the CHA-that-was.

## Groups within Groups

The organized circuits of a week's walks, rather like the organized Picturesque viewing stations, create a common space and time among the group and provide a modality of access among people who do not know each other. As procedures are reiterated each day (filling of thermoses, packing of lunches, polishing of boots, assembling in front of the house, sizing up the weather, puffing up hills, admiring the views, and so on), an assemblage of reciprocal relationships between the individuals brings about 'the group'. This particular 'here and now', so hugely at variance with regular daily life, becomes superimposed upon individualities. Shared biographical details are exchanges that progressively initiate some overarching sense of a collective. At the same time, there are constantly shifting cross-currents of subtle and not-so-subtle categories of inclusion and exclusion. *Communitas* and contestation co-exist; one does not preclude the other's emergence. Certainly, any notions I might have harbored about an unproblematic, 'feel-good' community of walkers, were laid to rest.

An activity that evolved both in the evenings and out on the walks in the first week at Buttermere was the swapping of Latin phrases and declensions in a display of friendly one-up-manship. Everyone's distant or not-so-distant educational backgrounds suddenly were brought to the fore as this activity divided those who knew Latin from those who did not. Below the level of consciousness, knowledge functioned as a sort of social orientation or act of classification (Bourdieu 1984). The 'Latinists' (who included the walk leader and whose ages ranged from mid-20s to mid-60s) seemed quite oblivious of their unspoken assumption that everyone would, like them, have taken Latin at school. They did not hear the silence it imposed upon a small segment of the group.

That it was a small segment was in turn a marker of the relative homogeneity of the group. Belonging is the experience of culture (Cohen 1982) and those who were not cultured in this particular way did not belong to the group for that display of cultural capital. The uncultured ended up walking by themselves as others, only merging back into the whole as the game petered out.

Cutting across this and any other configuration that the group experienced, was the way in which the group coalesced through Martin, a retired professional man in his late 50s, an unmarried, self-made millionaire as he described himself. Running as a sub-theme throughout the week was the social drama he initiated. Under the intensity of close living, people's traits and weaknesses are quickly exposed. Martin swiftly and relentlessly zeroed in on them which led to some fairly tense exchanges.[6] When late in the week I was able to ask Martin why he did this, his response was that by his stirring things up people were coming together. Did he see himself as the willing sacrifice for the good of the group? Was this egoism flecked with altruism?

If this was phase one of the social drama, as the week progressed we moved into phase two, 'a phase of mounting *crisis'* (Turner 1974: 38). One can 'just note the encounters and watch the occasional fireworks, but it is likely that there will come a point when the fireworks started exploding round you' (MacDonald 1987: 121). Knowing that I had introduced myself as an anthropologist, Martin, linking anthropology's early history with fascism and eugenics, spoke of the chaos of today's 'tribal Africa' as proof that blacks were innately of inferior intelligence to whites, and that this was caused by their different genetic makeup. I tried to counter this, only to be met with comments such as 'I'm not going to believe that I've got the same DNA as the jungle bunnies.'

Soon after, when we were all quietly eating our sandwiches and enjoying the view, Martin said that surely as an anthropologist I should be 'eating meat and chewing bones with the natives'. Scratching his armpit and making grunting sounds he then said, 'Shouldn't we be going uh, uh, uh, for you?' In a voice that even my own ears picked up as steely with anger, I shot back, 'Oh, but you are in your own way!' There was dead silence for a few seconds, then someone sitting behind Martin winked at me. I was momentarily an insider. The fireworks display thus erupting around me seemed to touch two buttons in the group: disgust at the deeply offensive content of what Martin said, and my status as a visiting 'American'. Several people in the group made it clear that as a guest in England – moreover, one who was specifically interested in walkers – they were anxious that I should not leave with the impression that Martin was representative of either 'Brits' or walkers.

After this incident Martin's verbal harassment of me ceased and we started having conversations. I think I became the only person he actually talked *with* rather than *at*. What Martin brought into focus for me by having invoked the archetypal anthropological field was the whereness/awareness of the geographical location of my fieldwork and the anxieties that 'real' fieldwork takes place 'somewhere else', not 'here'.

The more culturally exotic and geostrategically embattled parts [of the world] thus become proper "anthropological" field sites whereas Western Europe ... is a less appropriate "field", as the many Europeanists who struggle to find jobs in anthropology departments can attest.

(Gupta and Ferguson 1997: 12)

Fieldwork is anthropology's founding methodology for studying what were (erroneously or not) conceived of as small-scale societies. It is claimed to be anthropology's distinctive marker that serves to mark out and police disciplinary boundaries (Gupta and Ferguson 1997), although recent work suggests that fieldwork/ethnography may not be the exclusive trademark of the anthropologist (Bell 1994). Disciplinary insecurity about traditional fieldwork has been engendered by questioning the construction of the ethnographic text (Clifford and Marcus 1986), practices of power in the field (Crapanzano 1980), the assumptions lying behind the naturalized 'purity' of field sites (Gupta and Ferguson 1997) and the fact that

> the landscapes of group identity – the ethnoscapes – around the world are no longer familiar anthropological objects, insofar as groups are no longer tightly territorialized, spatially bounded, historically self-conscious, or culturally homogeneous.
>
> (Appadurai 1991: 191)

Within the landscape of walking-group identity, the social drama playing out around Martin arrived at the third phase: *'redressive action'* (Turner 1974: 39). On the last evening of a week when Martin had been getting under everyone's skin, antagonism towards him was articulated literally through contravening certain drinking 'rituals'. This was all played out among the men; the women were simply onlookers. As the whole group assembled to go to the pub a mile and a half away, Martin was told by one of the men he had been baiting that he would have to buy everyone the first round and that this was the cost of his coming along.

At the pub, though it was all done with a smile, the men proceeded to humiliate him with a few well-chosen home truths. The atmosphere became very tense and hugely awkward. A little later, tanked-up with gin-and-tonics – 'not that rubbishy beer you lot are drinking' – Martin returned the humiliation in kind, observing to the walk leader that, contrary to general custom, there had been no 'whip-round' to buy the week's leader a gift. It was the men's turn to feel embarrassed.

From then on Martin was ignored. He appeared hurt and upset, not understanding why he had been picked on. Turning to me he explained that at University, the thing had been 'to try to wind someone up 'til they broke, 'til the "red mist" descended and they got angry – then you'd won'. It seemed to me that one lesson he had not learned at University was that it was a game obviously best undertaken with like-minded players. From what he had told me of his (to my mind lonely) scramble up the economic ladder, 'winning' was the point of his game in whatever field of endeavor it was played. As it had been Martin versus the group, so it seemed to have been Martin versus the economic world.

A more sustained form of contestation arose the following week at Buttermere as the result of a clearly defined sub-group existing within the larger group. The sub-group were described to me as 'head bangers' – in other words, colloquially speaking they were considered crazy. They were a group of about a dozen fiercely fit people, most of them men in their thirties, who met up for the same week each year at this place. Their object was to cover the most ground in the least possible time. The head bangers had become great friends with the manager, I was told. He always led them and made it their week – regardless of who else came. Enquiries made to the manager and the current week's leader quickly established that I was not welcome to try to join the next week's group. I was told that I would be on my own. To be the object of exclusion in this way brought the otherwise academic notion of a dominant sub-group into rather clear and immediate focus.

The head bangers took over the largest table at both breakfast and supper, saving places for one another so that regardless of when they arrived, they would all be able to sit together. With rare exceptions they talked mainly among themselves in the sitting room after supper, and they went off to the pub as a group. The strangeness of being so overtly disconnected from the main group was mitigated by the presence of a friend who came up to rescue me. Since I saw people only at breakfast, supper and during the evenings, my roommate Elizabeth functioned as my source of information. She found the head banger's pace grueling but just about manageable. Before falling into a pre-supper deep sleep upon her return from each day's walk, Elizabeth would fill me in on the explosive dynamics that were developing between the head bangers and some of the other guests who were less able than she was to adjust to the pace.

People who could not keep up with the head-bangers were unceremoniously dumped. The group would get up and move off from a tea break as soon as the slowest person finally managed to catch up with them; in one instance, an outsider was literally left behind after being told to 'bugger off' and to stop trying to be part of the group. Sharp banter in the evenings made it plain who was not welcome on the walks. My roommate supplied the details. As the week wore on, those who were acceptable to the head bangers ceased to complain about the divisiveness of the situation and began to echo a similar line – 'if they can't keep up, they shouldn't be here' – as they recounted the physical challenges of the day. These people still did not manage to gain access to the dominant sub-group's table at mealtimes.

The head bangers' organizer, and one of the few women in the group, was Jean, who at fifty-three was the oldest among them. She kept in training for this one week by getting up, year-round, at 5 a.m., for an hour of step aerobics and a second hour of swimming or squash. Jean acknowledged how fiercely competitive she was, saying that when out on ordinary walks with her husband, 'if I see someone up ahead I start walking quickly to overtake them. I can't bear someone being in front of me'. For many of the walkers in the core population, what was regenerative about a week of walking was the way uncertainty and doubt were transformed into achievement. The head bangers had little or no uncertainty or doubt about their abilities. Rather, they seemed to gain a sense of power through their mastery of the landscape.

One evening I tackled the issue of exclusion with them. As a result I was invited to the pub with them. The mile and a half walk to the pub was more of a gallop. At the end of the evening, walking back along the road, Robert, a social worker from Manchester who was part of the head bangers' group, described walkers in fixed class terms. 'Walking has always been for me a working-class activity, but I think it's become middle class really. I think it was definitely related, from a Marxist point of view, with the alienation of the means of production.' Somewhat startled, I committed his words to memory thinking how glad I was that I had not had much to drink. He elaborated this thought with references to E.P. Thompson and Raymond Williams, the enclosure movement and the industrial revolution. He finished by saying that to his way of thinking, 'walking was a way of symbolically reclaiming the land'.

The only genuinely working-class person on that week's walks was George, a Londoner in his early seventies, a printer by trade but now retired. Not a head banger, George went out with that group on each day's walk and, I was told, managed to keep up with them. From the questionnaire he completed I learned that he jogged and took part in competition marathon-walking. George was very quiet and kept to himself. In the evenings he would sit reading a book in the midst of other people talking around him. Though friendly, he was difficult to draw out. But one evening he exchanged words with me for a few minutes about his early walking days. He said that as a youth he could not afford to come to the Lake District very often, but on the occasions when he could he would come up by train and then walk each day, spending the nights at different Youth Hostels spaced a day apart. His face and eyes became animated as he spoke of how much he had loved doing that, being out in the wide open, seeing the views from the tops. Then, like a door closing, he went back into his book.

In a final ritual of farewell for the last evening (and finally faring well as it turned out), Jean organized a meal at a fairly expensive vegetarian restaurant in Cockermouth (Wordsworth's birthplace), a good half-hour's drive away. No meal was served at the guest house that night. This meant that the people who had been the particular objects of the head bangers' exclusion and who opted not to join in the 'communal' meal, had to make their own alternative arrangements. But rather than being a meal shared by all the rest before reintegration into 'normal' life, the meal made manifest the divisions within the collectivity. The head bangers ate not only at their own table at the restaurant, but in a separate and inner room. Those who had been able to keep up with them were treated as honorary head bangers and invited to join them. Laughter from those who were 'high, inside and central by virtue of [their] very exclusions' (Stallybrass and White 1986: 22–3) reached the ears of the low, marginalized and outside group.

## Claiming Place

Having observed gendered competitiveness, I specifically sought to walk with a group organized just for women. Scanning web pages for the Lake District, my eye was caught by a walking outfit that carried what I recognized as the name of a Norse goddess. It was a walking-holiday outfit for women. Unlike the fracture lines created by a particular person or sub-group, walking for a week with a group of women, most of whom were lesbians, was made memorable by its peaceful sanity, the exquisite garden that we sometimes ate in, and the superb cooking. The internal workings of the group seemed less fraught, the cross-cutting elements of inclusion and exclusion less strident. But not entirely.

I noticed that my roommate Sarah, in a complex self-imposed modality of simultaneous inclusion and exclusion, spoke in front of other members of the group of taking holidays and so on with her 'companion', and in the privacy of our room she spoke of her 'husband'. Finally I asked her to explain this shift in terminology. Even after joining this walking holiday on three or four previous occasions, she felt uncomfortable making herself known as a heterosexual, and exclaimed with a flash of anger that 'not all heterosexual relationships involve women being dominated!' In order to be included, as she saw it, Sarah had to suppress a key ingredient of her own identity. Here was reverse closeting in face of the real or imagined pressures of a group of lesbians.

From conversations and notices on the bulletin board, and from our own walks which were by no means confined to popular routes or even definitive pathways at all, it became apparent that there was another mapping of the Lake District (and indeed the rest of the country). It was different from that of the CHA, the head bangers and all walkers I had met thus far. Walking outfits that cater primarily to lesbians form an overlay of an unseen series of pathways connecting lesbian-run bed-and-breakfast places, guest houses, tea rooms, restaurants and pubs. This hidden mapping of difference re-sites women in the practice of walking otherwise dominated by men as participants and leaders, and helps construct a community of landscape-located memory that privileges those who are usually silenced.

## Landscapes of Non-identity

The absence of ethnic minorities was discussed in structured interviews and informal conversations with representatives of Friends of the Lake District (FLD), Ramblers' Association (RA), Holiday Fellowship (HF) and Countrywide Holidays Association (CHA) as well as with local club representatives. Each organization referred to a national-level program instituted by the RA in the early 1990s called 'Let's Get Going' that built upon the Countryside Commission's 'Operation Gateway' experiment (Blunden and Curry 1988). Implicit in the imagery of opening a gateway is of course the presence of earlier gatekeepers. There were no blacks or Asians in the study population. Apart from one black rock climber and a young Asian couple I passed who were walking alone, the only members of ethnic minorities I saw were in school parties – some rock-climbing in the Peak District, some in a big summer campsite in the Lake District.

RA's project 'Let's Get Going' was specifically designed to bring into the countryside people 'who don't have a tradition of walking' but it had not yielded the desired results, in part because 'Asian women in particular do not go out without their menfolk, and if they are wearing saris, it makes it very difficult climbing over stiles' (Gunningham 1996). Another RA project called 'Family Rambling Days' had yielded better results. Its short two-to-four-mile-long walks were meant to attract families with young children and although there have been 'more black and Asian non-members on these walks over the last nine years . . . it's still a very small proportion of a small group. But there is an increase' (Gunningham 1996).

I asked fellow walkers if there were blacks or Asians in their home walking clubs, and what they made of the fact that there were none on 'our' week, nor were we meeting any in the course of our walks except for those in school parties. After regretful acknowledgments that there were no ethnic minorities in their home clubs, my companions would refer to the RA campaigns. As for their particular absence in the Lake District, a number of people explained that this was not a place that held 'their' history. In following up on this sort of response I found this to mean one of two things: they had no history of walking in the English countryside because they had not been brought up to it as children or young people, and/or they had no associational history with the countryside vis-à-vis early settlement, battles, literature, art, and agriculture. Blacks and Asians were seen to be urban.

Landscape was experienced by some people as a bastion of 'Englishness'. For them, it functioned as a temporary refuge not only from social and economic changes, but also from the demographic reality of urban England. A kind of patriotism crept in to people's responses when asked if they had ever gone walking abroad. Don, a retired man in his late sixties who was active in his local RA club and worked closely with the local county council's footpath officer, had never gone walking abroad. He said, 'I wouldn't give a quarter-inch of England for an acre of anywhere else, I really wouldn't'. Here was a flash of the ideological potency examined in Chapter 3, that exists when landscape is linked with nature, native, and nation. It indicates how nation/alism, mediated through cultural forms of engagement with landscape, gives rise to a particular form of belonging to something greater, be that the group or the country (as nation or landscape).

When Wordsworth termed the Lake District 'a sort of national property', the question that Chapters 3, 4 and 5 addressed was, 'whose nation'? Today race glosses class, and the question 'whose nation' carries a wider set of meanings that deal with ethnic and racial exclusions (Gilroy 1987). This issue is marked in stark visual and written terms by Ingrid Pollard, a black artist. Her holiday photographs, hand-tinted to recall old postcards or watercolors, show Pollard and other blacks in the English landscape. Their captions deal with power and powerlessness, appropriation and (im?)possible reappropriation. Referencing back to Wordsworth's 'I wandered lonely as a cloud/. . ./ When all at once I saw a crowd,/ A host, of golden daffodils,' one caption reads:

... it's as if the black experience is only lived within an urban environment. I thought I liked the LAKE DISTRICT, where I wandered lonely as a Black face in a sea of white. A visit to the countryside is always accompanied by a feeling of unease, dread.

(Pollard 1984 cited in Kinsman 1995: 301)

Other Pollard captions contain ironic references to William Blake's poetry. Her work is projected as an articulation of the 'collective experience of black people in Britain' (Kinsman 1995: 306). Whether such totalization is warranted I do not know, but the fact that I do not know – the fact that there were no blacks in my study population from whom I might have gathered a different perspective – only goes to support the view that Pollard's experience can be generalized. However, landscapes can be experientially reinterpreted and reclaimed by ethnic minorities:

A day's pony trekking for Muslim girls in the Brecon Beacons "reminded everyone of Kashmir and Mirpur where they used to live. The small villages, the streams, the green fields ... sometimes it leaves you lost: you feel just like you're home".

(Coster 1991 cited in Daniels 1993: 7)

## Silences and Privileging

Secular or sacred, mundane issues soon become apparent in extended walking. In hot weather it is easier for men to strip to a comfortable level of undress than it is for women (even in a women's group). Rest stops, or 'bracken breaks', take on particular importance in hot weather when one needs to stay well hydrated and drinks quite a bit. In an area with stands of dense bracken, there is no problem. But the same area in a different season affords no bracken cover. Women are at a distinct disadvantage.[7] In a virtually symbolic action of separation and boundary-making (Douglas 1970), even though screened from the men in their own group, whichever side of a wall or rocky outcropping women are directed to they are in full sight of anyone else coming up or down the fellsides.

A woman in one of the groups unexpectedly started menstruating and needed frequent stops. Too embarrassed to explain any of this to the leader (a man), various women in the group called for bracken breaks whenever she needed one. By the end of the week, the men were saying that they had never before walked with such a bunch of weak-bladdered women. They never knew otherwise. It prompted other women to say that they used birth-control pills for the weeks prior to coming away in order to avoid having to deal with the issue.

The avoidance and silence surrounding menstruation is maintained even in Eric Langmuir's compendious *Mountaincraft and Leadership* (1995), given to me to read at one of the walking centers by a walker who was himself undergoing leadership training. He referred to it as 'the mountain leaders' "Bible".' While going into great detail about the different caloric needs of male and female youths (15–18-year-olds) and adults (19–50-year-olds), how those needs vary under different weather conditions, and how mental and physical stamina differ between the age groups, there is nothing about the different needs that might be generated as the result of menstruation. (Nor was there anything about people over 50.)

The male-derived yardstick of ability, endurance and speed is another 'mismeasurement of man' (*sic*). Women in mixed groups, even when they are the majority, are still somehow the minority. They do not set the pace, they settle to the back of the group while the men 'naturally' gravitate to the front to accompany the leader, checking the route with him, and so on. (When we passed couples walking alone – that is, not in any organized group – it was always the man who was leading the way and reading the map.) This unspoken and competitive edge – men as map-readers, decision-makers, leaders – prompted some women in the mixed groups to speak of how much they liked walking with only women. They meant a locally based cluster of women. Such a group was 'more relaxed' and had a 'less competitive atmosphere' in which one could 'develop confidence in one's abilities'. But these women dismissed the idea of joining walking holidays organized only for women, because of their perception that such holidays were 'really' meant for lesbians and that they themselves would not be welcome.

Social rituals can carry gendered significance which are invisible to the outsider until made visible through their transgression. Buying a round of drinks for a small group, including one male, I asked for orders. One woman wanted a half-pint of a local beer. Everyone else agreed on the same. I ordered so many half-pints, at which point the lone male grew uncomfortable; embarrassed, he offered to pay the difference between a half and a full pint. Apparently, half-pints and maleness did not go together. Alerted by this incident, I observed that not only did most men drink pints, but even after having drunk six or seven they began to order a half, only to carefully pour the half-pint into a previously used pint glass. Since halves for women are served in differently shaped glasses (curved profiles instead of men's straight-sided glasses), there does not exist even a remote possibility that a male's half-pint could be mistaken for a female's half-pint. The symbolic enactment of difference does indeed exist in the most trivial action (Douglas 1970).

## Retiring Men

I met a number of men as leaders and fellow walkers who had been pushed into early retirement in their mid- to late fifties under the impact of England's economic restructuring. Despite their relative comfort, with decent pensions and reasonable financial security, many, though not all, were bitter about early retirement. Although they expressed anxiety about inflation in relation to pensions, most emphasized a personal rather than financial need to work. All were left seeking activities for their newly unstructured time. Where walking had been a recreational activity before retirement, it was pursued now as an avocation and as an avenue for restructuring both time and self-image.

Michael, a former air traffic control supervisor, put it this way: 'I'd been in a very stressful job, and when I retired, it went from that to deciding whether I should have a raspberry yogurt or a plain yogurt! So I thought it was time to begin this leadership thing.' One man who had taken up group leading upon retirement had, as a young man, led walks for organizations such as CHA. Many retirees had been introduced to recreational walking as children through their parents' involvement with various organizations, often CHA. Marion, one of the few female walk leaders I met, said that in her experience these retired men find it very difficult to adapt to a leisure situation:

> They still want to manage and they've got very set ideas – they're not flexible at all, and you have the devil's own job sometimes to persuade them to do something out of the norm. They've got this little tunnel and "this is my program, I only walk these walks, I only do this for entertainment for the evening, and I will only, that's my path." And if you suggest, 'Well how about if we did this?' they're all concerned because they've never done it before. And it's always men.

Men's managerial skills were being brought into national walking-holiday organizations as well as into local-level walking clubs. Through the clubs they often intersected with local politics in terms of access and planning issues – inherently contentious arenas. Stan, an early retiree and ardent member of his local walking club, had organized opposition to a proposed nearby major housing project in former protected countryside. Nigel, a retired Chief Executive Officer of a London Borough Council, was leading a fight against the proposed countryside siting of a hypermarket that would wipe out shops in the local high street (shopping area), alter the local landscape and vastly increase automobile and truck traffic in the surrounding area. He acknowledged that people such as himself, the ex-insiders with knowledge of the 'rules of the game', were 'the gamekeepers turned poachers'.

Some men were building a bridge into walk-leading prior to retirement, leading the occasional walk on an *ad hoc* basis to replace an indisposed scheduled leader. Some just stumbled into the role. Robin, an off-shore oil rig worker, had been on a walking holiday in Spain where 'the leader was awful,' with the result that the group of fourteen people 'had really bonded'. The next year most of them met up in Britain for a walking holiday together. They enjoyed it so much that they continued to meet up two or three times a year. Since Robin was the most experienced walker among them, he led the walks. Enjoying that experience, he began a mountain-walking leadership training program and planned to lead professionally after retirement, which he now does.

## Social *Movement* and *Social* Movement

While acknowledging that *communitas* and contention can co-exist, I have suggested that walking groups can be framed as sites of secular pilgrimage in which *communitas* may be experienced. Here I examine that idea within the extended temporal dimension of locally based walking clubs where people walk together over the course of several years or the larger spans of lifetimes. I wish to see whether walking clubs become a mediated space in which the structured hierarchical world is temporarily but repeatedly sloughed off, with concomitant entry into an experiential community of more egalitarian feeling.

From this perspective, week-long walking groups and locally based walking clubs throughout Britain may be posited as multiple and shifting points in a less visible network that maps out not only the 'why' but the 'how' of a social movement that, although it is non-political, has nonetheless the capacity to initiate policy reform. Certainly, some particular groupings within the walking movement do 'publicize the existence of some basic dilemmas of complex societies'

(Melucci 1989: 222). Considering walking as a social movement does not conform to traditional social movement theory that explains the origins of a movement – such as Chartism – through the existence of social grievances (Klandermans, Kriesi and Tarrow 1988; Melucci 1989). Rather, it fits more with the theorizing of new social movements that are marked by all or some of the following: a struggle over access to information, participation in 'the movement' as a goal in and of itself, participation merging into everyday life, and awareness of environmental issues (Melucci 1989).

Viewed at this broader level, walking as a social movement includes within itself the public and the private, and the metaphysical as well as the practical realities of life. It encompasses self-regenerating national-level organizations as well as naturally diminishing groups of women and men who walk together and sometimes admit no new members. In this social *movement* that is also a *social* movement, actors enter a field in which they produce meaning, negotiate life crises, and structure individual and group identities. Through walkers' organizations at local, regional and national levels, public space is created in which communication and debate takes place over issues such as access and planning. At the same time walking groups create private spaces (of either an ephemeral or a perduring nature) in which interpersonal relationships 'take place'.

What follows is drawn from observations of one of the most informally organized local clubs I walked with. Originally started in the early 1980s in Colwyn Bay, North Wales, as part of the local council's adult-education scheme called 'Focus', the walking club was for retired people. At the time that meant that members were women over sixty and men over sixty-five. Under changing patterns of employment brought about by downsizing, men and women in their fifties began to join the club. As it expanded, the younger retirees began to dominate, wanting to walk faster and further all the time. The leader of the club announced that he was leaving the council organization under which the club operated, and was forming an independent club for older retirees.

The 'Out of Focus' club – as its members then named themselves – has operated as a closed group ever since. It has some twenty members left. Sonia, a retired English teacher, explained, 'No one new can join. It's like family really – if one of us is ill and confined to bed, then others will do the shopping, or if there's a crisis, you know that there'll be people rallying round.' There had been three deaths in the group that year (1996). Usually when someone's spouse dies, others in the group such as retired accountants, solicitors and realtors, help deal with death's bureaucratic aftermath. Sonia told me that the members of the group intended walking together 'until the end, until no one is left'.

On the day-walks, members without a car were picked up by other members, and people shifted around into as few cars as possible at an arranged meeting spot before driving to the beginning of the day's walk. (Riders paid a token amount per mile to the driver.) As we were switching around between cars, one woman enquired numerous times after those missing from the group. Rose did not seem able to absorb that they had gone on a day trip to Dublin. People simply responded to her afresh each time with the facts of the matter.

Rather delightfully, we stopped for coffee and cakes before the walk began! In the tea room, Rose started gathering menus, having forgotten that she had already been given two or three (from her previous requests). Each time she was patiently dealt with, her odd behavior gently ignored. At some point she told me that I should write my impressions down because one's memory is not as good as one thinks it is: 'it's not that one forgets – one remembers very clearly, but then it's very distant for a while and then it's just gone'. She is quite right.

All now in their seventies, the 'Out of Focus' group kept up a steady pace, even on those sections which, though not severe, were uphill. I was told a group history story that combined issues of nation/native/nature with the element of bardic utterance. On a walk one day when the weather turned foul, the group was going up the edge of a very steep field after a cloudburst, so the path was literally running with mud. They went off the path and up along the edge of the crop. A farmer appeared and said, 'And what exactly do you think you are doing? English, I suppose, and you've come from London. Can't you see the path? It's clearly enough marked and you're walking onto my land.' One of the Out of Focus members who was not only Welsh but Welsh-speaking and a miner's daughter into the bargain, came forward and explained, in Welsh, who they were. The farmer, I was told, 'became like butter in her hand then, and we said, "Thank God for Lena!"'

As we walked along it became apparent that, like any family, they had had to learn to deal with each other's foibles. Indeed, that was the main reason they did not want any new members. They felt they were too old to start dealing with a new person's 'quirks' – they had spent so long learning to deal with each other's. Kathleen related that in the group's history only once had personality issues reached a point where someone was almost asked to leave. After a few years of difficulties caused by one woman, 'the menfolk finally put their foot down' and told her to pull herself together. She left the group only upon moving out of the area after her husband's death.

One man's verbosity was another woman's bane, and occasionally the air got a bit strained. But other people would draw the man off, engaging him in conversation – or rather, listening to him. It was explained to me that David had lost his wife the previous year and was 'not yet able to cope'. The only point when his bravura dropped was when he told his passenger at the end of day that he would not be able to pick her up the next week because he was going alone to Bruges. He said, 'It's my first journey alone you know – we'll see how it goes.'

Focusing my camera to take a photograph of the Out of Focus group as they were focused on the views at our lunchtime break, was like momentarily entering a hall of mirrors! These were people who through the medium of walking had formed their spirit of *communitas* by which they were also traversing the unknown territory of aging.

## Conclusion

Shorn of daily routine and set generally among people with whom there is no prior connection, the uncharted space of a week's walking encompasses both contention and something approaching *communitas*. Under the less intense conditions of locally based walking clubs, a supportive network can grow that functions to structure social life and a sense of belonging. Here is *communitas* without its pilgrimagistic framing, inserted into everyday life. In both study populations, taking income as an indicator of class (by which I mean the status distinctions or cultural capital accrued through education, professional training and so on which translates into economic capital), the walking group provides a space that cross-cuts class. A randomly selected one-week group from the core population showed a variation from the over-£50,000 category ($80,000) to the £5,000–10,000 category ($8,000–16,000). A randomly selected comparison population group – that is, a locally based walking group – showed income varying from the £35,000–50,000 category ($56,000–80,000) to under £5,000 ($8,000).

While fell-walking in organized groups can function as a temporary refuge from the loneliness and isolation of not having anyone to go on holiday with, local walking clubs help structure time year round, with their midweek and weekend walks. They mark the now desacralized ritual calendar with walking trips at Easter and Christmas, and social events such as annual general meetings are timed to coincide with (indeed are presented as) Harvest Suppers. Outfits such as CHA and HF also provide Easter, Christmas and New Year breaks. People's experience showed that this spatialized organization of time through membership in a local walking group became especially important in facing life after divorce, bereavement or serious illness. As Angela, a retired secretary, said, this was 'in part because people don't have their families nearby – children move away, so this does take the place'. This motif of the group replacing the family was summed up by the RA's Associate Director of Membership:

> I sometimes think that walking has taken the place of church. The walking group, generally of around forty people, has become the congregation, the extended family – people find it very supportive.
>
> (Gunningham 1996)

On the fell-walking weeks, sweating up steep hillsides, facing fear or unease negotiating a way up or down rock scrambles or scree, delighting in having succeeded, doing mile after mile in the heat or the pelting rain, receiving or lending a hand, waiting up for a straggler or being that straggler and having someone wait up for you – all this and more is part of a process of 'travelling together by primitive means' (see Olwig at this chapter's heading). Arriving at the top, there is a shared sense of accomplishment. These are moments when walking groups seem to come closest to *communitas*, to a feeling of 'egalitarian brotherhood' – though no one would dream of expressing it that way, particularly the women.

Shared experiences and sharing past experiences in which people present themselves in terms of walks taken, ascents made, weather conditions experienced, and people met, and dealing with the difficulties of the day adds multiple layers to past and present landscape-located memory. Everyone has the same mud splashed over them or is similarly bathed in sweat. Yet within this multi-faceted body-located commonality, differences of opinion and temperament have an uncannily fast way of making themselves known. Under these combined circumstances social boundaries thin out, get crossed – temporarily or otherwise – or remain confirmed in their impenetrability as multiple markers of social differentiation are on view close up. Language, accent, clothing, eating habits, understanding which jokes can be told at table or in what company – all these and more are the sitelines by which people take silent and unseen bearings on class.

Within this fluid social field a sense of community is constructed which gives an additional layer of meaning to life – be it the life of the temporally bounded group or the individual's life within or beyond that group. During one week, whenever we came to a cairn marking the top of mountain or ridge, or indicating the direction of an otherwise unidentifiable pathway, Sonia would always stoop down, pick up a stone, and add it to the cairn. I asked her why she did this. She said it was in memory of all the people who had walked that way before. This act of remembrance resonates to a Mexican Chalma pilgrimage practice that related to the belief that erstwhile pilgrims are turned into stones. Since they will regain human form only when they finally arrive at their original destination, pilgrims are beholden to kick a few stones along in the direction of the shrine (Turner 1974).

While fell-walking was experienced as being away from it all ('it' being the seemingly unrelenting stress of urban life), it was also experienced as holding the possibility of connecting to something larger, something beyond the mundanely personal. Although different people put it differently, a phrase that tended to occur in conversations about why one engaged in fell-walking, was that the effort of getting up into the mountains and seeing the panoramic views brought 'a different perspective' or 'a sense of proportion' to personal problems or worries. This was meant quite metaphorically. But I think it has a literal component.

I have already referred to another way people responded to having made the effort and their responses to the views as being variations upon 'I'm not religious but . . .'. Where these conscious and subconscious responses converge is in the word 'immanence', the quality or state of being immanent which is defined thus:

IMMANENT: Late Latin *immanent, immanens* the present participle of *immanere* to remain in place, from Latin *in* + *manere* to remain, to dwell – more at Mansion.

(Webster's New Collegiate Dictionary)

The etymology of 'immanent' is redolent with scriptural and psalmic overtones: 'In my Father's house are many mansions' (John 14: 1), and 'I shall dwell in the house of the Lord for ever' (Psalm 23: 6) are the first that spring to mind. Here is dwelling, indwelling, being in the world, being 'placed' differently: being re-placed, re-connected in and to one's self, in and to the visible world of Nature and through that to the invisible world of the 'mysterious creative power' that we can only apprehend, never comprehend.

A sense of place is arrived at once one is no longer 'apart from' but rather is 'a part of' the landscape. That subtle but all-important difference is the phenomenological experiencing of place: the lived sensing of self in the world (Basso 1996; Tilley 1994). In other words what in an earlier era was called a sense of the sublime, is gained by a particular 'rite which allows one to cross the limen or invisible boundary' (see Olwig, this chapter heading). In this instance, that rite is of course just plain slogging up the fell-sides to the tops of the mountains. Beyond simply registering a pounding heart and aching leg muscles, a new relation to self and the limitless surrounding briefly exists, in which one can feel part of – not separated from – that larger whole. The limen is the threshold. It is through organic impressions that one crosses the threshold, finds oneself opened to a different view. For all its being devoid of people, the view mysteriously includes self – though not the self of personal anxieties or aspirations.

As the Prologue made clear, views come inflected with all sorts of weather conditions. This is what Loutherbourg's *eidophusikon* strove to replicate. His theater without actors was only about six feet wide and had no stage apron, the better to focus the eye on the representational view. The withdrawal of the framing element helped eliminate an inevitable 'distancing' between viewer and view. Up on the tops, any frame of reference is totally absent. The panoramic views shared with just a few fellow sightseers are almost overwhelming. Self is a diminished center point for the dizzying rush of impression. The optical illusionism of the *eidophusikon* is reversed: rather than the view being made to appear larger, it is oneself that is reduced in size. The fundamentally empty and vast space of the theater of landscape reduces us, the actors-as-audience, to our true level of unscripted insignificance. Scale, permanence and impermanence are re-sited beyond our grasp, but within the view.

# Notes

1. I found this young man deeply distressing. He was so obviously on the edge of life. Terribly upset, I in turn had to be reassured by someone else in the group that this man *was* at least temporarily located within a group of people that broke the isolation that he obviously lived in. I could not help seeing him in terms of *beyond* those boundaries. I watched with gratitude the great kindness with which Geoff, our leader that week, dealt with him.

2. This is remarkably similar to a description by Herbert Spencer of a reflected sunset on the Sound of Mull in Scotland that he witnessed in 1861, and the effect it produced upon him:

> On the evening in question the gorgeous colours of clouds and sky, splendid enough even by themselves to be long remembered, were reflected from the surface of the Sound, at the same time that both of its sides, along with the mountains of Mull, were lighted up by the setting Sun. . . . The exaltation of feeling produced was unparalleled in my experience; and never since has pleasurable emotion risen in me to the same intensity.
>
> (Spencer 1904 (II): 78)

Here we have the same experience (over the course of 150 years) of distance between self and the phenomenological world being breached through the same landscape-located experience.

3. Of interest here is the different tone between the tongue-in-cheek quality of this British hi-tech clothing ad and American counterparts such as the full page advertisement for an Equinox sports store in Manhattan. Set in vastly more ad space, its major text runs:

> go on.
> be a hero.
> gear up.
> superior equipment.
> technically-correct apparel.
> expert advice.
>
> (*New York Times*, 17 November, 1996: 28)

4. As I was to experience later, CHA walk leaders still do conduct short Sunday services for those who are interested, so there is certainly no ban on them. I have no explanation for why this particular man felt he could no longer conduct services.

5. There were various permutations on this. Some leaders did mind if members of their group walked out in front, but mostly if there were people who were slightly faster than the rest of the group these people would then be told where they would have to wait up. Some leaders would make it very clear that the rest break would begin from when the end of the party arrived, and that no one was to leave before the break was over, that the group would start again *as* a group. The other side of this coin was that some people insisted on always walking up front with the leader and would resist anyone else's 'taking their place'. At times this reached quite ludicrous proportions as people were

actually jostled out of the way if it seemed they were taking over that space. Other leaders moved up and down the line or would walk at the back if someone was having trouble, but then they would have the front of the group wait up at a certain designated spot so everyone could catch up and 'regroup'. Generally someone would be appointed the 'whipper-in' to make sure no stragglers got lost.

6. These constituted the first phase of the drama, the '*breach* of regular, norm-governed social relations [by an individual who] always acts, or believes he acts on behalf of other parties, whether they are aware of it or not' (Turner 1974: 38). It is this altruistic quality that differentiates between a symbolic breach or a crime, the latter always being marked by some element of egoism (Turner 1974).

7. A woman friend in New York who had done some wilderness trekking had shown me a plastic device that (apparently) enables a woman to discreetly urinate standing up. This funnel contraption had been developed for use in pristine wilderness areas where everything you take in, including bodily wastes, you also take out. The other part of this 'piece of equipment' were the plastic bags into which the funnel would deposit urine. I declined her offer to bring it with me – even minus the bags. I described this device to the women on one of the walks, where it caused enormous hilarity, necessitating the call for yet another bracken break.

# Particular Points of View

When I was about fifteen I got on to Wordsworth . . . and the next time I went to the Lakes . . . I realised that on the map it said "Green Head Gill" and it struck me like a thunderclap really, that this was the Green Head Gill which is the scene of "Michael". And then the whole thing struck me that I could actually go up there and look at that old sheepfold, and that of course he's writing about Helvellyn and I'd like to go up Helvellyn! He's writing about his boat on Ullswater – I'd like to go and see! What were those mountains that worried him so much, and, therefore, I was then going up with the dual purpose – I was following the steps of Wordsworth and his contemporaries. And that gave a great new dimension to my walking.

Sonia Ankers

Walking is still my first love, it's a whole spectrum of things that I enjoy about walking. . . . It goes from meeting the people through the freedom. That's I think the main thing – it's space and freedom, and, to start on a hill, and look around, three hundred and sixty degrees, and there isn't another thing in sight except hills and beauty. And I think that really it hurts, it really does hurt because it's so lovely, and for that moment it's mine. And, I don't share that with anyone, so it's a selfish point of view, really.

Marion Canning

When I'm walking on my own, or particularly when I'm back packing or camping on my own, there's a very fine balance about what constitutes safety – I mean as a woman – because in general . . . especially if its coming on to evening and I'm going to be looking for somewhere to camp, for me [other walkers] represent threat actually, you know, because if I'm camping on my own, I don't want them to know where I am and where I'm camping and it's a funny one isn't it. Because you know from another perspective other walkers represent safety if I've broken my leg . . . but

I'm terribly aware of the animal-like need for camouflage . . . which is a gendered experience that relates to patriarchy and a culture of male domination, and women's fear of being attacked. Well that's all about access too isn't it.

Paula Day

## Introduction

Speaking *to* and speaking *for* is fieldwork's 'double ventriloquism' (Appadurai 1988: 16–17). What follows is an attempt to lessen the ventriloquist's act by presenting the voices of three women with as little interference as possible. It is a purposeful attempt to bring the margins to the center. The three women are Sonia Ankers, born in 1924 in Liverpool; Marion Canning, born in 1938 in what was then the village of Castle Bromwich, Staffordshire; and Paula Day, born in 1954 in London. Sonia is a fellow-walker; Marion leads walks on a voluntary basis for a national walking-holiday organization; and Paula runs her own women's walking holidays. Extended taped conversations with these three women yielded over 200 pages of transcripts. Rather obviously, choices have had to be made about what to present, what to drop – proof if it were needed that the ventriloquist is incapable of performing a disappearing act.

The central issue about which each woman speaks recapitulates in terms of her own life a particular theme carried in the exposition of one of the earlier chapters. That this is possible came about certainly not through any conscious forethought on my part but represents a fortuitous 'conjuncture of style, sensibility, and mood between the ethnographer and the society he or she encounters' (Appadurai 1988:18). The theme recapitulated by Sonia is the literary construction of the Lake District. Her early awareness of that constructed place was instrumental in shaping her life-course. The glimpses provided by Sonia's half-century of membership in Co-operative Holidays Association (CHA) complements its organizational history presented in Chapter 5.

Marion's organizing of a work-place walking club in the Midlands, and her deep involvement with leading walking groups all over the country, recapitulates the theme of 'repeopling' the landscape. Yet, as becomes apparent, this is not without its tension and internal contradictions. Access is the dominant theme of this whole work. Paula, while recapitulating that theme, adds to it a gendered view. The walking holidays that Paula runs for women, primarily lesbians, brings into focus current issues of access and discrimination: to be female, lesbian, black, or urban and in the landscape, is to run into rejection, ridicule or resentment.

## Sonia Ankers

*Sonia lives in the seaside village of Rhos-on-Sea situated on Colwyn Bay, North Wales. She retired in 1980 from Penrhos College, a girls' boarding school there, where she had been Head of the English Department. All I knew at the time of my arrival at Rhos-on-Sea was that Sonia had walked in the Lake District for decades and had been a member of CHA since she was a young woman. Within moments of starting the first of our taped conversations, the Lakeland poets were being placed in the context of British culture and Sonia's life.*

When you're talking about relationship of people both intellectually and spiritually and secularly to the landscape, you're basically talking about music, art, and poetry. Understand? And, in the Lakes, at a certain time in history, you got a particularly unique combination, a kind of mini-Renaissance. Now, there have been many great nature poets in Britain, mostly young, and um – that's quite a lot down south – who are nature poets in that they are writing poems about birds, about animals, specifically about trees, and there isn't any what I would call philosophy behind it, it's just a delighted reaction in the beauty of blossoms in the spring, Housman's 'Cherry blossoms', and so on. And there are people who love that, and I think we all do up to a point, and they read their work, and they'd be delighted to go and see the places where they sat by the river and heard the nightingale or they walked through the grove of cedars or whatever, but the Lakeland poets were different in that they had a philosophy.

And their giant as it were, their Wordsworth, wasn't a nature poet in that sense at all – though unfortunately in school everybody's taught 'Daffodils' (*I Wandered Lonely as a Cloud*) or 'To a Celandine' or some such charming little poetic stuff, flowers and trees – but he was undoubtedly pantheistic and his greatness lay in the 'Prelude', no doubt about that, (*the rest of this sentence is spoken with great emphasis*) and in the intellectual caliber of this meeting of some of the greatest writers this country has ever produced, so that you get the extraordinary phenomenon of a tiny cottage in a remote village in the mountains, owned by William Wordsworth, where his visitors are the crème de la crème of the literary world of the time.

Coleridge is not just the poet of the 'Ancient Mariner,' 'Christabel', and so on; he is a quite considerable nature poet, but he was also probably the greatest scholar I would say, all-round scholar, of the century. Coleridge, Hazlitt, Shelley, these were all gathering at the house at one time or another; Cooper, a lesser poet ... Lowndes, Scott, meeting, talking, discussing life, philosophy, walking together out on the hills. It is an extraordinary coming together of talent which was not unnoticed by the literati of the times, so that by the time Wordsworth is an old man his reputation is already fixed, and from then on, you are getting the legend of the cottage as some sort of symbol of nature worship or whatever.

*Today* you are getting not only the English, Scottish, Irish ... you are getting people from all over the world coming to his little cottage. Why? ... because Grassmere's a very pretty place, and the scenery's lovely, and you can buy some gingerbread, and you can look at the grave of the great Wordsworth, whose works you have not read, but you do know 'Daffodils', and you can go home, bearing a badge with Wordsworth on it. But the intellectuals are not for that at all, but to go around the cottage and think how restricted the space in that cottage was, how simple the life, how hard physically, what a rotten life they all had materially – what tragedy, what poverty – a great deal of their lives, and what glory came out of it.

... From a practical point of view, Liverpool is very near the Lakes and my generation did not have cars, but the trains and buses were always good. And people would go for day excursions, always have, and holidays to the Lakes, and from an early age the Lakes was one of our summer retreats. ... We were staying in a simple hotel, and we were walking. We were walking, we were not scaling the heights, but we were good walkers, and we would go round the Lakes, a lovely terrace kind of walk, I suppose you would say, a kind of 'C' walk, really, (*a reference to how CHA grades their walks*), only perhaps longer in distance, but just enjoying it.

When I was perhaps twenty-one I found out that CHA ... is a good way to go on holiday if you are alone and you want to walk. ... And so I joined the CHA, and they're pretty hearty people, and they're clomping along up to the top, and clomping along back, not on the whole literary people. Well, we go on for a long time then, and I teach English, and ... – you are not a good teacher of English literature if you can't act! Now my teaching is a highly dramatic thing (*she laughs*) and I taught through dramatic readings and sometimes acting the things out with the children, and, and then I was fortunate enough to have as an assistant a very brilliant woman. . . . And we made a wonderful team because we approached things in a different way. I'm talking about the sixth form (*high school senior years*). And if we were teaching in the sixth form, for one thing, she had her favorite authors and poets and I did, so it gave – you go to teach the things that you like most, if you don't like them to teach, you might as well not start in the first place, because the girls won't like it. And it widened what we could offer them from the set book range.

. . . And then I got a brilliant idea, because we had a new headmaster who was a mountain walker, he believed in, in, uh, canoeing, and abseiling (*rappeling*), and all the extra-curricular activity you could imagine. . . . And he very much wanted the staff not to be just teaching, but to be taking on activities. I don't just mean, a play-reading group, or discussion group or debating group, but something physical outside, because it was a boarding school. . . . Well by this time I wasn't young, and I had never been any good at sport, and I wasn't likely to be able to be in a canoe, or even take a rock-climbing course. Nevertheless I thought, well, I'm a good walker. I'm a very good walker, not of course now because I'm slow and older, but I was a very strong walker and I knew my mountains, and I got a brilliant idea.

So I said to Maureen, how would it be – we were studying Wordsworth for A-level, (*university entrance qualifying exams*) and part of the 'Prelude' in with it – if we had a weekend in the Lakes with our sixth form, and we combined . . . going out in the mornings . . . on a really decent climb there related to the poetry? We'll take them up Green Head Gill, up to Helen's Pike; we'll do Fairfield, or we'll go to Ullswater and we'll walk around. . . . And we'll work out what Wordsworth could've been looking at there, and relate it, and then when we come in in the evening . . . we'll have an evening meal, and then retire to the conference room and take that part of 'Prelude'. And the two of us would give a joint lesson, eh, I would read part, and I would interpret it, and then she would read part, and she would have, obviously, different ideas. In my opinion, those girls got some of the best lessons that anybody could ever have had because it was a combination of two minds that were very - we were very good teachers and we were expert at what we were teaching and those girls were lucky. . . . And we did that for several years . . . in the early '70s.

Now, while we're doing this, I always in the summer holidays had a fortnight at the CHA, and as I've been doing this over the years, I've got to know a lot of people. I don't mean as friends exactly, but I knew the leaders, and . . . I knew some of the people who came every year.

So, it was going home. After all, I knew the walks, I could take the walks and sometimes I did . . . but it wasn't that, it was the friendship and it was the, the excitement of all being together again another year, and you can't tire of the things you do in the Lakes. (*Sonia laughs.*) I just never tire of them.

I came across CHA when I was twenty-one, which means I was still at university. . . . I was beginning to get the feel of walking here, real walking. I cannot remember whether somebody told me, or I read about it, or I actually passed the place when I, probably on a holiday, and saw that it was a walking place. So the first time, I must have gone with great trepidation . . . I think the first time I went by bus, and I got off at The Swan (*a pub*). In those days, the principle of the CHA and the HF (*Holiday Fellowship*), and certainly the Youth Hostels, was to provide somewhere for – I don't want to say working-class people, quite – but people who hadn't got a lot of money, and who lived in the towns, and who wanted the opportunity of spending a holiday exploring the countryside, and of course having, not in the case of Youth Hostels, but of CHA and HF, a program that was guided, because in those days there weren't Americans, Germans, or . . . other people coming. It was for people in the towns, the cheapest holiday.

It was very basic, but it was nothing to what it had been. . . . When I went to CHA . . . the furniture was very simple. You had a bed and you had a bedroom chair, and you had a stick across the corner of the wall and a curtain on it, and that was a wardrobe. And you had a chest of drawers. You didn't have a bedside light, I think. And a bit of a carpet on the floor, and of course no washbasins in the room. . . . You had a breakfast, which is more or less what it is now, plunked down, and the evening meal was for quite a while very institutionalized . . . a great bowl of soup put down, and a ladle, and everybody plonked out. And always boiled potatoes, always boiled potatoes till people began to make songs about what do we have for evening meal? (*Sings out in a loud voice:*) Boiled potatoes, boiled potatoes! Cabbage, you can imagine. Eh, and, a slice of beef or a slice of some other meat, and of course traditionally in Grassmere, the rice pudding, which was always an alternative to some great heavy mucking piece of tart or some kind of trifle in a bowl where everybody's serving is slopped out from. And then you had entertainment which was usually of the jigging round, dancing, Scottish reels type, and then about quarter to ten, the host and hostess went to make a cup of tea and biscuits for the guests, and then they said, could somebody volunteer to wash up? That went on until very recently of course.

Also, there was a very strong Christian atmosphere . . . with both groups (*CHA and HF*). It was the kind of thing, I think they had the ideal of the Englishmen that Thomas Arnold had at Rugby – you know, a sound mind and a sound body, and the body has lots of cold showers and it doesn't think unclean sexual thoughts. And you go out (*here Sonia puts on a 'hearty' deep male voice*) and have a decent day on the hills, and you come in and you have a simple meal, and you've got your companionship, all very clean and upright and convivial. . . . Hardly anybody at first thought of going down for a drink to The Swan. Because that's the whole point, you see. They never had a TV or anything like that, because that doesn't go for community – they wanted you in the evening to be in.

On a Sunday evening . . . there was a service immediately after the meal, a kind of – from the Christian point of view – interdenominational service, in other words, Bible-reading, a few prayers, a few hymns, and there was always somebody playing the piano, and then there was the speech made for the appeal for the invited guests. And after that there were quiet games such as quizzes and paper games all day Sunday. Thursday was a concert, the guests you know got together and put on a show, and some of them were marvellous in their time. And the other days were as they are now pretty well . . . dancing, or a treasure hunt, or something like that. And at the end of the week you all gathered outside in the garden and you had a group photograph made, which was rather nice. I've only got one, because it was the same all the time (*Sonia laughs*).

There was every day, if you wished – indeed it depends on the leader now – prayers before breakfast in the lounge, and always grace, always at every meal. Until, oooh (*long pause*), ten years ago? There was this, this decidedly, it was a Christian . . . the founders of it were Christian. Fine if you weren't Christian, well that was fine because, I mean, you didn't have, certainly you didn't have to attend the services, and, I mean you can just sit through the grace, can't you? I've noticed that now how it's gone off, and, within the last, say the last six years, there have been leaders who haven't said grace or who haven't done anything at all, but there have been leaders who have said grace, and there have been leaders who have said for those who wish there will be morning prayers, and, and a little bit of a service after supper on a Sunday.

But the people who turn up for that are under ten, under ten in number, I would say, whereas in the past practically everyone went, of course. And that reflects the growing lack of religious belief in the country, of course. I think in many ways, walking (*long pause*) can be tied up with religion. There are so many hymns – if you've been out for a walk on the mountains and then you come back and you sing, 'All Things Bright and Beautiful', and you're having prayers for the, how lucky you are that you've had a holiday, and for the beauty of the mountains, the beauty of the hills, the beauty of the streams, for what we've seen today, the companionship on our walk - it lends itself, doesn't it?

You know, Holiday Fellowship and the CHA, . . . their song and hymn books have a lot of, not only hymns, but jolly songs, get-together songs that are about marching along the roads and the country ways. . . . And now, of course it's very sad, but there are fewer and fewer young people who are coming with their parents as they did in the olden days, it's like people attend church, and therefore obviously go on to be parents who bring their children and that will ensure that the group, the organization goes on. So they've had to alter the course in the last few years. The diehards, the devoted CHA people such as myself are getting increasingly old and that's why they're now running a 'C' party which is for those who are, have done every mountain and know them backwards like myself, and have been very strong walkers, and cannot walk them anymore but love the mountains and like to stay in the place and take part in all the activities, and go around to see them.

## Marion Canning

*Marion was one of three walk leaders taking an HF week that I was on. All such leading is done on a volunteer basis. In the evenings she and another of the leaders organized square dancing – something they also do for clubs outside of HF. Marion also gave a pre-breakfast exercise class each day. Both in conversation and letters Marion stressed that her involvement with landscape went back to her mother who was born on a farm. There had been a few sheep, a herd of cows, some pigs and fowl as well as arable land. Though her mother had left the farm, Marion grew up visiting grandparents and uncles who continued this mixed farming at the family place until the 1960s. Though the land has long since been lost to development, the farmhouse still remains, with a preservation order upon it. Others of her uncles and their sons were all farmers, and so, as she put it in a letter to me, 'my connections with the land "run in the blood"'.*

I have walked with a group I guess now for about twenty-five, perhaps thirty years. I was always most keen on leading – I wanted to lead before really I was capable of leading, and then I decided that I really ought to get something done, so I trained for mountain and compass work and gained all my certificates. And then . . . I put a notice up in the place where I worked and said 'I'm going for a walk on Sunday. If you'd like to join me, then do.' And that has evolved now into quite a large rambling club that I organize and run. I'm the committee, the treasurer, the chairman, the whole lot, because I don't want to be affiliated to Ramblers', I don't want to have a committee because they always make problems. So I organize the whole program. And we are . . . I think it's about forty-five, fifty members, which is quite a substantial club size. . . . We meet always once a month and occasionally twice a month. This year it's our tenth anniversary, and so that's something I'm quite proud about.

And because of that I've organized a special . . . walk, and it's called 'Walk X' . . . And there are ten sections of ten miles distance, and each person who wanted to lead drew a month, and it started in February which is our starting month, and it finishes in November, and the person leading doesn't divulge the end of the walk until the day they meet. So they meet where they finish last time you see and then it goes on from there. And it will finish back where we started, at the old headquarters of the office. . . . I'm thinking now that there are others coming in who may do it a little better than me, who can give it more time. . . . But, that was the start of my leading, really serious leading.

It started when I used to work for the Central Electricity Generating Board . . . and when the CGBs decided to privatize, they went over to PowerGen and that's when I left . . . but the walking group had to keep going, so . . . we had a competition (*for its name*) and 'Generators' won. It can be thought of in all sorts of ways – you generate power you know, you generate happiness. The camaraderie there is fantastic! We've got a doctor in chemistry, and we've got a chap who packed in a warehouse. When we're walking, everyone's the same. One of the members recently described it as 'my family.' And I thought, that is a nice thing you know . . . and I could believe that . . . because this person's involved with everything we do. . . . She has accompanied me on some of our long distance walks. She always protests . . . 'Oh I'll never be able to do that, I shall keep you all waiting.' And I realize that all she needs is, she wants you to say, 'Come on, you can do this'.

I've always enjoyed being in this country and travelling around this country. I like the villages and I like the open spaces, and I like the national parks. And so I, I just took it on from there, and because I became known as a leader then, you know word spreads very quickly, and then I became a guest leader for various groups and people would ring me and ask me to lead their walks which I did happily, and I do, or have done, a lot more, but occasionally I do some for the National Trust. We have a local center, quite a large center, seventeen hundred members, and I lead for their rambling group occasionally. I took it on for a couple of years, the whole thing, and enjoyed that.

And then I've led for various groups around, and only a couple of weeks ago I had a call from a lady in Malvern who's taking her walking group to the Quantocks and she asked if I would lead them down on the Quantocks. And I said, 'Yes, happily, I can drive from here to there.' And she said, 'Oh no, I want it for three days.' Right, fine. So she said, 'I want two walks on the Quantocks and one on Exmoor itself.' So I said, 'Yes, that's fine, that's no problem at all. What's the average age of your group?' 'Seventy-five,' she said. And I said, 'Oh, well, what kind of mileage are they thinking of?' And she said, 'Oh, about ten miles a day'. These are some very fit people, you know!

I kept being asked to lead more and more groups, and then this group that I, my own group, the 'Generators', they wanted to take a holiday with me leading. And I said, 'Yes, okay then', and I took them away on a week's holiday, and I led the whole time. When I got back I thought, oh, that wasn't bad, I quite enjoyed that really, I enjoyed showing them things and the camaraderie, and I thought, oh, that was great. So, I thought some more about HF then, and I applied to HF, and I went on the assessment, and that was quite rigorous, that put me through it.

They take you during the winter time, the winter months, and I had to go up to Coniston, in the Lake District, for a weekend, and they ask you to be there at five o'clock on a Friday afternoon. They don't want you there before, they don't want you there after. Five o'clock. Absolute chaos. We all arrived at five o'clock. But there were various leaders put, and if your name was Canning then you come into here with this leader. There's your room, there you are, we want you downstairs in ten minutes. And it was like that, that was the pace throughout the whole weekend.

Now at that time, I was fifty-three, and I was old compared with a lot of them. And we, that night we went out on the – ten o'clock we went out on night leading, we sort of did a treasure hunt trail. We were sorting out routes for the next day; I didn't get to bed until two o'clock in the morning. They kept the pressure on. Sort out this! Do that! Make a timetable for tomorrow's walk. Pick out your highlights and write them all down. I was up at six o'clock then the next morning sorting this out, and you had to be downstairs on duty, you know.

And all the time they were sorting out your weaknesses and your strengths. All the time, it was weakness here, weakness there. God, I

didn't realize I had so many weaknesses, you know. But I've got a few
strengths I didn't know about as well. And all the time this is going
on, you're being watched, not only by your own personal leader, but
by the powers that be that are going around making little notes. And
you realize, suddenly, it hit me like a bullet, I could fail. I had always
considered myself to be a good leader. I never lost anyone, I could use
a map and compass, I could get people out of trouble on top of a
mountain, whatever the weather conditions. I could do all of that, but
he could fail me, because I made some silly mistake.

And on the Saturday, we had to – a group of us, we were four in one
group, and we were given a route which we had worked out the night
before, and we then had to lead our leaders over this, and take it in
turns leading. And we were going up onto Wetherlam near to Coniston
and the chap who led in front of me, two chaps before me – because
there were three men and me – the first one went wrong, and he got
himself out of the trouble, but he was a bit surprised that no one had
told him that it was going on. But that was the idea – I mean you've
got to get yourself out of this trouble, matey! Because I could go wrong
and nobody's going to tell me about it. So, anyway, he got himself out
of it.

But, because he'd done that, I think he'd unnerved the next chap,
who took us up – it was the most scary path I've ever walked, and I
just felt out of control on it, and the weather was atrocious, it was
coming down and hitting the rock face and freezing, so it was we were
walking on ice. We hadn't got the proper crampons or anything.
(*Crampons are metal 'teeth' that fit on boots; they dig into the ice providing
some hold.*) And we were going up this path, and all this sleet, and I
was scared out of my wits, I really was. It was terrible! And I froze at
one point, and I thought, I am not going to tell anybody how scared
stiff I am here. And I really had to take control and say to myself,
'Right, get to the top then quick'. Which I did. And when I got to the
top I was like this (*she held her arms out, shaking*). I never before or
since have been in that state, ever.

And when we got to the top . . . my leader said, 'Right, Marion, then
you take over.' And I said, 'Well frankly, I would not have brought
leaders or guests up here, up this rock, and I certainly in this weather
condition would not take them any higher.' And I said, 'And I can't
take over the leading at the moment, I'm not in a fit condition.' 'Why?'
I said, 'Well, because I was scared coming up that part, it really unnerved
me, and the thought of bringing guests up there is just not on at all.'
So they said, 'Well what would you do?' I said, 'I'd take them down

now.' 'Well, show me the route.' So I said, 'Down there! That's the most obvious path straight down.' So he said, 'Well take us down, then.' Oh! Okay, so I took them down, and I got to a point, and I said, 'Well this is where I'd bring them to. From here it's quite, quite safe.'

At that moment he fell to the ground and said, 'I'm unconscious and breathing, deal with it.' Oh, so I dealt with it – I sent two off for an ambulance with the grid reference where we were, I got the others surrounding this chap and put him in the safe position and so on, dealt with all of that and he said, 'Okay, that's fine.' And, I thought, oh, I've blown this, I've blown the whole thing by my chatter earlier. So I thought, I don't care, I didn't really want to be an HF leader anyway.

And, as we were walking down, he said, 'Continue, and give us the descriptions as you're going down.' So I went down and I was showing them various things. And we got down to a road about four miles later, and he came to me and he said, 'If it's any consolation, Marion, I would have done exactly as you did.' Thank goodness for that. Well of course I passed! And I drove away from Coniston, on the, I think it was on the Sunday afternoon, I stopped about five miles down the road. I pulled into a lay-by and I just went across the steering wheel. And I thought, this is the first time I've relaxed since Friday afternoon.

(*The conversation switched to the experience of leading walking groups.*) I was up in Brecon last week and I was the first up a hill because the group were a bit slow and they were tired, and I stood waiting at the top, but I had the first view and all of these thoughts went through my mind then and I can remember quite clearly, I don't really want these people to catch up just now. You know, I was being very selfish, but I was just loving what I could see. . . . And I would, if they'd have said, 'Well, we're not coming up there,' I should have been quite happy.

I enjoy walking alone and I do walk alone, and that makes me very aware of my surroundings in a different way to taking a group and being aware of the surroundings then. Walking on my own, I'm totally immersed in the countryside, totally immersed. And, I'm watching for all sorts of things, and looking for, and observing things that I would not see when I'm walking with a group, because – and if I'm leading that group especially – because, I'm thinking of the comfort of my group: what do they want to see, what are they interested in? And you can stop and . . . talk to a group and say, that is a particular hill and there's an Iron (*Age*) Fort there, and then there's a castle, and later on they built another castle, but I'm sorry, sad to say it was ruined in the fifteenth century and all the locals pinched the stone and built their houses. They don't want to know. Ninety percent of the time they do not want to know. And I asked the group that I was leading on the one day, 'Are you interested in the bits of history?' 'Well, yes, I mean, if you say, that was the tree that King Charles hid in, on his run around, then yes, but no more than that.' They only want to know that, the gossip.

You have to assess the group, and I find that the short low-levels (*walks*) are generally, not always, but generally, they're the older groups, the older age group. Therefore they want to know everything because there's time. They want to go and inspect churches and they want to know about the churches, their history. Or they want – whatever's going on, they want to know about it because they've got time to absorb it. And I do reckon that these older people, they are a fountain of knowledge because they're doing this, listening and going on tours and trips all the time.

. . . Then you get the middle group who are trying, they can't quite manage the high-level long group walks, but they don't want to be on the low-level short walks, so, yes, they will rush through their walks, they don't want to know, really, what's going on – let's get this eight miles out of the way, you see, so they don't really want to listen. And they're of the age group, in that age group, thirty to fifty – they know everything anyway, you're not going to tell them anything. . . . Then you get the high-level long walks, yes, they want to know, but mostly want to get the head down and walk. They want to know what that hill is over there, because, yeah, we wouldn't mind walking there some time in the future, you know . . . that sort of thing.

A lot of people, as well, because they're coming on holiday, they walk perhaps once a month, and then they come on this annual holiday and they're walking every day for six days, and they tire very quickly. They don't realize how exhausting it is. And so, by Tuesday they're really very very tired. They need Wednesday to rest, Thursday they're really pulling themselves up . . . to get going again, and by Friday they're feeling quite fit. So, you watch this as well going through the week. So you have to be very careful with them on the Tuesday. I find that they're very touchy, you know – 'don't say anything because I'm very upset, I'm very tired, I don't want to walk really today, I'm having to push myself to do it'.

. . . There are a lot of people in authority, the bureaucrats, who are not seeing our world, they're not seeing its beauty. And that bothers me. You know that they can, at the flick of a pen, they can write off acres of land for building, without thinking about how can we build this little plot here elsewhere where we're not going to spoil the beauty?

And that, these sort of things all rush through my mind when I'm looking at one of these views.

## Paula Day

*Paula started her walking holidays for women as a way of funding herself while doing her doctoral studies at Lancaster University which she chose to attend in order to be near the Lake District. Initially a feminist, Paula now identifies as a lesbian-feminist. Her walking organization has gone through a similar transition, and now most guests are lesbians. However, her advertising brochure makes clear that all women are welcome. She neither wants 'lesbians only' to be read as the subtext of a 'women's walking group' nor wants to have heterosexuals 'freak out' as she put it. Her father was a serious amateur mountaineer. Brought up to walk and climb, she 'had to find her own way' relating to mountaineering, climbing, walking, and landscape itself. The first of our taped conversations started with my asking, When do you remember first walking for walking's sake?*

Well that immediately gets involved with my father and his mountaineering background and so on. It has me start there (*long pause*) and then there'd be another start, which is when I started to do it for myself which is quite a different one, and that was a kind of probably beginning to claim or reclaim it for me. . . . It would be being taken by him on weekends in the Lakes and Wales, yeah on weekends when he was going to rock-climb he'd take my mum and me. I suppose (*I was*) probably eight, nine or ten. The memory that comes very vividly is going with my school friend Juliette, for a weekend in North Wales . . . (and) her and me getting terribly excited about doing our own exploring up a streambed – actually following it to its source, sort of from the house, you know, so perhaps we could do some of our own exploring. . . . And that was a terribly important bit of becoming independent.

I'm going to start – all different sorts of connections all start to happen, because I guess that's the beginning of them, what I used to do with my school friends – which was go into the countryside going out on walks, climbing out of the window in the middle of the night to go to the Downs to see the sunrise and things like that, you know when we were about fourteen or, no, maybe younger, twelve or thirteen. Yeah, so I suppose there's two things aren't there, there's sort of him taking me and showing me about all this mountain stuff that he did . . . and then these other things about having exciting adventures with my friends.

He had a big thing about buying me proper walking boots, and . . . it was always a very special day when I put them on. . . . (*pause*) Yeah, because you know I was my father's daughter and supposed to be a chip off the old block and that meant proper walking boots . . . but there is something about his culture, you know, that's very important about his – his mountaineering culture which I've honestly been inspired by and also probably reacting against or exploring other ways of being ever since.

I used to go and climb in the Alps and things. Yes, so there was this tremendous sort of heroic imagery – Matterhorn and all that – and then later on I started to see it very differently (*pause*) later on ah . . . well I remember an occasion when I was 16, and a school friend and I went to the Dolomites and he (*Paula's father*) had an idea about me climbing mountains. He and I joined up with a mountaineering club (*to climb a mountain*) that we couldn't have done on our own . . . . but actually it was totally inappropriate – I didn't have any experience. And what happened was one of the Italian guides decided the foreigners had to be on his rope, and I didn't speak a word of the language . . . We got to the edge of a glacier and I didn't have crampons or an ice-axe, and I'd never done this kind of thing you see and my dad was somewhere miles back, so I started out across this steep ice. . . . I now know that it takes a long time for an individual person to discover what's possible for them on a particular kind of ground, and I was completely in the hands of that man that I knew nothing about and I just tried to follow.

I knew I was going to slip but I didn't speak Italian so I couldn't say, and I started to slip and fall and if he'd been ah, competent, he would've held me by sticking his – he'd have done an ice-axe arrest - he would have struck his ice-axe and held me and I would've just fallen just a little way. But being incompetent, though heroic-looking in his yellow socks, he began sliding as well and in the end he stabbed himself in the leg with his ice-axe. So there's this unforgettable image of these amazing yellow socks he had on all stained with blood while I slid – fortunately, don't know much about it – not knowing what was going on. My dad lower down thought – I mean there was a crevasse lower down – and he thought I was going to go in the crevasse – he started kind of running across the glacier lower down, he's all roped up to his poor Italian guide. I mean it was just awful. Fortunately I just came to a stop before I came to the crevasse. And the terrible thing about it was . . . the whole expedition, this whole club, all thirty of them, all turned around with 'the duce' all bleeding heroic you know, and my dad, as compensation I think, gave him his watch or something. I was just left feeling totally in the end that I had, I had just been humiliated. I now feel furious that I was put in that position. I think it's totally irresponsible of my father, totally irresponsible and incompetent of the leader, and I mean I was just putting myself in the hands of – because I learnt to – they were 'reliable' people. But you know they weren't, it was bloody dangerous and it totally put me off any kind of ice-climbing or that kind of scene, which was fine.

But I think, I probably didn't recognize it then, but later on, came to feel that there was a hell of a lot of all this, it's all about sort of heroic posing and stuff, and egos. . . . And I see it, I do see it on Striding Edge all the time – men taking their girlfriends you know, and for that woman it's not necessarily at all what she's ready to do or what she'd choose to do, but the guy – it's part of his sense of himself to be able to, you know, support someone who's scared stiff and get her up the mountain, a macho self-image that's nothing to do with actually helping her develop her confidence. I think, yeah, and I hope part of what I do in my work is, I hope I'm not doing that, because I just think it's . . . if there's someone more experienced taking someone who's less experienced, then the whole thing has to be about the needs of the less experienced person and giving them the support that they want, to go that bit further than they perhaps would on their own, you know. And if it's about the needs of the experienced person to be seen as wonderful, then I just think that's crap really.

I'm sure it happens between men as well but – perhaps it doesn't – I think it's a particular type of gender thing, isn't it. You know, I mean it would be men who'd more likely be competing . . . but the whole thing of 'taking' a woman who's less experienced, to a place that she doesn't feel safe on her own, that seems to me to be very much what happens. . . . So for me there's then a stage of very much needing to go up on my own to find out what I could do, wanted to do. . . . Especially when I first started the business and watching what's going on with groups walking in the hills, and it's just so often a sort of gendered thing, the dynamics going on – the man has the map and I've always, I always greet the woman who is usually behind and doesn't make eye contact at first because she is following – it's the man who makes the eye contact – so I always carefully avoid eye contact with him and greet the woman at the back you know.

. . . The walking I do for myself is actually still my own, exclusively mine. Yeah. I do it for a whole lot of different reasons. One of them being is I don't like being left behind and I don't like being in front *(laughs)*. I know that when I'm leading groups that that'll be an issue for the women in my group, but not for me because I'm their leader which means that I'm allowed to be in front and to be the benign person in the front if you see what I mean *(more laughter)*. . . . As a group leader . . . it's clear to me that I don't in any way value or admire women up in front more than the women at the back – I have just as much respect for them as I, you know what I mean. If I was in that position, situation in a group I think that I would think that the group leader – that I'd kind of have to be good at it for the leader to like me. But actually I know as a leader that it's not like that at all – I don't, yeah – I respect how people handle themselves, wherever they are.

   . . . *(Speaking of 'getting to the top')* I mean it's so funny, the idea that the top bit – the very high, the highest bit of the mountain is the important bit – it seems, it's taken as self-evident that the point of going near a mountain is to get on that particular rock on the top, you know, and of course we think that because all our language is full of land imagery. But it's a peculiar idea isn't it, that that's better than any other part. Often as not its got orange peel and graffiti, and stinks of pee *(laughter)* and there are wonderful places . . . and plants that are on the flanks. And of course then all that is deeply involved in gendered imagery right through our culture, and that's what part of my thesis is all about, you know. Mountains are seen as male and valleys as female – Tennyson saying 'Come down, O maid, from yonder mountain heights' and all that. Why shouldn't women go to the top? I think it's great that there are women's expeditions to climb Annapurna and all that, you know, and we've got every right to get onto the tops if we want to – as men have – but maybe I don't want particularly to go onto the top, you know.

   It's both isn't it, it's both about women having the right of access, you know, to everything that men might aspire to also, and at the same time questioning whether those are the bounds that we want anyway. . . . I remember, last year, there was a party of just two and we went up by Dungeon Gill, it was wonderful, though I hadn't been there for some years. There's a scramble and we were stopping and looking at some flowers because there are all sorts of special things there and these blokes – in an absolutely classic – I don't know if they were Army – but, ah young lads with an older chap, kind of stamping up there knocking all the rocks – actually doing some very bad hill-walking because they were being very clumsy and knocking down rocks and stuff. And as they kind of thundered past causing havoc to this fragile beautiful landscape, one of them actually turned round and said,

'Always trampling on all your flowers, ho ho ho' – it was just like, you know, a stereotype come alive, it was extraordinary. Yeah. Yeah. (*pause*) And, you know, there's such a dualism isn't there, that somehow to be, that those that do make it to the top means trampling on the flowers.

I'm sort of quite amused by the fact that I'm still running things, like holidays, like weekends, where the idea is to climb 'Big Lake District Mountains by the steepest way' and I kind of really enjoy it, and somehow I've got some kind of amusement about it, some kind of irony about it. . . . I'm not quite sure where I am with it as an idea, you know – (*whether*) this is the thing to do. *Well it's enabling.* It's absolutely! . . . I'm fine with me doing it because of lots of women want to do that, and it makes lots of sense that lots of women want to do it because it's the thing that the culture says is the epitome of hill-walking. And absolutely right that women should want to do what's the epitome of hill-walking, you know, and I'm very happy to enable that, great. But personally I'm not sure where I am with the idea of climbing the highest mountains by the steepest routes. So I suppose, you know, it's fine, it's fine, I'm very happy to do it.

. . . When I first started, one of the women had made a women's symbol banner, you know, and every time we got to the top, we'd climb up to the trig point and hold up this women's symbol banner and had ourselves photographed, and there was something kind of ludicrous about it, you know what I mean . . . And unconsciously I think, there's something about that, and that's great – I mean here we are, we're on the summit of Everest – and well, we're not really (*laughs*), and we're all wonderful and we shake hands with each other 'coz we've reached the summit, and take photos of ourselves and that's (*pause*) I suppose its, um, (*pause*) . . . I mean it's good fun. I think so, so perhaps that's what I mean about being amused by it – and I think I've always had that feeling. And yeah, I'm really happy to see it, yeah.

*I asked Paula about a holiday she had run for black women that she had mentioned on an earlier occasion.* It happened twice actually. But then I lost contact with the woman who initiated it, I lost contact. . . . There was a mixture, a lot of them she knew through the Re-evaluation Co-Counselling Community actually, so . . . *What's that?* You know about co-counselling? *No.* . . . Quite a few of the women who came had done a great deal of work in black women's groups on their identities as black women, and on looking at the ways they might still be oppressing themselves and then breaking out of that. So I mean they were wonderful wonderful role models of, well for me as well, of very clearly, very consciously stepping beyond what felt safe, you know, and so they were very conscious of coming to walk in the countryside being um a courageous thing to do as black women. And they supported each other a lot. . . . There was such consciousness about being a group (*pause*) and that what they were doing (*pause*) was courageous and a break (*pause*) I mean they were, (*there was an*) absolutely amazing atmosphere here, absolutely amazing because – yes, so that what could easily be seen as a very short local walk . . . was quite clearly for some of them a big challenge which was taken on with immense courage and enthusiasm.

The woman who initiated it actually, you know, was very challenged simply by, ah, by walking on rough ground and encountering mud and stuff. And that's not unique to her as a black woman, that's – I've had white women who come on holidays who've never been in the country before, you know, for whom getting over a stile or getting through mud was a big challenge because that doesn't happen in London, on the street. And um, yeah, (*pause*) you know, I really respect that. That's just as big a challenge for them as doing huge long walks would be for somebody else, you know.

So its about being, um, how the woman experienced walking being a city experience and then encountering these unfamiliar physical things in the country – that I guess that the black women, they were also identifying that there wasn't any physical time to lose their challenge about feeling safe enough in an environment where, you know, there weren't black people, and where the culture seemed to be telling them they belonged in the inner city and not in the countryside.

. . . Most of them were Afro-Caribbean, and um yeah there were two Asian women as well, yeah. And then you see, the other difference as well, I mean this wasn't visible to me (*at the beginning*) but there were very different kinds of identity among the Afro-Caribbean women, because some of them were people who had grown up in the Caribbean, and were very recent immigrants and felt that home was the Caribbean, and others were sort of second-generation immigrant background so they felt completely British and quite divorced from any sense of roots elsewhere. I mean I hadn't realized that was quite a different kind of identity.

. . . One of my ideas when I um set it up, which was at this woman's initiative but I thought it was great because I'd been aware how few black women came on my holidays, and I thought this might be a way of opening it up. And I suppose I thought perhaps some of those women would come on other holidays I run, but then I thought about it. And they were saying, you know, the real lack of a black space in the country, a centre or some such thing, for black people in a rural area in the country. When I thought about it, I thought well you know, I've been on mixed . . . courses and so on, and then you know now, having gone through all that and gotten confidence in myself, my choice isn't at all to go on mixed courses but to do things with women, so why would I expect black women having just gotten over their fear, you know, of feeling less equal and less confident um, then choose to go off and be with white women when they could find ways to go off and be with other black women? That makes total sense, and I don't think that is ah, *(pause)* why should we um, ( *pause*) engage ah, I don't know, what would be the point given the choice of being with people with whom you feel strong and comfortable um, to not do that but to go and spend time with people with whom you have a struggle? . . . And I think that, that actually given the world that we live in now, there needs to be loads more opportunities to make that choice.

. . . I mean, what I see as my job is making space, you know, the physical space in the house, and then a space in the sense of access to the space out there, and that people come into that, really come into that space. So I suppose I'm sort of saying a held space, and then they do whatever they bring, don't they, and that may *(pause)* that'll be all sorts of things, yeah.

I just thought – there are some areas actually, in this area, not so much the Lakes, there are places I take guests in which feel to me very personal because they are places that aren't necessarily in guidebooks, and it's always one of my joys making up walks that aren't in guide-books – just because I've lived in this part of the world for a long time and you know, there are places that are important to me. So I suppose in some ways there is something about, I've always felt that I feel good about taking groups of women to those places, but I certainly wouldn't want to write a guidebook and publicize them to the world, and I probably wouldn't take mixed groups. The reason is always something about the landscape to me, in some ways part of my home. . . . I was just thinking that.

*Yes, that there's a public and a private landscape out there.* Yeah, yeah. *(pause)* So in some ways I am sharing a personal – the landscape is personal to me so I am sharing something that is personal to me. I think that is something I like, 'coz really it wouldn't be the same to me to kind of run holidays abroad or somewhere I'd gone and done some research . . . and was 'doing a decent job'. That wouldn't feel the same as showing this particular landscape that means a lot to me. *But within – you have the different kinds of weeks – and in those there's generally a mix of the public landscape and the private landscape?* Yes I suppose so really. I think that's rather a good way of describing it. Yes, I'm often aware of trying to get a balance between – OK people probably want to go to the highest hill or the well-known hill in the area that they've read about, and I'm willing to do that, and that's usually much busier. And then the days that I really enjoy showing are the ones which are much less well known which are much more personal. . . . *So how would you characterize those landscapes, which ones are they? What type of landscape are they?* All kinds of imagery starts coming in, which is alright isn't it, but it does make me smile.

*Paula then went off on another track. A few minutes later I asked the question again,* Well that's where I started getting embarrassed, because I realised that what comes to mind is some of these amazing streambeds in the Dales that are very very secret – hidden away, you know, so there's a wonderful sort of vulval imagery there especially um in some of the limestone places like (*name removed*) which is a dry limestone streambed ravine which I think is absolutely magical and incredibly sculptural, with amazing limestone rock walls, you know, and it's very much a hollow – so it's the most amazing kind of womb imagery kind of place, and some of the women who I've taken there respond to it in that way. Yeah, so certainly there I wouldn't be – I suppose it feels intimate and I dunno, I suppose it's probably a whole mix.

*. . . I reminded Paula of her having said that the fastest way up a mountain was slowly. This prompted her to recount the following.* We were having our stop and the guys came storming up the path with a real sense – the one in the front setting up a really formidable pace and the others struggling along to keep up with him, you know, looking as if they were highly uncomfortable really, racketing up the path at that rate, and um – but couldn't possibly be left behind, and then past they went. And then well back was this one black guy kind of sweating along, but as he passed us . . . he looked at us and caught our eye, and we were kind of laughing – well I was laughing . . . and he said 'I think it must be male bonding' (*laughter*). And we fell about laughing, and caught up afterwards. They were going too fast and in the end had to slow down. And it was just a lovely moment of recognition somehow. And that was just wonderful that he was the one black guy and that somehow he was able to have a little bit of distance and see what was going on . . . A little bit of distance from the values of the group.

# Conclusion

A staunch member of the Conservative Party and an Anglo-Catholic, Sonia Ankers voiced regret about the England that had passed. She lamented mothers' inability to stay home with their children; the word 'forename' having replaced 'Christian name' on forms; women having entered the priesthood; polytechnics having become universities overnight and their granting of 'rubbishy degrees'; the breakup of the Commonwealth; and Britain's loss of sovereignty through its membership in the European Union. Sonia related to walking through literature, not only in the sense of the great writers but also in books about the landscape, about mountaineering, about walking, about the National Parks. In these lay the untouched verities, for contemporary Britain is a far cry from the world that Sonia grew up in or knew most of her adult life.

Much as Marion Canning railed against planners and their wind farms and motorways, building sites and developments and their corresponding lack of inner-city development, her love of the English landscape did not extend to embracing those who would defend it with militant tactics. She related the vast overuse of the national parks to the generalized despoliation of the countryside beyond their boundaries that was going on under the rubric of planning. Though she could see no solution to the problem, she was adamant that we cannot keep 'poaching the landscape' with impunity.

Walking as a form of engagement with the landscape operated at a variety of levels for Paula Day. The exploration of the streambed as a child and the private landscapes only to be shared with women form but one level of landscape's foundational importance in the construction of her identity. My last week of fieldwork walking was with Paula's outfit. Towards the end of a blazing hot day, I was at the back of the line. As we made our way single-file up a steep path, the line bore sharply to the left. There in front, some way ahead of me and silhouetted against the sky, was Paula – absolutely straight, hands on her hips, going up the path with slow deliberation.

It was an immensely striking image that carried within it movement and stillness, a centeredness that seemed to pivot around each foot's placement on the ground. Paula was teaching by example what she months later spoke to me about as 'being in sync with the body . . . going back inside and finding the heartbeat, finding the breathing rate, and then . . . slowing to the pace that's actually going to be comfortable . . . regardless of what anyone else is doing . . . a way of moving [where there is] the possibility of being present in each step'. Here is walking as a practice of an inner journey, another kind of secular pilgrimage.

# Conclusion: Envisioning/ Re-visioning Community

Gregory Bateson, the anthropologist, who was no believer, once pointed out how the erosion of the concept of divine immanence in nature led men to see the world around them as mindless, and therefore not entitled to moral, aesthetic, or ethical consideration. This led them to see themselves as wholly set apart from nature; when this loss of a sense of organic unity was combined with an advanced technology Bateson argued, 'your likelihood of survival will be that of a snowball in hell'.

Fuller 1985: 282–3

... "the real England" refers less to a bounded place than to an imagined state of being or moral location ... there can be little doubt that the explosion of a culturally stable and unitary England into the cut-and-mix "here" of contemporary [reality] is an example of a phenomenon that is real and spreading ... as actual places and localities become ever more blurred and indeterminate, *ideas* of culturally and ethnically distinct places become perhaps even more salient. It is here that it becomes most visible how imagined communities come to be attached to imagined places, as displaced peoples cluster around remembered or imagined homelands, places or communities in a world that seems increasingly to deny such firm territorialized anchors in their actuality.

Gupta and Ferguson 1992: 10–11

By trespassing across disciplinary boundaries it has been possible to bring into focus the multidimensional interplay of representation, meaning and power that attach to strategies and ideologies embedded in landscape, especially more or less unpeopled landscapes. The margins of particular landscape representations and the 'marginalized within' thus became visible. In a sense, this transdisciplinary approach permitted a return of the perspectival gaze, challenging the depicted silences that had 'gone without saying' as cultural capital became inextricably linked with landscape. This approach followed the shift from landscape as theater of power to landscape as theatrical entertainment, and from that to landscape as panorama – those theaters without actors where the unpeopled view was all-important. It then charted the spatial and social dispersal of such unpeopled landscapes to wider audiences.

The cultural production of the Lake District was mapped on a template triangulating between the rise of British nationalism, the Picturesque aesthetic, and antiquarianism. Geographical space and social place intersected to construct a network of exclusions through a complex grid of linkages and influences. The transformation of space to place was the shaping of a moral order, a re-enchantment of nature within which recreational walking and touring were reiterated performative modes of identity construction and maintenance. Such re-enchantment supported social and class differentiation even as the valorization of the Lake District began to move into the realm of social memory through the ever-widening dissemination of a Picturesque aesthetic to literate and non-literate publics alike.

Contesting ideologies of nation were located in and performed upon the land. The political fiction of Great Britain is a useful instrument by which to get at various versions or visions of what constituted 'England' and the strategies of behavior used by different communities as they laid claim to 'their' Englands. Moving between the nascent centralizing nation-state, cultural nationalisms, and the Dissenters' culture of otherness, exposes aesthetic, cognitive and moral tensions and anxieties that masked class antagonism. A particular example of such interlocking frictions may be found in the consumption and commoditization of the view and the re-enchantment of nature as the Lake District was further incorporated into a capitalist logic of tourism.

The Lake and Peak Districts were central to the nineteenth-century struggle for access to and conservation of the English landscape. Within that struggle, despite differences in immediate objectives, working-class activists, parliamentary reformers, members of the legal profession, and academics entered a swirl of legal and extra-legal practices aimed at maintaining or regaining access to open landscapes, commons, and footpaths. The specificities of nineteenth- and twentieth-century legislative and extra-legal battles over access to and conservation of the Lake and Peak Districts have extensive significance for clarifying the links between spatial and political geographies of exclusion. The contested processes of representation, incorporation and legislation of landscape aesthetics calls into question the apparent democratization of access to landscapes freighted with symbolic value.

The re-emergence in the 1990s of a fierce debate over access – its use as a means of destabilizing ideas of private property, and the State's legislative response that makes illegal the spatial practices of certain groups – shows that landscape still functions as a repository of group identity which under particular circumstances barely, if at all, masks class antagonisms. Paradoxically, research data showed that walking groups can and do cut across class, that the well-booted and the Wellington-booted occasionally meet in a single social space.

The many links between body, imagination and place observed throughout the study were reinforced through participant-observation with walking groups set within a well-defined landscape. The contested terrain of temporary and permanent walking groups can usefully be framed in terms of secular pilgrimage in which the potential exists for walkers to experience a particularized sense of belonging. In their quotidian and lifetime-framed journeys through the landscape, walkers create structure, meaning and a sense of community through their walking groups. Warning that 'the "secular pilgrimage" should not be taken merely as a fanciful trope,' Benedict Anderson writes of it as being made up 'by the constant flow of pilgrims moving towards [a specific place] from remote and *otherwise unrelated* localities' (Anderson 1991: 53–5, emphasis in original). This is a close description of the Lake District study population, some with an affective affiliation to that place which has been bringing them back over twenty, thirty or forty years, in a few instances even longer. Their actions refute modernism's and postmodernism's claim that we live in a free-floating state of un- or non-attachment, where everything is ephemeral, disposable, and temporary – including attachment to place (Urry 1995).

At heart are issues of fragmentation and homogeneity. The illusion of there being an 'English' culture has shattered under the impact of Americanization, immigration, globalization, imposition of European Union regulation, and loss of status as a political and economic power. In the past, the essentialist mantle of the English landscape became a place of temporary refuge for a cultural elite. In the present, at an unremarked-upon level, the landscape serves a similar function for a wide segment of the population that cuts across class but not yet ethnicity. Even the conservation of traditionally farmed upland land-scapes in such places as the Lake and Peak District National Parks can be read as thinly veiled romanticized icons of national identity, a threnody to the England that once was.

Intense commercialization of walking has slowly captured the Lake District's symbolic value, converting it to actual value through its indirect incorporation into the marketplace. Whether landscape's incorporation into the marketplace will move into a more direct mode, in which people will have to pay for access, remains to be seen. From the perspective of white Britons, stratification of access is hardly yet an issue: the sheer number of walkers attests to that. Indeed, the Lake District is now so densely saturated with walkers that capitalist penetration of other putative 'empty' spaces through commercialized walking is well underway globally. The mountain highlands of Scotland, Ireland, Eastern Europe, Nepal, New Zealand and Peru are marketed as alternatives to the crowded and therefore less pristine mountain-walking areas of the Lake District and the Alps. The quintessence of this fetishization of landscape is what has been called 'Explornography' (Tierney 1998).

This work began by moving between dyadic sets of relationships operating around landscape representations. Doing so showed that the eighteenth-century English cultural elite shared in an imagined community of painted, printed and actual unpeopled landscapes. From this complex of hierarchically organized 'sightings', the Lake District emerged as a new site of assembly for that elite. The epigraph taken from Gupta and Ferguson, given at the head of this concluding chapter speaks to the present-day salience of 'the real England' as a place of moral location and locality of imagined community. While the Lake District certainly functions as a location of this mythic England, it is certainly not a 'blurred and indeterminate' place for those who go fell-walking there year after year.

In a curious inversion of the way community is generally thought of, the core study population consisted of outsiders. They had come to participate in excursive walking in the Lake District for a variety of reasons – the panoramic views, literary associations of place, personal challenge, loneliness, re-engagement with nature, meeting up with like-minded walking friends, a whole gamut of things. They were sweaty and sometimes even vulgar. Their polyphony of lively, sad, ribald and 'cultured' voices jostled for emplacement in the landscape. As all pilgrims – secular or otherwise – come to understand, though the journey is undertaken in groups, no one else can take your steps for you. Everyone has to find her or his own particular pathway up and down fellside and mountain. Who leads a group can be critical – not simply in terms of safety, but in terms of experiencing walking as something more than simply covering a certain amount of ground in a certain amount of time. Also, in metaphorical as well as literal terms, the boots you wear and the load you carry are other key factors in what you will experience.

The opening chapter concluded with observations concerning British Rail's InterCity poster on 'English landscape art. A private view' to get at the dual and conflated embodiment of class and England as located in landscape. The jacket art of a recent book on non-places (Augé 1995) – which are defined as non-relational, ahistoric and not concerned with identity – recalls the poster. The upper band of the poster's landscape image shows a view of the sky as seen in a flash through a train window. The upper band of the book jacket shows an airport boarding-gate area with a view out through a narrow window onto a waiting jet. In the flash of a second that high-speed InterCity travel affords, the poster image's lower band shows a ploughed field. The book jacket's lower band is a close-up shot of the green industrial-type carpeting in the non-place's waiting area. The regular lines of the field's plough marks find their echo in the weave of the carpet seen close up. The one cannot be reached, the other is walked over unknowingly.

Poster art and cover art are flooded with anonymity, boundaries, and framings. Whether from train or plane, the view is beyond direct experiencing, especially when what is on offer is a bird's-eye view from 30,000 feet – cloud-cover permitting. The re-engagements with nature that walking groups allow are intervals in such everyday constraints of confinement and conformity. Walking groups allow for transgression of anonymity and boundaries – the latter sometimes quite literally. Within the walking group, landscape views become an experiential reality bound up with a social organization that can cross-cut class. This is the repeopling of those 'more or less' unpeopled landscapes that were themselves reflections of landscape paintings.

New social movements act to buffer the insecurities engendered in modern societies that by their very nature destroy tradition and traditional ways of being in the world and relating to it (Melucci 1989). From this perspective, the innumerable locally based walking groups and the several million walking holidays sold in Britain each year can be considered points in a web that add up to a *social* movement and a social *movement* that cut across national, social and cultural landscapes and breach solitary individuality. Not only does the dense network of pathways crisscrossing England lead to places-in-nature, but the human movement along them creates the very places to which they lead. The equally dense network of walkers, their shared experiences and their creation of memories and histories together create a 'bass line . . . indicating the passage and continuation of time' (Augé 1995: 77) within which there is place for recreating a sense of the social – in effect, for reimagining and reconstructing community.

# Appendix

## Questionnaire

Nearly all questions operated on a yes/no or five-choice basis that moved from strong approval or agreement to strong disapproval or disagreement, or from shorter periods of time/distance to longer ones, or from never to always. Where a list of options was given, room was left for 'other' responses, and space for additional comments appeared throughout the questionnaire. The following is a somewhat abbreviated form of the questionnaire.

## I. General statistical information

included age; sex; employment status; occupation/former occupation; household income

## II. How did you get started in walking?

1. Through family, school friends, friends at work, youth groups?
2. At what age?
3. Did you start walking because you thought it would improve your health?
4. Do you engage in any other form of outdoor exercise such as bicycling, golfing, bird-watching?
5. Are you involved with charity walks?
6. Do you take part in competition walking?
7. To what extent have walking contacts developed into social activities outside of walking?
8. Have you arranged walking holidays with people you have met through walking but whom you do not see outside of a walking setting?

## III. Clothing

9. Have you bought or been given any of the following items specifically for walking? (A range of nine items followed.)
10. How much do you spend a year on average to purchase walking gear?
11. What is your reaction when you see walkers in hi-tech gear?
12. Do you agree/disagree that present-day walking gear is more elaborate, comfortable, expensive, colorful, practical than in the past?

## IV. Participation in walking in groups in England under the direction of a leader or guide

13. What is the extent of your participation? (Range: never to always.)
14. What is the frequency of your participation? (Range: once a year to more than once a month.)
15. What is the duration of your participation? (Range: one day to more than three weeks.)
16. What is your preferred level of difficulty? (Range: strolling to steep scramble.)
17. What is the average distance of a day's walk? (Range: 4–8 miles to over 20.)
18. What is your average expenditure on guided walking trips in England, including travel costs?

(The same group of questions was asked about walking in led groups outside of England; non-guided walking in England; and non-guided walking outside England.)

## V. Landscape preferences in England

19. Do you prefer upland and mountain settings or lowland and coastal settings?
20. How much of your walking is done in the various settings and which is your home setting?

(The same group of questions was asked about landscapes outside England.)

## VI. **Landscape, reading and the Web**

21.   Do you read novels or poetry by authors associated with the areas you walk in and if yes, what have you read recently?
22.   Do you read up on local history of the areas you walk in and if yes, what have you read recently?
23.   Do you read 'countryside' books or magazines and if yes, which ones?
24.   Do you communicate with other walkers via the Web?

## VII. **Membership organizations**

25.   Are you involved in any organizations dedicated to the protection of and access to the countryside?
26.   How active are you in them and do you think they are doing a good job?
27.   Do you belong to any of the following national walking, environmental or countryside organizations? (Range: Council for the Protection of Rural England; Friends of the Earth; Friends of National Parks; Long Distance Walker's Association; National Trust; Ramblers' Association; Royal Society for the Protection of Birds; other.)
28.   Do you belong to any local nature trusts, conservation or footpath societies and if so, which ones?

## VIII. **General**

29.   Do you ever walk in groups that are only the same sex as yourself, and if so then why and in what way is the experience different?
30.   Have you ever taken any map-reading or orienteering courses, and if so then where?

## IX. **Attitudes about the countryside**

How strongly do you agree or disagree with the following statements.

31.   In voting for a political party, people should take into account its stand on environmental issues.
32.   Farmers should receive subsidies to engage in environmentally sound agricultural practices.
33.   Subsidies for intensive agriculture should be decreased.

34. Walking is the most challenging activity I undertake.
35. Current intensive farming practices are detrimental to the environment.
36. Environmental issues are important to me.
37. The countryside of the north-west of England is most typically 'English'.
38. Vegetarianism is a good idea.
39. There was a greater variety of butterflies in the countryside when I was younger.
40. Removing field hedgerow boundaries to make larger fields makes economic sense.
41. The English landscape used to look much more attractive when I was younger.
42. I prefer the countryside where it is divided into small fields.
43. Walking is more fulfilling than my everyday work activity.
44. How the countryside looks should take second place to efficiencies of agriculture.
45. Large fields planted with one crop, like rapeseed, look attractive.
46. There has been a great deal of change in the landscape since I was younger.
47. Change in the landscape is necessary to produce cheap food.
48. Changes to the countryside are a loss of history.
49. Loss of hedgerows to make larger fields has negatively altered the look of the landscape.
50. There was a greater variety of wild flowers in the countryside when I was younger.
51. We should be preserving the landscape for future generations.
52. The countryside of the south-east of England is most typically 'English'.
53. Walking gives me a greater sense of well-being or accomplishment than my job.
54. I would be willing to pay more for food if it meant the countryside would not be subject to such drastic alteration through agriculture.
55. Commercial conifer plantations should be interplanted with broad-leaf trees.
56. The rolling hills of the Cotswolds and the South Downs is a 'typical' English landscape.

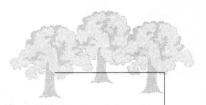

# Bibliography

Abrams, Harold M. (1959) *Britain's National Parks*, London: Country Life Limited.

Abrams, M.H. (gen. ed.) (1968; 1986) *The Norton Anthology of English Literature*, NY: Norton.

Acheson, James M. and Bonnie J. McCay (eds) (1987) *The Question of the Commons: The Culture and Ecology of Communal Resources*, Tucson: University of Arizona Press.

Addison, Joseph (1712) "Essay on the Pleasure of the Imagination", *Spectator*, Nos. 411–21.

Aers, David, Jonathan Cook, David Punter (1981) *Romanticism and Ideology: Studies in English Writing 1765–1830*, London: Routledge & Kegan Paul.

Allen, B. Sprague (1937) *Tides in English Taste*, Cambridge, Mass.: Harvard University Press.

Anderson, Benedict (1991) *Imagined Communities*, London: Verso.

Anderson, Patricia (1991) *The Printed Image & Transformation of Popular Culture*, Oxford: Oxford University Press.

Andrews, Malcolm (1989) *The Search for the Picturesque Landscape: Aesthetics and Tourism in Britain 1760–1800*, Aldershot: Scolar Press.

Appadurai, Arjun (1988) "Introduction: Place and Voice in Anthropological Theory," *Cultural Anthropology* (3) 1: 16–20.

Appadurai, Arjun (1991) "Global Ethnoscapes: Notes and Queries for a Transnational Anthropology," in Richard G. Fox (ed.), *Recapturing Anthropology: Working in the Present*, Santa Fe, N.M.: School of American Research Press.

Appleton, Jay (1986) "Some thoughts on the geology of the picturesque," *Journal of Garden History* (6) 3: 270–91.

Archer, John E. (1989) "Poachers abroad," in G. E. Mingay (ed.), *The Unquiet Countryside*, London: Routledge.

Archer, John E. (1990) *By a Flash and a Scare. Incendiarism, Animal Maiming, and Poaching in East Anglia 1815–1870*, Oxford: Clarendon Press.

Arensberg, C.M. and S. Kimball (1940) *Family and Community in Ireland*, Cambridge, Mass.: Harvard University Press.

Arnold, Matthew ([1869] 1994) Samuel Lipman (ed.), *Culture And Anarchy*, New Haven: Yale University Press.

Ashcroft, Peter (1998) "U.K. Day Visits Survey," *Countryside Recreation Network News* (6) 1, Spring issue, n. p.

Atherton, Herbert M. (1974) *Political Prints in the Age of Hogarth: A Study of the Ideographic Representation of Politics*, Oxford: Oxford University Press.

Augé, Marc (1995) *non-places: introduction to an anthropology of super-modernity*, trans. John Howe, London: Verso.

Austen, Jane ([1813] 1956) *Pride and Prejudice*, Mark Schorer (ed.), Boston: Houghton Mifflin.

Backscheider, Paula R. (1993) *Spectacular Politics: Theatrical Power and Mass Culture in Early Modern England*, Baltimore: Johns Hopkins University Press.

Bailey, Peter (1978) *Leisure and Class in Victorian England: Recreation and the Contest for Control, 1830–1885*, London: Routledge & Kegan Paul.

Barker, F.R. and N.D.M. Parry (1996) "Open Access, Rights and Legislation," in *Web Journal of Current Legal Issues* (2), www.nd.ac.uk/~nlawwww/1996/issue2/parry2.html

Barnes, Trevor J. and James Duncan (1992) *Writing Worlds: discourse, text & metaphor in the representation of landscape*, London: Routledge.

Barrell, John (1980) *The Dark Side of the Landscape*, Cambridge: Cambridge University Press.

Basso, Keith H. (1996) *Wisdom Sits in Places*, Albuquerque: University of New Mexico Press.

Bate, Jonathan (1991) *Romantic Ecology: Wordsworth and the Environmental Tradition*, London: Routledge.

Baum, Joan (1994) *Mind-Forg'd Manacles: Slavery and the English Romantic Poets*, NY: Archon Books.

Beard, Geoffrey (1980) "The First Watercolourists," in *The Viewfinders: An Exhibition of Lake District Landscapes* Exhibition catalogue 31 May–27 July 1980, Kendal, Cumbria: Abbot Hall Art Gallery.

—— (1991) *Attingham: The First Forty Years 1952–1991*, London: The Attingham Trust.

Bell, Michael M. (1994) *Childerly: Nature and Morality in a Country Village*, Chicago: University of Chicago Press.

Bender, Barbara (1993) "Introduction: Landscape – Meaning and Action," and "Stonehenge – Contested Landscapes" in Bender (ed.), *Landscape: Politics and Perspectives*, Oxford: Berg.

Bennett, Gillian (1993) "Folklore Studies and the English Rural Myth," in *Rural History* (4) 1: 77–91.

Beresford, M.W. (1961)"Habitation versus improvement: the debate on enclosure by agreement," in F.J. Fisher (ed.), *Essays in the economic and social history of Tudor and Stuart England, in honour of R.H. Tawney*, Cambridge: Cambridge University Press.

Bermingham, Ann (1986) *Landscape and Ideology: The English Rustic Tradition 1740–1860*, Berkeley: University of California Press.

—— (1994) "System, Order, and Abstraction: The Politics of English Landscape Drawing around 1795," W.J.T. Mitchell (ed.), *Landscape and Power*, Chicago: University of Chicago Press.

Berry, Geoffrey and Geoffrey Beard (1980) *The Lake District: a Century of Conservation*, Edinburgh: John Bartholomew.

Betjeman, John ([1937] 1988) "Slough," in Richard Ellmann and Robert O'Clair (eds), *The Norton Anthology of Modern Poetry*, NY: W.W. Norton.

Bewell, Alan (1989) *Wordsworth & The Enlightenment: Nature, Man & Society in the Experimental Poetry*, New Haven: Yale University Press.

Bicknell, Peter (1987) *The Picturesque Scenery of the Lake District 1752–1855*, Cambridge: private printing.

—— and Robert Woof (1982) *The discovery of the Lake District 1750–1810: A context for Wordsworth*, Exhibition catalogue 20 May–31 October 1982, Cumbria: Trustees of Dove Cottage.

—— and Robert Woof (1983) *The Lake District Discovered 1810–1850: The Artists, the Tourists and Wordsworth*, Exhibition catalogue 20 May–31 October 1983, Cumbria: Trustees of Dove Cottage.

—— (ed.) (1984) *The Illustrated Wordsworth's Guide to The Lakes*, NY: Congdon & Weed.

Birkett, Norman, Sir (1945) *National Parks and the Countryside*, Cambridge: Cambridge University Press.

Blacksell, Mark (1982) "Leisure, recreation and environment," in R.J. Johnston and J.C. Doornkamp (eds), *The Changing Geography of the United Kingdom*, London: Methuen.

Blake, William (1794) "London" from *Songs of Experience*.

Blunden, Edmond (1935) *The Legacy of England*, London: Batsford.

Blunden, John and Nigel Curry (eds) (1988) *A Future for Our Countryside*, Oxford: Blackwell in association with the Countryside Commission.

Boland, Eavan (1995) "Jewels set in blood," *The Observer Review of Books*, 13 August 1995: 16.

Bourdieu, Paul (1984) *Distinction: A Social Critique of the Judgement of Taste*, Cambridge, MA.: Harvard University Press.

Bowen, Margarita (1981) *Empiricism and geographical thought from Francis Bacon to Alexander von Humboldt*, Cambridge: Cambridge University Press.

Bowie, Fiona (1993) "Wales from Within: Conflicting Interpretations of Welsh Identity," in Sharon Macdonald (ed.), *Inside European Identities*, Oxford: Berg.

Brewer, John (1997) *The Pleasures of the Imagination: English Culture in the Eighteenth Century*, NY: Farrar, Straus & Giroux.

—— (1992) "Review of Linda Colley, *Forging Britons*," in *The Times Literary Supplement*, October 16, 1992: 5–6.

*Britannica Curiosa* (1777) 6 vols, London: Fielding & Walker.

British Mountaineering Council (1997) *Access Charter*, Manchester: BMC.

Broad, John (1990) "The Verneys as enclosing landlords," in John Chartres and David Hey (eds), *English rural society 1500–1800, Essays in honour of Joan Thirsk*, Cambridge: Cambridge University Press.

Bromley, D.W. (ed.) (1992) *Making the Commons Work: Theory, Practice, and Policy*, San Francisco: ICS Press.

Brownlow, Timothy (1983) *John Clare and Picturesque Landscape*, Oxford: Clarendon Press.

Brydon, Anne (1995) "Inscriptions of Self; The Construction of Icelandic Landscape in Nineteenth-Century British Travel Writings," *Ethnos* (60) 3–4: 243–63.

Bunce, Michael (1994) *the countryside ideal: Anglo-American images of landscape*, London: Routledge.

Burke, Edmund ([1757] 1990) *Philosophical Enquiry into the Origin of our Ideas of the Sublime and Beautiful . . .* , Oxford: Oxford University Press.

Burnett, John (1979) *Plenty & Want: A social history of diet in England from 1815 to the present day*, London: Scolar Press.

Butler, Marilyn (1982) *Romantics, Rebels and Reactionaries: English Literature and its Background 1760–1830*, Oxford: Oxford University Press.

—— (1988) "Romanticism in England," in Roy Porter and Mikulás Teich (eds), *Romanticism in National Context*, Cambridge: Cambridge University Press.

Butlin, R.A. (1979) "The enclosure of open-fields and extinction of common rights in England, circa 1600–1750: a review," in H.S.A. Fox and R.A. Butlin (eds), *Change in the Countryside*, Special Publication No.10 London: Institute of British Geographers.

Butts, Mary (1932) *Warning to Hikers*, London: Wishart.

Cafritz, Robert C. (1988a) "Netherlandish Reflections of the Venetian Landscape Tradition," in *Places of Delight: The Pastoral Landscape*, Exhibition catalogue November 6, 1988–January 22, 1989, Washington, D.C.: The Phillips Collection.

—— (1988b) "Classical Revision of the Pastoral Landscape," in *Places of Delight: The Pastoral Landscape*, Exhibition catalogue November 6, 1988–January 22, 1989, Washington, D.C.: The Phillips Collection.

——, Lawrence Gowing and David Rosand (1988) *Places of Delight: The Pastoral Landscape*, Exhibition catalogue November 6, 1988–January 22, 1989, Washington, D.C.: The Phillips Collection.

Campbell, M. (1942) *The English Yeoman under Elizabeth and the Early Stuarts*, New Haven: Yale University Press.

Cannadine, David (1992) *G.M. Trevelyan: A Life in History*, London: HarperCollins Publishers.

—— (1995) "British History as a 'new subject': politics, perspectives and prospects", in Alexander Grant and Keith Stringer (eds), *Uniting the Kingdom? The Making of British History*, London: Routledge.

Cantor, Leonard (1987) *The Changing English Countryside 1400–1700*, London: Routledge & Kegan Paul.

Carter, Harold and C. Roy Lewis (1990) *An Urban Geography of England and Wales in the Nineteenth Century*, London: Edward Arnold.

CHA (1895) *Holiday Committee, Minutes*, December 30, 1895; January 4 and 5, 1897; February 27, 1897; October 23, 1897. Greater Manchester Public Records Office, unaccessioned material, no catalog number, no box number, no item number.

CHA (1897–9) *Domestic Committee, Minutes*, February 1897, 1899. Greater Manchester PRO.

CHA (1898–9) *Executive Committee, Minutes*, February 19, 1898; October 8, 1898; March 24, 1899; November 4, 1899. Greater Manchester PRO.

CHA (1899) *Lecturers Committee, Minutes*, March 24, 1899. Greater Manchester PRO.

CHA (1914–1946) *Free Holiday Committee, Minutes*, various; November 1945; June 1946. Greater Manchester PRO.

Chadwick, Edwin (1834) evidence given to the Select Committee on Drunkenness, *Parliamentary Papers*, 1834, Volume VIII, question 325.

Chadwick, Owen (1997) "God is in the Detail. And in the Footnotes," *Observer Review*, 20 March 1997: 16.

Chapman, Malcolm (1993) "Copeland: Cumbria's best-kept secret," in Macdonald, Sharon (ed.), *Inside European Identities*, Oxford: Berg.

Charlton, D. G. (1984) *New Images of the Natural in France: A Study in European Cultural History 1750–1800*, Cambridge: Cambridge University Press.

Ching, Barbara and Gerald W. Creed (eds) (1997) *Knowing your place: rural identity and cultural hierarchy*, NY: Routledge.

Clark, Anthony M., edited and prepared for publication by Edgar Peters Bowron (1985) *Pompeo Batoni: A Complete Catalogue of his Works*, NY: New York University Press.

Clark, Kenneth (1949) *Landscape into Art*, Harmondsworth: Penguin Books.

Clifford, James and George E. Marcus (eds) (1986) *Writing Culture: The Poetics and Politics of Ethnography*, Berkeley: University of California Press.

Clout, Hugh (1984) *A Rural Policy for the EEC?*, London: Methuen.

Cohen, Anthony P. (1985) *Symbolic Construction of Community*, London: Tavistock Press.

Cohen, Anthony P. (1982) "Belonging: the experience of culture," in Anthony P. Cohen ed. *Belonging. Identity and Social Organization in British Rural Cultures*, Manchester: Manchester University Press.

Cohn, Bernard S. ([1980] 1987) "History and Anthropology: the State of Play," in *An Anthropologist among the Historians and Other Essays*, New Delhi: Oxford University Press.

—— ([1981] 1987) "Anthropology and History in the 1980s: Towards a Rapprochement," in *An Anthropologist among the Historians and Other Essays*, New Delhi: Oxford University Press.

—— (1996) *Colonialism and Its Forms of Knowledge: The British in India*, Princeton: Princeton University Press.

Colley, Linda (1992) *Britons: Forging the Nation 1707–1837*, New Haven: Yale University Press.

Collini, Stefan (1992) "Like family, like nation – The national past as seen from Northumbria," review of David Cannadine (1992), *G.M. Trevelyan: A Life in History*, London: HarperCollins Publishers, in *The Times Literary Supplement*, October 16, 1992, 3–4.

Comment, Bernard (1993) *Le XIX^e siècle des panoramas*, Paris: Adam Biro.

*Comradeship*, bound collection 1911–1925, Greater Manchester PRO.

*Comradeship V*, September 1911, "CHA," 1: 3.

*Comradeship XVII*, March 1914, "Open Sesame," 4: 52.

*Comradeship IX*, October 1915, "Letters," 1: 14.

*Comradeship XV*, October 1924, "York Group Report," 5: 16.

*Comradeship XXIII*, December 1931, "Holidays by Instinct," 2: 11–12.

*Comradeship XXIII*, December 1931, "World Disarmament," 2: 5.

*Comradeship XXIV*, May 1933, "Letters," 4: 15.

Cook, Dave ([1974] 1978) "The Mountaineer and Society", address given at the 1974 National Mountaineering Conference, in Ken Wilson (ed.), *The Games Climbers Play*, 461–472, London: Diadem Books.

Cooke, Richard and Fiona Gough (1997) "Permissive Access to Agricultural Land Provided Through Agi-Environment Schemes: The Current Position in England," in *Countryside Recreation Network News*, (5), 4 : 1–6.

*Copper Plate Magazine* (1774–1778; 1792–1802) London: G. Kearsly, break in publication then, London: J. Walker.

Corrigan, Philip and Derek Sayer (1985) *The Great Arch: English State Formation as Cultural Revolution*, Oxford: Basil Blackwell.

Cosgrove, Denis (1988) "The geometry of landscape: practical and speculative arts in sixteenth-century Venetian land territories," in Cosgrove and Stephen Daniels (eds), *The iconography of landscape*, Cambridge: Cambridge University Press.

——, Barbara Rosco and Simon Nycroft (1996) "Landscape and Identity at Ladybower Reservoir and Rutland Water," *Transactions* of the Institute of British Geographers, N. S. (21), 3: 534–51.

Coster, Graham (1991) "Another country," *Guardian Weekend*, 1–2 June, 1991: 4–6.

*Country Walking* (1996) Karrimore K-SB walking boot advertisement, June 1996: 38–9.

Countryside Commission, *Press Releases*, http://www.countryside.gov.uk

—— (1998) *Press Release* 98/23 New National Framework Needed for Open Access, 1 June 1998.

—— (1998) *Press Release* 98/24 Paths 21 – Rights of Way for 21st Century's Users, 12 June 1998.

—— (1998) *Press Release* 98/38, Eight Propositions for Planning and the Countryside, 19 September 1998.

*Countryside Recreation Network News*, http://www.sosig.ac.uk/crn/news/

Craig, David (1992) "Coming Home: the Romantic Tradition of Mountaineering," in Keith Hanley and Alison Milbank (eds), *From Lancaster to the Lakes: the region in literature*, Lancaster: Centre for North-West Regional Studies, University of Lancaster.

Crapanzano, Vincent (1980) *Tuhami: Portrait of a Moroccan*, Chicago: University of Chicago Press.

Craton, Michael (1974) *Sinews of Empire: A Short History of British Slavery*, NY: Anchor Books.

Cunningham, Hugh (1980) *Leisure in the Industrial Revolution c. 1780–1880*, London: Croom Helm.

Cust, Lionel (1898) *History of the Society of Dilettanti*, London: Macmillan & Co.

Daniels, Stephen (1993) *Fields of Vision: Landscape Imagery & National Identity in England & The United States*, Princeton: Princeton University Press.

—— (1993) "Re-Visioning Britain: Mapping and Landscape Painting, 1750–1820," Katharine Baetjer (ed.), *Glorious Nature: British Landscape Painting 1750–1850*, NY: Hudson Hills Press in association with The Denver Art Museum.

Darby, Wendy Joy (1988) *The Hartsop Valley: A Programme for Cultural Landscape Conservation*, unpublished master's thesis, Columbia University, Graduate School of Architecture, Planning and Preservation.

—— (1992) "A Reading of Edward Lange's Landscapes: Text and Context," in *Long Island Historical Journal* (4), 2: 185–99.

Darian-Smith, Kate, Liz Gunner and Sarah Nuttall (eds) (1996) *text, theory, space*, London: Routledge.

Daumal, René, trans. Roger Shattuck (1974) *Mount Analogue*, London: Penguin.

Ditt, Karl (1996) "Nature Conservation in England and Germany 1900–1970: forerunner of Environmental Protection?" in *Contemporary European History* (5), 1: 1–29.

Dodd, Philip (1986) "Englishness and the National Culture," in Robert Colls and Philip Dodd (eds), *Englishness: Politics and Culture 1880–1920*, London: Croom Helm.

Douglas, Mary (1970) *Purity and Danger*, Middlesex: Penguin.

Dower, John (1945) *National Parks in England and Wales*, London: HMSO.

Duncan, James S. (1989) "The power of place in Kandy, Sri Lanka: 1780–1980," in John A. Agnew and James S. Duncan (eds), *The Power of Place: Bringing together the geographical and sociological imaginations*, Boston: Unwin Hyman.

Dyos, H.J. and D.A. Reeder (1986) "Slums and Suburbs," in Pat Thane and Anthony Sutcliffe (eds), *Essays in Social History*, Vol. 2, Oxford: Clarendon Press.

Epstein, James A. (1994) *Radical Expression; Political Language, Ritual, and Symbol in England, 1790–1850*, Oxford: Oxford University Press.

Etchell, Catherine (1997) "Access 2000: Improving Countryside Access," in *Countryside Recreation Network News* (5), 1: 1–2.

Evans, Eric (1995) "Englishness and Britishness: National identities, c.1790-c.1870," in Alexander Grant and Keith J. Stringer (eds), *Uniting the Kingdom? The Making of British History*, London: Routledge.

Everett, Nigel (1994) *The Tory View of Landscape*, New Haven: Yale University Press, for The Paul Mellon Centre for Studies in British Art.

Eversley, George John Shaw-Lefevre, Lord (1910) *Commons, Forests and Footpaths: The Story of the Battle during the last Forty-five Years . . .*, London: Cassell.

Farndale, Nigel (1995) "Back on the warpath – Rambling as to war," *Sunday Telegraph Magazine*, 17 September 1995: 12–18.

Fedden, Robin (1974) *The National Trust Past & Present*, London: Jonathan Cape.

Fernandez, James (1988) "Andalusia on Our Minds: Two Contrasting Places in Spain As Seen in a Vernacular Poetic Duel of the Late 19th Century," *Cultural Anthropology* (3)1: 16–20 theme issue: "Place and Voice in Anthropological Theory."

Finlay, Nancy and Roberta Waddell (1996) *The Romance of the Stone: Lithography, 1769–1825*, exhibition notes, New York Public Library, Miriam and Ira D. Wallach Collection.

Foucault, Michel (1980) Colin Gordon (ed.), *Power/Knowledge: Selected Interviews & Other Writings 1972–1977 of Michel Foucault*, trans. Colin Gordon, Leo Marshall, John Mepham, Kate Soper, New York: Pantheon Books.

Fox, J. R. (1967) "Tory Island" in B. Benedict (ed.), *Problems of Smaller Territories*, Institute of Commonwealth Studies: Papers, No.10, London: Athlone Press.

Frankenberg, Ronald (1957) *Village on the Border*, London: Cohen & West.

—— (1966) *Communities in Britain*, Baltimore: Penguin.

Fraser, Iain (1996) "Quasi-markets and the provision of nature conservation in agri-environmental policy, in *European Environment* 6: 95–101.

Frykman, Jonas and Orvar Löfgren (1987) *Culture Builders: A Historical Anthropology of Middle-Class Life*, trans. Alan Crozier, New Brunswick: Rutgers University Press.

Fuller, Peter (1985) *Images of God: the Consolations of Lost Illusions*, London: Chatto & Windus.

Funkel, Alicia (1996) *Romantic Stages: Set and Costume Design in Victorian England*, London: McFarland & Company.

Gadian, David (1986) "Class formation and class action in north-west industrial towns, 1830–1850," in R.J. Morris (ed.) *Class, power and social structure in British nineteenth-century towns*, Leicester: Leicester University Press.

Geertz, Clifford (1988) *Works and Lives*, see especially Chapter 4: "I-Witnessing: Malinowski's Children", Stanford, Ca.: Stanford University Press.

*Gentleman's Magazine* (1731–1825) London: various publishers.

Gerzina, Gretchen Holbrook (1995) *Black London: Life before Emancipation*, New Brunswick: Rutgers University Press.

Gilroy, Paul (1987) *'There ain't no black in the Union Jack': the cultural politics of race and nation*, London: Hutchinson.

Girouard, Mark (1980) *Life in the English Country House*, Harmondsworth: Penguin Books.

Gluckman, Max (1962) "Les rites De Passage," in Max Gluckman (ed.), *Essays in the Ritual of Social Relations*, Manchester: Manchester University Press.

Goddard, Victoria A., Josep R. Llobera and Cris Shore (1994) *The Anthropology of Europe: Identities and Boundaries in Conflict*, Oxford: Berg.

Goldsmith, Oliver (1773) "The Deserted Village".

Gonner, E.C.K. (1912) *Common Land and Inclosure*, London: Macmillan.

Grant, Alexander and Keith Stringer (1995) "The enigma of British History," in Grant and Stringer (eds), *Uniting the Kingdom? The Making of British History*, London: Routledge.

Green, Nicholas (1995) "Looking at the Landscape: Class Formation and the Visual," in Eric Hirsch and Michael O'Hanlon (eds), *The Anthropology of Landscape: Perspectives on Place and Space*, Oxford: Clarendon Press.

Grove-White, Robin (1996) "A New Culture?" in *Countryside Recreation Network News* (4) 3: 1–3.

Guha, Ranajit (1987) "Introduction", in Bernard S. Cohn, *An Anthropologist among the Historians and Other Essays*, Delhi: Oxford University Press.

Gunningham, Catharine (1996) Assistant Director – Publicity and Development, Ramblers' Association, London. Interview, September 13th, 1996.

Gupta, Akhil and James Ferguson (1992) "Beyond 'Culture': Space, Identity and the Politics of Difference," *Cultural Anthropology* 7 (1), 6–23.

Gupta, Akhil and James Ferguson (1997) "Discipline and Practice: 'The Field'" as Site, Method, and Location in Anthropology," in Gupta and Ferguson (eds), *Anthropological Locations: Boundaries and Grounds of a Field Science*, Berkeley: University of California Press.

Hardin, Garret (1977) "The Tragedy of the Commons," in Garrett Hardin and John Baden (eds), *Managing the Commons*, San Francisco: W.H. Freeman.

Harley, J.B. (1988) "Maps, Knowledge and Power," in Denis Cosgrove and Stephen Daniels (eds), *The iconography of landscape*, Cambridge: Cambridge University Press.

—— (1992) "Deconstructing the Map," in Trevor J. Barnes and James S. Duncan (eds), *Writing Worlds: discourse, text & metaphor in the representation of landscape*, London: Routledge

—— and G. Walters (1982) "Welsh Orthography and Ordnance Survey Mapping. 1820–1905," *Archaeologia Cambrensis* 121: 120–l.

Harris, John and Gervaise Jackson-Stops (eds) (1984) *Britannia Illustrata*, Bungay, Suffolk: The Paradigm Press.

Harvey, David and Martin Whitby (1988) "Issues and policies," in M. Whitby, and J. Ollerenshaw, (eds), *Land Use and the European Environment*, London: Belhaven Press.

Hastrup, Kirsten (1987) "Fieldwork among friends: ethnographic exchange within the Northern civilization," in Anthony Jackson (ed.), *Anthropology at Home*, ASA Monograph 25, London: Tavistock Publications.

Hawes, Louis (1982) *Presences of Nature: British Landscape 1780–1830*, New Haven: Yale Center for British Art.

Hay, Douglas (1975) "Poaching and the Game Laws on Cannock Chase," in E.P. Thompson et al. (eds), *Albion's Fatal Tree: Crime and Society in Eighteenth-Century England*, NY: Pantheon.

Healey, Patsy, Paul McNamara, Martin Elson and Andrew Doak (1988) *Land Use Planning and the Mediation of Urban Change: The British planning system in practice*, Cambridge: Cambridge University Press.

Hearn, Francis (1978) *Domination, Legitimation, and Resistance: the Incorporation of the 19th century English Working Class*, Westport, CT.: Greenwood Press.

Hechter, Michael (1975) *Internal Colonialism: The Celtic Fringe in British National Development, 1536–1966*, Berkeley: University of California Press.

Helsinger, Elizabeth (1994) "Ruskin and the Politics of Viewing; Constructing National Subjects," in *Nineteenth-Century Contexts* 18 (2), 125–146.

—— (1994) "Turner and the Representation of England," in W.J.T. Mitchell (ed.), *Landscape and Power*, Chicago: University of Chicago Press.

Hemingway, Andrew (1992) *Landscape imagery and urban culture in early nineteenth-century Britain*, see especially Chapter 5: 'Philosophical criticism and the science of landscape', Cambridge: Cambridge University Press.

Hill, Christopher (1992) *The English Bible and the Seventeenth-Century Revolution*, Middlesex: The Penguin Press.

—— (1996) *Liberty Against the Law*, Middlesex: The Penguin Press.

Hill, Howard (1980) *Freedom to Roam: the Struggle for Access to Britain's Moors and Mountains*, Ashbourne, Derbyshire: Moorland Publishing.

Hill, Octavia (1877) *Our Common Land*, London: Macmillan & Co.

Hipple, Jr., Walter John (1957) *The Beautiful, The Sublime, & The Picturesque in Eighteenth-Century British Aesthetic Theory*, Carbondale, IL: Southern Illinois University Press.

Hirsch, Eric (1995) "Introduction. Landscape: Between Place and Space," in Eric Hirsch and Michael O'Hanlon (eds), *The Anthropology of Landscape: Perspectives on Place and Space*, Oxford: Clarendon Press.

Hirschman, Albert O. (1977) *The Passions and the Interests*, Princeton: Princeton University Press.

Hobsbawm, Eric and George Rudé (1969) *Captain Swing: a Social History of the Great English Agricultural Uprisings of 1830*, New York: Pantheon.

Hodge, Ian (1986) *Countryside Change; A Review of Research*, London: Economic and Social Research Council.

Hodgen, Margaret T. (1964) *Early Anthropology in the 16th–17th Centuries*, Philadelphia: University of Pennsylvania Press.

Hoecker-Drysdale, Susan (1992) *Harriet Martineau: First Woman Sociologist*, Oxford: Berg.

Hogarth, William (1753) *The Analysis of Beauty, Written with a View of Fixing the Fluctuating Ideas of Taste*, London.

Hogg, Robert (1974) *The Landscape of Cumbria*, Exhibition catalogue, Carlisle Art Gallery 7 November–7 December, 1974, Carlisle: Charles Thurnam & Sons.

Holt, Ann (1990) *A charter for whom? The access provisions of the National Parks and Access to the Countryside Act, 1949*, London: Ramblers' Association.

—— (1995) *The Origins and Early Days of the Ramblers' Association*, London: Ramblers' Association.

Horn, Pamela (1980) *The Rural World 1780–1850: Social Change in the English Countryside*, New York: St. Martin's Press.

Hoskins, W.G. (1955) *The Making of the English Landscape*, Harmondsworth: Penguin.

Howkins, Alun (1986) "The Discovery of Rural England," in R. Colls and P. Dodd (eds), *Englishness; Politics and Culture 1880–1920*, London: Croom Helm.

Hull, William (1834) *The History of the Glove Trade*, London: Effingham Wilson.

Hume, David ([1741–2] 1985) *Essays, Moral, Political, and Literary*, especially "Of the Delicacy of Taste and Passion," and "Of the Rise and Progress of the Arts and Sciences," Eugene F. Miller (ed.), Indianapolis: Liberty Classics.

Hume, David (1751) *An Enquiry Concerning the Principles of Morals*, London: A. Millar.

Hussey, Christopher (1927) *The Picturesque: Studies in a Point of View*, London: Putnam.

Hutcheson, Francis (1725) *An Inquiry into the Original of Our Ideas of Beauty and Virtue*, London.

Hutchinson, Horace G. (1914) *Life of Sir John Lubbock, Lord Avebury*, 2 vols, London: Macmillan.

Hyde, Ralph (1988) *Panoramania! The Art and Entertainment of the 'All-Embracing' View*, Exhibition catalogue, 3 November 1988–15 January 1989, London: Trefoil Publications and Barbican Art Gallery.

Jackson, J.B. (1980) "Landscape as Theater," in *The Necessity for Ruins*, Amherst: University of Massachusetts Press.

Jeans, D. N. (1990) "Planning and the Myth of the English Countryside, in the Interwar Period," in *Rural History* (1) 2: 249–64.

Jeffrey, Ian (1983) "Public Problems and Private Experience in British Art and Literature," in Judy Collins and Nichola Bennet (eds), *Landscape in Britain 1850–1950*, Exhibition Catalogue, 10 February–17 April 1983, Hayward Gallery.

Jones, Stephen G. (1988) *Sport, politics and the working class*, Manchester: Manchester University Press.

Joppien, Rüdiger (1973) *Philippe Jacques de Loutherbourg, R.A., 1740–1812*, Exhibition catalogue, 2 June–13 August 1973, London: Greater London Council.

Joyce, Patrick (1994) *Democratic subjects*, Cambridge: Cambridge University Press.

*Karrimor International Limited* (1994) insert in "Polartec Action Base Layer" garment packaging.

Keith, W.J. (1980) *The Poetry of Nature*, Toronto: University of Toronto Press.

Kinsman, Phil (1995) "Landscape, race and national identity: the photography of Ingrid Pollard," *Area* (27), 4: 300–10.

Kip, Johannes and Leonard Knyff (1708) *Nouveau théâtre de la Grande Bretagne: ou, Description exacte des palais de la reine, et des maisons les plus considerables des seigneurs & des gentilshommes de la Grande Bretagne . . .*, London: David Mortier.

Klandermans, Bert, Hanspeter Kriesi and Sidney Tarrow (eds) (1988) *International Social Movement Research*, Vol. I, London: JAI Press.

Knight, Richard Payne ([1805] 1972) *An Analytical Inquiry into the Principles of Taste*, Westmead: Gregg International.

Kroeber, Karl (1975) *Romantic Landscape Vision*, Madison: University of Wisconsin Press.

Kuklick, Henrika (1991) *The Savage Within: The Social History of British Anthropology 1885–1945*, Cambridge: Cambridge University Press.

*Lake District Mountain Rescue Team Association* (1995) Kendal, Cumbria: Stramongate Press.

*Lake District National Park Plan* (1986) Kendal, Cumbria: Lake District National Park Authority.

Lakeside Railway Society, *Heritage Series* of posters reproduced as postcards.

Lee, Anita Armstrong and John Houfe (eds) (1994) *A Century of Footpath Preservation*, Manchester: Peak and Northern Footpaths Society.

Lee, Donald W. (1976) *The Flixton Footpath Battle*, Stockport: The Peak and Northern Footpaths Society.

Lees, Susan and Sutti Ortiz (eds) (1992) *Understanding Economic Process*, NY: University Press of America.

Lees-Milne, James (1968) "Chatsworth, Derbyshire" – IV, *Country Life*, Vol. CXLIII: 1110–2.

Lefebure, Molly (1977) *Cumbrian Discovery*, London: Victor Gollanz.

Leonard, T.A. (n.d., c. 1910) *CHA: Please Read this! Both New and Old Members Should Know How it Came, and What it Stands For*, Manchester: The William Morris Press.

Lloyd, Richard (1992), Interview at the Countryside Commission, Cheltenham, August 5, 1992.

Lovell, Nadia (ed.) (1998) *Locality and Belonging*, London: Routledge.

Lowe, Philip (1988) "Environmental concern and rural conservation politics," in M. Whitby, and J. Ollerenshaw (eds), *Land Use and the European Environment*, London: Belhaven Press.

—— (1989) "The rural idyll defended: from preservation to conservation," in G.E. Mingay (ed.), *The Rural Idyll*, London: Routledge.

—— and Jane Goyder (1983) *Environmental Groups in Politics*, London: Allen & Unwin.

Lowenthal, David (1991) "British National Identity and the English Landscape," *Rural History* 2 (2) 205–30.

—— (1994) "European and English Landscapes as National Symbols," in David Hoosen (ed.), *Geography and National Identity*, Oxford: Blackwell.

Lowerson, John (1980) "Battles for the Countryside," in Frank Glover-smith (ed.), *Class, Culture and Social Change: A New View of the 1930s*, Sussex: Harvester Press.

Lucas, John (1990) *England and Englishness: Ideas of Nationhood in English Poetry 1688–1900*, London: The Hogarth Press.

Lui, Alan (1989) *Wordsworth: The Sense of History*, Stanford: Stanford University Press.

MacDonald, Maryon (1987) "The politics of fieldwork in Brittany," in Anthony Jackson (ed.), *Anthropology at Home*, ASA Monograph 25, London: Tavistock Publications.

Macdonald, Sharon (ed.) (1993) *Inside European Identities*, Oxford: Berg.

MacEwen, Ann and Malcolm MacEwen (1987) *Greenprints for the Countryside? The story of Britain's national parks*, London: Allen & Unwin.

MacNicol, Ian (1996) "Access 2000: The Way Forward," speech given by Ian MacNicol, Deputy President of the Country Landowners' Association, November 27, 1996, London: Country Landowners' Association.

Malone, Caroline (1989) *English Heritage Book of Avebury*, London: Batsford.

*Man* (Old Series) (1901–1955) Journal of the Royal Anthropological Institute of Great Britain and Ireland.

Manwaring, Elizabeth (1925) *Italian Landscape in Eighteenth Century England*, NY: Oxford University Press.

Marcus, George E. (1995) "Ethnography In/Of the World System: The Emergence of Multi-Sited Ethnography," *Annual Review of Anthropology*, 24: 95–117.

Marsh, Jan (1982) *Back to the Land: the Pastoral Impulse in England, from 1880 to 1914*, London: Quartet Books.

Marshall, J.D. and John K. Walton (1981) *The Lake counties from 1830 to the mid-twentieth century*, Manchester: Manchester University Press.

Martineau, Harriet (1855) *Complete Guide to the English Lakes*, London: Whittaker & Co.

Marx, Karl ([1852] 1972) *The 18th Brumaire of Louis Bonaparte*, NY: International Publishers.

Matless, David (1993) "One Man's England: W.G. Hoskins and the English Culture of Landscape," *Rural History* (4) 2: 187–207.

Matless, David (1995) "The Art of Right Living: landscape and citizenship 1918–39," in Steve Pile and Nigel Thrift (eds), *Mapping the Subject: geographies of cultural transformation*, London: Routledge.

McCay, Bonnie J. (1992) "Everyone's Concern, Whose Responsibility? The Problem of the Commons," in Sutti Ortiz and Susan Lees (eds), *Understanding Economic Process*, Lanham, MD.: University Press of America.

McGann, Jerome J. (1983) *The Romantic Ideology: A Critical Investigation*, "Introduction", Chicago: University of Chicago Press.

McGowan, Kris (1996) "Mountain Biking – Perceptual Problem, Passing Fad or Positive Management?" *Countryside Recreation Network News* (4) 1: 1–3.

McWilliam, Neal and Alex Potts (1983) "The landscape of reaction: Richard Wilson and his critics", *History Workshop Journal* 16: 171–5.

Mellor, David, Gill Saunders, and Patrick Wright (1990) *Recording Britain: A Pictorial Domesday of Pre-War Britain*, London: David & Charles in association with the Victoria and Albert Museum.

Melucci, Alberto (1989) *Nomads of the Present*, John Keane and Paul Mier (eds), Philadelphia: Temple University Press.

Mewett, Peter G. (1986) "Boundaries and discourse in a Lewis Crofting community," in Anthony P. Cohen (ed.), *Symbolising Boundaries. Identity and Diversity in British Cultures*, Manchester: Manchester University Press.

Miles, Gary B. (1980) *Virgil's Georgics: A New Interpretation*, Berkeley: University of California Press.

Miller, Simon (1995a) "Urban Dreams and Rural Reality: Land and Landscape in English Culture, 1920–45", *Rural History* (6) 1: 89–102.

—— (1995b) "Land, Landscape and the Question of Culture: English Urban Hegemony and Research Needs," *Journal of Historical Sociology* (8) 1: 94–107.

Milner, Douglas (1986) "The Art and Sport of Rock Climbing in the English Lake District," in *The Lake District: A sort of national property. Papers presented to a symposium held at the Victoria and Albert Museum 20–22 October 1984*, Cheltenham, Glos.: Countryside Commission and London: Victoria and Albert Museum.

Milner, Marion (1955) "The Role of Illusion in Symbol Formation," in M. Klein (ed.), *New Directions in Psychoanalysis*, NY: Basic Books.

Mingay, G.E. (1976) *Enclosure and the Small Farmer in the Age of the Industrial Revolution*, London: Macmillan Press.

—— (1989) "'Rural war': the life and times of Captain Swing," in Mingay (ed.), *The Unquiet Countryside*, London: Routledge.

Mitchell, J. Clyde (1956) *The Kalela Dance*, The Rhodes-Livingstone Papers No. 27, Manchester.

Mitchell, Jon P. (1997) "A Bridge Too Far? The Relationships Between History and Anthropology," *Contemporary European History* (6) 3: 405–411.

Mitchell, W. J. T. (1994) "Introduction" and "Chapter One: Imperial Landscape," in W.J.T. Mitchell (ed.), *Landscape and Power*, Chicago: University of Chicago Press.

Monk, Samuel H. (1960) *The Sublime: A Study of Critical Theories in XVIII-Century England*, Ann Arbor: University of Michigan.

Morgan, Prys (1983) "The Hunt for the Welsh Past in the Romantic Period," in Eric Hobsbawm and Terence Ranger (eds), *The Invention of Tradition*, Cambridge: Cambridge University Press.

Mormont, Marc (1983) "The emergence of rural struggles and their ideological effects," in *International Journal of Urban and Regional Research* (7)4: 559–76.

Morris R. J. (1990) "Clubs, societies and associations," in F.M.L. Thompson (ed.), *The Cambridge Social History of Britain 1750–1950*: *Social Agencies and Institutions*, Vol. 3: 395–443.

Murdoch, John (1984) *The Discovery of the Lake District: a Northern Arcadia and its Uses*, Exhibition catalogue, Winter 1984–Spring 1985, London: Victoria and Albert Museum.

Murdoch, John (1986) "Foregrounds and focus: Changes in the Perception of the Landscape c. 1800," in *The Lake District: A sort of national property. Papers presented to a symposium held at the Victoria and Albert Museum 20–22 October 1984*, Cheltenham, Glos.: Country-side Commission and London: Victoria and Albert Museum.

Newby, Howard (1987) *Country Life: A Social History of Rural England*, London: Weidenfeld & Nicolson.

Newhall, Beaumont (1964) *The History of Photography*, New York: The Museum of Modern Art.

Newman, Gerald (1987) *The Rise of English Nationalism: A Cultural History 1740–1830*, NY: St. Martin's Press.

Nicholson, Andrew (ed.) (1991) *Lord Byron: The Complete Miscellaneous Prose*, Oxford: Oxford University Press.

Nicholson, Norman (1955) *The Lakers: The Adventures of the First Tourists*, London: Robert Hale.

Nicolson, Marjorie Hope (1959) *Mountain Gloom and Mountain Glory: The Development of the Aesthetics of the Infinite*, Ithaca: Cornell University Press.

North, Mick (1991) "Ordnance Survey in the Northern Counties," in William Scammell (ed.) *The New Lake Poets*, Newcastle-upon-Tyne: Bloodaxe Books.

Olsen, Gerald Wayne (ed.) (1990) *Religion and Revolution in Early-Industrial England: The Halévy Thesis and Its Critics*, New York: University Press of America.

Olwig, K. (1993) "Sexual Cosmology: Nation and Landscape at the Conceptual Interstices of Nature and Culture; or What does Landscape Really Mean?" in Barbara Bender (ed.), *Landscape: Politics and Perspectives*, Oxford: Berg.

*Oxford English Dictionary* (1971) Oxford: Oxford University Press.

Palmer, Bryan (1990) *Descent into Discourse*, Philadelphia: Temple University Press.

*Parliamentary Debates*, 3rd Series, Commons (1837) 37: c.162–164.

*Parliamentary Debates*, 6th Series, Commons (1983) 61: c. 924.

Parmenter, Barbara McKean (1994) *Giving Voice to Stones: Place and Identity in Palestinian Literature*, Austin: University of Texas Press.

Parris, Leslie (1973) *Landscape in Britain c.1750–1850*, Exhibition catalogue, 20 November 1973–3 February 1974, London: The Tate Gallery.

Payne, Christiana (1993) *Toil and Plenty: Images of the Agricultural Landscape in England 1780–1890*, New Haven: Yale University Press.

Pearlman, Jerry (1992) *Give us some 'Quid' for our Quo!*, London: Ramblers' Association.

Peel, J.D.Y. (1971) *Herbert Spencer: the evolution of a sociologist*, London: Heinemann.

Pepler, G.L. (1950) "Forty Years of Planning," *Town and Country Planning Textbook*, Association for Planning and Regional Reconstruction, London: The Architectural Press.

Phillips, J. (1987) "Enough Grousing," in *Shooting Times and Country Magazine*, December 3, 1987: 25.

Phythian-Adams, Charles (1991) "Local History and National History: The Quest for the Peoples of England," *Rural History* (2) 1: 1–23.

Pickard, Tom (1982) *Jarrow March*, London: Allison and Busby.

Pickles, John (1992) "Texts, Hermeneutics and Propaganda Maps," in Trevor J. Barnes and James S. Duncan (eds), *Writing Worlds: discourse, text & metaphor in the representation of landscape*, London: Routledge.

Picozzi, N. (1970),"Breeding Performance and Shooting Bags of Red Grouse in Relation to Public Access in the Peak District National Park, England," *Biological Conservation* III: 211–15.

Piggott, Stuart (1950) *William Stukeley, An Eighteenth Century Antiquary*, London: Thames and Hudson.

—— (1976) *Ruins in a Landscape: Essays in Antiquarianism*, Edinburgh: Edinburgh University Press.

Pittock, Murray G.H. (1994) *Poetry and Jacobite Politics in Eighteenth-Century Britain and Ireland*, Cambridge: Cambridge University Press.

Polanyi, Karl (1944) *The Great Transformation*, Boston: Beacon Press.

Poore, Duncan and Judy Poore (1987) *Protected Landscapes: The United Kingdom Experience*, Cheltenham: Countryside Commission.

Price, Uvedale (1794) *An Essay on the Picturesque*, London: J. Robson.

Prince, Hugh (1988) "Art and agrarian change, 1710–1815," in Denis Cosgrove and Stephen Daniels (eds), *The iconography of landscape*, Cambridge: Cambridge University Press.

Prynn, David (1976) "The Clarion Clubs, Rambling and the Holiday Associations in Britain since the 1890s," *Journal of Contemporary History* 11: 65–77.

Radcliffe-Brown, A.R. and C.D Forde, (eds) (1950) *African Systems of Kinship and Marriage*, Oxford: Oxford University Press.

Raeburn, Michael (1995) "The Frog Service and Its Sources," in Hilary Young (ed.), *The Genius of Wedgwood*, Exhibition catalogue, London: Victoria and Albert Museum.

Ramblers Association (1994) internal document entitled *membership questionnaire*, and dated September 1994.

—— (1995) *Draft: Access to the Countryside Bill*, London: Ramblers' Association.

—— (1996) *Rights of Way – Reporting Problems and a Brief Guide to the Law*, London: Ramblers' Association.

Ravenscroft, Neil (1994) *Leisure, Consumerism and Active Citizenship in the UK*, Working Paper No. 28, University of Reading: Department of Land Management and Development.

Reed, Francis (1991) *On Common Ground*, London: Working Press.

Reed, Michael and Roger Wells (eds) (1990) *Class, Conflict and Protest in the English Countryside, 1700–1880*, London: Frank Cassell.

Rhyne, Charles (1986) "The Drawing of Mountains: Constable's 1806 Lake District Tour," in *The Lake District: A sort of national property. Papers presented to a symposium held at the Victoria and Albert Museum 20–22 October 1984*, Cheltenham, Glos.: Countryside Commission and London: Victoria and Albert Museum.

Robbins, Keith (1988) *Nineteenth-Century Britain: Integration and Diversity*, Oxford: Clarendon Press.

Robinson, Mike (1992) *The Greening of British Party Politics*, Manchester: Manchester University Press.

Rogers, Alan (1989) "A planned countryside," in G.E. Mingay (ed.), *The Rural Idyll*, London: Routledge.

Rosand, David (1988) "Giorgione, Venice, and the Pastoral Vision," in *Places of Delight: The Pastoral Landscape*, Exhibition catalogue November 6, 1988–January 22, 1989, Washington, D.C.: The Phillips Collection.

Roseberry, William (1989) "Marxism and Culture," in *Anthropologies and Histories*, New Brunswick: Rutgers University Press.

—— (1991) "Potatoes, Sacks, and Enclosures in Early Modern England," in Roseberry and Jay O'Brien (eds), *Golden Ages Dark Ages*, Berkeley: University of California Press.

Rosenfeld, Sybil (1972) "Landscape in English Scenery in the Eighteenth Century," in Kenneth Richards and Peter Thomson (eds), *The Eighteenth-Century English Stage*, London: Methuen.

Rosenthal, Michael (1993) "Landscape as High Art," in Katharine Baetjer (ed.), *Glorious Nature: British Landscape Painting 1750–1850*, NY: Hudson Hills Press in association with The Denver Art Museum.

Rothman, Bernard (1982) "The day we took Kinder," in *The Countryman* (87)1: 102–109.

Royal Commission on the Poor Laws (1834) "Answers to Questions Circulated in Rural Districts", Appendix B.1. Parts I–V *Parliamentary Session Papers*, vols 30–4.

Rüdig, Wolfgang (1995) "Between Moderation and Marginalization: Environmental Radicalism in Britain," in Bron R. Taylor (ed.), *Ecological Resistance Movements*, Albany, NY: State University of New York Press.

Rudwick, Martin J. S. (1985) *The Great Devonian Controversy: The Shaping of Scientific Knowledge among Gentlemanly Specialists*, Chicago: Chicago University Press.

Ruskin, John (1876) *A protest against the extension of the Railways in the Lake District*, Windermere: Somervell.

Russell, Gillian (1995) *The Theatres of War: Performance, Politics, and Society 1793–1815*, Oxford: Clarendon Press.

Sahlins, Peter (1989) *Boundaries: The Making of France and Spain in the Pyrenees*, Berkeley: University of California Press.

Said, Edward (1979) *Orientalism*, New York: Vintage Books.

Sales, Roger (1983) *English Literature in History 1780–1830: Pastoral and Politics*, London: Hutchinson.

Salveson, Christopher (1965) *The Landscape of Memory: A Study of Wordsworth's Poetry*, Lincoln: University of Nebraska Press.

Samuel, Raphael (1989) *Patriotism: The Making and Unmaking of British National Identity*, London: Routledge.

—— (1994) *Theatres of Memory: Past and Present in Contemporary Culture*, London: Verso.

Sandby, Paul (1778–81) *The Virtuosis Museum*, London: G. Kearsly.

Saunders, Gill (1990) "Introduction," in David Mellor, Gill Saunders, Patrick Wright *Recording Britain: A Pictorial Domesday of Pre-War Britain*, published to coincide with an exhibition, Recording Britain, at the Victoria and Albert Museum, 1 August–18 November, 1990, London: David & Charles in association with the Victoria and Albert Museum.

Schama, Simon (1996) *Landscape and Memory*, NY: Alfred A. Knopf.

Schneider, Jane (1991) "Spirits and Spirit of Capitalism," in Eric R. Wolf (ed.), *Religious Regimes and State-Formation: perspectives from European Ethnology*, Albany, NY: State University of New York Press.

Schwarzkopf, Jutta (1991) *Women in the Chartist Movement*, London: Macmillan Academic.

Shaftesbury, Anthony Ashley Cooper, Lord (1723) *Characteristics of Men, Manners, and Opinions*, London: J. Darby.

Short, John Rennie (1991) *Imagined Country: Environment, Culture and Society*, London: Routledge.

Sidaway, Roger (1990) *Birds and Walkers: A Review of Existing Research on Access to the Countryside and Disturbance to Birds*, London: Ramblers' Association.

Sider, Gerald (1986) *Culture and Class in Anthropology and History*, Cambridge: Cambridge University Press.

Simmons, I.G. (1975) *Rural Recreation in the Industrial World*, NY: John Wiley & Sons.

Slater, T.R. (1987) *Batsford's "Face of Britain": Topographical Writing 1930–1960 and Images of Britain*, Working Paper Series No. 37, University of Birmingham: Department of Geography.

Small, John (1990) "Geology and landforms," in Nicholas Stephens (ed.), *Natural Landscapes of Britain from the Air*, Cambridge: Cambridge University Press.

Smith, Adam ([1776] 1985) *An Inquiry into the Nature and Causes of the Wealth of Nations*, Richard F. Teichgraeber (ed.), NY: Modern Library.

Smith, Bernard (1985) *European Vision and the South Pacific*, New Haven: Yale University Press.

Smith, Walter Raymond (c. 1922) Manuscript diary of a walking tour of the Lake District made in July, probably in 1922. .

Solkin, David H. (1992) *Painting for Money: The Visual Arts and the Public Sphere in Eighteenth-Century England*, Paul Mellon Centre for Studies in British Art, New Haven: Yale University Press.

Southall, Humphrey (1996) "Agitate! Agitate! Organize! Political travellers and the construction of a national politics, 1839–1880,"

*Transactions* of the Institute of British Geographers NS (21)1: 177–93.

Speake, Robert (1993) *A Hundred Years of Holidays: 1893–1993: A Pictorial History of C.H.A.*, Manchester: Countrywide Holidays.

Spencer, Herbert (1855) *Railway Morals and Railway Policy*, London: Longman, Brown, Green, & Longman.

—— (1904) *Autobiography*, 2 vols, NY: D. Appleton & Company.

Springhall, John (1977) *Youth, Empire and Society; British Youth Movements 1883–1940*, London: Croom Helm.

Stallybrass, Peter and Allon White (1986) *Transgressions*, Ithaca, NY: Cornell University Press.

Standring, Timothy J. (1993) "Watercolor Landscape Sketching During the Popular Picturesque Era in Britain," in Katharine Baetjer (ed.), *Glorious Nature: British Landscape Painting 1750–1850*, NY: Hudson Hills Press in association with The Denver Art Museum.

Stanners, David and Philippe Bourdeau (eds) (1995) *Europe's Environment: The Dobris Assessment*, Copenhagen: European Environment Agency.

Stedman Jones, Gareth (1983) *Languages of class: Studies in English working class history 1832–1982*, Cambridge: Cambridge University Press.

—— (1997) "Anglo-Marxism, Neo-Marxism and the Discursive Approach to History," in *Was bleibt von marxistischen Perspektiven in der Geschichtsforschung?*, Göttingen: Max-Planck Institut für Geschichte.

Stephens, Nicholas (ed.) (1990) *Natural Landscapes of Britain From the Air*, Cambridge: Cambridge University Press.

Stocking, Jr., George W. (1987) *Victorian Anthropology*, New York: The Free Press.

Stone, Laurence and Jane C. Fawtier Stone (1986) *An Open Elite? England 1540–1880*, Oxford: Oxford University Press.

Strathern, Marilyn (1981) *Kinship at the Core: An Anthropology of Elmdon, Essex*, Cambridge: Cambridge University Press.

Stuart, David C. (1979) *Georgian Gardens*, London: Robert Hale.

Summerson, Sir John (1983) *The Classical Language of Architecture*, Cambridge: M.I.T. Press.

Symes, Michael (1991) *The English Rococo Garden*, Princes Risborough, Buckinghamshire: Shire Publications

Tashjian, Georgian R., David R. Tashjian, and Brian J. Enright (1990) *Richard Rawlinson, A Tercentenary Memorial*, Kalamazoo, MI: Western Michigan University New Issues Press.

Tate, W.E. and M.E. Turner (1978) *Domesday of Enclosures*, Reading: University of Reading Press.

Tate Gallery, London (1996) Exhibition: "Mountain Gloom, Mountain Glory".

Tayler, Edward William (1961) *Nature and Art in Renaissance Literature*, NY: Columbia University Press.

Taylor, Bron Raymond (ed.) (1995) *Ecological Resistance Movements*, Albany, NY: State University of New York Press.

Taylor, Harvey (1997) *A Claim on the Countryside: A History of the British Outdoor Movement*, Edinburgh: Keele University Press.

Thacker, Christopher (1989) *England's Historic Gardens*, Dorking, Surrey: Templar Publishing.

*The London Magazine* (1732–1784) London: J. Wilford.

Thomas, Keith (1983) *Man and the Natural World: A History of Modern Sensibility*, NY: Pantheon.

Thomason, David and Robert Woof (1986) *Derwentwater: The Vale of Elysium, An Eighteenth-Century Story*, Exhibition catalogue, 8 June–31 October 1986, Grasmere and Wordsworth Museum, Cumbria: Trustees of Dove Cottage.

Thompson, B.L. (1946) *The Lake District and the National Trust*, Kendal: Titus Wilson.

Thompson D. (1984) *The Chartists*, London: Temple Smith.

Thompson, E. P. (1966) *The making of the English working class*, NY: Vintage Books.

Tierney, John (1998) "Explornography: The Vicarious thrill of Exploring When There's Nothing Left to Explore," lead article in *The New York Times Magazine*, July 26, 1998, 6: 18–23, 33–4, 46–8.

Tilley, Christopher (1994) *A Phenomenology of Landscape*, Berg: oxford.

Trevelyan, G. M. (1937) "Amenities and the State," in C. Williams-Ellis (ed.), *Britain and the Beast*, London: J. M. Dent & Sons.

Trevor-Roper, Hugh (1983) "The Invention of Tradition: The Highland Tradition of Scotland," in Eric Hobsbawm and Terence Ranger (eds), *The Invention of Tradition*, Cambridge: Cambridge University Press.

Trueman, A.E. (1971) *Geology and Scenery in England and Wales*, Harmondsworth: Penguin Books.

Trumpener, Katie (1997) *Bardic Nationalism: The Romantic Novel and the British Empire*, Princeton: Princeton University Press.

Turner, Graham (1996) photograph of child actors in the Young National Trust Theatre's play *Flowers and Slaves* at Claydon House, Buckinghamshire, in *The Guardian*, April 26, 1966: 8.

Turner, Michael (1980) *English Parliamentary Enclosure: Its Historical Geography and Economic History*, Folkestone: Archon Books.

—— (1984) "The Landscape of Parliamentary Enclosure," in Michael Reed (ed.), *Discovering Past Landscapes*, London: Croom Helm.

Turner, Victor (1974) *Dramas, Fields and Metaphors: Symbolic Action in Human Society*, Ithaca NY: Cornell University Press.

—— and Edith Turner (1978) *Image and Pilgrimage in Christian Culture: Anthropological Perspectives*, Oxford: Basil Blackwell.

Tylor, Edward B. (1891) *Anthropology*, NY: D. Appleton & Company.

Urry, James (1993) *Before Social Anthropology: Essays on the history of British anthropology*, Chur, Switzerland: Harwood Academic Publishers.

Urry, John (1995) *Consuming Places*, London: Routledge.

Van Gennep, Arnold (1960) *The Rites of Passage*, trans. Monika B. Vizadom and Gabrielle L. Caffee, London: Routledge & Kegan Paul.

Van Keuren, David Keith (1982) *Human Science in Victorian Britain: Anthropology in Institutional and Disciplinary Formation, 1863–1908*, unpublished doctoral thesis, University of Pennsylvania.

—— (1984) "Augustus Pitt-Rivers, Anthropological Museums and Social Change in Later Victorian Britain," *Victorian Studies* 28: 171–89.

Vardi, Liana (1995) "Imagining the Harvest in Early Modern Europe," unpublished paper presented to the Program in Agrarian Studies, Yale University, 7 April 1995.

Vernon, James (1994) "Who's afraid of the 'linguistic turn'? The politics of social history and its discontents," in *Social History* 19 (1): 81–98.

Vincent, Joan (1990) *Anthropology and Politics*, Tucson: University of Arizona Press.

Vitruvius, Pollio, Morris Hicky Morgan trans. (1960) *De architectura. Vitruvius: the ten books on architecture*, NY: Dover .

Wainwright, Martin (1996) "'Spy' stiles to log Yorkshire Dales hikers,' *Guardian*, April 29, 1996: 5.

Wallace, Anne D. (1993) *Walking, Literature and English Culture*, Oxford: Oxford University Press.

Walvin, James (1978) *Leisure and Society 1830–1950*, London: Longman.

Watkins, Charles (ed.) (1996) *Rights of way: policy, culture and management*, London: Pinter.

Watson, Adam (1991) *Critique of report: "Moorland recreation and wildlife in the Peak District" by Penny Anderson, Peak Park Join Planning Board, 1990*, London: Ramblers' Association.

Watson J.R. (1970) *Picturesque Landscape and English Romantic Poetry*, London: Hutchinson.

Webster, Mary (1976) *Johan Zoffany 1733–1810*, Exhibition catalogue, 14 January to 27 March 1977, London: National Portrait Gallery.

*Webster's New Collegiate Dictionary* (1973) Springfield MA.: Merriam-Webster.

Wells, H.G. (1935) *Tono-Bungay*, NY: The Modern Library.

Welsh, Frank (1989) *The Companion Guide to the Lake District*, London: Collins.

Wetherell, D. and C. Carr-Gregg (1990) *Camilla: a Life, C.H. Wedgwood 1901–1955*, Kensington, Australia: New South Wales University Press.

Whitby, M. and J. Ollerenshaw (eds) (1988) *Land Use and the European Environment*, London: Belhaven Press.

Whitby, Martin (1997) "Countryside Access; a traditional asset but growing fast?" *Countryside Recreation Network* 5: 4, October 1997, n. p.

Whitney, C.R. (1997) "Alpine Thrills Attract an Untiring Visitor: Death," *NY Times*, August 17, 1997.

Whymper, Edward ([1871] 1981) *Scrambles Amongst the Alps in the Years 1860–1869*, Berkeley: Ten Speed Press.

Wiener, Martin J. (1981) *English Culture and the Decline of the Industrial Spirit 1850–1980*, Cambridge: Cambridge University Press.

Wilberforce, William ([1779] 1983) *Journey to the Lake District From Cambridge 1779: A Diary*, C.E. Wrangham (ed.), London: Oriel Press.

Wilcox, Scott B. (1988) "Unlimiting the Bounds of Painting," in Ralph Hyde, *Panoramania! The Art and Entertainment of the 'All-Embracing' View*, Exhibition catalogue, 3 November 1988–15 January 1989, London: Trefoil Publications and the Barbican Art Gallery.

Williams, Raymond (1973) *The Country and the City*, Oxford: Oxford University Press.

Williams, Raymond ([1968] 1989) "The Idea of a Common Culture," in Robin Gable (ed.), *Resources of Hope: Culture, Democracy, Socialism*, London: Verso.

Williams, W. (1956) *The Sociology of an English Village: Gosforth*, London: Routledge & Kegan Paul.

Williams-Ellis, Clough (1947) *On Trust for the Nation*, London: Paul Elek.

Wolf, Eric R. (1982) *Europe and the People Without History*, Berkeley: University of California Press.

Woodbridge, Kenneth (1989) *The Stourhead Landscape*, London: The National Trust.

Wordie, J. R. (1983) "The Chronology of English Enclosure, 1500–1914," *The Economic History Review*, 2nd series, 36 (4), 483–305.

Wordsworth, Dorothy ([1802] 1971) *The Journals of Dorothy Wordsworth*, Mary Moorman (ed.), Oxford: Oxford University Press.

Wordsworth, William ([1835] 1984) *A Guide Through the District of the Lakes in the North of England with a Description of the Scenery, etc. For the Use of Tourists and Residents*, Kendal, Westmorland: Hudson & Nicholson.

Wright, Patrick (1985) *On Living in an Old Country: the National Trust in Contemporary Britain*, London: Verso.

Young, Hilary (1995) "Introduction. From the Potteries to St. Petersburg: Wedgwood and the Making and Selling of Ceramics," in Young (ed.), *The Genius of Wedgwood*, Exhibition catalogue, London: Victoria and Albert Museum.

# Index

Note: Page numbers in italics refer to figures.

Chiswick, 45n11
Churchill, Winston, 205n6
Clare, John, 29, 105
Clarion Ramblers clubs, 135
Clark, Kenneth, 186
class, issues of, 3–4, 38, 63, 64, 107,
    115–17, 253
  of access, 118–19, 133–7, 139,
    150–1, 155–7, 165, 173–5, 195
  in group configuration, 238, 242
  leisure and, 158–66
  in linkage of religion and
    recreation, 132
  in London-based culture, 70–1
  public transportation and, 88, 89
  of reform or revolution, 120–4
  in re-visioning of the past, 76–7
  in Romanticism, 84
  rural myths and, 124–5, 138
Claude glass, 59
Claude Lorraine, 28, 46n13, 57, 60,
    66n11
Climbers' Club, 164
clothing, walkers', 231–2
Coleridge, Samuel Taylor, 83, 90,
    92n3, 93n9, 262
  and slavery, 73, 98n28, 140n4
  on walks with Wordsworths,
    144n23
Combe, William, 64
commedia dell'arte, 31
commons, 30, 107, 109–10, 126
  definition of, 185
  development of, 126
  enclosure of, see enclosure
  legislation, 109–10
  mass demonstrations on, 120–1,
    124
  in Peak District, 128
  preservation of, 4 (see also
    Commons Society)

Commons Amendment Act (1893),
    126
Commons, Open Spaces, and
    Footpath Preservation
    Society,(Commons Society), 130,
    152, 154, 167, 172, 178n18,
    179n23, 180n25
Communist Party, 137
communitas, 228–30, 238, 249, 252,
    253
Complete Suffrage Union, 115, 116
Comradeship, 161–3, 175, 178n15
Congregationalists, 76, 115
Conservative Party, 199, 280
Cook, Captain James, 16, 47n20
Cook, Thomas, 36
Co-operative (later Countrywide)
    Holidays Association (CHA),
    158–63, 171, 177n12, 178n14,
    206n12, 244, 253, 260–6
  founding of, 158–9
  Disarmament Conference
    (Geneva, 1932) and, 162
  national parks advocated by, 172
  publication of, (see Comradeship)
  religious activities of, 159–60, 235,
    256n4
  reorganization of, 233–4
  walking holidays run by, 222–3,
    226, 234–7, 248
Copper Plate Magazine, The, 31, 38,
    40, 41, 47n19, n21, 55, 93n8
Copyhold Act (1887), 126
Cornish, Vaughan, 171
Corresponding Societies, 115
Corrigan, Philip, 70, 184, 196
Cotton Famine, 134
Council for British Archaeology,
    201
Council for the Preservation (later
    Protection) of Rural England

St. Barbe, Charles, Jr., 47n22
Sandby, Paul, 29, 38, 55, 66n9,
    96n22
Sandford, Lord, 192, 193, 206n12
Sannazaro, 14
Sayer, Derek, 70, 184, 196
Scafell Pike, 165, 179n20
Schama, Simon, 216
Scott, Walter, 66n10, 262
Scottish Cairngorms Club, 158
Scottish Mountaineering Club, 158
Scott report, 183, 187
*Seasons, The* (Thompson), 49, 85
secular pilgrimage, 66n12, 226–31,
    249–52, 280, 283
Seebohm, Frederic, 107, 139n1
Shaftsbury, Earl of, 52
Shaw-Lefevre, George, 130
Sheffield and District Ramblers'
    Federation, 136
Sheffield Clarion Ramblers (SCR),
    135
Shell Oil, 176n4
Shelley, Percy Bysshe, 83, 262
Shenstone, William, 83
Sider, Gerald, 69
Silbury Hill, 55, 80, 127
Silkin, Lewis, 188–90
Simmons, I.G., 184
sites of special scientific interest
    (SSSIs), 192
slavery, 26, 73
    opposition to, 115, 122
Slingsby, Cecil, 164
Smith, Bernard, 33
Smith, Colonel Charles Hamilton,
    90
Smith, Thomas, 57–8, 60
Smith, Walter Raymond, 179n22,
    230
Snowdonia National Park, 4, 191

Socialist Party, 136
social movements, 249–52, 285
Society of Antiquaries of London,
    65n4
Society of Antiquaries of Scotland,
    65n4
Society of Dilettanti, 27–8
Society for the Encouragement of
    Arts, Commerce, and
    Manufactures in Great Britain, 56,
    91n2, 91n3
Society for the Preservation of
    Ancient Buildings, 180n25
Society for the Preservation of
    Liberty and Property Against
    Republicans and Levellers, 113
Solly, Godfrey, 164
Somervell, Robert, 152
*Songs of Experience* (Blake), 30
Southey, Robert, 65n9, 73, 83, 90,
    93, 122, 166
*Spectator*, 71, 92n6
Spencer, Herbert, 115–16, 148, 150,
    178, 256n2
Stallybrass, Peter, 19, 32
Starkey, Phyllis, xix
Steele, Richard, 71, 92n6
Stephens, Leslie, 163, 168, 178n18
Stephenson, Tom, 189, 206n8
stiles, definition of, 186
Stone, Jane C. Fawtier, 38
Stone, Lawrence, 38
Stonehenge, 55, 80, 127, 143n14
Stopping-Up of Unnecessary Roads
    Act (1815), 130, 131
Stourhead, *25*, 26
Stukeley, William, 55, 57
Sturge, Joseph, 115
suburbs, development of, 168–9
Sunday Tramps club, 168, 178n18
Surveyors' Institution, 179n25